Michael F. Gray

Michael F. Gray

The magic of
ESOPs and LBOs

The magic of
ESOPs and LBOs

the definitive guide to Employee Stock Ownership Plans and Leveraged Buyouts

By Robert A. Frisch

FARNSWORTH PUBLISHING COMPANY
a subsidiary of Longman Financial Services Publishing, Inc.

DISTRIBUTED BY
the ESOT group, inc.
PUBLISHING DIVISION
3580 Wilshire Boulevard, Ste. 1410
Los Angeles, CA 90010-2515
1-800-621-0849 ext. 333
(213) 384-1126

© 1985, Robert A. Frisch.
All rights reserved.
Published by Farnsworth Publishing Co.
A subsidiary of Longman Financial Services Publishing, Inc.
Rockville Centre, New York 11570.
Library of Congress Catalog Card No. 85-80623.
ISBN 0-87863-244-1.
Manufactured in the United States of America.
No part of this book may be reproduced
without the written permission of the publisher.

FOR LEONA, DANA, AND RANDI

Contents

Preface

ESOPs

An employee stock ownership plan (ESOP) is a tax-qualified corporate employee benefit plan that is unlike any other. An ESOP actually creates working capital and cash flow while benefiting the employees and the owners of the company.

A corporation can make tax-deductible contributions to its ESOP in the form of cash or its own stock. Company contributions are allocated to the accounts of the employee-participants. The taxes saved and the multiple effect those savings have when put to proper use increase the size of the corporate pie. It is this newly formed capital that makes it possible for the employees to share in the stock of the company with no contribution on their part and without taking equity away from the stockholders.

ESOPs have become increasingly popular as their virtues have been discovered. They are different things to different companies. Owners of private corporations think of ESOPs as a means of selling their stock on a gradual basis while continuing to control the company. Others may wish to sell all of their stock to an ESOP and make way for their heirs or executives to take over the corporate reins. Some might wish to buy out minority stockholders.

Private companies may want to become stronger and put themselves in better positions to capture larger shares of the market. There are those who find the ESOP a magnificent tool for making acquisitions with pretax dollars. Still others would have their employees experience the pride of ownership in the corporation as well as the security such equity affords. By having an in-depth understanding of how an ESOP works and what it can accomplish, one can perceive a logical interrelationship between ESOPs and leveraged buyouts (LBOs).

LBOs

An LBO constitutes the technique by which a company, an individual, a partnership, or an investment group can acquire a corporation. It involves the use of a loan, the collateral for which is the underlying assets of the acquired company. The debt service is accommodated by the cash flow to be generated by the corporation.

LBOs are frequently used by executives to acquire divisions or subsidiaries of corporations or, in some cases, the corporation itself. They are equally applicable in acquisitions involving public or private companies. Size is of little importance if the asset value, earnings capacity, and management talent combine to make sense to a lender. The similarity of $100,000 LBOs and $5 billion deals is masked by the degree of sophistication and the number of players involved. Yet an LBO is an LBO, irrespective of the size of the prize.

Takeover attempts by corporate raiders often serve as catalysts for initiating LBOs as possible deterrents and, indeed, alternatives to selling the company to unfriendly parties. The buyouts that avoid the takeovers are goldfish-bowl transactions visible for all to see. For

1

every LBO involving a large public corporation, there are more than 1,000 LBOs that go unheralded within the confines of either private corporations or small public corporations.

LESOPs

ESOPs, as tax-qualified plans, are unique in their ability to borrow money. This trait is not enjoyed by pension or profit-sharing plans. The implication of the ESOP's cost effectiveness as a leverage device is readily apparent. Since the corporation's cash contributions to the ESOP are tax deductible, its payments for both principal and interest are made with pretax dollars by the corporation. This can effectively reduce the aftertax cash requirement for repaying principal by half that amount needed for a non-ESOP loan. The ESOP uses the loan proceeds to purchase stock or assets from the seller. The leveraged ESOP has been assigned the acronym, LESOP.

With this in mind, the ESOP coupled with an LBO creates a synergistic marriage. If an LBO will work in a given situation, there is little doubt that an ESOP would improve its effectiveness. Giving the employees a piece of the action should improve their productivity. This will further enhance the likelihood of a successful buyout. A congressional act that gives a tax break to ESOP lenders can lead to a lower interest rate for the ESOP. This also translates into a positive effect on the corporation's ability to service the loan costs.

LBOs are daily news items in the financial press, and they are being implemented with greater frequency in connection with ESOPs. ESOPs can be the adrenalin that helps an LBO accomplish its wonders. LBOs that could not quite be done by themselves are often made possible by the added ingredient of an ESOP. ESOPs tend to add class to LBOs. LBOs by themselves are often done for the benefit of one or perhaps a handful of investors who want to make a killing even if it requires liquidating the acquired company and dispersing its employee population.

Other LBOs are nobler of the heart and are done by management to thwart an attempted LBO by outsiders. ESOPs can still allow a few at the top to enjoy a large element of control coupled with incentive equity while spreading the major portion of the equity to the employees at large. The employees become capitalists overnight. The day after a LESOP buyout occurs, it is business as usual. Neither the employees nor the management team has faced dislocation. The customers, the suppliers, the subcontractors, and the name of the concern remain unchanged. The community still retains its taxpaying corporate citizen. The social fabric of the area has not been unwound.

The federal government has been quite consistent in its tendency to liberalize laws that relate to ESOPs. Government at the federal, state, and local levels has learned more about ESOPs in recent years and has come to recognize the importance of letting employees retain a portion of the fruits of their productivity. The capital appreciation they receive is a magnificent incentive for employees to give themselves more by producing more. This improves the tax base of the corporation and, as dividends or equity is distributed to the workers, they pay more taxes and spend more money in the community so that the merchants will pay greater amounts of revenue to the government. As the corporation expands, it will hire additional employees, thereby lending a multiple effect to the capital created by the ESOP.

Magic of ESOPs and LBOs describes the workings of ESOPs and LBOs separately and in concert with each other. Creative uses to which these financial vehicles can be put are emphasized.

This book is also designed to update the reader as to the many recent positive changes that have occurred. It contains examples of companies that have gone the ESOP or LESOP route and the reasons for doing so. In some cases, LBOs by themselves would not have worked, but because of the additional tax and other advantages inherent in an ESOP, its inclusion made the buyouts practicable.

It is the author's intent that this technical subject be readable and understandable. It should be useful to corporate managers, investors, bankers, attorneys, accountants, politicians, life insurance agents, and employees whose jobs may be threatened by possible closures or transitions. Corporate owners who have potential estate liquidity problems and those concerned with the perpetuation of their companies will find possible solutions here that can easily be implemented. Proper use of some of these concepts might help corporate owners create hundreds of thousands, or perhaps millions, of dollars for themselves that will become spendable during their lifetimes without giving up their "toy" in life, their businesses. At the same time, they will benefit loyal employees and the community at large.

In a broad sense, this subject matter involves not only practicability but a philosophy as well.

The Status of Employee Stock Ownership Plans

Employee stock ownership plans (ESOPs) have become a movement unlike any this country has seen for many decades. A steamroller effect has become evident among an ever-increasing number of our legislators who hope to broaden the ownership of capital among the millions of employees who help create it. A breakthrough of momentous proportions came about with the enactment of the Deficit Reduction Act of 1984. It was signed into law on July 18, 1984, by President Ronald Reagan. It included provisions of an act that had been spearheaded by Senator Russell E. Long and co-sponsored by 47 other senators. Interestingly enough, the sponsorship was bipartisan, with backers ranging from those as different as their outlooks as Senators Edward Kennedy and Paul Laxalt, Senators Lloyd Bentsen and Mark Hatfield, and Senators Donald Riegle and John Tower. Liberals, conservatives, and those in between were well represented in the group of supporters. A similar bill encouraging ESOPs had been co-sponsored by 24 members of the House of Representatives.

The act is so broad in scope as to widen and resurface the path laid down by ERISA in 1974. ERISA stated congressional intent—namely, to broaden the base of capitalism—when it formalized the acronyms ESOP and ESOT (employee stock ownership trust) a decade earlier.

The ESOP is quite simple in its concept. It merely involves a tax-qualified plan under which an employer may make tax-deductible contributions of cash or employer stock to a trust. The trust assets are allocated among the employee participants, who will receive distributions of cash or stock upon their termination, death, or retirement. Hopefully, the trust assets will have risen in value prior to that time. Distributions of stock for which there is no public market are generally readily redeemable into cash.

Unlike other tax-qualified plans, the ESOP can borrow cash from any source, including the corporation or stockholders, in order to buy stock from the corporation or from stockholders for the benefit of the employee participants. Since the ESOP is a tax-qualified trust, cash contributed to it by the corporation to service the loan is tax deductible. Both principal and interest can be paid with deductible dollars, thereby permitting the loan to be discharged at about half the usual cost.

By contributing stock to the ESOP, the corporation saves taxes with no disbursement of cash. Tax savings increase the size, value, and earning capacity of the company. The effect is to create new capital that employees can own without reducing the wealth of the owners of the business.

The Credibility Gap

Relatively few employers were willing to put their companies on the line with a program that seemed too good to be true. A no-action, wait-and-see approach seemed appropriate.

For other entrepreneur-founders of private companies, putting stock in the hands of employees did not come naturally. To employees, cash in hand was better than idle paper that paid no dividends. From IRS's standpoint during that early period, there was suspicion that tax savings without a cash expenditure spelled S-C-A-M. The Department of Labor, very protective of its employee flock, also cast a wary eye on a plan whereby employees might possibly become the beneficiaries of overvalued employer securities in exchange for their expended labor.

In retrospect, all of these parties could have afforded to be much more optimistic. Indeed, the history of ESOPs in use has demonstrated that an overwhelming percentage of ESOPs has been highly successful in benefiting employee, employer, and the U.S. Treasury. In only an insignificant number of instances has there been a willful misuse of the ESOP concept to the detriment of employees. ESOPs have worked out so well for such a large variety of corporations and its employees that the government has enacted a stream of favorable legislation to encourage more widespread adoption of ESOPs.

Credibility is no longer a factor among companies who are considering the possibility of adopting an ESOP. It is estimated that ESOPs have saved more than 70,000 jobs during the 1974-1984 decade. Aside from this, ESOPs have created thousands of new jobs because of the capital they have brought to about 6,000 ESOP companies in that time period.

ESOPs—An Answer to Social Security

ESOPs can become the greatest boon to capitalism since the country adopted that philosophy as its mode of economic development. By broadening capital ownership, ESOPs give more than mere lip service to the term. For the 6% of the population that owns 72% of the nation's corporate stock, capitalism works. This startling statistic of the minimal participation by Americans in significant ownership of corporate America is the result of a study by the Joint Economic Committee.

The Federal Reserve Board reports that the average American family has cash savings and investment in stocks and bonds valued at approximately $24,000. Little can be gleaned from averages. A median figure of $2,300 in such family savings becomes more meaningful. Yet, even this modest figure paints too glowing a picture of the assets families in this country have to fall back on. A further breakdown of the financial picture leaves less than $1,000 in the hands of 39% of American families.

Fifteen percent of the populace owns 85% of corporate stock. The vast majority of the 85% of the citizens of America are dependent on their ability to earn a current livelihood through their labor. Once that finite fuel for production wanes, it is replaced by the fragile fabric of Social Security. This system has bounced along from funding crisis to funding crisis.

The solution has always been an easy, if unimaginative, one. Simply fund Social Security currently, and have employers and employees ante up more cash as needed. This is all well and good, but, to the extent that businesses put more into the Social Security fund, they reduce working capital and cash flow. This inhibits the business's ability to expand and create more jobs. Productivity is curtailed.

Improved life expectancy is also creating a greater dependency on the Social Security fund. With more and more people dependent on fewer and fewer workers, businesses will be called upon to support more of the retirement benefit in the years ahead. Sir Winston Churchill's observation is appropriate: "Never before have so many owed so much to so few." This will further reduce working capital. Something will have to give. It is only a matter of time.

To the extent that employees own capital, they will become less dependent on Social Security. A reduction of the number of those on the Social Security rolls would correspondingly decrease the amount of capital needed to fund the program. The capital contributions to the public system that is saved by employers would be put to better use in their own corporations. Employees would have more disposable income to invest for their future security.

ESOPs have proven to be the most cost-efficient means of placing capital into the hands of employees. This is due to the fact that the capital they receive does not come from existing stockholders but is derived from capital that would not have existed were it not for the ESOP. Millions of employees of ESOP companies are now capitalists who would not have been so characterized just a few years earlier. Many additional millions of employees will join their ranks as ESOPs continue to proliferate.

ESOPs and Motivation

Numerous studies have shown that improved productivity is a byproduct of stock ownership among employees. According to a study by the Survey Research Center at the University of Michigan, companies, the majority of whose stock is substantially owned by its employees, are one-and-one-half times more profitable than comparable companies that are conventionally owned.

It was also determined that the greater the amount of equity the employees owned, the greater the corporate profitability. Approximately 10% of all ESOPs are in companies wherein the majority of the stock is owned by the employee trust. MBA candidates at the UCLA Graduate School of Management have correlated improved employee motivation with stock ownership by the employees.

7

The Journal of Corporation Law at the University of Iowa School of Law issued a survey of 229 ESOP companies. The study showed increased productivity among ESOP companies during the period between 1975 and 1979 in contrast to comparable non-ESOP companies where productivity was on the decline.

The Use of ESOPs to Save Jobs

ESOPs have been used with increasing frequency in leveraged buyouts (LBOs) of companies by their employees. This typically occurs when the founder wishes to retire and becomes interested in looking for outside buyers. Many ESOP LBOs come as a result of a corporation's decision to relocate to a better labor or economic environment. Employees in such situations would face mass localized unemployment.

State and local governmental agencies often encourage and help finance employee take-overs because of the potential harm a corporate relocation could create. Unions have joined the ESOP movement in order to maintain jobs among their membership. They have even encouraged reinvesting capital in the business rather than negotiate exclusively for higher wages to assure the long-range well-being of the union members.

Unions have found that they can flourish as representatives of management and labor since, in an ESOP company, they can be one and the same. In a number of employee buyout instances, the unions have actually encouraged the employees to give up wages to help finance the acquisition. They do this primarily in the face of potential plant closures. The unions and the employees have an incentive to make the company succeed, since they will be getting a slice of the equity pie. They will become capitalists in the truest sense.

ESOPs are being implemented overwhelmingly in healthy, growing corporations, companies with good management and a bright future. This is the most efficient means of putting stock into the hands of many employees. These plans require no contribution from the employee, but the tax savings and increased productivity repay the company and its principal owners for contributing stock to the employee trust. ESOPs are proving their worth to corporations, major stockholders, employees, and the community at large. Their flexibility and value as instruments of corporate finance have given ESOPs a permanent status in this country.

From the government's standpoint, tax revenue increases with corporate productivity. As ESOPs help companies become more profitable, the companies invest in capital equipment, expand, and hire more people. The corporations pay more taxes, as do their subcontractors and suppliers. Employees must work in order to provide revenue for the government.

ESOPs—
What They Are About

What if there were a way that would let the owner of a private corporation—

• Increase the company's working capital and cash flow with no cash expenditure and no additional productive effort?

• Buy out minority or majority stockholders with pretax dollars?

• Cut the cost of borrowing essentially in half by deducting loan principal payments as well as interest?

• Reduce the interest rate on loans by as much as 25%?

• Recover taxes paid in prior years with no cash expenditure?

• Transform the assets of the corporation's profit-sharing plan into working capital?

• Make acquisitions with pretax dollars?

• Sell stock of the company, pay no tax on the proceeds, and still keep control?

• Make life insurance premiums tax deductible?

• Provide the employees with equity at no cash outlay on their part or the owner's part?

• Deduct the payment of dividends from taxes?

• Transfer the estate tax obligation to the employees, with the government making them a low-interest loan to pay the tax and then picking up half of the principal and interest?

And what if there were a means whereby a public company could—

• Divest itself of unwanted divisions or subsidiaries and let the government pay half the buyer's cost, or

• Have the government pay the corporation to take over other companies?

And what if employees or executives with little or no cash could buy a division, a subsidiary, or a corporation with other people's money (OPM), with the government paying half the cost of the loan and the business paying the rest?

Too good to be true? The ESOP makes it all happen and does so with the sanction and encouragement of the United States Congress. ESOPs and ESOTs are tax-qualified plans and trusts, respectively, which are created by corporations for the benefit of their employees. Because of the unique nature of these plans, they benefit the corporation and stockholders as well.

Unlike typical pension and profit-sharing plans, an ESOP is mandated to invest its assets primarily in stock of the employer. It is a seeker of stock and can obtain it from the corporation in the form of newly issued stock or treasury stock contributions. The company gets a tax deduction based on the value of the stock or cash it contributes. Another source of stock is from stockholders who are willing to sell some or all of their holdings.

ESOPs—
Now Let's Get Technical

Many tax-qualified plans that are structured as stock bonus plans are loosely referred to as ESOPs. Actually, an ESOP is a defined-contribution plan that is a stock bonus plan or a combination of a stock bonus plan and money-purchase plan designed to invest primarily in qualifying employer securities.

In a company whose stock is not readily traded, "qualifying employer securities" denotes common stock of the employer corporation that has voting power and dividend rights equal to or greater than that of any stock in the company that has the greatest voting power and dividend rates. Callable preferred stock that may be converted to such common stock is also a form of qualifying employer security so long as the conversion price is a reasonable one. Public company stock that is readily tradeable is also eligible for ESOP purchase.

With a defined-contribution plan, the company can vary its tax-deductible contribution and make no commitment to the employee as to a precise retirement benefit. This is in contrast to a money-purchase plan in which the plan's formula determines the contribution. A defined-benefit pension plan promises a specific benefit and adjusts contributions in an amount needed to achieve the benefit promised.

Stock bonus plans, profit-sharing plans, thrift plans, and money-purchase plans fall into the general category of defined-contribution plans. An ESOP must invest primarily in qualifying employer securities, which it can obtain from the corporation or from stockholders who are willing to sell their stock.

The corporation can make tax-deductible contributions of authorized but unissued stock, treasury stock, or cash to the ESOP. If a parent company owns 50% of the stock of another corporation, they are categorized as members of a controlled group and the securities of any member may be contributed or purchased by an ESOP for all the members. Cash is useful in that it can be used to pay administrative costs or purchase stock from shareholders or from terminated employees who may have had stock distributed to them.

More often, cash is distributed to the participants upon termination, disability, death, or retirement. An ESOP is an eligible individual accounts plan whose assets can be 100% invested in employer stock.

Control and Responsibility

The trustee is appointed by the board of directors of the company and performs transactions only at the direction of the Administrative Committee, which is appointed by the board of directors. All have fiduciary responsibilities in the management and control of ESOP assets, bearing in mind that ESOPs, or any qualified plan for that matter, must be for the exclusive benefit of the participants and their beneficiaries.

Nonetheless, an ESOP enjoys freedom from various restrictions pertaining to parties-in-interest transactions that are disallowed in pension and profit-sharing plans.

The Asset Diversification Exemption

One of the most important ways in which ESOPs differ from other forms of corporate qualified plans is the fact that they have been granted an exemption from the diversification rules. The ESOP assets can be composed totally of employer stock. An ESOP's purpose is to provide ownership of company stock to the employees. Pension plans and traditional profit-sharing plans are precluded from having more than 10% of assets in the form of employer stock. Their assets are thereby invested away from the company while the ESOP invests its assets back into the company.

The regulations say that the assets of the ESOP must be invested primarily in employer stock but do not define what "primarily" really means. Practitioners have generally perceived this to mean that 51% of the assets in company stock is a good, safe number for meeting this specification. If there is a good rationale for cash even in excess of this percentage, it can probably be justified on audit. The ESOP's assets can also be partially composed of cash, or cash equivalents, or other assets easily changeable into cash so that liquidity will be available to the ESOP to enable it to redeem stock of ESOP participants who terminate, die, or retire.

The ESOP's fiduciaries are not insulated from the diversification rule as it applies to assets other than employer stock. Another area of departure between ESOPs and other qualified plans is the fair-return-on-investment rule. Accumulation of equity in the corporation for the benefit of employees is the rationale for ESOPs. It is understood that relatively few privately owned corporations pay dividends. It is hoped that the ESOP will assist companies to increase the per-share value of their stock. The employees or their families will benefit from any capital appreciation that might occur in their ESOP accounts when they terminate, die, or retire.

Contribution Limits in the Nonleveraged ESOP

Under the stock-bonus-plan aspect of an ESOP, the corporation can make tax-deductible cash contributions in varying amounts but subject to a general limitation of 15% of participants' annual payroll. This is a rather flexible arrangement since the employer is not locked into a specific amount that must be contributed each year. The employer can make the contribution in the form of employer stock, cash, or a combination. The employee is not taxed on the employer's contribution to the ESOP until the stock is distributed to him or her at termination or retirement or to the beneficiary at death.

The upper limitation of the deductible contribution is 15% of covered payroll but with an added provision that credit carryovers can be used from prior years wherein the maximum was not contributed.

Carryovers can bring the maximum contribution up to 25% of annual compensation, including forfeitures. Forfeitures refer to nonvested portions of the accounts of employees who terminate prior to becoming fully vested. Forfeitures are reallocated among the other participants.

The flexibility achieved by carryovers is useful to corporations since the employers can make minimal contributions in some years with the assurance that they will be able to someday use the rest of the tax-shelter opportunity as needed, so long as there are unused carryovers.

As noted, the ESOP can also be partially composed of a money-purchase plan in addition to the stock bonus plan if the employer desires to structure the ESOP with a combination of the two plans. The money-purchase plan is less flexible than the stock bonus plan in that the plan defines the percentage of compensation that must be contributed yearly. The corporation must make contributions to this side of the plan whether it would normally wish to or not.

A typical combination plan might be a mandatory employer contribution of 10% of covered payroll with the balance subject to the stock-bonus-plan limit. This means that an additional amount ranging from 1% to 15% can be contributed under the framework of the stock bonus plan at the discretion of the company. The corporation can make tax-deductible cash or stock contributions ranging from 11% to 25% through a combination ESOP described above.

Combination plans are seldom used since the stock-bonus-plan ESOP provides the carryovers, which, if available, permit corporations to contribute up to 25% of covered payroll. The majority of ESOPs are of the stock-bonus-plan variety. A company cannot establish a money-purchase-pension-plan ESOP unless it is accompanied by a stock-bonus-plan ESOP.

Contribution Limits in the Leveraged ESOP

Leveraged ESOPs (ESOPs that borrow) have been granted favored treatment exempting participants from the 15% or 25% contribution limitation. Employer contributions to an ESOP for paying interest under an ESOP loan, the proceeds of which are used to purchase employer stock, are deductible. In addition to this, the corporation may deduct up to 25% of covered payroll if the contribution is used to pay principal under an ESOP loan. This is true in the case of either a stock-bonus-plan ESOP or a combination plan. The exemption on the deductibility of the interest applies over and beyond the contribution the corporation makes to other qualified plans. An exemption to the 25% rule also applies to allocation of forfeitures of stock that have been released as collateral under a leveraged transaction.

This exclusionary rule is applicable if officers, shareholders holding more than 10% of the employer's outstanding stock, and highly compensated employees do not receive allocations that, in the aggregate, exceed 33⅓% of employer contributions that are used to repay the loan in a given year. This is another example of the benevolent way in which the government looks upon ESOPs as instruments of corporate finance.

Voting the ESOP Shares

If the company is publicly traded, its ESOP participants must be permitted to vote the stock that is allocated to their accounts. For ESOPs or stock bonus plans of privately owned companies that have issued no registration-type securities, the vote need not be passed through to the participants except in those states that require the vote of more than a majority of stockholders on certain grave issues. These major issues generally concern mergers, sale of most of the corporate assets, or discontinuance of operations, depending on the particular state. This limited voting right does not apply to ESOP stock acquired prior to December 31, 1979. It is important to note that the limited vote passthrough does not apply to unallocated stock such as in a loan transaction wherein the stock may not be released prior to the loan being amortized.

In all other situations, the trustee votes the ESOP shares at the direction of the administrative committee, which is appointed by the board of directors.

Eligibility

An ESOP must include all employees who have reached the age of 21 and completed one year of service during which they worked at least 1,000 hours. There are certain exceptions. Employees in a plan that grants complete vesting immediately upon participation may be excluded until they have completed three years of service. Seasonal industries are an exception to the 1,000-hour rule.

Although there is a minimum age, 21, there is no maximum age above which an employee meeting the other requirements can be excluded from the plan. They become eligible on the earlier of: (a) the first day of the plan year after completion of the service requirement, or (b) six months after completion of the service requirement. Nonresident alien employees whose earned income is derived entirely from sources outside of the United States border are to be excluded from participation in an ESOP.

A plan may specify that employees who are members of a collective bargaining unit may be excluded from the ESOP so long as retirement benefits had been the subject of good-faith bargaining between the union and the employer.

An alternative to the foregoing qualification items is the percentage test that assures satisfaction of the coverage requirement if the plan covers either 70% or more of all employees, or 80% of all eligible employees, assuming 70% or more of the employees are eligible.

Prior to November 1, 1977, ESOPs were permitted to be integrated with Social Security, which could have the effect of eliminating from eligibility those employees whose compensation was below the Social Security base. Subsequent to that date, ESOPs were precluded from integrating with Social Security; however, those established prior to that cutoff date may continue as integrated plans. The minimum employee participation standards must be met on at least one day of each quarter.

ESOPs may provide that participants who have incurred a break in service (failure to complete more than 500 hours in a specified 12-month period) will no longer be considered plan participants. In order to become eligible again, the former participant may be required to complete a year of service following the break.

4

Allocating the Stock to Participants' Accounts

Assets of the ESOP are allocated to participants' accounts in accordance with their compensation, service with the company, or a combination of both. Most generally, compensation is the only criterion that is used.

Typically, the total covered payroll is divided into units equaling $100 of annual compensation. The amount of corporate contribution allocated to a participant's account will be determined by the ratio that his or her unit count bears to the total. The more highly compensated individuals will receive the greatest allocation.

Forfeitures from those employees who terminate prior to becoming fully vested are reallocated among the remaining participants in a stock-bonus-plan ESOP. Allocation of forfeitures is computed in the same manner as for corporate contributions. This rewards tenure and loyalty. Employers should place emphasis on this desirable end result in selecting the types of benefit programs they wish to adopt.

Forfeitures are treated in different ways, depending on the type of qualified plan. In a defined-contribution plan, e.g., stock bonus plan or ESOP, forfeitures are reallocated to the accounts of the remaining participants unless the contributions are limited by formula in the plan's design, in which case forfeitures are used to reduce the employer's contribution for the plan year. This same reduction of employer contribution treatment is true of money-purchase plans, e.g., money-purchase ESOPs.

In a leveraged ESOP, shares that are used to collateralize a loan are allocated to participants' accounts as the shares of stock are released from pledge as the loan is repaid. This is done on a pro rata basis and in accordance with the same allocation method used for employer contributions and forfeitures.

The amount of employer contribution and forfeiture that can be allocated to the account of a participant in a defined-contribution plan is limited to 25% of the employee's compensation or a dollar amount, whichever is less. The dollar limitation schedule has called for $30,000 in 1985 and an annual cost-of-living adjustment beginning in 1988.

```
MODEL:

                    Allocation of Shares to Corp, Inc.,
                 Employee Stock Ownership Trust Participants

Payroll of ESOP Participants: $1,000,000
Corporation Contribution to ESOT: 15% of payroll, or $150,000.
```

| | | | Amount
Credited |
Employee	Salary	% of Payroll	to Account
Vice President	$ 70,000	7.0%	$10,500 (7% × $150,000)
Department Head	35,000	3.5%	$ 5,250 (3.5% × $150,000)
Clerk	14,000	1.4%	$ 2,100 (1.4% × $150,000)
Others (in aggregate)	881,000	88.1%	$132,150 (88.1% × 150,000)
Total:	$1,000,000	100%	

Distribution of ESOP Benefits

The Economic Recovery Tax Act of 1981 (ERTA) permits ESOPs to make distributions of their cash assets in the form of either stock or cash subject, however, to the right of the participants to demand distributions of stock. This is modified by the proviso that if the employer's charter or bylaws provide that only employees or the qualified trust may own "substantially all" (probably 80% or more) employer stock, then the ESOP may make its contributions in cash but with no right on the part of the employee to demand stock. Upon termination of employment, employee participants seldom wish to have distributions in the form of stock that is not publicly traded and that possibly pays no dividends. They want spendability. Aside from this, they will be taxed on the distribution and will need cash for that purpose as well.

ESOPs of companies whose stock is not readily tradeable on a public market must give the participants a put option that would require the employer to purchase their ESOP account shares within 60 days after they are distributed to the employee. If the option is not exercised within that time frame, the terminated employee must receive another put option for an additional 60-day period during the following plan year and subject to a new valuation of the employer's stock.

Some states require that corporations redeem stock essentially only out of retained earnings. If a corporation's retained earnings are inadequate in this context, the company may defer the put options until it can meet the retained-earnings requirements. This applies to nontradeable shares that the ESOP acquired after December 31, 1979.

ESOPs cannot be required to purchase stock at some future unknown date at an undeterminable price. For this reason, a put option cannot be imposed upon an ESOP. The ESOP may have the right to purchase stock from the terminated participant if the corporation is unable to do so. In this same context, an ESOP cannot enter into a mandatory buy-sell agreement that would require it to buy the stock upon a stockholder's retirement or death.

In the event an employee exercises the right to demand stock at the time of distribution, he or she still must be given a put option. Employers seldom wish to have stock in the hands of terminated employees. As a result, the ESOP regulations provide them with a safeguard under which the employer or the ESOP may be given a right of first refusal to reacquire the stock from the distributee or from his or her ESOP account at fair market value. If the distributee receives a bona fide offer from a third party, the company or the ESOP may meet the higher price within 14 days of receiving written notice from the distributee concerning the offer.

ESOPs of public companies do not require put options since their stock is readily tradeable in the public marketplace. If the stock is subject to certain trading limitations, the plan must provide a put option covering those shares. ESOPs and banks are not required to contain a put option where such banks are precluded by law from redeeming their own shares.

Payment for repurchased stock can be made in a lump sum or on an annual installment basis of up to 10 years. Adequate security must be provided if the installment period exceeds five years.

The ESOP trustee will look to the corporation for liquidity in order to make cash distributions or repurchase stock from those participants who are disabled, die, or retire. The corporation can oblige by making tax-deductible cash contributions to the ESOP to the extent needed within the limitations set forth by the regulations. Some firms choose to establish sinking funds comprised of liquidity instruments ranging from CDs to annuities to life insurance held within the corporation or by the ESOP. There are pros and cons to the various approaches and these will be discussed in Chapter 34. The liability will not generally be pronounced in the early stages of the ESOP due to the younger average ages of the ESOP population and the shallow vesting at that stage. Nevertheless, the problem should be anticipated and provision made to accommodate the future cash-out needs.

5

Vesting of Benefits

Qualified plans, whether they be pension plans, profit-sharing plans, or ESOPs, are seldom designed so as to be fully vested in the first year. This would be unduly costly, but, possibly more important, it would not meet with most employers' desire to use benefit plans as "golden handcuffs" to help dissuade employees from terminating. They would have too much to forfeit if they left the firm prior to being fully vested.

ERISA provides a guideline in the form of three minimum vesting schedules. An ESOP's vesting provision must be no more stringent than any of these in order to be considered non-discriminatory. ERISA also provides a safe-harbor vesting schedule, the so-called 4-40 vesting. This schedule provides that those participants with fewer than four years of service will have zero vesting. They will become 40% vested after four years of service, 45% after five years, 50% after six years, and in increments of 10% thereafter with full vesting after 11 or more years of service.

The three other schedules are:

(1) Ten-year vesting—under which there is zero vesting for a participant with less than 10 years of service. One becomes fully vested upon completion of 10 years of service.

(2) Five- to fifteen-year vesting—zero vesting for less than five years of service and 25% upon completion of five years. The schedule increases by 5% increments each year thereafter until one becomes fully vested upon completion of 15 years of service.

(3) Rule of 45—provides for 50% vesting upon the earlier of (a) completion of five or more years of service if the sum of the employee's age and years of service equals or exceeds 45 or (b) completion of 10 years of service. Vesting increases an additional 10% for each subsequent year of service.

Class vesting is also available under which 100% vesting is provided within five years after the end of the plan year for which contributions are made.

The 4-40 vesting schedule appears to be the most popular among the corporations structuring new plans. In the case of an ESOP that has been converted from a profit-making plan, the participant in the ESOP will retain the vesting status that he or she had in the profit-sharing plan. By freezing the assets of the profit-sharing plan, a new vesting schedule can apply to subsequent employer contributions to an ESOP.

Complete vesting for all participants will be triggered by the act of terminating the ESOP. This is true of all other tax-qualified plans.

The vesting guidelines set forth by ERISA are useful in helping plan designers avoid the pitfalls that might lead to discriminating in favor of officers, shareholders, or highly compensated employees. The vesting schedule and all other provisions of the ESOP must fit fundamental requirements of being for the benefit of employee participants and their beneficiaries.

How an ESOP Increases Working Capital and Cash Flow

Assuming a corporation is in the 50% federal and state tax bracket and contributes stock to its ESOP valued by independent appraisal at $200,000, it saves $100,000 in taxes. Instead of the money going to taxes, it remains in the corporation as working capital and cash flow. By contrast, $200,000 of cash contributed to a pension or a profit-sharing plan reduces working capital and cash flow by $100,000 after taxes. The difference between the stock-contribution plan and the cash-contribution plan is $200,000 for the year.

A 10-year projection of this corporation shows a $2 million working capital gap in the ESOP's favor. The difference becomes more pronounced as annual increases are factored in along with the time value of money. These could easily cause the $2 billion figure to double. This is an example of capital formation at its finest. If the corporation were in the 44% combined federal and state bracket, a contribution of $227,272 would accomplish the same thing.

How an ESOP Can Create a Market for a Stockholder's Stock

In lieu of contributing stock to its ESOP, a corporation can make deductible contributions of cash. The cash can be used to acquire stock of shareholders who wish to divest themselves of some or all of their stockholdings. It is difficult for holders of a private company stock to sell their stock. A sale of part of one's stock to the corporation is treated like a dividend for tax purposes. A sale to others generally means giving up control. Finding a buyer for minority shares of a private nondividend-paying company is like searching for the Holy Grail.

A majority owner or a minority stockholder can sell stock to the ESOP and receive either favorable capital gains tax treatment, or, under certain circumstances, may not be taxed at all.

This is a great way for an owner to transform paper into cash and diversify his or her estate while at the same time pass the company down to heirs or a second-line management team. By so doing, the owner can enjoy the spendability of his or her equity, assure perpetuation of the company, cash out minority stockholders, and still control the assets that are not in the ESOP. As we will see, this will enable the owner to effectively control the corporation.

How a Corporation Can Cut the Cost of Borrowing in Half

Neither pensions nor profit-sharing plans can borrow, but ESOPs are permitted to do so if the proceeds of the loan are used to purchase employer stock. Tax-deductible corporate cash contributions to the ESOP are employed by the plan trustee to buy stock from the corporation or from stockholders. The deductibility of the amount needed to service principal payments in addition to interest reduces the cost for repaying the loan by the taxes saved. One dollar of cash flow can go twice as far in accommodating debt retirement.

How Owners of Private Companies Can Get a 50% Discount on Estate Taxes

One of the provisions of the Tax Reform Act of 1984 that will be most meaningful to owners of private companies is the estate tax assumption aspect of the law. A lingering fear of many such owners is that since so much of their estates is locked into illiquid stock the company may have to be sold or liquidated in order to provide for estate taxes.

The government has long recognized the fragile nature of the entrepreneurial enterprise, the entity whose continued viability all too often parallels the finite existence of its founder. The estate tax invoice is levied, courtesy of the U.S. Treasury Department, at or near the moment of death. This tax is the most insidious of all, since the government requires no one to set aside a reserve for estate taxes as it does for income taxes. Yet the obligation is just as certain.

When one prepares a financial statement, the reserve for income taxes is noted but there is never an indication of the fact that as much as half of the net estate assets really belongs to the government. Estate taxes are often a blind spot, a manifestation of wishful thinking, a maybe-they-will-go-away syndrome. Estate taxes have the same effect on the family as though half the assets created by the breadwinner were lost in the stock market.

Once the estate planners do all that they can think of doing to reduce taxes, the bottom-line amount remains. Entrepreneurs seldom like to freeze their estate values at current levels if there are workable alternatives to keep the estate whole. Freezing the value means contemplating no future growth. It takes the fun out of the game, a game that is nearing its end.

The government has provided some help in alleviating the trauma of paying estate taxes so that closely held companies can stay afloat after the owner dies. I.R.C. §303, often referred to as the "bail-out provision," permits privately owned corporations to redeem sufficient stock from the owner's estate to pay federal estate taxes, state inheritance taxes, funeral expenses, and settlement costs. The redemption would not result in a taxable event. This is an exception to the treatment afforded partial redemptions wherein any appreciation over the basis would be taxed as a capital gain.

Thirty-five percent of the adjusted gross estate must be in the form of the company stock in order to qualify for this means of paying taxes.

25

An alternative is available for those estates with the same prerequisites as those qualifying for the §303 redemption. I.R.C. §6166 permits federal estate taxes to be paid on an installment basis over a 14-year period from the date of death. In essence, the government lends the executor the money for the taxes—at interest, of course. There is a five-year interest-only moratorium on principal. The interest rate applicable to estate taxes on the first $1 million of taxable estate is only 4%. The interest rate charged on the balance of the unpaid taxes is a floating prime rate.

Although §6166 offers relief for those who are unprepared from a liquidity standpoint, the interest can actually double or triple the cash requirement for paying death taxes.

How an Owner of a Private Company Can Transfer Estate Taxes to an ESOP

If there are estate taxes that must be paid, the Tax Reform Act of 1984 has made their payment almost a comfortable experience where owners of ESOP companies are concerned. Estate taxes can now be transferred over to the ESOP for payment, thereby cutting the cost for paying taxes in half.

Here is how the estate tax transfer can be accomplished:

> An executor of the estate of a stockholder of a private company may transfer qualifying securities to the ESOP of that company in exchange for the ESOP's agreeing to assume payment of the decedent's federal estate tax equal to the amount of securities transferred.

The ESOP administrator must agree in writing that the ESOP will assume the tax liability, and the employer of the ESOP participants must guarantee in writing that it will make the payments necessary to cover the tax and interest, if any.

The amount of securities transferred must equal the federal estate tax assumed by the ESOP. The ESOP will assume tax equal to the value of the securities transferred or the estate tax (reduced by any statutory credits that may be allowed), whichever is less.

Statutory credits that are allowed include:

• The unified credit;

• Credits for state death taxes, gift taxes that have been paid, foreign death taxes, tax on any prior transfer, and taxes on remainders or revisionary interests.

This procedure for paying death taxes places the burden of payment on the corporation's successor management. From this standpoint, the owners-to-be must be in a position to accommodate the demands of the written obligation. Insurance on the owner's life could be a means of preparation.

If the estate qualifies for I.R.C. §6166 treatment, the ESOP's administrator may pay the taxes by this means.

The transfer of the stock to the ESOP by the executor is actually treated as a sale. The price or consideration involved is the ESOP's agreement to pay the estate taxes. The transaction is also considered a loan for purposes of bypassing the prohibited-transactions rules. This treatment is also applicable to cooperatives.

The ability to transfer estate taxes to the ESOP is a means of transforming nonspendable stock into the equivalent of cash at short notice. Yet the company will not be forced into liquidation. Jobs will remain intact and the employees rather than the outsiders will be the equity owners. The community will reap the benefits of retaining local consumers and spenders and the federal government will harvest a greater amount of corporate and personal income taxes than it would have had the company been liquidated to pay the owner's estate taxes.

How You Can Sell Some or All of Your Private Company to Your Employees for Cash and Avoid All Taxes

The tax laws have been responsible for many private companies being sold to other corporations rather than to their own employees. If an owner of a company sells 80% or more of the outstanding stock to another corporation for stock in that company, there will be no capital gains tax until the shares acquired in the transaction are sold. If, on the other hand, the owner sold less than a substantially disproportionate share of his or her stock to his or her own corporation, the proceeds of the redemption would be taxed as a dividend, subjecting the owner to ordinary income tax.

The more appealing approach from a tax standpoint has been afforded under the ESOP rules, which permit a stockholder to sell any or all shares of qualifying employer securities to an ESOP. This transaction would be treated as a third-party sale, and the appreciation above the cost basis would be taxed under the more favorable capital gains rules.

Thousands of owners of private companies have taken this route to provide employee participants with equity in the company that they will continue to help build in the years ahead. This would have the additional beneficial effect of giving them an incentive for greater productivity, which would increase the value of any remaining shares still held by the remaining shareholder.

An improvement of windfall proportions has been brought about by the Deficit Reduction Act of 1984 and would affect stock sold by a shareholder to an ESOP after July 31, 1984. This is the tax-free rollover provision, which, as the name implies, would, under proper circumstances, give the same tax break to an owner who sells shares to an ESOP that is enjoyed by the owner who sells shares to another corporation. Actually, the sale to the ESOP is more advantageous in that an owner does not have to sell 80% of his or her stockholdings in order to receive favorable tax treatment. The only quantitative prerequisite is that the ESOP own 30% or more of the company's stock after the sale has been accomplished. It does not matter how the ESOP accumulated the shares so long as the 30% mark has been obtained.

For example, the ESOP may have received stock from the corporation as a contribution or a sale. It might have purchased shares from various stockholders. The ESOP must retain at least 30% of the outstanding stock of the company for a three-year period. A reduction below the 30% mark that may have been brought about as a result of statutory distributions occasioned by terminations, retirement, or death is not considered as a reduction for this purpose.

In order for the seller of the stock to avoid the tax upon sale of his or her shares, the seller must invest in stock or other qualified replacement property of another domestic corporation within 12 months from the time of sale, or, more precisely, within 15 months commencing three months prior to the transaction. Qualified replacement property includes not only corporate stock but corporate stock rights, bonds, debentures, notes, certificates, or other evidences of indebtedness in registered form or with coupons attached. The foregoing must be issued by a domestic corporation having no more than 25% passive income for the tax year of issuance.

The stock sold by the stockholder under this provision must have been held for at least one year and may not include stock that he or she had acquired under an option or any other right that the employer may have granted the stockholder. It must not have been stock that he or she received as a result of a distribution for a qualified plan and must not be stock that is readily tradeable on a securities market.

The rollover provision has erased the discrimination that had existed in favor of selling corporations to other corporations instead of to employees. The owner can still retain as much as 70% of the stock and have the benefit of any future appreciation. The owner can, if he or she wishes, sell incremental shares in the future in order to receive a tax-free supplement to taxable compensation. The corporation would, of course, make tax-deductible contributions of cash to the ESOP, which would be transferred over to the selling stockholder tax free.

The seller of the stock may not have the benefit of any of the stock sold being allocated to his or her ESOP account or to the ESOP accounts of any family members or to any other person who owns more than 25% of the outstanding stock of the corporation.

Prior to the 1984 Act, ESOPs had served to perpetuate companies and keep them in the hands of the founder's family, executives, and other employees. This trend will be accelerated by the tax-free rollover provision created by the 1984 Act, further broadening the base of capital ownership among the nation's employees. The law permits and encourages corporate owners to make partial sales of their companies, which has the positive effect of a gradual transition rather than a traumatic one that would come from a full sale. This will help assure corporate stability and continuity of the growth pattern that had existed prior to the sale. The owner will have an incentive to make the shares retained appreciate in value. This will be good for the ESOP equity holders as well.

In a sale to outsiders, the first heads to roll will generally be the key executives'. Relocations of companies that are sold to outside corporate or individual buyers of companies is a frequent aftereffect that will call for family upheavals if the employee is to remain with the corporation. This scenario is avoided by the owner's ability to obtain cash for the stock equity that he or she holds. The continued interrelationships with local suppliers, subcontractors, and banks make the rollover far more preferable than the outright sale to corporations in other locations. Many communities recognize these attributes and have passed legislation beneficial to ESOPs. The tax-free rollover will help keep companies in the community.

A point is reached when nearly every owner of a private corporation strongly ponders the advisability of selling the company. The owner is often asset rich and cash poor. Income from labor is a poor trade-off for capital that is tied up in the company.

So long as the owner does not sell the company, he or she cannot capitalize assets. Yet the capital the owner would release to himself or herself upon sale can far exceed the salary he or she will continue to receive from the business, and it could be tax free as opposed to being taxed as ordinary income. A partial sale, perhaps through an LBO coupled with an ESOP (LESOP), can capitalize his or her wealth without turning off the faucet.

8

How a Company Can Increase Working Capital and Cash Flow by Converting Its Profit-Sharing Plan to an ESOP

ESOPs are mandated to invest primarily in company stock, while other forms of qualified plans are generally restricted to 10% of their assets being in employer securities. The analogy in Chapter 5 bears reemphasizing. Contributions of cash to a qualified plan result in a tax deduction for the corporation but nonetheless reduce working capital and cash flow. If the corporation is in the combined 50% state and federal tax bracket and contributes $100,000 of cash to a qualified plan, it will, nonetheless, decrease working capital and cash flow by $50,000. A corresponding contribution of employer stock to an ESOP in the same amount will increase its working capital and cash flow by $50,000, since neither the cash contribution nor the tax payment leaves the pockets of the corporation. The difference between the two plans from a working-capital and cash-flow standpoint is $100,000 in favor of the ESOP. This amounts to over $1 million of increased working capital in the course of a decade, assuming no change in payroll or annual contributions.

If covered payroll increases at a 10% compounded rate and a proportionately greater annual contribution is made, working capital would be improved by $1.7 million over the decade. If the corporation is able to earn 10% net on the capital that it gained as a result of choosing an ESOP over another form of qualified plan, this will add an additional $1.7 million of working capital, for a total of $3.4 million over the 10-year span.

Studies have demonstrated dramatic productivity improvements among ESOP companies. If this is factored into the subject company's working-capital improvement, the $3.4 million gain noted above would be further enchanced. The studies of this nature were discussed in Chapter 1. Although this is a compelling feature of the ESOP, it should not be treated in isolation of other characteristics of the various forms of qualified plans.

Profit-sharing plans can be converted to ESOPs and their assets used to buy employer stock, assuming it is deemed to be in the best interest of the participants. Assuming there is no fiduciary question about the advisability of the transaction, the assets of the profit-sharing plan could be used to purchase stock from the corporation or from stockholders who are willing to sell. The purchase price must be no more than fair market value. Purchase of stock from the corporation will infuse working capital and cash flow into the company. The improved working capital position could possibly benefit the participants significantly. Assuming this to be the reality of the situation, the argument for the transition of the assets would be fortified.

The vesting status of the profit-sharing plan is protected. Those employees who are in the prior plan will have the same degree of vesting in the ESOP as they enjoyed in the profit-sharing plan. In a conversion, the assets of the prior plan can be, but need not be, used to purchase employer stock. The assets of the previous plan could be frozen in a separate account with separate records being maintained. At some future date it might be considered more timely to use some or all of the assets of the former plan to purchase employer stock from the company or from stockholders. Distributions to terminating employees would be made from the stock account and from the other asset account.

The corporation can implement the ESOP and still retain the profit-sharing plan, in which case contributions would be made to each plan subject to the overall contribution limitation prescribed by the regulations. In this case, the ESOP could have a completely different vesting schedule from the profit-sharing plan. Moreover, employee-participants of the profit-sharing plan who were partially or fully vested would not necessarily retain that status in the ESOP.

Conversion of money-purchase pension plans or defined-benefit pension plans is treated as a termination of the plans, and this act would trigger immediate and full vesting of all participant accounts. The company can also retain a pension plan as well as a profit-sharing plan and ESOP subject to the rules governing total contributions to qualified plans as discussed in Chapter 3.

When considering whether to convert a profit-sharing plan to an ESOP, the question will arise as to whether the employees should participate in the decision. An election on the part of the employees to convert profit-sharing plan assets into an ESOP may be considered an offering of stock that would require that the company stock be registered with the Securities and Exchange Commission and under state securities laws unless the company could qualify for an exemption.

If the fiduciaries use the assets of the existing plan to purchase employer securities without seeking the participants' approval and the account balances are decreased as a result of the conversion, there could possibly be a cause of action against the fiduciaries under the prudent person rule or because the conversion was not for the exclusive benefit of the employees. This may be difficult to establish if the stock was purchased at fair market value in accordance with an independent appraisal. The independence of the appraisal cannot be overemphasized. One should remember that shares of employer stock are as valuable as an equivalent dollar amount of shares of listed companies if the appraisal is thorough. Private company stock might have the advantage of not being quite so subject to the emotional whims of the public marketplace.

A "partial" conversion is one whereby the assets of the profit-sharing plan are maintained in a separate cash account in the newly created ESOP, and new contributions are made to the ESOP in the form of stock or cash, which is used to purchase stock. The assets in the cash account can continue to be invested in money instruments or diversified securities other than qualified employer securities. The fiduciary responsibility must be maintained to assure diversification and a fair return on investment in connection with the nonemployer security assets.

A technique that might be considered would be to allow the employees to compare the investment gain in the cash account and the stock account for one or two years after the conversion. A conversion might be less traumatic to the employees if the annual valuation attests to the fact that the employer stock had appreciated to an amount at least equivalent to the investments in the cash account. Thereafter, the use of the cash account to purchase employer stock might pose no problem. Certainly this would tend to build an argument for prudency.

Employers tend to make more generous contributions to ESOPs than they had been making to profit-sharing plans due to the fact that ESOPs permit the cash to remain in the corporation while profit-sharing plans are a drain against the cash flow and working capital of the corporation. If, for example, a corporation had been contributing 5% of covered payroll to its profit-sharing plan and subsequently contributes 15% to an ESOP, the plan participants would be essentially just as well off if the stock value declined by approximately 66⅔%.

Of course, this is a theoretical example and the employees would undoubtedly feel very uncomfortable about the decline in the value of the stock. It is quite likely that if the company were doing that poorly, many of the employees would have already been discharged. By the same token, since contributions to a profit-sharing plan can only be made out of profits, it is obvious that the employer would not be in a position to make further contributions to the profit-sharing plan until such a time as the company turned around. A contribution of the employer stock to an ESOP would tend to increase working capital and cash flow and should offer further security to the employees as a result of its improved capital position.

While profit-sharing plans can be converted, the Pension Benefit Guaranty Corporation will deem the conversion of a defined-benefit pension plan to an ESOP as a termination, and all of the account balances of participants will become fully vested subject to distribution.

How to Convert or Terminate an ESOP

A question frequently arises as to how one might convert or terminate an ESOP in the event it does not work out as well as the employer had hoped. Just as profit-sharing plans can be converted to ESOPs, the converse is also true. The assets of ESOPs can be frozen and new cash contributions can go into the profit-sharing plan to which the ESOP has been converted. Alternatively, the ESOP can be terminated, in which event the assets will become fully vested and distributed to the participants or rolled over into an individual retirement account (IRA) as the participant may direct within 60 days of distribution.

MODEL:

Conversion of a Profit-Sharing Trust to an ESOP Using Assets
to Increase Company Working Capital

$300,000 ASSETS

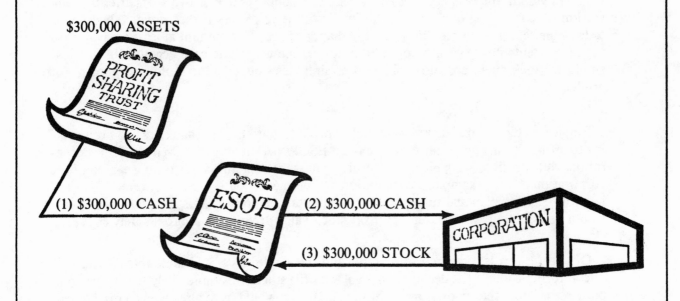

—Corporation has a profit-sharing trust with assets of $300,000.
—It forms an Employee Stock Ownership Plan.
—Assets are converted from the profit-sharing trust to the ESOP.
—Assets are liquidated and used to purchase stock of sponsoring corporation.
—Employer-participants retain vesting standing they had prior to the conversion.

Summary:

The corporation's cash flow, working capital, and net worth are increased
by $300,000.

The employees participate in the growth of their company.

9

How to Value the Stock of a Closely Held Company

ESOP companies are parties to various types of transactions involving the sale or purchase of employer securities. These include the contribution of employer stock to an ESOP or the contribution of cash, which is used by the ESOP to purchase stock from the corporation or from stockholders other than stock held by the ESOP trustee, cash that the trustee distributes to ESOP participants in lieu of employer stock, and cash used to purchase stock from ESOP distributees.

All of these transactions have one thing in common—they must be done for adequate consideration. "Adequate" has been defined by ERISA as "the fair market value of the asset as determined in good faith by the trustee or named fiduciary pursuant to the terms of the plan and in accordance with the regulations promulgated by the Secretary" (of the Treasury).

As of the publication of this book, regulations pertaining to ESOP valuation have been neither proposed nor issued. Although there are no regulations to the effect that an independent appraisal firm must value the stock, the determination of the value of the stock is more defensible if an independent appraisal firm is used.

Firms specializing in the appraisal of privately owned companies use the same guidelines for ESOP valuation as for gift tax and estate tax determination. *Revenue Ruling 59-60* refers to fair market value as the price at which the property would change hands between a willing buyer and a willing seller when neither is under any compulsion to buy or to sell, both parties having reasonable knowledge of the relevant facts. The ruling indicates that valuation of stock of a private company should take eight basic items into consideration, as follows:

(1) The nature of the business and the history of the enterprise from its inception;

(2) The economic outlook in general and the condition and outlook of the specific industry in particular;

(3) The book value of the stock and the financial condition of the business;

(4) The earnings capacity of the company;

(5) The dividend-paying capacity of the company;

(6) Whether or not the enterprise has goodwill or other intangible value;

(7) Sale of the stock and the size of the block to be valued; and

(8) The market price of stocks of corporations engaged in the same or similar lines of business having their stocks actively traded in a free and open market, either on an exchange or over the counter.

Valuation experts delve deeply into numerous other factors such as the firm's share of the market and its potential for maintaining that share. They look at the first-line and second-line management team and consider the various aspects of management succession and perpetuation of the company. The corporation's technological capabilities, research and development status, lines of credit, adequacy of the physical plant, and potential for expansion are some of the other considerations in arriving at fair market value of the company. The use of a formula in valuing a company does not relate to many of the tangible and intangible factors of the immediate and distant economic and political environments that can influence the company's future. Appraisal by formula can fall apart and lacks the credibility inherent in independent appraisals.

The transactions that the trustee usually engages in involve minority interests that have no control over important decisions such as compensation, dividends, or determination of corporate policy. As a consequence, the valuation specialists will most likely assign a minority discount to the value of the stock. Others contend that, taken as a whole, if the ESOP has a controlling interest, each participant's share should be valued on an enterprise or control basis.

Some appraisers contend that a minority discount is not called for if the private company stock valuation takes into consideration the value of comparable public company stocks. They point out that stocks listed on major exchanges reflect a minority discount; consequently, an additional discount would be redundant.

If there is little or no market for the shares, one might impute a discount of 10% to 35% off of public company stock that is actively traded. This discount could be reduced or eliminated by other factors.

A good funding program for the ultimate purchase of the stock in the ESOP account can have a positive effect on the value of the stock in that it may reduce the discount for lack of marketability. A put option for the distributee can justify a further reduction in the marketability discount—more so if the financial condition of the company warrants a realistic expectation of its ability to repurchase the stock.

When a company takes a tax deduction for its contribution of stock to the ESOP, it had better be certain that fair market value is the criterion on which the amount of the deduction is based. If the stock has been valued at too high a price, a disallowance of the deduction may be the unpleasant result. If a major stockholder sells stock to the ESOP at a price that is greater than fair market value, the stockholder may be asked to pay an excise tax.

Conversely, if the ESOP trustee purchases stock from a terminating employee-participant at a price below fair market value, the former participant may litigate for a more favorable price. Use of an annual valuation will generally be adequate for transactions that do not involve a party-in-interest (the corporation or an officer, director, or 10% or more stockholder). But for one that does involve a party-in-interest, the value must be updated as close to the date that the transaction occurs as possible. Ninety days is probably acceptable if no events have occurred in the interim that might materially affect the outcome. For routine transactions such as redeeming a participant's stock, an annual valuation should suffice.

Companies whose stock is listed on a national exchange pose no problem in valuation. For ESOP purposes, fair market value will be considered to be the average of the closing prices of the stock in question for 20 consecutive trading days immediately preceding the date of the ESOP transaction.

Formulas will, over a period of time, produce unrealistic valuation results because of a changing environment. For this reason they are not recommended for establishing fair market value.

10

How to Feel Loved and Needed After Selling the Company—Keep Control

Control is everything. This has become a cliche because it has a basis in fact. Equity is important, but with control, equity frequently follows. The downside of equity in the form of private company stock is that it is, in a practical sense, a liability. It triggers a governmental invoice demanding as much as 50 cents of cash for each $1 of nonspendable paper held in the estate at the time of death. It is this fact that drives owners of private companies to seek ways of transforming their paper into cash. If there were a way that would permit them to cash out as they see fit without losing control, this would be a way to have one's cake and eat it too. A sidelight, not to be discounted, is the self-assurance that is purchased by control. Whether one is loved and adored matters little so long as he or she has control.

A nonleveraged stock bonus plan combined with creative planning is an ideal vehicle to enable an owner of a private company to unleash his or her nonspendable stock asset and transform it into cash without relinquishing corporate control. This combination can also serve to assist in the orderly transition of ultimate control of the company, placing it in the hands of the owner's children who have demonstrated an aptitude and desire to carry on the family tradition. Key executives might also fall into a similar category.

It is Mr. Big's desire to perpetuate the firm, and find a means whereby he can reward the employees for their loyalty and at the same time give them an incentive to continue to build the company. He wants to ultimately place control in the hands of his two children, both of whom are active in the business. He cannot afford to give his stock away, in that it represents his only significant asset. Above all, he has a strong feeling about retaining control of the company for as long as he lives.

How Mr. Big Can Remove His Capital, Retain Control, and Perpetuate the Company

The corporation can rearrange its capital structure by creating a new class of stock, class B nonvoting common. The corporation will declare a stock dividend of nine shares of class B nonvoting common stock for each share of stock outstanding. This means that 100% of the

41

voting capacity rests in 10% of the equity, namely in the class A voting stock. Mr. Big recognizes that his children have insufficient cash to buy out his interest in the business. Yet Mr. Big cannot afford simply to give the stock to his children, or, for that matter, to executives.

He solves the problem by selling his class B stock to the stock bonus plan, which is a non-leveraged ESOP. The corporation will make deductible cash contributions to the plan, which the trustees will use to purchase class B nonvoting stock from Mr. Big. This process will continue indefinitely, since the amount he sells each year roughly parallels the annual appreciation of his holdings. He will be taxed on the appreciation that will have occurred in the value of the stock he sells above its cost basis. The transaction will be subject to capital gains tax treatment.

A stock purchase agreement provides that the children who are in the business will purchase the class A voting stock from the executor of Mr. Big's estate. The class A stock would have a very small value relative to the total value of the company. This could be funded by insurance owned by the children on Mr. Big's life. The balance of the class B stock that is not sold during his lifetime could be redeemed by the ESOP, using corporate deductible dollars to accomplish this. Since the corporation is not to redeem the stock, there should be no attribution problem, which would have meant adverse tax treatment.

The end result coincides with Mr. Big's goal. The stock will be reduced to liquid form so that he will be able to enjoy the diversification that cash brings. He will be able to maintain control for his lifetime. The children will acquire control at very little cost, since the life insurance premiums will be bonused to them by the corporation. The employees will gain a lion's share of equity, which will be destined to give them the incentive to become more productive. The family, the executives, and the rank-and-file employees will have greater peace of mind in knowing that the company's perpetuation will be assured and dislocations will not occur.

Mr. Big will feel loved and needed...even after selling his shares.

11

How to Sell Your Company and Still Keep It

Your Corporation—An Asset/Liability

A well-run corporation is a virtual money machine. It provides the working owner with reasonable compensation and capital appreciation. The former is spendable, but the latter can become spendable only if all or part of the company is sold. It is difficult and unusual to be able to sell a portion of the company to outsiders. Outside buyers generally want at least 51% or nothing. They want to be the ones to do the voting. Employees may be willing to purchase minority interests, but usually only if the stock is bonused to them. Even then they may eventually feel that their capital is tied up and, absent dividends, will often feel resentful of the fact that their capital might be put to better use. They will possibly even look upon the investment as a loan to their employer.

Going public is seldom the answer to getting one's capital out of the company. Assuming the corporation is sufficiently charismatic to have a successful offering, it is difficult for a member of the control group to sell his or her own stock because of the stringent restrictions that govern such shares.

If the major stockholder sells a minor portion of his or her stock to the corporation, it will be treated as a dividend. He or she will be taxed as though it were ordinary income and not deductible by the corporation.

The downside effect of maintaining stock as a primary asset in one's estate is that the government will not accept it as legal tender for paying estate taxes. The government wants cash, not stock. Taxes are due nine months from the date of death. This is a frequent cause for families to sell or liquidate good going businesses at a distressed price. It is an opportunity avidly sought by sharp-eyed vultures.

I.R.C. §6166 permits a stockholder's executor to pay taxes over a 14-year period with a five-year interest-only moratorium. Interest is at 4% on the first $345,000 of taxes and at a floating government rate on the balance. Although this gradual payment schedule can triple the cost of paying taxes, it is useful if immediate liquidity is not available. Section 6166 eligibility requires that stock in one's company make up 35% or more of the adjusted gross estate.

Let's assume that Mr. Big owns 100% of the stock of his corporation but would like to have more cash to spend during his lifetime and more liquidity in the event of his death. Moreover, he does not care for the idea of taking on new stockholders who might interfere with his style of building the company, and he would consider selling the company only as a last resort. Here is what he can do to solve his problem under the ESOP provisions of the 1984 Deficit Reduction Act.

• He can sell a large portion of his stock and receive tax-free cash on the transaction;

• He can maintain effective control of his company;

• He can obtain bank financing at approximately 80% prime;

• The corporation can deduct its payments for both principal and interest;

• The corporation will be able to deduct its payment of dividends to the ESOP participants, including the stock that had been allocated to Mr. Big's ESOP account; and

• Upon Mr. Big's death, the estate taxes can be transferred to the ESOP to be paid either in a lump sum or, if the estate is eligible, it may elect to use I.R.C. §6166, the installment arrangement.

Additional facts are these:

• The corporation has established an ESOP that is a stock bonus plan for the current year;

• The covered annual payroll is $2 million;

• An independent appraisal has determined the fair market value for the corporation is $3 million;

• Pretax earnings are $1,250,000 and are expected to grow at a 10% annual compounded rate;

• Prime interest at the time is 12%; and

• There are 400,000 shares of stock outstanding. Mr. Big has offered to sell 80% of his 400,000 shares of stock, whose fair market value has been determined to be $7.50 per share to the ESOP. He conveyed the offer to the administrative committee and it was agreed that if suitable financing could be obtained, the trustee would be instructed to proceed with the purchase of the 320,000 shares for $2.4 million.

A bank was found that was willing to pass three-fourths of its tax savings under the ESOP provisions of the 1984 tax act onto the ESOP. Under the 1984 act, the bank could deduct 50% of its interest income for loans made to an ESOP for acquiring stock. The bank would have been willing to make a loan to the corporation at the prime rate, which at that time was 12%. Fifty percent of the interest the bank was to receive was tax deductible. The lending committee agreed to pass three-fourths of the 3% tax savings, or 2.25%, onto the ESOP. This netted out to a 9¾% interest rate.

The bank stipulated that the corporation must agree to make annual cash contributions to the ESOP to service both principal and interest for the seven-year period of the loan. The payments for principal and interest on the $2.4 million seven-year loan amounted to $39,565 per month, annualized at $474,403.

The Economic Recovery Tax Act of 1981 increased the deductible limitation under a stock-bonus-plan ESOP from 15% to 25% of covered payroll for servicing principal on a leveraged ESOP transaction. In addition, interest could be deducted irrespective of the limitation. The $2 million annual payroll could accommodate as much as $500,000 annual contribution for principal alone. The servicing obligation for the loan would fit well into this limitation. The $1.25 million pretax earnings would offer a comfort zone to the company with respect to its contributions to the ESOP. Mr. Big proceeded to invest in a portfolio of qualified domestic company stocks and bonds within 12 months from the time of the sale of his stock. This made it possible to receive the tax-free rollover.

By continuing to own all of the outstanding stock not held by the ESOP, Mr. Big maintained active control of the company except for those grave issues such as merger or liquidation on which more than a majority of stockholders must act, since on those matters the vote would be passed through to the employee participants. The vote passthrough would pertain only to those shares that had been released by the bank as the note is amortized. It would still be a few years before Mr. Big's holdings went below the 51% mark. On all other matters the ESOP participants would have no vote.

If the terms of the loan agreement permitted, the corporation could declare dividends and deduct those going through the ESOP to the participants. This would be a direct reflection of the employees' productivity and should serve as an additional incentive to them. Improved productivity would make Mr. Big's remaining 20% more valuable.

Upon Mr. Big's death, the executor of his estate could transfer the federal estate tax obligation attributable to the securities remaining in his estate at his death to the ESOP. The executor would pay for the taxes by merely transferring the stock in Mr. Big's estate to the ESOP. The taxes could therefore be paid by tax-deductible corporate contributions.

The arrangement was far better than an outright sale of the company from the standpoint of Mr. Big and the employees. Mr. Big continued to run the company as he always had, and the employees were delighted because there were no dislocations or relocations of management or rank-and-file employees. Moreover, the employees were destined to own the equity of the company in addition to receiving original compensation for their labor and a passthrough dividend as well. There was no pressure brought to bear to sell the company upon Mr. Big's death because his estate was quite liquid. Mr. Big netted as much after tax as he would have had he sold the company to outsiders based upon the capital gains tax rules. He continued to receive his usual compensation for the rest of his life in addition to the capital he released from the corporation.

Although the government helped tremendously with tax relief, the perpetuation of the corporation and continued expansion were destined to result in the hiring of many more people who would pay more and more in taxes just as the corporation itself would. The government was destined to make a recovery of deferred revenue in the many years ahead. The community at large, including the state, would not lose the enterprise to outsiders.

Stock Redemption by an ESOP—Getting an Advance Ruling

The IRS will issue an advance ruling to the effect that sale of stock to an ESOP by a shareholder constitutes a third-party sale rather than a redemption. To obtain such a ruling, the conditions delineated in *Revenue Procedure 77-30* must be met. Here are the conditions:

☐ The beneficical interest in a plan for a selling shareholder and all related persons must not exceed 20% of the total assets of the plan. This requirement is not satisfied if:

• The combined covered compensation of the selling shareholder and related persons exceeds 20% of total covered compensation under the plan;

• The total account balances (vested and nonvested) of the selling shareholder and related persons exceed 20% of the total of all employee account balances (vested and nonvested) in the plan; or

• The combined interest (vested and nonvested) of the selling shareholder and related persons in any separately managed fund or account within the plan exceeds 20% of the total net assets in that fund or account.

☐ Any restrictions on dispositions of the stock in the plan, and on stock received by the employees from the plan, can be no more onerous than the restrictions on at least a majority of the shares held by other shareholders.

☐ It must be stated that there is no plan, intention, or understanding for the employer to redeem any of the stock from the employee plan.

Revenue Procedure 77-30 applies to all corporate qualified plans and not simply to ESOPs. While there is no requirement that calls for obtaining an advance ruling, there may be some comfort in doing so. Some questions had been left up in the air, which were brought down to earth with the publication of *Revenue Procedures 78-18* and *78-23*.

Revenue Procedure 78-18 clarified the provision dealing with the "more onerous restrictions" as it applies to the right of first refusal. If the "right" complies with the final regulations, the "more onerous" provision is not applicable.

One of the questions concerned itself with replacement of a profit-sharing plan by an ESOP in which the assets of the former plan are frozen with no further contributions going into it, and the profit-sharing assets are maintained with separate accounting under the ESOP. *Revenue Procedure 78-23* indicates that the 20% limit is not applicable to a separate profit-sharing-plan account.

These revenue procedures have proven to be guidelines that add comfort to broad utilization of ESOPs for many creative purposes. Among these are:

- Buying out a minority or a majority stockholder.

- Providing estate liquidity for stockholders.

- Transferring ownership to successor management.

- Selling the company in its entirety to an ESOP.

Prior to publication of the revenue procedures, there was a great deal of speculation as to how the IRS might view stockholder sale transactions.

12

How a Company Can Pay Dividends—
And Deduct Them

ESOPs have the unique attribute of building a capital nest egg for employees without their contributing any cash. The employer is the sole source of the equity contribution and in a broad sense one can think of it as additional tax-deferred compensation. The employee receives taxable wages for his or her labor. A third element of compensation comes as a result of extraordinary effort that results in increased productivity. This, in turn, is reflected in the appreciation in the value of the stock allocated to his or her ESOP account.

The fourth form of benefit can now be expected in the form of tax-deductible dividends, an immediate or nondeferred return on equity. This is the element that had been missing in ESOP. It is difficult for employees with limited patience to rely solely upon the value that can be realized sometime in the future.

What is also often needed in order for one to appreciate one's wealth is tangible evidence of its existence. This comes most effectively in the form of current spendability. The deductibility of dividends had been talked about for years, but when the first realization of the tax break came, it was for the benefit of ESOP companies.

The Deficit Reduction Act of 1984 permits a corporation to pay dividends to an ESOP and deduct them from corporate taxable income, provided that they are passed through to the employee participants. Dividends have heretofore created a double taxation event. The corporation received no dividend reduction and the recipient was taxed. The dividend passed through still leaves the employee participants with the burden of paying taxes upon the receipt of the dividend, but the corporation is no longer inhibited from distributing some of its excess earnings to those who now produce the earnings.

The law prescribes that the dividend, in order to be deductible, must be passed through the ESOP within 90 days of its being contributed to the ESOP. Alternatively, the ESOP may use the dividends to make loan payments for the acquisition of employer's stock within that period of time, although they would not be tax deductible. The shares of stock would be allocated to employee accounts, thereby enhancing their equity position. An issuance of dividends treated in this manner does not count as part of the contribution limitations.

The payment of tax-deductible dividends is an ideal way to help avoid a penalty tax for excess accumulations of retained earnings in the company. The dividend pass-through provision provides the corporation with another distinct advantage. Employees will come to a better understanding as to the meaning of equity ownership. They will quickly learn that dividends will be paid on their shares in a manner commensurate with corporate profits. The fact that dividends are related to additional productivity will not be lost on them.

The deductibility of the dividend is applicable only to shares in the ESOP and has no applicability to shares held by stockholders other than the ESOP.

13

How to Make an Acquisition With Pretax Dollars

A corporation cannot deduct the cost for acquiring another company. It can deduct its contributions to an ESOP, however, and the ESOP can acquire the company. The degree of simplicity or complexity of the facts surrounding the components of the acquisition determines the degree of sophistication that will be put into the transaction. Here is a simple example of how a corporation with an ESOP might acquire a company and get a tax deduction for doing so.

Alpha Corp. has an ESOP covering 100 employees with a $2 million payroll. Alpha's ESOP has $1 million of Alpha Corp. stock. The pretax earnings of the company are $1 million, and its net worth is $2 million. Alpha Corp. wishes to expand and would like to acquire Beta Corp., whose book net worth and pretax earnings are $3 million and $2.5 million, respectively. Beta Corp. has a qualified profit-sharing plan with $1 million of assets in the trust covering a payroll of $3 million. The company is owned by its 70-year-old founder, who thinks the time has come to retire. He has no heirs in the business nor does he have an executive that he feels has all the talents required for a chief executive officer. A deal is struck. Mr. Beta will sell his corporation to the smaller Alpha Corp. for $5 million, having determined that the bank financing is available. Here is how the financing is arranged.

Alpha Corp. plans on converting Beta Corp.'s profit-sharing plan to its ESOP. The assets of the converted plan will be liquidated and used to acquire Alpha Corp. stock, thereby infusing $1 million of working capital into Alpha Corp. Alpha Corp. will use the $1 million of proceeds from the conversion as its downpayment for Beta Corp. The bank will make a $4 million seven-year loan to Alpha's ESOP, which the ESOP will use to buy Alpha stock from Alpha. Alpha will then use the $4 million to complete the purchase of all of Beta's stock. The two ESOPs probably would then be consolidated into one ESOP with Alpha Corp. as the sponsoring corporation and Beta Corp. as participating employer. The ESOP's shares will be pledged as collateral to be released as the loan is amortized. The bank will look to Alpha's and Beta's ability to contribute cash to the ESOP in sufficient amounts to service the loan.

Alpha's pretax earnings will be increased by $2.5 million and its net worth by $3 million. By consolidating warehousing, accounting, and other functions, Alpha's pro forma projects a substantially increased pretax earnings picture for the following year. Its increased payroll will add to its ability to service principal and interest with pretax dollars. The interest rate charged by the bank is more favorable than it would have been had an ESOP not been involved to reduce the cost of servicing the loan. The bank also receives a tax deduction on its interest income from an ESOP loan. This will be discussed at length in Chapter 18.

All in all, the ESOP makes it feasible for Alpha Corp. to more than double its net worth and its earnings. Debt service is cut in half because of the tax savings. The employee-participants are destined to increase their productivity as their equity ownership becomes more apparent. This is destined to enhance the growth in the value of the stock. It is a win-win deal for Alpha's stockholders, who increase their capacity for net worth. Mr. Beta obtains his liquidity immediately. Beta Corp.'s employees receive equity instead of mere compensation for their labor. The bank makes a profitable loan. And the government gives up some tax revenue temporarily but is destined to make up the deferral of its income many times over. The increased taxable corporate earnings coupled with the expanded taxpaying work force and its taxable retirement equity will make the initial tax incentives all worthwhile from the government's viewpoint.

The ESOP's magic ingredient for accomplishing these results is its unique ability to create capital.

14

ESOPs—A Way to Acquire Key-Executive Insurance at No Net Aftertax Cash Outlay

The death of a key profitmaker could cause the value of the stock in the ESOP to drop, thereby eroding the security of the ESOP participants. It is for this reason that the final regulations permit ESOPs to own key-executive life insurance subject, of course, to the prudence tests.

It is generally more desirable that the insurance be owned by the corporation than by the ESOP. This bypasses any question of prudence. Another reason is not as readily apparent.

Death proceeds of ESOP-owned insurance provide cash that will prove useful in redeeming the decedent's stock from his or her estate. The effect of this is beneficial to the ESOP's participants by infusing greater equity into their accounts. The estate heirs will be grateful for the cash.

The corporation and its direct stockholders will not fare quite so well. A new liability will be created by the very liquidity that flowed into the ESOP. Someday the participants' enhanced accounts must be purchased by the corporation or by the ESOP. Although the corporation is relieved of the obligation to redeem the decedent's shares, a new liquidity problem of similar or greater magnitude still looms ahead.

Corporate Ownership: The corporation can own insurance on the lives of key profitmakers. The proceeds of the insurance can be used to:

☐ Fund a buy-sell agreement so that the decedent's shares can be acquired by the corporation. The trustees of an ESOP cannot enter into a mandatory buy-sell agreement to purchase shares upon the contingency of a stockholder dying at some unknown date and subject to an unknown value. A corporation may agree to purchase the stock subject to the ESOP having an option to buy it. The insurance can therefore be owned by either the corporation or by the ESOP.

☐ Maintain financial stability upon the key profitmaker's death. This will help keep the lines of credit open. The influx of tax-free proceeds will have a positive effect upon the stock's value and, in turn, upon the morale of the ESOP participants.

☐ Enable the corporation to make deductible cash contributions to the ESOP to purchase the shares allocated to the decedent's ESOP account.

Two Dollars for One: One dollar of corporate-owned insurance proceeds can serve the purpose of two dollars of any other form of liquidity, since the insurance proceeds are tax free. Two dollars of insurance proceeds can be contributed to the ESOP at an aftertax cost of one dollar. The ESOP will have two dollars with which to buy the decedent's stock.

Corporate Insurance at No Net Aftertax Outlay: Let's say the corporation wishes to purchase insurance on the key executive's life. The premium is nondeductible, since the policy's cash value is to be owned by the corporation and the death proceeds payable to it. By using the ESOP in conjunction with the purchase of the corporate-owned insurance, we can eliminate any aftertax cash outlay. Let's assume an annual premium of $20,000.

Corporation to ESOP: The corporation makes a deductible $20,000 cash contribution to the ESOP at an aftertax cost of $10,000.

ESOP to Corporation: The ESOP purchases $20,000 of stock from the corporation.

Corporation to Insurance Company: The corporation, ahead $10,000 because of tax savings, pays $20,000 to the insurance company for a policy it will own on the key executive's life.

Insurance Company to Corporation: The insurance company sends a policy to the corporation, the corporation to own the policy and cash value.

The Corporation Recovers Its Net Outlay: The corporation borrows sufficient cash value from the policy to recover its aftertax cost on average as well as the aftertax cost of the interest.

Result: There is no net aftertax cost for the insurance. Also, there is an impressive two-for-one liquidity in the use of the death proceeds.

A Liquidity Reserve: In addition to the foregoing, there is an additional important function that corporate-owned life insurance will serve. The policy's cash value can be considered a liquidity reserve for the emerging repurchase liability to buy the stock of terminating ESOP participants.

15

How to Get Personal and Corporate Tax Deductions That Exceed the Value Of Your Gift

An ESOP can help you help your college, hospital, church or temple, or other favorite charitable organizations...and yourself.

If you are a stockholder, you can donate shares of your appreciated stock to a qualified public charity and get a tax deduction equaling the current value of the gift. If you have held your appreciated stock long enough for it to be considered long-term gain property, your limit for the deduction under most circumstances is 30% of your adjusted gross income. The limit for cash gifts is 50% of the adjusted gross. Excess amounts can be carried over for five years plus the current year. The gift eliminates capital gains tax on the appreciation over the base cost of the stock. The charitable act also serves to reduce your taxable estate.

If the security that is given to the charitable institution is publicly traded stock, the recipient, such as a college, sells it in the open market to reduce the gift to usable cash. If the stock is thinly traded, it may be difficult to sell a significant block of stock without affecting the stock's price adversely.

A donation of a minority interest in a nonpublic company is all but useless to a charitable organization, since there is virtually no market for the stock. The charity needs cash—not just a vote as a minority stockholder.

A gift of stock may be made in such a way that it is essentially the equivalent of cash. Let's assume that the donor is the controlling stockholder in a closely held nonpublic corporation that installs an ESOP. He gives some of his personally owned stock to his favorite university, a qualified public charity under the Internal Revenue Code. This entitles him to a federal income tax deduction on the gift up to 30% of his adjusted gross income for the current year plus five years of carryovers. He pays no capital gains tax on any appreciation in the value above his base price.

The university may then sell the stock to the ESOP, a logical marketplace. The ESOP pays the university an amount of cash equal to the appraised value of the securities. (It is assumed here that the ESOP has no obligation to purchase the stock.)

The ESOP could obtain the liquidity for the purchase from corporate cash contributions not to exceed 15% or, if applicable, 25% of covered payroll.

Tax Effect on the Donor

The donor receives an income tax deduction for the current value of the gift. Though the donated stock may have cost only $2,000, if it is currently valued at $10,000, the donor is entitled to a $10,000 income tax deduction. If the donor is in the 50% federal tax bracket, he or she saves $5,000 in income taxes. And the estate tax is also reduced by the removal of this asset from the estate.

Tax Effect on the Corporation

The corporation contributes $10,000 of cash to the ESOP, thus providing the liquidity with which the trust can pay for the shares. If the company is in the 50% federal and state combined tax bracket, it saves $5,000 in taxes.

The tax effects can be summarized as follows:

• The combined income tax deduction is 200% of the value of the gift.

• The combined income tax savings are 100% of the gift.

• The estate tax savings, assuming donor is in the 50% estate tax bracket, are $5,000.

• There is no capital gains tax on the transaction.

• The public charity gets $10,000 worth of stock that it can sell to the ESOP for $10,000 in cash, assuming the ESOP trustees are willing to buy the shares.

Another Idea

The charity could establish a gift annuity. The donor could contribute stock to the charity in a single transaction or in annual installments, earmarking part of the contribution as a gift and part as a purchase of an annuity from the charity. As the charitable institution is able to obtain cash from the ESOP as payment for stock, the charity pays—at a predetermined rate and in accordance with the IRS published annuity tables—a monthly or annual lifetime income to the annuitant. Such payments can be treated partially as return of capital, a portion as ordinary income, and part as capital gains.

Any part of the contribution that was not used as an annuity purchase will constitute a deductible donation within prescribed limits. The gift remainder portion could be calculated so that the deduction would offset the income tax on the annuity.

The Charity Buyout Arrangement

The stockholder can donate stock in a private corporation to a charitable remainder unitrust of a public charity. The unitrust will then seek a buyer of the stock which may be the corporation or the ESOP. The unitrust can give the donor a stated income of not less than 5% of the value of the gift on each trust annual valuation date for life. A favorite charity as remainderman can receive the amount remaining at the donor's death, thereby reducing estate taxes. The donor receives a current income tax deduction of up to 30% of adjusted gross income with five years of carryover deductions.

Since the stock is donated rather than sold to the unitrust, the donor pays no capital gains tax. Thus, there is a greater trust corpus from which to receive a larger income. The donor can use the tax savings to buy life insurance equal to the value of the gift. The insurance can be owned by an irrevocable trust, naming his or her children as beneficiaries so that they receive the full value of the gift.

The advantages can be summarized as follows:

• Current income tax savings.

• No capital gains tax.

• Probably greater lifetime income.

• Reduction of estate tax.

• All without disinheriting the family.

If the ESOP technique is employed, the purchase is made with 50 cents on the dollar.

Certain charities are better than others in this regard. Some public charities exist that have no specific charitable cause of their own such as cancer, heart, etc. They merely serve as a conduit...an umbrella. A donor who directs the charity as to where the funds should go from year to year is not locked into any single charity but can get an immediate write-off.

These charities will accept real estate or other property as well; thus capital gains can be eliminated. A buyer can buy from the charity. A pooled-income fund can provide the lifetime income and the estate exclusion as well as the current deduction. The corporation can be the buyer and can sell stock to the ESOP to recoup its deducted dollars.

It is even possible to have a buy-sell agreement between a future buyer and the charity, to be triggered by the donor's death. Thus, the corporation or the stockholder's grandchildren could agree that the stock will be purchased from the charity when the stockholder-donor dies. The ESOP could be given an option to buy if the others do not buy. Insurance can fund the various arrangements.

MODEL:

How to Get Personal and Corporation Tax Deductions That Exceed The Value of Your Gift to an IRS-Qualified Public Charity

• Donor gives public or private corporation stock, which he or she owns, to a qualified public charity. Value of stock is $10,000.

• Corporation whose stock is gifted has an ESOP to which charity sells its stock.

• Corporation contributes $10,000 in cash to ESOP, which corporation deducts from taxable income.

Income Tax Deductions:

DONOR'S DEDUCTION	
(For contribution to charity)	$10,000
CORPORATION'S DEDUCTION	
(For contribution to ESOP)	10,000
TOTAL DEDUCTIONS	$20,000

NOTE: Donor reduces gross estate by $10,000.
    Estate tax savings: $5,000
    (50% estate tax bracket)

Income Tax Savings:

DONOR (50% bracket)	$ 5,000
CORPORATION (50% bracket)	5,000
COMBINED INCOME TAX SAVINGS	$10,000

Summary:

Value of gift	$10,000
Total deductions	20,000
Total income tax savings	10,000
Estate tax savings	5,000
Donor's current cash outlay	ZERO
Corporation's cash outlay	$10,000

16

ESOP Loans for LBOs

Qualified plans other than ESOPs are precluded from borrowing. ESOPs are permitted to borrow from a party in interest such as the sponsoring employer or major stockholders. The terms of the loan must be on an arm's-length basis and just as favorable as would be the case between independent parties.

The loan can be in the form of a direct loan, a loan guarantee, or an installment sale. The ESOP may not pledge any collateral other than the stock that was acquired with the loan proceeds or stock that had been released as collateral for a previous loan as a result of the new loan proceeds. The ESOP's liability for servicing the loan interest and principal is limited to the cash contributions it receives from the employer or the earnings on those contributions. Dividends on the stock held by the ESOP can also be used to repay the loan. The loan must not be a demand loan except where default is concerned. The loan must be structured for repayment over a specified period of time.

Although the employer is not required under regulations to make contributions sufficient to service the ESOP loan, from a practical standpoint, lenders look to the corporation as their ultimate source of repayment. Creditors are therefore likely to stipulate that the corporation must make cash contributions at least equal to the amortization payments. ESOPs are considered by the regulations to be conduits of loan proceeds. Accordingly, they are treated in much the same manner as conventional borrowers.

Independent lenders can accelerate the loan repayment in the event of default, while for parties in interest loans, only such assets as are required to cover the amount of the default may be transferred from the guarantor or from the sponsoring corporation itself. The financed stock may be allocated as the loan is repaid, the allocation being based on principal and interest. Another method permits allocation to be based entirely on principal payments. There are stipulations that must be applied to the latter method that preclude using it for loans in excess of 10 years. A suspense account is created from which shares are released as the debt is paid.

The ABCs of a Leveraged ESOP Transaction

The procedure to follow for using a leveraged ESOP transaction is outlined below.

☐ The corporation agrees to sell and the ESOP trustee agrees to buy from the employer a specific number of qualifying employer shares of stock for fair market value.

☐ A loan is arranged between the ESOP and a lender for the purpose of purchasing the shares that are then pledged as collateral for the loan. The employer corporation will guarantee the loan.

☐ The ESOP trustee uses the loan proceeds to acquire the stipulated shares from the employer corporation.

☐ The corporation will make tax-deductible cash contributions to the ESOP in an amount equal to the servicing requirement for the ESOP to pay principal and interest on the loan.

This is a typical leveraged ESOP procedure to enable the proceeds to be transferred from the bank to the ESOP to the employer. The loan would be paid with pretax dollars by corporate contributions using the ESOP as a conduit to the lender. As the loan is repaid, shares will be released from a suspense account and allocated to the ESOP participants.

Corporate Loan Compared With a Leveraged ESOP Loan

If the corporation borrows money directly, it cannot deduct principal payments but can deduct payments for interest. It should be noted, however, that if the corporation does have an ESOP it can make annual tax-deductible contributions of stock to the trust in an amount equal to its principal payments to the bank. The aftertax effect is the same as though principal and interest were being deducted through an ESOP loan.

This route is not so dilutionary as the ESOP loan transaction described above, assuming the stock is growing in value. In the ESOP loan transaction, stock in the full amount of the loan is transferred immediately, whereas in the corporate loan scenario the shares are transferred gradually as they increase in value, thereby requiring fewer shares to accomplish the same end result.

The 15% of payroll limitation (or 25% with either carryovers or a combination ESOP) would prevail. This in in contrast to the 25% limitation for principal plus the amount needed for interest in the ESOP over and beyond contributions to other qualified plans, assuming the loan is channeled through the ESOP.

17

Leveraged ESOP Versus a Corporate Loan to Cash Out a Stockholder

Cost of an ESOP Loan Compared With a Corporate Loan

The cost of an ESOP loan is reduced by the corporation's tax bracket. In the case of a combined 50% corporate state and federal bracket, a $1 million loan requires an aftertax payment for principal of $500,000. This should shorten the period for repaying the loan when compared with a direct corporate loan. This would, in turn, reduce the dollar amount of interest that must be paid over the repayment period. The leveraged ESOP loan requires significantly less cash flow than does the direct corporate loan. From an overall cost standpoint one should remember that in a leveraged ESOP transaction, the corporation would transfer to the ESOP an amount of stock equal to the loan principal as collateral, which would ultimately be released to the employees' accounts.

Thus, a $1 million loan would require the transfer of $1 million of stock. If the corporation did not have an ESOP or any other type of qualified plan, the cost of borrowing would be the aftertax cost of principal and interest. A direct loan by the corporation in the amount of $1 million at 12% interest for a 10-year period would require a gross cash flow outlay of $1,721,652. The aftertax cash flow requirement would be $1,360,826. A leveraged ESOP transaction would require aftertax cash flow of $860,826, a difference of $500,000 in favor of the ESOP transaction.

If the corporation were going to contribute $1 million over a 10-year period to an ESOP or other qualified plan while doing a conventional corporate loan transaction, the overall cost of the corporate loan would be higher than the ESOP loan.

Another cost factor that should be considered is the time value of money. If the aftertax cash flow savings were put to use in the company, this would further enhance the advantage on the ESOP loan side.

Leveraged ESOP Loan Versus Public Equity Financing

A public corporation can reach out to the public for equity financing. Alternatively, it can go to venture capitalists as can a private company. Where applicable, this can be a viable alternative to leveraged ESOP debt financing.

In the case of a public offering, the corporation would raise $1 million of cash by selling that amount of stock on the open market. It is always problematical as to whether a corporation will be able to realize the true worth of its stock in an initial offering. Assuming that the public pays the fair market value, this would infuse into the corporation $1 million. For purposes of this example we will ignore the significant costs of underwriting the issue with the brokerage firm.

The only cost to the corporation for this form of equity financing is the $1 million cost of the shares since the corporation incurs no debt. A complete comparison would have to take into consideration the question of whether the corporation has a qualified retirement plan for its employees that might have been replaced by an ESOP. The contributions to the plan should also be factored into the cost equation. The $1 million of equity would go to the public instead of to the employees. If it had gone to the employees, it is quite possible that the equity in the hands of the employees would replace the benefits that the corporation would otherwise have had to purchase in order to maintain comparable employee benefits when compared with similar corporations.

A leveraged ESOP transaction generally affords greater flexibility when the proceeds are to be used to acquire shares from a major stockholder of a private company. If the corporation were to redeem the major stockholder's stock in an amount that would not be considered a substantially disproportionate share of his or her holdings, the transaction could be taxed to the stockholder as ordinary income. If an ESOP borrowed the money to buy his or her shares, it would be treated as a capital gains event rather than as a dividend. Under circumstances that would comply with the rollover provisions of the 1984 Tax Reform Act, there would be no taxes to be paid if the ESOP buys the stock.

A purchase of a stockholder's shares by the ESOP has an additional advantage over the corporate redemption in that it leaves the corporation in a better financial condition, since the corporation cannot deduct its cost for redeeming stock, but it can deduct the contribution to an ESOP. A plus factor in favor of the corporate redemption is that by pulling stock into treasury, the other stockholders would be in an improved equity position over the ESOP route.

MODEL

How Corporation With an ESOP Can Repay Loan Principal and Interest With Pretax Dollars

Assumption: $1 million covered payroll

1. SELLS SHARES VALUED AT $½ MILLION 2. PLEDGES SHARES

4. PAYS $½ MILLION FOR STOCK 3. LENDS ESOP $½ MILLION

5. CONTRIBUTES AND DEDUCTS 6. REPAYS ($150,000)
$150,000 CASH ANNUALLY (NET PRINCIPAL & INTEREST
AFTERTAX COST $75,000)

7. RETURNS STOCK WHEN
DEBT IS RETIRED

—Corporation requires money for expansion.
—Corporation sells shares of its stock to ESOP.
—ESOP pledges stock for bank loan.
—ESOP uses loan to pay corporation for its stock.
—Corporation makes annual tax-deductible cash contribution to ESOP in amounts up to 25% of covered payroll for principal in addition to the amount needed to pay interest.
—ESOP repays bank loan as scheduled.
—Bank returns stock to trust when debt has been retired.

Summary:

Corporation repays loan principal and interest with pretax dollars.

Net aftertax cost to repay each dollar of principal and interest is 50 cents.

Cost to pay $500,000 of principal is $250,000 plus aftertax cost of interest.

15% is illustrated but more is permitted.

18

How Your Company Can Borrow at Well Below Prime With an ESOP

The ESOP provisions that were included in the Tax Reform Act of 1984 have broadened the appeal of ESOPs among commercial lending institutions and their corporate clients. Heretofore, banks and insurance companies have demonstrated little interest in the subject of ESOPs from a marketing standpoint. Many banks have had ESOPs implemented for themselves as a means of creating working capital and broadening the market for their stock, but have not promoted and capitalized on the basic leverage enhancement qualities of the ESOP as they might apply to potential customers.

The 1984 Act has provided an incentive for banks that have made them sit up and take notice of this potential bonanza. The trickle-down effect has manifested itself among thousands of corporations that heretofore took little notice of the ESOP as a means of solving corporate and estate planning problems.

Loans made by commercial lenders to ESOPs or to corporations that re-lend to the ESOPs receive tax-sheltered treatment under the Act. Specifically, the eligible lenders can deduct 50% of all interest they receive or accrue from loans made to ESOPs or to employers who re-lend the proceeds to the ESOPs. A prerequisite is that the loan proceeds must be used to purchase stock for the ESOP.

In order to be eligible, the lender must be a bank, an insurance company, or other corporation that is actively engaged in the business of making loans.

The following parties to the loan agreement are ineligible for the 50% deduction:

• Members of the ESOP and the sponsoring corporation that employs any of the ESOP participants;

• Any member of a controlled group that includes ESOP participants; or

• Corporate members of the same controlled group that includes the employer of any ESOP participant.

By permitting the loan to be made to the corporation, the cap on the amount that can be contributed to an ESOP will not be an inhibiting factor on the servicing requirements.

Let's assume a bank is in the combined 50% federal and state tax bracket. Further assume a prime rate of 12% and a 1% surcharge, for a total interest rate for the ESOP or the ESOP corporation of 13%. Half of the interest income the bank receives is deductible. This amounts to a deduction of 6.5% of the loan principal or a tax savings of 25% of the interest charge.

If the bank is willing to pass the full tax break on to the borrower, this could reduce the interest rate well below prime. From the bank's standpoint, giving its tax savings to the borrower would add to the security of the loan in that the ESOP company could more easily service the note. Of course, any of the tax savings the bank retains would enhance its own bottom line. Banks have actually begun to look for ESOP loan opportunities and to compete for them. Those banks that are in low tax brackets because of loan interest reserves or other taxable earnings depressants will not be as competitive as those banks that are in a top tax bracket.

The Parsons Story

The first known large leveraged transaction to take advantage of this tax savings aspect of the 1984 Act was Parsons Corporation, one of the world's largest construction and engineering companies. Its 1983 revenue was $839.8 million. Parsons' ESOP was implemented some years earlier to create a market for the stock in the estate of its founder, Mr. Ralph Parsons. This was supplemented by a public offering. The ESOP covered approximately 7,000 employees and owned 29% of the company when it was decided to go private.

The ESOP made a successful $32 per share tender offer and became the owner of 93.6% of the 24.7 million shares outstanding. Independent appraisal determined this to be fair market value for control shares, notwithstanding the fact that the stock had been trading at a lower price on the public exchange. The total cash transaction for the buyout required $557 million of long-term and short-term financing; $300 million of this was arranged at a rate that was 82.5% of prime for the five-year loan. The bank gave Parsons' ESOP the benefit of approximately 3/4 of its tax savings provided under the 1984 law.

Parsons Corporation is one of the largest employee-owned companies. It was felt that the employees would rather control their own retirement destiny than be at the whim of Wall Street.

Offer to Purchase for Cash
All Outstanding Shares of Common Stock, $1 par value
of
THE PARSONS CORPORATION
and
All Outstanding Common Shares, no par value
of
RMP INTERNATIONAL, LTD.
by
The Parsons Corporation Employee
Stock Ownership Plan and
the Trust Established Thereunder
and
The Ralph M. Parsons Company
at
$32 Net Per Unit of such Paired Shares

The Offer Will Expire at 12:00 Midnight, Los Angeles Time, on Thursday, October 25, 1984, Unless Extended. Withdrawal Rights Will Expire at 12:00 Midnight, Los Angeles Time, on Thursday, October 18, 1984.

THE OFFER IS CONDITIONED UPON, AMONG OTHER THINGS, A MINIMUM OF 6,500,000 UNITS BEING PROPERLY TENDERED AND NOT WITHDRAWN PRIOR TO THE EXPIRATION OF THE OFFER.

Special Committees of the Boards of Directors of The Parsons Corporation ("Parsons") and RMP International, Ltd. ("International") have each unanimously recommended the Acquisition, including the Offer and Purchase Price (as such terms are hereinafter defined), to their respective Boards of Directors as being fair to the two companies' respective public stockholders. Based upon such recommendation and certain other factors, each of these Boards has unanimously recommended acceptance of the Offer by such stockholders. Each Board suggests that such stockholders, in determining whether or not to tender their Units, consider the following:

1. The premium being offered over the historical market price for the Units.

2. The opinion of Lehman Brothers of Shearson Lehman/American Express Inc. that the $32 per Unit Offer price is fair, from a financial point of view. (See copy of such opinion attached as Annex C.)

3. The possible absence of any active trading market for the Units after completion of the Offer.

4. The significantly increased indebtedness of Parsons after the Offer.

5. The Financing Arrangements may preclude dividends.

6. The possibility that intervening events could delay or prevent consummation of the Merger, Asset Sale and/or Liquidation.

7. The other factors described under "SPECIAL FACTORS," "THE FINANCING" and "THE ACQUISITION AGREEMENT."

IMPORTANT

The shares of Parsons and International are subject to a Pairing Agreement which provides that such shares may be traded or transferred only in units consisting of one share of each company. Therefore, any stockholder desiring to tender his shares must tender only in such Units. Each outstanding certificate for such shares represents an equal number of the shares of Parsons and International.

Any stockholder desiring to tender all or any portion of his Units should either (1) complete and sign the Letter of Transmittal or a facsimile thereof in accordance with the instructions in the Letter of Transmittal and mail or deliver it with his stock certificate(s) and any other required documents to the Depositary or (2) request his broker, dealer, bank or other nominee to effect the transaction for him. A stockholder having Units registered in the name of a broker, dealer, bank or other nominee must contact his broker, dealer, bank or other nominee if he desires to tender such Units.

Questions and requests for assistance or for additional copies of the Offer to Purchase and the Letter of Transmittal may be directed to the Information Agent and the Depositary. The addresses and telephone numbers of the Information Agent and the Depositary are set forth on the back cover page of this Offer to Purchase.

THIS TRANSACTION HAS NOT BEEN APPROVED OR DISAPPROVED BY THE SECURITIES AND EXCHANGE COMMISSION NOR HAS THE COMMISSION PASSED UPON THE FAIRNESS OR MERITS OF SUCH TRANSACTION NOR UPON THE ACCURACY OR ADEQUACY OF THE INFORMATION CONTAINED IN THIS DOCUMENT. ANY REPRESENTATION TO THE CONTRARY IS UNLAWFUL.

19

The Magic of LBOs

Leveraged buyouts, LBOs, have been used for decades as a means of transferring corporate ownership. In the late 1970s, and more particularly in the decade of the 1980s, LBOs have become an office-hold word due to the crescendo of activity in this area.

LBOs have developed an aura because of the mystique in being able to magically transform corporate ownership into the hands of unlikely acquiring parties.

The explanation of the "magic" unfolds as the supporting performers are introduced from the wings of the stage. These are the venture capitalists, the bankers, the accounting firms, the attorneys, the valuation firm, and the conceptualizer. It is the conceptualizer who pulls the players together and makes the dramatic event materialize.

An LBO involves the acquisition of a company, the assets and cash flow of which are used by an investor to obtain and service the financing required to make the acquisition.

LBOs have been on the financial scene for many years, but until recently, were often referred to simply as "getting a loan to buy a business." The acronym LBO has helped popularize this method of acquiring companies to an extent unknown in the past. A great deal of sophistication has been added over the years to facilitate the leveraged transfer of the stock or assets of companies from one party to another.

Leverage can be accomplished through the use of third-party investment loans. Businesses are seldom bought without the use of outside funds, since buyers seldom have adequate cash on hand. Even if they did, it is almost invariably more advantageous to use other people's money (OPM), since this expands one's capability to make larger acquisitions than would otherwise be possible.

Quite frequently, acquisitions can be made on a shoestring or in some cases on no string at all. The price must be right. The financing must be well tailored and the new owners must be capable of churning out a profit sufficient to make the transaction worthwhile for all parties.

If the recipe is right and the potions are stirred and brewed, a truly magical transformation can occur. A large corporate enterprise can be made to rest in relatively small hands. Indeed, an LBO can permit an individual with limited resources to acquire an extraordinarily large firm.

Many LBOs are the unsung smaller deals that never even hit the last page of the financial section. The prerequisites for newsworthiness are much more stringent than they were in the 1970s. The fees for putting an LBO together today are often larger than the whole financing package was in those days. A billion dollar acquisition price is in the ho-hum category.

The LBO field in the 1970s was limited to a handful of very creative investment bankers. They were joined in the early 1980s by a large percentage of the other major investment banking houses and smaller "specialty shops."

Although the more sizable LBOs are usually structured by the investment banker, smaller ones can be put together essentially in-house but with outside advisers. The large buyouts involve venture capitalists, banks, and insurance companies that provide the capital source and are rewarded by high interest rates and equity kickers such as convertible debentures or preferred stock, giving them a piece of the action upon ultimate sale.

Outside investment groups, management teams, or the employees are the buyers. Management and employee buyouts are becoming a more frequent occurrence as the viability of the technique emerges.

The leverage involved in LBOs can be awesome. A one-to-one or two-to-one debt to asset ratio is textbook for an established, well-run corporation. Nine or ten to one is not an uncommon leverage ratio for some of the large LBO transactions. Somewhere about midway offers a comfort zone for the less adventuresome players. The debt loan must be supportable if the deal is to succeed. The underlying assets and the cash flow are the determinants of this.

Cash flow rides on the backs of management as does the security and profitability for the lenders and investors. Their management and operating talents are often a mandatory ingredient. The top executives are therefore frequently given the opportunity to cash in on the big capital gains stakes. The financial participation sometimes comes out of their pockets to make them try harder. For the most part, their net outlay, if any, is zeroed out by incentive bonuses.

The act of public companies going private has become commonplace. The stock of many public companies is underpriced, selling far below liquidation value. The company's assets may provide sufficient collateral for financiers. The enhancement of the deal could come from a strategic performance study involving a paring down of expenses coupled with a good marketing plan to increase cash flow. This could portend a return trip from being private to going public or selling out to a larger corporation as a means of cashing out the lenders and entrepreneurs.

The smaller LBO transactions have the same basic prerequisites for success as those of behemoth proportions. The degree of sophistication and the number of players grow exponentially with the size, however. A large financing might involve venture capitalists, pension funds, and insurance companies that take a subordinate position to the commercial banks, with each represented by separate counsel. A relatively small LBO might involve only an individual buyer (who may or may not take back some of the paper), a seller, the bank, and their respective counsel.

The leveraged ESOP buyout (LESOP) lends itself remarkably well to the acquisition of public and private companies by its management and employees. The technique improves the do-ability of the deal and has many social attributes that are lacking in other forms of LBOs by outsiders.

The LBO Candidate—In Profile

The Public Corporation as an LBO Candidate

LBOs assume many characteristics. They involve transactions ranging in value from $100,000 to billions of dollars. The company being acquired might be a small, medium-sized, or large manufacturer, financial institution, service company, retail chain, or wholesale chain. Geography is not an inhibiting factor. LBOs are permitted in every state. They can be done by anyone. There is no legal barrier.

An LBO opportunity often exists when a large public company makes a decision to divest itself of one or more divisions or subsidiaries. The reasons are varied. These units may not be profitable. On the other hand, they may be very profitable but require too much of the parent company's attention, capital, or both. The parent may wish to concentrate its energies in another direction. It may want to raise capital to make acquisitions that are better suited to the company's blueprint for the future.

Obsolescence of products occurs almost as soon as a technical product is introduced to the public. This occasions management's thinking in the direction of a spinoff unless some alternative use can be found for equipment and personnel that has greater bottom-line gratification.

An ideal buy is a division that is at the receiving end of an economic downswing, once having been a good performer and possessing the potential of becoming one again. The parent wants to massage its annual report and rid itself of the subsidiary often at a bargain-basement price. A talented operator who has a knack for rekindling situations of this kind can build up the bottom line to make a killing on resale several years hence.

Public companies can range in size from a $500,000 market value to one in the megabillions. Those on the lower rung can be closely controlled, but with a relatively large number of outside stockholders to whom the major stockholder must report. These companies can be essentially private in effect. The major stockholder, often the founder, has no practical means of selling his or her stock because of the SEC restrictions and the thin market. A secondary stock offering of this stock can become a sell signal to other stockholders who stampede the market and depress the stock price before the founder has a chance to sell his or her securities.

This is sufficient motivation for a control group to seek an outside buyer for the whole company. Such a scenario is not uncommon. It is applicable to small and medium-sized public corporations.

The larger the company, the less likely it is that an individual stockholder holds sufficient stock to control the company. Many companies listed on the NYSE, AMEX, NASDAQ, and all regional exchanges are potential takeover targets. Some are willing or friendly candidates, but many are not willing to be absorbed by another corporation or an investment group.

It requires a great deal of defensive maneuvering to avoid an unfriendly marriage. Mergers all too often mean severe dislocations of management even if this is not a stated intent during the courting period.

In order that takeovers be thwarted, public companies sometimes seek to go private. This can be more difficult for management to accomplish than it was for them to take the company public.

The restrictions that must be overcome are awesome, but companies can and do go private by a tender offer to the stockholders coupled with a leveraged buyout by a control group of management or an outside investment group.

It is common for large public corporations to acquire each other in the form of giant mergers effectuated by stock swaps. More and more companies, however, are going private through LBOs. ESOPs are being used with great frequency to make the deal work.

The Private Corporation as an LBO Candidate

Private companies can almost invariably be considered the lengthened arm of an individual, probably the founder. The company takes on the founder's characteristics and the corporate personality is as distinguishable as his or her own. The owner's goals are mirrored in the philosophy that governs the direction of the company.

A private business, aside from legal definitions, has a finite existence. Unless it is endowed with a strong second-line management team, it is as fragile as the thin life thread of its founder.

An entrepreneur's major asset is often his or her corporate stock. While the owner is alive and productive, the corporation is a virtual "goose that laid the golden eggs." It continues to spin off income within the limits of reasonable compensation set forth by IRS. The owner is paid for his or her labor—not ownership. Unlike public corporations, private companies seldom pay dividends.

The owner's ownership of the company stock is a paradox. It is an asset, but it is nonspendable so long as he or she controls the company. It is in another sense a liability. It will be taxed in his or her estate, notwithstanding the fact that the owner could not use it during life for capital gains without relinquishing the company to others. The bottom line is that the owner was compensated for labor and not for capital while he or she was a major stockholder.

One seldom wishes to acquire less than 51% of a private company. If the owner sells controlling interest, he or she is generally out of a job. An entrepreneur would find it difficult to work for others in any event. Individuals can sell all other forms of property such as real estate, automobiles, coin collections, or sailboats without forfeiting their vocation or their potential for earned income. Not so with the entrepreneur's private company. The sale of their life's blood, their "toy" in life, is the biggest decision that many entrepreneurs face.

Aside from the emotional attachment to the company, the owner must weigh the financial price he or she is willing to pay for keeping the capital in a nonspendable form. If the company is worth $5 million, it is costing approximately $5 million of otherwise spendable funds, ignoring taxes.

Business owners are experiencing the frustration of being wealthy but nonliquid. They face the specter of estate taxes, essentially a nine-month call on half their assets by the government at an indeterminate time. The Treasury Department will not accept stock certificates. It relates only to cash. An owner's failing health may become the catalyst for considering the subject of mortality and perpetuation of the company.

The need for liquidity to pay estate taxes is a most compelling reason for selling a private corporation. Sometimes companies are sold by the executors at a distressed price. More often, a business is sold by the founder while he or she is still very much alive and able to negotiate a better price. The owner may not be actively pursuing an opportunity to sell the company, but will be receptive if a prospective buyer broaches the subject in a serious vein. A new owner might require the founder's talents for a period of time in order to assure a smooth transition. The founder's availability would enable him or her to command a more attractive price for the company.

If the founder has one or more heirs, whether they are offspring or other executives who have demonstrated their ability to take over as chief executive officer, the founder will in all likelihood be motivated to retain the company for their benefit. This is a problem. He or she can't afford to give them the company, and they don't have the cash to buy the stock.

Private firms that were built with the help of capable, loyal, long-time executives explore every possible technique to permit the executives to buy the owner out. Some of these transfer arrangements are so generous that the owner all but gives the company away, thereby depriving his or her family of the true worth of the accumulated wealth. An ESOP-assisted LBO might be a viable alternative.

Since there are many more private companies than public ones, it follows that there are more private companies overtly for sale. There are also more reasons for selling companies that are privately owned. A private company is an extension of an individual, an entrepreneur whose working career is finite.

21

Who Are the Prospective Buyers?

Logical purchasers of the company might be other corporations that wish to increase their market share of the product involved. Or perhaps the products fit synergistically with the acquiring company's product line. It is quite common for an outside group of investors to purchase spinoffs or entire major corporations.

More and more frequently, key executives who have been involved in the running of corporate departments, divisions, or subsidiaries have been purchasing these divestitures and continuing to operate the business as new companies. Corporations find the LBO an intriguing vehicle for consuming their competitors.

Whole companies are often acquired by their employees, as a group. This is a relatively recent phenomenon and an exciting one.

Public and private companies are eyed as challenges to would-be buyers who feel that if they buy low, pare the company's staff to the bone, improve efficiency by streamlining manufacturing techniques, and develop a viable marketing plan, the company can be built to its full profitable potential. Such a company may be held permanently by the acquiring parties, sold for a substantial capital gain, or even taken public after having gone private.

22

How ESOPs Can Make an LBO Work

ESOPs are leverageable tax-sheltered instruments of corporate finance. They can borrow, and yet contributions made to them by corporations are, within prescribed limits, tax deductible. The result is that payments to service loan principal, if paid by an ESOP, become tax deductible to the corporation. This reduces the amount of corporate earnings needed to discharge the indebtedness by the amount of taxes saved. The deductibility also has the complementary effect of justifying a larger financing package.

Debt servicing makes up a major cash flow requirement of a leveraged buyout. The state and federal governments must be paid before anything can go towards servicing principal. To the extent that taxes can be eliminated from the buyer's obligation, the burden of purchase can be made more benign. Correspondingly, a larger acquisition can be made with a given amount of pretax earnings. Financing that would otherwise be delayed because of high interest rates can perhaps proceed, since the tax savings on the principal payments might be considered an offset to the higher interest.

In an LBO, the corporation provides not only the collateral, but the cash flow to service the debt. It is to the buyer's advantage to maximize the amount of earnings that can go into aftertax working capital so as to expand the company's earning capacity. This will make the underlying acquisition a more valuable property for the acquiring parties. A dollar diverted to pay taxes is a dollar less for expansion. By maximizing a corporation's aftertax cash flow and working capital, an ESOP can approximately double the leverage in an LBO transaction.

The Leveraged ESOP Buyout

Here is how a leveraged ESOP buyout (LESOP) might work. Let's assume a corporation wishes to divest itself of a profitable division that it feels does not fit synergistically with the parent corporation's future growth pattern.

The parent corporation decides to give the first opportunity for purchasing the division to the management team that has demonstrated an ability to make the entity run at a profit. The division's five senior executives have marginal net worth, but as a group they manage to borrow $250,000.

An independent appraisal determines the value of the division to be $12 million. It has experienced a 10% annual compounded growth in net worth over the previous five years, and this growth rate is projected for the next five-year period. The annual payroll is $6 million and is projected to increase 7% annually over the next five years. Pretax earnings of the division for the prior year amounted to $3.4 million. The purchase price for the division is set at $12 million.

Doing the Deal

The divisional management team forms a new corporation, Newco, for which it implements a stock bonus plan ESOP. A bank agrees to lend the ESOP $11.75 million payable over 10 years if the executives contribute $250,000 for the purchase of equity. The lender also requires that Newco stock be pledged as collateral and that Newco agree to make annual cash contributions to its ESOP sufficient to service principal and interest.

The bank expresses a willingness to pass three quarters of its tax savings to the ESOP under the terms of the 1984 Tax Reform Act's ESOP provisions. The law permits the bank to deduct half of the interest income that results from an ESOP loan. Instead of charging the prime rate, which at the time is 11¾%, the bank charges the ESOP trustee only 9.5%.

> The Economic Recovery Tax Act of 1981 (ERTA) increased the amount of the deductible contribution to a leveraged ESOP from the former 15% of covered payroll to 25% for servicing principal. Any amount of contribution over and beyond this that is required for interest payments may be deducted as well.

The ESOP trustee promptly uses the loan proceeds to purchase stock from the corporation, the stock to be pledged as collateral. The bank could release the stock from pledge as the amortization payments are made. Those shares would then be allocated to the ESOP participant's accounts.

The corporation is required to contribute $152,040 monthly ($1,824,480 annualized) to the ESOP, which the trustee will pay to the bank to service principal and interest. The contribution is less than the percentage of payroll limitation, and the aftertax annual cost is $912,240.

The executives use the $250,000 of borrowed funds to acquire founders' stock whose value has a negative book value. They anticipate that the future growth of their stock will make the extra effort they put into the company over the next several years worthwhile, and will eventually make them quite wealthy.

The employees not only will be able to look forward to reasonable compensation from their labor, but they can also anticipate receiving a second tier of income from dividends created as a result of extraordinary productivity. The ESOP provisions of the 1984 Act permit the corporation to deduct dividends if passed through to the ESOP participants. The employees' big kicker comes to them in the form of equity when the loan is retired and growth of the stock allocated to their ESOP accounts accelerates.

This scenario is quite different from what might have been. Had the parent simply liquidated the unwanted division or sold its assets to another corporation in a different state, the executives and other employees would be on the labor market. They might be consuming the bounties of welfare instead of contributing to welfare as taxpayers. Wage earners support the many local businesses, which in turn pay more taxes.

The company's subcontractors and suppliers are better off with the revenue they derive from its continued productivity than they might have been without it. So are the federal, state, and local taxpayers. The multiple spinoff effects of this LESOP divestiture are enormous and lasting. A group of employees such as those of this corporation, an ESOP company, are likely to regard the Social Security system as no more than an unneeded luxury fund.

24

How a Corporation Can Sell Its Division to the Employees Through a LESOP

Corporations frequently sell divisions or even liquidate them when they do not produce the return on investment or return on equity that the parent corporation desires. Spinoffs often occur for the simple reason that top management's time allocation would be better placed in other endeavors. Irrespective of the reason, great opportunities abound for the acquirer of profitable entities that simply do not mesh with the parent's corporate guidelines. Corporations would generally prefer to sell their division on an "as is" basis without spending initial time and dollars in reshaping it into a more salable package. Once a decision has been made to divest itself of the subsidiary or division, top management wants to get the deed done and get on with other things. If a buyer is not found promptly, a company may simply dismantle a division and write off the loss since time is also money.

Given a reasonable choice, a corporation would often prefer to sell a division to the employees who have been running the operation rather than create grave dislocations among the personnel. When a division is sold or relocated, the parent company frequently puts its human resource department to work in an attempt to find new employment for the affected employees. Aside from the human element, the cost for unemployment insurance can become a matter of consideration for the parent corporation. The primary reason for wanting to sell to the employees is that they have been loyal and know their jobs better than anyone else, and it is the right thing to do if it is at all possible.

Since the employees cannot be expected to have sufficient cash to acquire the division being divested, the purchase would have to be done with borrowed capital secured by the assets and cash flow of the division.

Outlined below is the procedure for a LESOP divestiture transaction:

• The parent company creates a new corporation, Newco.

• Newco establishes an ESOP.

• ESOP borrows sufficient cash from a lender, commercial or otherwise, or possibly from the parent corporation, which will take back a note. Quite possibly a combination of sources would compose the lender. It is quite likely that the parent corporation would guarantee the loan. If the parent is unwilling to do this, Newco would guarantee the loan.

• The ESOP would acquire the assets from the parent company that would be put into Newco.

• The ESOP would exchange the acquired assets for Newco stock.

• Newco would make annual deductible cash contributions to the ESOP to service loan principal and interest.

When the loan has been amortized completely, the employee-participants of the ESOP will own Newco. If the deal was right, the corporate earnings should be sufficient to service the obligation until the debt is retired.

As an alternative to acquiring the assets, the ESOP could use the proceeds of the loan to purchase Newco's stock. Newco would then use the funds to acquire the assets. This would work out the same way. The note would be discharged with pretax dollars, cutting the cost of the acquisition in half.

Quite often employees will take a reduction in their compensation to help with the repayment of the loan. The LBO/ESOP combination provides an ideal means for a corporation to divest itself of a unit. This broadens the base of capitalism.

25

How LESOPs Can Be Used to Thwart Hostile Takeovers

Traditionally, employees can vote with management on major issues. It is for this reason that ESOPs are being used with greater frequency to ward off unwanted suitors. This technique has proven to be useful when implemented properly, but offers no assurance that it is without downside risks.

Typically, companies that consider themselves targets for unfriendly takeovers should consider implementing an ESOP well in advance of its being needed for this strategic purpose. A corporation should try to get as many of its shares allocated to its employees' accounts as might be needed for this block vote purpose. The ESOP should be well communicated to the employees, and they should be brought into the decision process whenever possible. In this way, employees will identify with the company and the privileges of equity ownership.

In order to get the block of stock into the ESOP, the trustees may wish to borrow a substantial sum of cash to purchase stock from a large available block holder on the open market. The corporation would make tax-deductible cash contributions to the ESOP so that the trustees could repay the indebtedness. As the loan is amortized, the shares would be allocated to employees' accounts and voted by the employees. The balance of the shares, representing the portion that has not yet been amortized, would be voted by the trustees.

Fiduciary Aspects

If the price offered for the shares by the contender for the company is attractive, there is no guarantee that the employees will not vote in favor of being acquired.

The trustees may find themselves on the horn of a fiduciary dilemma. They should bear in mind that the ESOP is primarily for the benefit of the participants and their beneficiaries.

If the price offered is too good to refuse, the employees might be reluctant to vote against the takeover. On the other hand, one of the principal purposes of an ESOP is to disseminate equity ownership among employees. It is quite possible that a takeover might have a chilling effect on the furthering of this goal.

The trustees will have more unallocated shares to vote immediately following the leveraging of the ESOP, since relatively few shares will have been allocated. Structuring the ESOP well before the need arises will permit the employees to have a greater allocation and might tend to reduce the vulnerability of the trustees and other fiduciaries.

A shareholder vote is not required in the event of a tender for shares. Therefore, the participants need not make a decision in connection with a tender offer. The decision is made for them by the trustees. Some practitioners feel that ESOP documents can be designed so that tenders can be passed through to the participants.

The proper design of the ESOP cannot be overemphasized if the plan is to achieve the purposes for which it is intended.

26

Classic Executive/LESOPs

The LBO coupled with an ESOP has proven to be a winning team for making it possible for executives and other employees to buy out companies. From a broad perspective, the economy as well as the social fabric of the country is far better off when the ESOP is involved in a corporate takeover. The economy is weakened by a traditional LBO simply because the ownership is reduced to perhaps one individual or at best a handful of investors. The ESOP broadens the ownership and places equity in the hands of employees, where it will do the most good.

LESOP takeovers often place 55% to 85% of the equity ownership in the ESOP for the benefit of the employees at the time of the implementation. The balance, or at least most of it, will be made available to key executives. Perhaps a modest amount of equity will be channeled to those who procure the financing or to the lenders themselves.

The shares that go to the executives might be sold to them on attractive terms. The stock would quite possibly be of a different class that would have a built-in incentive for achieving certain profit goals. The executives typically spearhead the drive for buying out a company, a subsidiary, or a division. Providing them with additional motivation can be better for the rank-and-file employees in the long run.

LESOP transfers of ownership are for the most part friendly buyouts or takeovers. These are in the best interests of all concerned since the atmosphere is more conducive to getting off to a good emotional start with a free mind for production. Some of the larger LESOP buyouts have become classics. Certain smaller company buyouts are also classic examples but are not newsworthy. Dan River Inc., and Raymond International Co., Inc., are somewhat similar in nature as to the structuring of the LESOP.

Dan River Inc.

This East Danville, Virginia, textile firm with 12,000 employees was a gleam in the eye of a takeover expert, Carl C. Icahn, when it was decided that the ESOP concept would provide a means of thwarting the hostile takeover of the company. Icahn owned 29%, 1.6 million shares, of the 5.8 million outstanding shares. He had threatened the possibility of dismantling the 100-year-old company and eliminating the jobs of its employees. An LBO was approved by the stockholders and it was agreed to sell all of Dan River's shares to a newly

Dan River Inc.

2291 Memorial Drive
P.O. Box 261
Danville, Virginia 24543

Dear Stockholders:

April 28, 1983

The enclosed Proxy Statement and Notice of Annual Meeting provide detailed information about matters to be considered at the Annual Meeting of Stockholders to be held on the campus of Averett College at Pritchett Auditorium in Danville, Virginia on May 24, 1983 at 11:30 a.m. I sincerely hope you will be present or represented by proxy at this very important meeting.

This year, in addition to the usual business, you will vote on an Agreement of Merger providing that all present Dan River stockholders will receive $22.50 in cash for each share of Common Stock and $1.10 Cumulative Convertible Series Preferred Stock, and $3.25 in cash for each share of Cumulative Convertible Voting Preferred Stock, $0.375 Series B, owned by them. Under this Agreement, Dan River would become a subsidiary of a new holding company owned almost entirely by an employee stock ownership plan for Dan River employees and certain members of present Dan River management. If this Agreement is approved and the merger is consummated, stockholders will receive their cash without paying any brokers' commissions out of the proceeds of their shares.

The Board of Directors of Dan River recommends this merger to you. We emphasize that more than two-thirds of the outstanding voting stock must vote in favor of this merger if it is to take place. Achieving this vote will require the enthusiastic cooperation of all Dan River stockholders who favor the merger.

As you received offers from the Icahn Group in recent months, Dan River's Board of Directors on each occasion instructed me to advise you not to sell your shares as we did not believe that those offers were fair and in the best interest of all of the stockholders of the Company. After receiving the favorable recommendation of a committee of non-management directors of your Company, the Board concluded that the Agreement of Merger that you will be asked to vote on at the Annual Meeting *is* fair to and in the best interests of the holders of shares of voting stock. As directors, we had the benefit of advice and assistance from two prominent investment banking firms.

In summary, the Board of Directors believes this merger will provide all of our present stockholders with fair treatment while preserving the Company as an active corporate citizen in the many communities in which it operates. The price to be paid holders of Common Stock and $1.10 Preferred Stock is 25% higher than the $18 per share price offered by the Icahn Group for Common Stock.

We urge you to consider your vote very carefully. Regardless of the size of your holdings, it is imperative that your shares be voted at the meeting. To vote for the merger, check the box marked FOR on the enclosed proxy card. Whether or not you plan to attend the meeting, please be certain to complete, sign, date and mail your proxy in the prepaid envelope provided.

On Behalf of the Board of Directors
Sincerely yours,

David W. Johnston, Jr.

DAVID W. JOHNSTON, JR.
Chairman of the Board

THIS TRANSACTION HAS NOT BEEN APPROVED OR DISAPPROVED BY THE SECURITIES AND EXCHANGE COMMISSION NOR HAS THE COMMISSION PASSED UPON THE FAIRNESS OR MERITS OF SUCH TRANSACTION NOR UPON THE ACCURACY OR ADEQUACY OF THE INFORMATION CONTAINED IN THIS DOCUMENT. ANY REPRESENTATION TO THE CONTRARY IS UNLAWFUL.

formed holding company, which would establish an ESOP. A $150 million loan was arranged to tender for the outstanding stock. Mr. Icahn made a profit of approximately $8 million on the transaction. The pension plan had been determined by actuaries to be overfunded by approximately $16 million. It was terminated and replaced by the ESOP. The overfunding provided the down payment on the loan.

The ESOP owned 70% of the stock after the successful tender offer, executives owned approximately 25%, and the investment bankers received the balance. A significant portion of the debt has been repaid with pretax earnings by channeling the repayment through the ESOP. The employees were not represented on the board because top management felt that a corporation should not be run by committee.

After the LESOP was effectuated, profitability increased. The stated reason being given is the improved interest in company productivity on the part of the employees, who now have a stake in the company's finances. A pro forma suggests that the employees retiring under the ESOP will have three to four times greater benefits than they would have had under their old plan. Interestingly, the employees had voted to cancel the pension plans in favor of the ESOP since they feared that the takeover by Mr. Icahn would break up the company and eliminate their jobs. Time will tell whether the move was productive. From the standpoint of both management and the other employees, it certainly seemed better than the alternative.

Raymond International, Inc.

The desire of Raymond International, Inc., to be private was not motivated by a hostile takeover attempt but was rooted in a more philosophical bent. Raymond International, an engineering and construction company, the stock of which was traded on the New York Stock Exchange, also had approximately 12,000 employees on its payroll. The management wanted to place its greater amount of shares in the hands of employees. This was impractical for a company whose stock was traded on the big board. The management style of a public company must cater to the outside stockholders, who are more interested in quarterly earnings improvements than they are in long-term gains. The company had considered going private through a management LBO but later discovered the virtues of an ESOP for facilitating reaching the goal of becoming private.

Raymond Holdings, Inc., a holding company, was established for the purpose of acquiring the stock of Raymond International, Inc., which it would maintain as a wholly owned, operating subsidiary. Approximately $180 million in bank loans was arranged in addition to approximately $6.2 million of equity investment of which $5 million came from management and the balance from the investment banker group. The equity participants obtained all of the class B common stock in the holding company. Initial funding for the buyout of the stock came as a result of converting the profit-sharing plan to an ESOP and using its assets to buy class A holding-company stock. The pension-plan assets were used to buy a single-premium annuity to fund the pension benefits.

The excess came back to the company and was taxable but was offset by a contribution to the ESOP in that amount, which was deductible. This negated the taxable income. The pen-

Raymond International Inc.

Galleria Towers East • Suite 1225 • 5065 Westheimer • Houston, Texas 77056

September 15, 1983

Dear Stockholder:

You are cordially invited to attend a Special Meeting of Stockholders of Raymond International Inc. ("Raymond"), to be held on Friday, October 7, 1983 at 10:00 A.M., local time, at the Westin Galleria Hotel, 5060 West Alabama, Houston, Texas. At the meeting, stockholders will be asked to approve the proposed merger of Raymond Acquisition Subsidiary Inc. with and into Raymond, pursuant to which holders of Raymond Common Stock will be entitled to receive $27.50 in cash for each of their shares and holders of Raymond Series A Convertible Preferred Stock will be entitled to receive approximately $132.53, plus accrued dividends, for each of their shares. As a result of the merger, Raymond would become a wholly owned subsidiary of a new privately held holding company principally owned by certain members of present Raymond management and by an employee stock ownership plan for eligible Raymond employees. Details of the merger and other important information appear in the accompanying Proxy Statement.

A Special Committee of independent directors of Raymond has carefully reviewed and considered the terms and conditions of the proposed merger and has received opinions from its financial advisors, Kidder, Peabody & Co. Incorporated and Merrill Lynch Capital Markets, that the price to be paid in the merger is fair to Raymond stockholders. In light of the unanimous recommendation of the Special Committee, the Board of Directors has authorized and approved the Agreement and Plan of Merger and recommends to the stockholders of Raymond that they adopt such Agreement. For a discussion of the interests of certain directors and officers of Raymond in this transaction, see "Special Factors—Interests of Certain Persons in the Merger; Conflicts of Interest" in the attached Proxy Statement.

Your Board of Directors recommends you vote FOR the merger. The merger will not be effected unless it is adopted by (i) the holders of a majority of the outstanding Common Stock and the holders of two-thirds of the outstanding Series A Convertible Preferred Stock, each voting as a separate class, and (ii) a majority of the outstanding Common Stock and Series A Convertible Preferred Stock, all voting as one class. All shares of Common Stock and Series A Convertible Preferred Stock beneficially owned by members of Raymond management who agree to acquire a direct equity interest in the holding company which will own Raymond after the merger will be voted in the same proportion as all other shares of such respective classes are voted.

We urge you to read the enclosed material carefully and request that you complete, sign, date and return the enclosed proxy as soon as possible. Your vote is important regardless of the number of shares you own.

Sincerely yours,

Henry F. LeMieux

Henry F. LeMieux
*Chairman of the Board and
Chief Executive Officer*

THIS TRANSACTION HAS NOT BEEN APPROVED OR DISAPPROVED BY THE SECURITIES AND EXCHANGE COMMISSION NOR HAS THE COMMISSION PASSED UPON THE FAIRNESS OR MERITS OF SUCH TRANSACTION NOR UPON THE ACCURACY OR ADEQUACY OF THE INFORMATION CONTAINED IN THIS DOCUMENT. ANY REPRESENTATION TO THE CONTRARY IS UNLAWFUL.

90

sion plan was terminated as the ESOP was adopted. Approximately $21 million in the thrift plan was reinvested and used to purchase series A preferreds in the holding company. A stock bonus plan yielded $932,580 for the purchase of series B preferred stock. All of the classes of stock purchased as a result of using assets of the other qualified plans yielded $59.2 million in additional capital. The ESOP acquired 100% of the class A common and gave the holding company a note for $100 million.

Raymond International, Inc., the operating company, began making its cash contributions to the ESOP, which the ESOP used to pay off its note to the holding company. The holding company used the cash to service its own note with the banks. The subsidiary contribution amounted to 25% of covered payroll. This route was taken in order to enable the note and bank obligations to be discharged with pretax dollars. The consequence of this was a reduction in the company's cash flow requirement, which made the deal more likely to succeed.

The transformation resulted in pulling in stock that was owned by outside investors who had no stake in the company and putting those shares primarily in the hands of the employees through the ESOP trustee. The employees' share of the company at the conclusion of the buyout was 80%. Henceforth they will have the right to feel like the capitalists they are and will have a better feeling for working for the company they own. The management people have a special incentive built into their stock purchase, giving them a great potential for capital gains. It is a real golden handcuff for keeping the management team intact which, in turn, serves the best interests of all of the employees.

Observations

Media attention is often directed at employee buyouts of failing companies. Dan River and Raymond International are two examples of highly successful public companies whose shares were transformed from benefiting shareholders who were not directly involved with the company to benefiting the employees who devote their working careers toward the common effort of making the company perform for their own benefit. Dan River was within a hair of being taken over so that an individual might receive the fruits of the company's historical existence. It was targeted because it was a profitable enterprise. In neither case do the employees have a voting right. Management does the voting. In essence, owners of stock of public companies do not get much use out of their ability to vote the stock since it is so widely held. Individual stockholders who purchase their stock through their favorite stockbrokers seldom have the inclination to make a thorough study of ongoing corporate activities and as a result simply permit their proxies to be voted by the board of directors.

Management had felt that the marketplace did not adequately reflect the true value of the company, and time will tell whether the annual independent valuations of these now private companies will give more satisfactory indications of actual value.

It is estimated that 98% of the ESOPs that have been implemented have been structured in profitable companies. In examining many of those corporations, productivity has improved as a direct result of employee equity ownership.

ESOP Case Histories

Fastener Industries, Inc., Berea, Ohio

It can be said that the leading industrial weld fastener manufacturer in the country is a 100% ESOP-owned firm. It was founded in 1905 and incorporated as The Ohio Nut and Bolt Company, which is now one of Fastener's primary divisions. The company had been owned by the R.J. Whelan family, and in 1979, Roderick Whelan, Jr., decided to retire. The firm's treasurer, Richard G. Biernacki, approached Mr. Whelan on the idea of an employee buyout through an ESOP. The concept was well received.

The company's profit-sharing plan was converted to an ESOP and 85% of the assets used to buy stock from the Whelan family. The corporation also borrowed $4 million from its local bank.

There is very little turnover among the participants, who number approximately 125. This is not surprising since their average wages exceed industry averages in addition to the equity they own through the ESOP. Employees become 100% vested after one month of service and the vote is passed through to the employees.

The company had been profitable historically and continues to be so with the ESOP. It broke even during the 1982 recession but none of the employees were laid off. Dividends, which had first been paid in 1981, were not paid that year but have continued to be paid in subsequent years.

The company also has paid substantial bonuses, which have been as high as three-and-a-half weeks' salary. The productivity is exceptionally high though the production employees work only 35 hours per week. The company has a generous fringe-benefit program.

The need for supervision is minimal; for example, in one plant employing 45 workers, there is no shop foreman in the organizational set-up between the plant manager and machine operators. Every employee participates in small, semiannual group meetings with the corporate president to cover any topic they wish, and the employees are involved in discussions before buying new equipment or making significant changes. They are provided with quarterly statements concerning the financial condition of the company and are thoroughly informed as to the workings of the ESOP.

Maximum contributions are made to the ESOP to service its debt for the buyout.

The employees have expressed a deep sense of security and have a magnificent esprit de corps.

ComSonics, Inc., Harrisonburg, Virginia

Warren Braun, President, founded ComSonics after having worked as an executive in the radio and TV industry. He had designed and operated radio and TV stations for others but had no ownership in the entities and decided to start a company that would involve the employees in the ownership.

The formula has worked well. *Inc Magazine* included ComSonics in its 1982 list of the fastest growing private companies. The corporation had achieved a 30% compounded growth rate for the prior five-year period.

The firm implemented its nonleveraged ESOP in 1974, and the plan is 95% invested in company stock.

Participants are 30% vested after five years with gradual increase until the participant is fully vested after 15 years.

ComSonics operated on a management-by-objectives approach under which the annual operating plan is based upon known facts concerning its expenses, contracts, and prices. Its long-range plan is derived as a result of examining actual facts but tempered with aspirations of the level of production and sales that is determined by a composite plan assembled by Strategic Planning Units, which individually have time lines unique to the specific SPUs. Therefore, there is no reason for three-, five-, or seven-year plans, which system was abolished last year. Management formulates the objectives with Mr. Braun finalizing the plans for the appropriate time periods.

The company has instituted a communications program that emphasizes the benefits as well as the risks associated with equity ownership. Recently the company has emphasized employee training at the entry level to understand stock ownership.

The ESOP philosophy is a logical ingredient in the participatory management philosophy at the company. The executives are imbued with tremendous responsibility as a consequence of the participatory ownership and management way of life at ComSonics. Each executive is subject to a review and open critique by his or her peers covering a well-defined checklist. Each manager has a stake in the others, and the system has created an unusually open atmosphere for productivity growth.

A knowledge on the part of the employees that what is good for a company is good for their cache of equity is conducive to a great dedication to the firm that they own.

ComSonics' employees, without the participation of its president, wrote the firm's creed, "Roles and Missions," which is displayed prominently throughout the company headquarters.

Roles and Missions

To operate profitably a Dynamic, Progressive, Growth Oriented, Employee-Owned Corporation in the Electronic and Communications Industry within a framework of high ethical standards of conduct which:

* Increases the value of all assets (Tangible and Intangible) thus improving the Employees' equity over the long period of time.

* Creates and sells innovative, quality products to the Industry worldwide.

* Provides our Customers with the best technical service available in the Industry through high quality repair or rebuild of their equipment.

* Maintains and improves customers' service to the public by providing prompt, competent field service support.

* Furthers the State-of-the-Art in the Industry by aggressive research and development.

* Develops and provides marketing worldwide to insure a continuing demand for our products and services.

* Provides an environment for all employees which stimulates and challenges each to use his or her abilities to achieve personal growth and the company's goals.

* Demonstrate how employees from a variety of origins can work together for their separate and combined benefit.

* Strengthens the community in which we operate.

Serving the World of Visual and Aural Communications

Canterbury Press, Inc., Rome, New York

A company founded in 1950 in upstate New York has become one of the largest and most prestigious lithographers in the area. Its modernization program has made the company a formidable competitor principally as a printer of periodicals. The firm established its ESOP in 1975 for the purpose of acquiring 100% interest in the company. The 70 or so employees in the ESOP now own Canterbury. The ESOP was leveraged by a $350,000 corporate loan in order to purchase the remaining shares of the previous owner. The loan has now been retired and the company is concentrating its earnings on the acquisition of even more modern and substantial equipment.

The company works on a four-day work week, but the presses roll for at least five to six days a week. The company provides excellent fringe benefits, but the ESOP has the major philosophical and emotional effect on the employees. The ESOP committee comprises the president, the secretary/treasurer, and a shop member. There is no voting passthrough for the ESOP participants, but the company does issue special annual reports to keep the participants apprised of company financial matters. There has been a noticeable improvement in the quality of the employees' output, which management attributes to the ESOP. The employees know that this is truly their company, and it is evident in their daily activities.

28

Going Public as an Alternative to a Sale

An owner who wants to exchange stock for cash will consider the possibility of going public. In order for this to be a serious consideration, the company should have management strength, financial stability, good prospects for growth, and should be in an economic environment that is conducive to a successful public offering.

Going public is not a panacea. It is costly and the results are uncertain. If the objective is to get capital out of the corporation by creating a market for the stock, the entrepreneur may be disappointed. The offering price is determined at the due diligence meeting of the underwriters. The determining factor is the marketability of the issue. This, in turn, is related to the then-current status of the stock market. The stock would quite possibly be offered through a regional exchange and there would be a thin market for the stock. A sale of a significant portion of the owner's stock at the initial offering would be suspect. If the company is so good, why is the owner selling?

The market for the stock would be thin and would not absorb large blocks of the securities. The price that the entrepreneur could hope to receive for his or her holdings might be well below liquidation value.

Assuming the offering has been successful, it would still be impractical for the founder to plan on selling his or her stock because of the rules prohibiting control persons from selling more than a fairly insignificant amount of their stock at any point in time.

Underwriters do not come cheaply. They frequently demand a portion of the company in addition to their large fees.

The ongoing costs for meeting the requirements of the securities laws are first noted with the filing of the 10K. The nonproductive expenses continue ad infinitum with public-relations-oriented annual and quarterly reports for the stockholders and more filings with regulatory agencies.

One of the most dramatic aspects of going public from the entrepreneur's standpoint is the move from the picket-fence home to the goldfish bowl. The owner will be under public scrutiny and will no longer be able to run the company on a shoot-from-the-hip basis.

This is not to say that private companies should never go public. Some corporations are made to order for having their stock widely held. Sadly, the ones that make it to the extent intended are few and far between. A private company has greater control over its true value than a public company because the latter is subject to the whims and vagaries of the public marketplace. Notwithstanding this, the valuation of private companies partially reflects the value of public corporations in related industries.

It is important to remember that none of the companies on the New York or American Stock Exchange started there. There was a long road between the regional or over-the counter and the big board. Those companies had the staying power to reach that austere status that made it big for their original stockholders.

Upon analysis, going public would probably be relegated to a distant second position when compared with the alternatives of selling to an outside investor, a group of investors, or the company's employees through an ESOP-assisted LBO or partial buyout.

29

What Effect an ESOP Has on the Sale of the Company

An ESOP can have a salutary effect on a corporation that may be considering purchasing the ESOP company. There are many scenarios that might be pertinent. Let's look at a few.

Scenario I: A private company, Buyer Corp, acquires a private corporation wherein the ESOP holds some of the stock. Buyer Corp purchases the stock of the stockholders other than that held by the ESOP trustee. Buyer Corp establishes an ESOP. The stock held by the seller's ESOP is rolled into Buyer Corp's ESOP and is exchanged for Buyer Corp's stock of equivalent value. This reduces the amount of cash needed by Buyer Corp for the transaction, since it had to cash out only the non-ESOP stockholders.

Scenario II: Public Corp buys privately controlled Seller Corp. Whether the acquisition is for cash or stock of Public Corp, the ESOP can be terminated and both the non-ESOP stockholders and the ESOP trustees can be cashed out and the account balances distributed. Alternatively, the ESOP account balances can be exchanged for Public Corp stock and rolled into another qualified plan of Public Corp, such as an ESOP, a profit-sharing plan, or an IRA.

30

How Banks Can Benefit From ESOPs

As a Lender to ESOP Companies

Banks are on the receiving end of one of the biggest tax benefits that has ever been given to any institution. The ability to deduct half of the interest income that it receives from loans to ESOPs or ESOP corporations is a tax break that requires giving up nothing in return. The banks do not even have to make a contribution of earnings to a trust in order to obtain the tax savings. A dollar of taxes saved is a dollar of capital created, which, in turn, means several dollars of newly created lending capacity.

The 1984 Deficit Reduction Act created this bonanza not only for banks but for other commercial lenders, including insurance companies as well as commercial lenders, whose primary business is lending. This should encourage a lending institution to seek loan customers of this type to a greater extent than any other, assuming the bank is or will soon be paying taxes. If the lender is not now in a positive tax bracket but expects to be in the near future, the deductions can be carried over as losses and are just as good as "money in the bank."

In order to attract even greater revenue and clientele, a bank may be willing to pass some or all of its tax savings on to the borrowing company or to its ESOP trustee. This can be one of the more inexpensive ways of attracting business.

Why a Bank Should Have an ESOP

The interest deductibility provision has served as a catalyst for banks to investigate and implement ESOPs for their own employees. Some banks have indeed gone so far as to borrow money from other banks that were willing to pass on the tax savings. These leveraged transactions have been used for financing the LBOs of other banks, thereby increasing the acquiring bank's scope of operations and lending capacity. This, in turn, leads to greater earnings.

The multiple effect is probably more applicable to the banking industry than to any other. A bank's lending capacity is a magnified reflection of its reserves, which, in turn, come from earnings. This leverage capability can be given great impetus by the adoption of an ESOP whether it borrows money or not.

For a bank in the 50% combined state and federal tax bracket, an ESOP can create $1 of tax savings by making a deductible contribution of $2 of newly issued stock to the ESOP. This increased working capital and cash flow lets the bank expand its lending ability three-, four- or five-fold. If the bank has a qualified profit-sharing plan and converts it to an ESOP, this can provide even greater cash flow. The assets of the profit-sharing plan could be used to purchase the bank's newly issued stock, thereby improving its lending power.

The shares owned by the ESOP may become a major voting block on behalf of management since the trustee could vote the shares in accordance with the committee's direction. In any event, employees tend to vote in favor of management when a vote is passed through. This is useful in unfriendly takeover situations.

The fact that productivity would be expected to be enhanced by the equity ownership enjoyed by ESOP participants should have a salutary effect on earnings and lending capacity.

Stockholders of the bank would be afforded a marketplace for their shares without the need for the bank to go public. This would serve as an alternative to going public or selling the bank to outsiders in order to create a market for the stock.

The effect on the employees' morale should be positive and significant since the shares held by the ESOP trustee in their accounts can become their retirement nest eggs.

Banks are often precluded by law from redeeming their own stock. This had proven to be an impediment to their establishing ESOPs. This was due to the fact that a leveraged ESOP permitted employees to demand stock upon distribution. Banks are given an exception when state law prohibits banks from redeeming stock. ERTA deletes the put-option requirement when ESOPs provide that participants may receive cash as their distributions.

How a Bank's Trust Department Can Become More Profitable Through ESOPs

As executor and trustee of many estates, a bank finds itself in many "can-of-worms" situations that cause trust officers sleepless nights. It is not uncommon to find estates with a majority block of closely held stock or thinly held public stock having no way of cashing out at other than a distress price. On the one hand, there is no market for the nonpublic stock. And on the other, offering a large block of thinly held public stock would tend to depress the price. The bank can be criticized if it holds on to a stagnant stock ... and subject to litigation if it sells at what might be a ridiculously low price. So it's damned if it does and damned if it doesn't.

If the corporation behind the stock has a decent track record and is paying taxes in the top bracket, an ESOP might be just what the doctor ordered. Here is how the "bail out" of a widow's stock works:

The corporation installs an ESOP to which it contributes deductible cash in amounts not to exceed 15% of covered payroll. The ESOP purchases stock from the executor of the estate at a price determined by third-party appraisal, thereby avoiding criticism. This provides liquidity with which the executor can pay taxes or diversify the holdings in the estate. An LBO/ESOP might also have come into play if needed. The executives and other employees become the new owners, and the bank's trust department breathes a sigh of relief. In upholding its fiduciary role, the bank no longer needs to choose between two equally unappealing solutions, liquidating or selling to outsiders, to see that the widow's best interests are served.

Without a mechanism such as an ESOP, the business might be subject to liquidation to pay the estate taxes. With it, the corporation maintains its executive staff, which might have drifted away because of the uncertain future of the stock's control. Chances are, the bank will retain a corporate customer that might otherwise have been lost.

If the corporation had a profit-sharing plan, a game plan could have called for converting it to an ESOP and, with IRS approval, transferring the assets from the profit-sharing plan to the ESOP. The trust would then liquidate the assets for the purchase of stock from the estate. Additional cash contributions could also be used to buy stock.

31

Security Law and the ESOP

The Securities and Exchange Commission has taken a stance in various "no action" letters that contributions to an ESOP do not constitute an offer to sell or a sale under the 1933 Securities Act so long as the plan is qualified under I.R.C. §401(a) and employees are not permitted to make contributions to the plan or have any choice as to receiving cash or stock from the plan. The important fact here is that the employees should have no choice or discretion concerning the shares, nor should the shares be granted to employees as repayment for specific services rendered. Collective bargaining resulting in the adoption of an ESOP could result in the SEC's taking the position that an offer has been made under the 1933 Act, since the shares are being made available to the employees for value received.

When stock is distributed to participants of a private company's ESOP, it is generally subject to an investment letter that prevents resale of the securities to a third party. The put option as well as right of first refusal prevents the stock from reaching third-party hands, as does the bylaw or charter amendment.

ESOPs of public companies are considered to be affiliates and the registered shares fall under Rule 144, which inhibits their tradeability unless an independent trustee acquires the stock and subsequently sells it. If the trustee is not considered to be absolutely independent, the participant's shares may be subject to Rule 144, in which case they must be held for at least two years and subsequently sold as a broker's transaction. Some companies feel it is wise, safe, and relatively simple to register all the stock under a Form S-8 Registration. It is advisable to consider use of a bank so that the exemption for registration can apply even if voluntary contributions by employees are provided for in the plan document.

All qualified plans have been declared exempt from registration under the Investment Company Act. If such a plan provides for voluntary employee contributions, it will probably fall under the 1933 Act and be exempt from reporting under the 1934 Act. ESOPs are exempt from insider-trading rules if the plan has been approved by the shareholders. This rule is not applicable if stock is distributed to an outsider at the time of retirement, or if the outsider does not sell the stock for six months before or after the date of distributions. This is pursuant to Rule 16(b).

Blue Sky Laws

Blue Sky laws of the various states should be researched thoroughly for any possible application to ESOPs. These laws vary from state to state and should be reviewed carefully. For example, the attorney general of New York State has determined that broker-dealer registration requirements must be adhered to by any corporation, firm, association, or person that issues securities in connection with ESOPs. It considers an ESOP to be a dealer since it buys, maintains, and distributes securities.

Although New York general business law requires that dealers become registered before offering or selling securities—either from New York or operating within the state—it does not require that the securities be registered. ESOPs sponsored in New York that emanate from outside the state, but that cover corporations as well as those employees who are residents and employees of the state, must register as broker-dealers or apply for an exemption for securities that are issued in connection with ESOP, pension, profit-sharing, thrift, or any other plan of this general category.

The SEC issued a "no action" letter to DeCouper Industries, Inc., on December 22, 1975, pertaining to the conversion of its funded profit-sharing plan. A key to this case was that the employees did not have a choice with regard to the conversion, notwithstanding the fact that some of the employees' accounts were vested, according to Section 4(2) of the Securities Law.

The SEC has granted a "no action" letter to a corporation, which reversed its earlier position. In this letter, the Commission pointed out that, due to the small amounts of company stock distributed to the employees, the transactions would not fall under the 1933 Securities Act or, more specifically, under Rule 144 of the Act. The SEC indicated that this ruling would be applicable to all similar situations.

The SEC issued a "no action" letter to another company advising the corporation that it need not register the interests in its TRASOPs (Tax Reduction Act ESOP) or the shares upon distribution. It did point out that the staff felt that the shares distributed to the participants would be "restricted" for purposes of Rule 144 and that the two-year holding period for shares distributed would begin to run when the shares became fully vested. Although this speaks of a TRASOP, it might serve as an indication of the agency's thinking in connection with a tax-credit ESOP (PAYSOP). The SEC subsequently agreed that it was not necessary to register shares of stock procured by a tax-credit ESOP in the open market so long as the employer's participation was limited to performing basic administrative functions and the employer was not directly involved in the payment for the stock that the tax-credit ESOP has acquired.

The foregoing is not to be considered conclusive or all-encompassing, and all aspects of the securities laws should, of course, be cleared with counsel.

32

The Fallacy of the Free Lunch—
The Downside of ESOPs

"There is neither good nor bad; our thinking makes it so." Shakespeare's observation is appropriate when considering the applicability of ESOPs in a given situation. One's perception of what is to be accomplished in a corporate environment will determine the viability of an ESOP for achieving a stated goal. If the ESOP can do what the owners want for their company, their employees, and themselves, the upside potential of its use may more than compensate for any problem to be overcome as a result of implementing the ESOP.

A quip, "AESOP's Fables," is used frequently to characterize the too-good-to-be-true or free-lunch quality that, upon shallow analysis, might seem applicable to ESOPs. This is far from the truth. Anything that is worthwhile does not come easily. Here are some ESOP problem areas that must be addressed.

Valuation Problem

Contributions to an ESOP for a company whose value is very low can cause an adverse dilution of the stock, from the owner's standpoint. The employees, from their perspective, will benefit by having stock allocated to their accounts that has been valued on the low side if the upside potential for growth is destined to be realized. Assuming a given dollar value of the contribution, they will receive a greater number of shares that will be worth more in the future. Conversely, if little or no appreciation occurs, the ESOP could foster animosity rather than goodwill.

Valuation of the stock is a problem, but one that can be solved by independent valuation firms. It is important that a defensible valuation be arrived at and updated annually. The ESOP fiduciaries must be in a position to adhere to the requirement that the trustee can purchase securities for no more than fair market value. If the trustee pays more than fair market value, an excise tax could be incurred. A worst-case circumstance could be disqualification of the plan. In actuality, this would happen only in rare cases. The subject of valuation is addressed in greater depth in Chapter 9.

Dilution Problem

This is a downside that must be dealt with when considering an ESOP. When a corporation issues new shares of stock, it cuts the corporate pie into additional slices. Upon contributing those shares to the ESOP for the benefit of its employees, the corporation reduces the size of the slices owned by the non-ESOP shareholders. The "free lunch" is in the form of tax savings created by the stock contribution. These savings can be more than offset by the equity that the outside owners lose if the corporation does not put its newly created working capital to productive use. Doing so, however, could result in a multiple effect that would increase the value of the stock of all concerned, including that of the outside owners. The judicious use of this new capital can more than offset the diminution of the portion of the pie still retained by the non-ESOP owners.

A further offset to dilution that should be considered is the likelihood that the corporation would have another form of tax-qualified plan to which it would be making cash contributions for the employees. This would reduce the company's working capital and cash flow by its net aftertax expenditure. A technique for reducing the effect of further dilution is to have the corporation redeem the shares from those employees who are eligible for statutory distributions. The corporation would make its next contribution of stock to the ESOP after the subsequent valuation occurred, at which time, it is hoped, the stock will have risen in value. This would require a contribution of a smaller number of shares to achieve a given tax deduction.

It is evident that although dilution is a problem, it can be reduced in its importance by modifying factors.

Control

Control is an issue that should be well thought out but need not be a problem. The corporation's board of directors appoints the ESOP's administrative or management committee, which directs the trustee as to how to vote the stock. The major stockholder can hold all these positions, but he or she must be careful to wear different fiduciary hats. It is generally advisable to have an independent third party such as a bank serve as trustee.

The employee participants of the ESOP do not physically hold the stock. The assets of the trust are held by the trustee on behalf of the participants. The plan may provide that the trustee must take its direction from the administrative committee, which, in turn, is appointed by the board. Only in those states where more than a majority of stockholders must vote on certain grave issues such as merger or liquidation is the vote passed through to the ESOP participants. Some advisers feel that this provision applies to all states. This viewpoint seems to be quite conservative but should be considered.

In a practical sense, on all other matters the control rests ultimately in the hands of the non-ESOP major shareholders who control the corporate board that appoints the committee that directs the trustee. Fiduciary responsibility must be borne in mind at all times. Shares pledged as collateral continue to be voted by the non-ESOP shareholders.

The corporation or the ESOP can have a right of first refusal to purchase stock from terminated employees. Moreover, the corporate charter or bylaws can be amended to restrict stock ownership to current employees or to a trust. This would have the effect of making it mandatory that the stock remain with the corporation or the ESOP for continued control.

ESOP participants are given a put option enabling them to look forward to cash rather than stock. Since the employees will be taxed upon a distribution, they will tend to want cash rather than the stock. This is an additional factor in recycling the stock back for further control by the non-ESOP stockholders.

Repurchasing the Stock From Participants

There will come a time when the stock in a private company's ESOP must be repurchased by the corporation or by the ESOP. Employees want to know that when they become disabled, die, terminate employment, or retire, there will be a market for their stock.

The cash must be provided for this purpose. This is a problem, but one that can be solved quite easily if addressed well in advance. Public corporations whose stock is widely traded do not face this problem, since there is a ready market for the stock allocated to ESOP accounts.

This subject is treated in greater depth in Chapter 34, "The ESOP's Emerging Repurchase Liability."

33

Where ESOPs Do Not Apply

Noncandidates for ESOPs in General

Corporations with a poor earnings track record and whose prospects are not likely to improve are not prospects for an ESOP. It is important that a company be in a position to demonstrate historical and sustainable stability for purposes of valuing its stock.

Companies that have very few employees and therefore a low coverable payroll would be unable to generate sufficient tax savings to make an ESOP worthwhile. A stock-bonus-plan ESOP permits a maximum annual contribution amounting to 15% of covered payroll. If the corporation is in a 50% combined state and federal tax bracket, and has a covered annual payroll of $200,000, a 15% contribution of $30,000 would give the company a $15,000 tax savings. This may not be worth the effort. If, on the other hand, the company were likely to grow rapidly, there might be some justification for implementing the ESOP and making minimal contributions of perhaps a small percent of covered payroll so as to accumulate carryovers that could be used in future years. This would permit the corporation to contribute as much as 25% of covered payroll in subsequent years when its payroll and earnings will likely be significantly greater.

Corporations whose owners have no desire to permit rank-and-file employees to share in the harvest of equity appreciation are certainly not candidates for an ESOP irrespective of how they themselves might benefit. They would never consider their own rewards to be sufficiently adequate to offset their anguish at relinquishing any equity to the employees.

S Corporations

S corporations are ineligible for ESOPs due to the limitation as to stock ownership by a trust. Legislation had been introduced as part of the 1984 tax package that would have permitted S corporations to adopt ESOPs but this was thwarted in the final bill.

Professional Corporations

Professional corporations have not been eligible for ESOPs because of the rules governing stock ownership by nonprofessionals. Certain states have passed enabling legislation that would appear to eliminate this problem. The antidiscrimination rules would apparently preclude the adoption of a different form of qualified plan for nonprofessional employees while covering only the professionals under the ESOP. Such is not the case if the two plans are a profit-sharing plan and a stock bonus plan that is not an ESOP. The possible distribution of stock to nonprofessional employees upon termination, disability, death, or retirement need not occur if the charter or bylaws preclude this. Yet, state laws vary as to the rules governing specific professions. These laws change and should be reviewed periodically.

34

The ESOP's Emerging Repurchase Liability

The piper must be paid. The stock allocated to ESOP accounts must be purchased by the ESOP or by the corporation. If the ESOP has been good for the employees, it will have been due to the appreciation of the stock. This will be more costly to translate into cash when the stock is due to be distributed.

If the stock is to be repurchased by the corporation, it will have to be done with aftertax dollars since a corporate redemption is not a deductible transaction. If the stock is to be redeemed by the trustee, it will be done with pretax dollars that the corporation contributes to the ESOP.

The problem is frequently addressed by making cash contributions to the ESOP and maintaining an amount of cash that will anticipate the repurchase requirements for several succeeding years. The amount of cash to be contributed is determined by projecting forthcoming retirements and using turnover, mortality, and morbidity factors. The growth of the stock must also be taken into consideration. As the corporation grows it will be in a better position to provide the cash. This will keep the problem in check so long as the corporate cash flow continues to increase. As cash contributions are made, however, they will reduce working capital and cash flow and can have the effect of retarding the increase in the value of the stock.

A sinking fund is, in essence, a profit-sharing plan rather than an ESOP. It does not address the long-range obligation to buy back the share of the corporation that is owned by the employee trust. The valuation will eventually reflect the unfunded repurchase liability unless a far-sighted program is adopted that will create as much capital as is projected to be owned by the ESOP over a minimum period of two decades. If such a program is implemented, the owners of the company will be more apt to use the ESOP to its greater capital-formation potential. A well-designed repurchase liability funding program can also enable the corporation to recycle the stock to counteract the effect of dilution. This is true for corporations whether the ESOP owns a portion of the stock or 100% of it.

The selection of a funding program to cope with the ESOP's emerging repurchase liability is one of the most important aspects that must be dealt with both by companies that are considering the implementation of an ESOP as well as companies that have had a plan in effect for some years.

The problem is insidious in that there is relatively little in the way of repurchase obligation during the first 8 or 10 years. Yet this is the time when the funding technique should be effectuated, since it will be far less costly than when the barn is truly on fire. A simple actuarial study of the kind used for other qualified plans will not address the total financial interrelationship between the corporation and the ESOP. The downstream effect of the valuation, the sale of the stock by owners, estate planning of major stockholders, and perpetuation of the closely held company must be factored in.

The ESOP, unlike a pension plan, is not a fund-as-you-go plan. This is why capital can be created with an ESOP but not with a pension plan. It is of a different breed and must be funded accordingly with a philosophical approach that will not usurp its basic capital-formation characteristic.

A properly designed funding program will reduce or eliminate the discount that a valuation firm might assign the stock because of the unfunded repurchase liability that would otherwise loom ahead. This is another problem that is quite easily solvable if addressed early and with a long-range viewpoint in mind.

35

Profile of Likely Candidates for ESOPs

The ESOP is not for every company. A profile of likely candidates provides an overview of firms that should explore an ESOP's possibilities. It is especially important to determine the basic goals of those who control the corporation being evaluated as an ESOP candidate.

The strength, structure, and earning capacity of a company must be considered as well. The Employee Stock Ownership Feasibility Checklist on subsequent pages can be useful in uncovering these facts.

Following are some specific qualities to consider before matching a company with an ESOP.

☐ The corporation should be in the top income tax bracket, with likelihood of remaining profitable.

☐ The corporation must be taxed as a corporation—not as an S corporation. (S corporations do not qualify. An S corporation restricts stock ownership to a limited form of trust.)

☐ It must be a domestic corporation.

☐ The corporation may be privately or publicly owned.

☐ It may be desiring to make acquisitions. (The corporation can do this with pretax dollars.)

☐ It may be seeking to make a divestiture. (The corporation can facilitate this by making it possible for buyers to take over with pretax dollars.)

☐ If it is a private corporation, it should have major or minor stockholders who wish to cash out. (The ESOP provides a private pretax method for accomplishing this.)

☐ It may be a public corporation wishing to avoid takeover. (An ESOP can tender for shares. Present management would appoint the committee that directs the voting of the trust. However, the vote must be passed through to participants in a public-company ESOP.)

☐ It has major stockholders who desire creative and tax-advantageous methods in their estate planning.

☐ It may be looking for ways to service incurred debt or future financing. (Principal and interest can be serviced with pretax dollars through the ESOP. Five hundred thousand dollars of principal can be serviced with $500,000 by using the pretax dollar approach through the ESOP. Without this method, a corporation would be required to earn $1 million to repay principal on a $500,000 loan.)

☐ The corporation may have a profit-sharing plan. (It may be possible to convert to an ESOP, thereby using the assets to buy company stock.)

☐ It wishes to increase working capital and cash flow.

☐ If it is a private corporation, it has an owner who wants to make way for successor management such as working heirs or other key executives.

☐ In many cases, the owner simply wishes to transfer ownership to the employees.

☐ The corporation is a profitable public company that feels its stock price on the stock exchange does not reflect its true value, or management is convinced that it would be more advantageous to be goal-oriented for long-term results rather than quarterly profits that are demanded by outside stockholders for quick profits. Such a company might want to go private through a leveraged ESOP buyout.

☐ The corporation is failing, and the employees, who face imminent unemployment, wish to acquire the company.

☐ The corporation, for altruistic reasons, wants to have the employees own a greater piece of the action.

36

How to Implement an ESOP

A corporation's board of directors, often after having considered a feasibility study, would resolve to adopt an ESOP. The plan and trust documents should be designed by the company's counsel or by the counsel of a firm specializing in ESOP implementation. It should then be presented for board review prior to submission to the local District Director of Internal Revenue for a letter of determination.

Fiduciaries, including the administrative committee members and the trustee, would be named in the document. The members of the administrative committee need not include any specific category of individual such as rank-and-file employees. Such employees are sometimes included on the committee, however. Though it is advisable to use a corporate trustee such as a trust department of a bank, an individual can serve in this capacity. It makes it easier to separate the fiduciary responsibilities if a corporate trustee is used.

Although the trustee can be given complete responsibility for managing all of the assets of the ESOP, the plan generally provides that the trustee will be subject to the administrative committee's direction as noted earlier.

The annual administration can be done in-house, since this is rather perfunctory by nature and somewhat similar to the administration of a pension or profit-sharing plan. The administrator must have software capable of tracking the values of the assets.

For this and other reasons it may be advisable to use an outside administrator who is well-versed in ESOPs. Participants to whom stock is distributed will be subject to ordinary income taxation on the base cost and capital gains on the appreciation when they sell the stock. It is therefore mandatory to maintain year-by-year records as to the cost basis.

The administrators should keep abreast of administrative requirements since these change from time to time. They must file annual tax forms similar to those required in connection with other forms of qualified plans and submit these to the IRS and to the state of corporate domicile.

The most visible duty of the administrator is to compute the number of shares that are allocated to the trust and the value of those shares as well as the number and value of the shares to be allocated to each participant's account. This includes the allocation of forfeitures from terminated employees as well.

A valuation of the shares of the corporation should be performed prior to the board's determination as to the amount of stock to be contributed to the ESOP.

Summary of steps to implement an ESOP:

• Feasibility study.

• Resolution by board of directors to adopt an ESOP and have it drafted by counsel.

• Design of the plan.

• Communication of the provisions of the ESOP to the employees.

• Valuation of the corporate stock.

• Submission to IRS for letter of determination.

• Contribution by the corporation during the tax year.

• Administration and trusteeship of the plan.

Because an ESOP, unlike other qualified plans, is an instrument of corporate finance rather than a retirement plan, it should be implemented only after taking into consideration the effect the ESOP might have on corporate financial goals, executive benefit planning, corporate ownership succession, and estate planning for major stockholders. Perhaps this should be done with a new dimensional outlook of specialists.

37

How to Communicate ESOP Benefits to Employees for Greater Public Relations

ESOPs can be left to gather dust in the bottom drawer or can be placed on a pedestal as a constant reminder that the employees own equity in the company. Some companies go so far as to capitalize on this fact by proclaiming themselves to be ESOP companies. This carries with it the implication of better quality control and the suggestion that, all things being equal, an ESOP company is better for the consumer. ESOP companies do give their employees an incentive to achieve perfection in their work, thereby becoming more competitive and more profitable.

If employees and the community at large are constantly reminded of the fact that the employees have a stake in the company, productivity should result, with a commensurate increase in the value of the stock allocated to participants' accounts in addition to increasing sales.

The IRS and Department of Labor, underscoring the need to communicate benefits, have set forth minimum requirements for disclosure of key elements of the ESOP to employees. They can be capsulized as follows:

• Employees must be notified of the intent to adopt an ESOP.

• Notice to interested parties must be posted or distributed.

• A summary plan description must be provided for each participant.

So much for the mandatory aspects of disclosure. Let's move on to the nonmandatory and equally important facets of communication ... the meat of the program that brings on the fun part of ESOPs. The enjoyment comes when the employer begins to notice improved morale and greater productivity brought about by employees feeling that they have a piece of the action.

If the plan participants are uncertain as to what their "action" consists of—or indeed whether or not it really exists—a benefit plan can become counterproductive. By merely stopping at the Summary Plan Description (SPD) as required by federal law, the employer may be taking too much for granted. The employer may be giving the employees too much credit for basic knowledge about mundane facts. Many surprisingly simple questions have been brought up at employee meetings. Questions like these:

- What is stock?

- What are dividends?

- How are profits determined?

- How does management decide how much to contribute to the plan?

The first commandment among news professionals demands that a story respond to the questions that flash into every reader's mind ... What? Who? When? Where? Why? Employees ask the same questions at meetings but add others to the list. How? What if? What is meant by?

The SPD does a fair job at getting communications on a proper track, but it falls short at the point where subjective thinking begins. There is just no substitute for eyeball-to-eyeball sessions, preferably at small gatherings, which tend to reduce inhibitions among the attendees. The larger the number of questions, the greater the interest and appreciation of the program. A lack of questions at the meeting does not necessarily mean that they will not be asked somewhere else or at some other time. And when they are, those responding to such queries will lack the expertise that the well-informed conductor of an organized meeting will have. That's why careful consideration should be given to selecting the meeting leader.

Bulletins relating to various areas of employee interest are always well received and well read if they are interesting. Employees enjoy being the first to hear about the new defense contract that was awarded to their firm, or about the public's response to the new product that has just been unveiled by the marketing division. A point of interest about the ESOP should be interspersed between items in the bulletin.

Posters are powerful instruments of communication. And while they are used with great success as brainwashing devices in dictatorial states, no inference of bad intent should be drawn here when it comes to using posters to convey the spirit of employee ownership. Perhaps a poster contest to kick off the ESOP might help get everyone off and running. The more involvement, the better.

Slide and other audiovisual presentations are available—some more effective than others. It is quite possible that the sponsoring company may wish to design its own slide show, or have a custom show created by an outside resource. The program should be made part of the indoctrination of new employees even though they may not yet be eligible to participate in the ESOP. It shows them what lies ahead.

An employee benefit booklet can range from being devoid of graphics to incorporating expensive layouts that run the cost through the roof. In any event, the booklet should be thoroughly informative; otherwise it might raise more questions than it answers.

Communications deserve time and thought. A well-conceived information program can more than pay its cost in improved productivity and employee morale. Management should factor in measuring devices to see what kind of feedback it is receiving. The tried-and-true suggestion box can tell a great deal. After all, it is the ESOP participants who will gain by the company's overall progress and well-being.

38

ESOP and Tax-Credit ESOP Accounting Basics

Effect on the Balance Sheet

If the corporate contribution is in the form of authorized but unissued stock, the following will result:

• Reduction of taxable income.

• Reduction of aftertax profits.

• Increase in cash.

• Increase in capital stock.

• Reduction in retained earnings.

If the corporation makes a cash contribution, the following will result:

• Taxable income is reduced.

• Aftertax profits are reduced.

The American Institute of Certified Public Accountants (AICPA) issued its statement of position on accounting practices for certain ESOPs on December 20, 1976. This was later reaffirmed in the Statement of Financial Accounting Standards #32. The statement clarified the AICPA position as to how the corporate financial statements should record a leveraged ESOP transaction. It was recommended that if the corporation guarantees the obligation or commits itself to make future contributions to the ESOP in an amount sufficient to equal the debt service requirements, the transactions should be recorded as a liability, but it goes on to say that it does not follow from the above that the assets held by an ESOP should be included in the financial statements of the employer. Such assets belong to the employees.

The statement recommends that the offsetting debit to the liability recorded by the employer should be accounted for as a reduction of shareholders' equity. It points out that when new shares are issued to the ESOP by the employer, an increase in shareholders' equity should be reported only as the debt that financed the increase is reduced. The offsetting debit is shareholders' equity, which, in this case, is akin to unearned compensation. It states that when outstanding shares as opposed to unissued shares are accounted for by the ESOP, the shareholders' equity should similarly be reduced by the offsetting debit until the debt is repaid.

It further states that the liability recorded by the employer should be reduced as an ESOP makes payments on the debt. Therefore, it should not be reduced until payments are actually made. Similarly, the amount reported as a reduction in shareholders' equity should be reduced only when the ESOP makes payments on the debt.

The amount contributed or committed to be contributed to an ESOP with respect to a given year should be the measure of the amount to be charged to expense of the employer. This is also true of nonleveraged ESOPs. Such contributions measure the amount of expense irrevocably incurred whether or not they are used concurrently to reduce the debt guaranteed by the employer.

Since the debt of the ESOP is, in essence, the employer's debt, the employer should report separately the compensation element and the interest element of the annual contributions, and should disclose the related interest rate and the terms in the footnotes.

Shares held by the ESOP should be treated as outstanding shares in the determination of earnings per share. An ESOP is a legal entity holding shares issued by the employer whether or not those shares have been allocated to the employee accounts. Dividends paid by shares held by an ESOP should be charged to retained earnings. Such dividends should not be included as compensation expense.

The additional investment tax credit should be accounted for (to the extent that it is available and utilized) as a reduction of income tax expense in the same year in which the contribution to the ESOP is charged to expense, irrespective of the accounting for the normal investment tax credit on property acquisitions.

Excess contributions, as defined, made in any one year may be carried over to future periods for income tax purposes. The financial statements of the employer should reflect the tax effect of timing differences.

39

How an ESOP Can Recover Taxes Paid in Prior Years (With No Cash Expenditures)

ESOPs differ from profit-sharing plans in a way that is useful for recovering taxes or creating a loss to be carried forward for future years. A corporation can make contributions to a profit-sharing plan only out of profits. It can make contributions to an ESOP even in years when there is no profit. Furthermore, the contribution to the ESOP need not be made in cash.

Corporate losses can be carried back three years and forward 15 years. Let's assume a corporation has paid taxes in each of the prior three years but has a current year of no earnings.

The corporation could make a tax-deductible contribution of stock to its ESOP this year, thereby creating a loss that can be carried back three prior taxpaying years. The current contribution to the ESOP would go to offsetting the taxable income of the earliest of the three years and then the other two most recent years sequentially. The taxes could be recovered with no cash contribution using this methodology.

MODEL:

How an ESOP Can Make It Possible to Obtain a Tax Refund

Year	Taxable Income	Contribution to ESOP (Installed 1985)	Federal Taxes Paid
1982	$ 90,000	— 0 —	$22,250
1983	110,000	— 0 —	30,350
1984	100,000	— 0 —	25,750
SUB TOTALS	$300,000	— 0 —	$78,350
1985	— 0 — (A)	$300,000 (B)	

(A) Corporation broke even in 1985.

(B) Corporation installed an ESOP in 1985, to which it contributed 15% of payroll or $300,000 in cash or stock.

(C) Corporation is entitled by the Internal Revenue Code to a refund of federal taxes paid for three preceding years because the ESOP contribution in 1985, a break-even year, offset the taxable income in those years. The refund in this model is $78,350.

MODEL:

Effect of Contribution to Qualified Trusts on Company Statement

	ESOP	Profit-Sharing Trust	No Qualified Trust
Pretax Income	$250,000	$250,000	$250,000
Less Contribution	150,000 (Stock)	150,000 (Cash)	0
Net Taxable Income	100,000	100,000	250,000
Income Tax (federal & state)	50,000	50,000	125,000
Net Aftertax Income	50,000	50,000	125,000
Cash Flow	$200,000*	$ 50,000	$125,000

The $150,000 stock contribution remains at work in the corporation.

40

ESOP Legislation at the State And City Level

Various state legislatures are taking a page from the Federal Register. California, Delaware, Illinois, Maryland, Massachusetts, Michigan, Minnesota, New Jersey, Pennsylvania, and West Virginia are among states that have adopted ESOP legislation. New York City was the first municipality to have its own ESOP law. The enactments are generally quite different from one another but with the underlying commonality of encouraging the use of ESOPs.

Under the California law, the State Department of Economic and Business Development must help employee buyout situations along by making available revenue-bond-based financing for the purchase of the plan. Filing procedures involved in complying with various governmental agency requirements will also be expedited. Unemployment benefits will continue under law while the negotiations take place between the employees and the present owner on the transfer of the company in question. California will also make available planning money for employee-owned companies.

The state of Delaware adopted a broadened ownership act patterned after the one that Maryland had enacted. Maryland's act declares broadened ownership of companies by their employees to be of special importance and it calls upon various state agencies to report on their efforts to assist in broadening ownership. Reporting must be done annually. The law also exempts ESOPs from all state security laws. It amends the antitakeover disclosure act so as to allow the state securities department to require the potential buyer of a business to notify the target company's management that it may use an ESOP as a defense against the takeover attempt. The act precludes the Maryland public utility commission from requiring that companies pass on to consumers a utility's savings that may have occurred as a result of its maintaining an ESOP.

Illinois, New York, and Michigan have laws somewhat similar to the one described for California. The Massachusetts law permits a PAYSOP (tax-credit ESOP) trustee to vote the stock of the plan participants. This deviates from the state's corporate law whereby companies are prevented from voting their own stock either directly or indirectly. This legislation does not apply to a statutory ESOP, however. New York City has become the first municipality to adopt special legislation encouraging ESOPs.

Other states have considered the adoption of ESOP legislation and it is quite likely that new laws will be placed into force that will further enhance the value of ESOPs.

41

The PAYSOP

The PAYSOP is a name given to the tax-credit ESOP, which replaced the TRASOP (Tax Reduction Act ESOP) as a result of the Economic Recovery Tax Act of 1981. The PAYSOP became effective as of January 1, 1983. As the name implies, PAYSOPs were designed to permit corporations to receive a tax credit as a result of contributing stock to a tax-credit ESOP based on covered payroll of its employees. This is in contrast to the TRASOP, wherein the employer was permitted a tax credit for stock contributions to a trust for its employees, the upper limit of which was related to the corporation's investment in capital equipment. The TRASOP was of particular importance to capital-intensive companies. The PAYSOP, on the other hand, was designed to benefit payroll-intensive companies.

The PAYSOP originally permitted a tax credit for 1983 and 1984 of up to one half of 1% of the compensation of the participants, and for 1985 through 1987, the credit was increased to three quarters of 1% and was scheduled to expire after 1987 unless renewed by Congress. The 1984 Deficit Reduction Act maintained the percentage for which a tax credit would be allowed at one half of 1% with no escalation. The credit was scheduled by that Act to expire after 1987 subject to Congress voting to end it or continue it.

The PAYSOP tax credit is in addition to the allowable deduction limitation under the ESOP. The PAYSOP can exist on its own even if there is no ESOP. The PAYSOP is a defined-contribution plan designed to invest primarily in employer securities and is allocated to participants' accounts in the same way allocations are made in other qualified plans. Benefits are fully vested immediately and the vote passed through to the participants. The same rules pertain to PAYSOPs as to ESOPs concerning the right of the employee-participants to demand stock upon distribution. PAYSOPs of public or nonpublic companies whose stock is not readily tradeable are subject to a put-option requirement.

Securities in a participant's account must not be distributed to the participant until 84 months after it has been allocated to the account unless the employee terminates, dies, is disabled, or if the corporation is sold or certain pertinent divisions are sold. The employee is not taxed on the stock or any dividends credited to his or her PAYSOP account until the assets are distributed to the employee. At that time, the employee will be taxed.

The contribution limitation for which tax credits were allowed made both the TRASOP and PAYSOP significantly more appealing to large public companies than to private ones.

In the case of the PAYSOP, the payroll would have to be extraordinarily large in order for the tax credit to be worthwhile. The PAYSOP is a foot in the door and may lead to future thoughts of larger limits so as to broaden the base of capital ownership among the employees.

42

ESOPs and Other Executive Incentive Plans

An ESOP, though tied into ERISA requirements as to its being nondiscriminatory, does indeed provide greater benefits for more highly paid employees. Since the ESOP is almost invariably noncontributory, it requires no burdensome near-term or long-term capital outlay by the executive. This is quite unlike a stock option plan wherein, if the stock appreciates, the executives will have to come up with a bundle of cash in order to take advantage of the appreciation. An ESOP participant can look forward to the ultimate distribution of his or her vested interest with no coinciding monetary obligation.

Since the executive will be receiving a greater portion of the nonvested forfeitures of those who terminate, the ESOP becomes even more meaningful. The executive will receive ESOP participation statements at the end of each year showing ever-increasing values, assuming the stock valuation has not declined sufficiently to offset the quantity of shares added to his or her account. A plan document that gives the administrative committee the right to refrain from making a distribution to a terminating employee until normal retirement age would discourage an executive from quitting in order to obtain the vested portion of his or her account.

The incentive characteristic of an ESOP varies somewhat in proportion to the valuation of the stock. Noting that greater earnings increase the value of the stock, the executive will be predisposed to enhance the value of his or her account through greater productivity. The executive might go so far as to keep a weather eye out for those employees who do not carry their weight, thereby leveraging the productivity factor. The executive will also think long and hard before terminating employment, an act that would trigger forfeiture of the nonvested interest in the trust.

From the corporate vantage point, the ESOP offers the advantage of being able to prepare for the liquidity required for distributions on a gradual basis. The company need not make distributions until normal retirement age, and even at that time, is permitted to dole out the distribution over a period of years. An actuarial study should be performed periodically on the liquidity requirement. The other types of stock-oriented plans tend to tie up cash on a near-term basis since the spread between the point of grant and the measurement point is narrow.

The corporation normally seeks an incentive program that has long-range retention goals, whereas the executive likes the idea of as much cash up front as possible, as well as a program that will satisfy his or her natural desire for security. The ideal incentive package is one that can satisfy both desires.

A combination of an ESOP and, say, a participating units plan* might be an example of such a combination. The latter provides the sweet smell of cash and the ability to use it in the not-too-distant future, while the ESOP's deferred aspect tied to normal retirement age gives the executive greater freedom to spend and enjoy the fruits of the more current distributable awards under the participating units plan.

A current cash distribution plan brings with it current tax payments and, for one who is in the top tax echelon, the resulting erosion of purchasing power detracts from its glamour in the year received.

Other Incentive Plans

In order to gain a perspective of the ESOP as an incentive program, it is important to understand other stock-related executive incentive perquisites.

The ESOP and the fringe benefit programs described in this chapter are not mutually exclusive. Interesting combinations can be created.

Here are some of the more viable stock-oriented executive incentive programs that incur little or no corporate cash outlay initially. The cost factor manifests itself in the near-term future or, in some cases, substantially later.

The History of Qualified Stock Option Plans

The Revenue Act of 1950 enacted provisions of the restricted stock option plan. The Act provided tax incentives when options were given to executives. The search for alternative executive incentive compensation packages was given a new urgency in 1976, when the death knell of newly adopted qualified stock option plans was sounded. And while the existing plans were grandfathered, options under any then-existing plan had to be exercised by May 21, 1981.

It is estimated that between two-thirds and three-fourths of public companies had qualified stock option plans prior to 1976. Under such a plan, a corporation granted stock options to favored executives based upon current value, with no tax to the employees until they exercised the option after three years but within five years. The executives received capital gains tax treatment on the appreciation above option price. They had to come up with hard cash for the purchase of the stock at the time they exercised the option. The corporation received no deduction on buying the stock from the executives.

The 1976 Tax Reform Act removed the favorable tax treatment and changed the tax on the gain to earned income instead of capital gains treatment. All new stock option plans became nonqualified because of the 1976 regulation.

Participating units plans are discussed on page 135.

The 1981 Act's Restricted Stock Option Plan

The Economic Recovery Tax Act of 1981 restored the tax luster to restricted stock option plans.

Observations on Stock Options

From the corporate viewpoint, costs are deferred between the date of grant and the date of exercise. However, the latter date may come as a surprise, and fiscal control can be affected adversely.

Options can lose their luster if the stock does not increase in value. The greater the appreciation, the greater the amount of money the executive will have to come up with upon exercise of the option. In the event of the executive's death prior to exercise, the difference between the fair market value and the value at the time of grant will be includable in the executive's estate, notwithstanding the fact that the stock option had not been exercised during his or her lifetime. Valuation of the stock for a closely held company pursuant to stock option plans can be as serious a concern as valuation for an ESOP.

Phantom Stock Plan

This is really a form of deferred compensation whereby the company agrees to pay selected executives an amount of cash in the future equal to the value of a determined amount of stock in the company, including dividends that would have been paid on that block of stock. The stock, however, is not distributed to the employee. Thus, it has sometimes been referred to as "phantom stock."

Job performance criteria generally govern the number of phantom stock units to be awarded the employee. One unit might equal one share of stock. A vesting schedule can be included. Cash payout can be in the form of a lump sum, but it is more likely to be doled out in annual installments beginning at the end of the deferral period. Young companies with little track record—and with a young executive staff—quite frequently have a short deferral period of just a few years, whereas older companies with older executives tend toward normal retirement age maturities.

The executive is not taxed until he or she receives cash payments, at which time the payout is considered earned income for tax purposes. The corporation takes a tax deduction in the year of the payout to the employee. The expense is accrued annually and the income statement is charged based on the year-end value of the phantom stock units allocated to the employee. Nonvested forfeitures are credited since those amounts had been expensed out previously. At payout time, the income statement is not affected because the charge had already been made.

One of the advantages that this form of compensation package has over stock options is that this is truly a cash transaction. Security regulations are not applicable to phantom stock, whereas they do apply to stock options.

Appreciation Rights Plan

Appreciation rights are identical in essentially every respect to phantom stock...with the exception that the former are based upon the increase in stock price plus dividend equivalents, whereas the latter is based upon the full stock value plus the dividend equivalents. In this regard, stock appreciation rights are a less costly increment to compensation than phantom stock. Both are taken into consideration by the IRS in determining the reasonableness of compensation. Neither creates stock dilution as do stock option plans. They do, however, require concern as to maintenance of liquidity in order to avoid fiscal surprises in the event executives who are partially or fully vested terminate. Liquidity can be maintained on a reasonably sound basis by using turnover and mortality factors in anticipating requirements.

Stock Bonus Plan

Stock bonus plans are relatively common fringe benefits used primarily in large public companies, but they are useful in a number of private companies, as well. For public companies, the stock market price usually governs the fair market price. For private companies, valuation is in accordance with a formula such as book value or fair market value as established by independent appraisal.

Actual shares are granted by the corporation to the executive with no monetary contribution on his or her part. The stock bonus plan, as a nonqualified plan, does not have to be submitted to IRS for special tax treatment since there is none. The allocation of shares can be based upon performance or simply on the basis of position so long as the element of compensation reasonableness is maintained.

The shares can be granted outright or placed on a vesting schedule, the latter being popular when employee retention is a goal. An executive will think long and hard about leaving the firm if he or she must suffer substantial forfeitures under the program. The stock bonus plan is something used to recruit prime candidates who are looking for a "piece of the action." It is used more often, however, as an incentive, tied into the executive's performance and the achievement of certain production or profit goals.

The corporation deducts an amount equal to the market value in the case of a public company, or fair market value when used in privately owned companies. The tax deduction takes place in the tax year in which the shares are granted to the employee. The executive receives earned income tax treatment based upon the market value as the shares are granted, and capital gains treatment on the gain at the time of sale of the shares.

The shares are unrestricted. The executive can sell them at any time without putting up any capital to acquire the shares, as would have to be done in the case of options. For this reason, an outright bonus is more meaningful to the executive than options that may prove worthless. With actual shares of stock, the executive is assured of market value, which is subject to fluctuation.

A stock bonus plan in a public company offers a marketplace in which executives can sell their stock. Such a plan for a privately owned company would be likely to include a right of first refusal of the corporation to buy the stock from the executive at the agreed upon formula or price. The owner of a closely held corporation may not be enamored by the prospect of having to accept a minority shareholder, and for this reason, is not nearly so likely to adopt a stock bonus plan as is a public company.

Shareholder approval is required, and the shares must be registered. The owners of the stock are subject to SEC rules relating to insider trading.

From an accounting standpoint, the compensation liability is accrued as are dividend equivalents credited from the point of grant. This statement reflects a compensation cost as the shares are accrued annually.

As the stock is issued, the accrued compensation expense is credited to capital stock. The issuance of the stock under the stock bonus plan is dilutionary and does not bring capital into the corporation. It is discriminatory, which adds to its appeal from the owners' standpoint.

Performance Share Plan

This is merely a form of stock bonus plan wherein units are granted in accordance with executive performance as measured by a predetermined method. It is used as an incentive for the executive to achieve greater heights.

The shares are granted after the deed has been accomplished and are not taxed to the executive until he or she actually receives them. The plan is identical in all other respects to the stock bonus plan as described earlier.

Participating Units Plan

One of the shortcomings of stock-oriented incentive programs is that the executive has little control over the fair market value of the shares. The participating units plan contemplates a bonus in the form of cash to be delivered to the executive at a future date, in accordance with a formula conceived with corporate growth objectives in mind.

Each unit can have a zero value at the base period or a starting value of, say, one dollar or ten dollars. The unit increases or decreases in value in proportion to the executive's success in meeting the assigned goal. The goal can be contained within a section or a division, or it can encompass the whole company. The change in unit value is measured from the date of award to the end of the deferral period, which can be any number of years such as two, three, four, or five years.

Vesting can be utilized, and part or all of the vesting amount can be distributed in the form of cash from year to year, at which time it is received as earned income by the executive and expensed out by the corporation. The amount accrued for the executive at the end of the deferral period can be paid in installments, thereby enhancing the company's working capital by the further deferral. Units start out with a new base value each year and achieve their own new value during the deferral period. The unit value at the end of each year is accrued on the corporate books, and the income statement is charged for the unit values as they are allocated to the employee. The income statement is credited with those amounts that are forfeited, rather than being charged at the time of cash distribution to the executive.

Since stock is not involved, SEC regulations are not applicable. The corporation must nevertheless be diligent in arriving at a formula that will limit its additional compensation costs to the extent that is prudent from a fiscal standpoint, and reasonable as to compensation from both the corporation's and the employee's standpoint. The plan can provide great incentive for achievement, and is reasonably popular primarily in medium and large corporations. The concept is conducive to improving tenure among executives who are reluctant to forfeit nonvested benefits.

Supplemental Executive Retirement Plans (SERPs)

The inadequacy of retirement benefits has become quite apparent in our society. It is highly visible among executives who are accustomed to high living standards and find themselves incapable of setting aside an amount sufficient—after taxes—to provide adequate income at retirement. This is particularly true when one considers the impact of inflation on retirees who rely on fixed income plans.

A supplemental executive retirement plan (SERP) provides an income over and beyond the amount that can be provided under qualified pension plans, profit-sharing plans, or ESOPs. Qualified plans must be nondiscriminatory. SERPs can discriminate in favor of the prohibited group (highly compensated executives).

The various tax acts that have been enacted have left the nonqualified compensation plan, or SERP, attractive and unscathed. Under this concept, the corporation agrees that if the executive continues to be employed by the corporation for a stated number of years (generally to normal retirement age), the corporation will, commencing upon fulfillment of his or her service obligation, pay to the executive an annual income for a defined period such as 10 or 15 years. In the event the executive predeceases the payout period, the income that he or she would have received would be payable to the surviving spouse or other named beneficiary.

In order that the income not be taxed to the executive until the money is actually received, there must be a reasonable element of forfeiture on the executive's part. An example of this is the forfeiture that would occur if creditors had prior right to corporate assets and earnings that might otherwise be used to pay the executive. Thus, in the event of the company's bankruptcy, the executive might be left out in the cold with no income.

Funding for the obligation must be accomplished in such a way that the funds are not construed as belonging to the executive. Any funding is accomplished with aftertax dollars; however, the payout to the executive is treated as a deductible compensation expense to the company and is taxed to the executive or to the surviving spouse as earnings in the year the income is received. The deferred compensation or SERP package is subject to IRS scrutiny

136

in terms of reasonableness, along with all other compensation. This form of benefit is more cost effective than the others.

There are numerous ways in which the corporation can make provisions to have the funds on hand at the time they are needed. One of the more common ways is by obtaining insurance on the executive's life and making itself owner, beneficiary, and premium payer. The cash values—which accrue in the company's surplus tax free—provide a substantial offset against premium outlay. Alternatively, they can be borrowed to enhance corporate cash flow. The policy can be paid up at the executive's retirement, and at the time of his or her death, the insurance proceeds go into corporate surplus tax free, enabling it to meet the deductible payments to the executive's surviving spouse. The cash value can also be used in the event of the executive's retirement toward paying out two dollars of deductible compensation for each dollar of cash reserve. Or the company could meet its payout obligation with then-current income, retaining the policy, which will have been paid up at retirement. At the executive's subsequent death, the policy's proceeds will flow into corporate surplus tax free to enable the company to recover the cost of the compensation program.

A vesting schedule can be included, or if preferable, the plan can be entirely forfeitable. A nonqualified deferred compensation plan is useful as an incentive tool in that it is flexible in design, simple to administer, free of SEC problems, and requires no prior IRS letter of determination. The executive finds it appealing since it is tailored to his or her individual needs. This program makes a splendid "fit" with an ESOP.

Dividing the Profits Via Scanlon Plan

A productivity-oriented concept that provides employees with a bonus based on an elaborate formula was introduced to a number of corporations during the late 1940s by Joseph Scanlon, an educator. The Scanlon Plan offered an elaborate, though flexible, approach that could be varied from company to company and from time to time, depending upon the economic climate.

The bonus is in the form of cash and is based upon a ratio that can be measured from base period to base period, usually against the previous year's ratio. The improvement represents the sum, part or all of which is placed into a pool to be divided among all employees, including management.

A formula that has been used by some companies involves a ratio of payroll to net sales, plus or minus any inventory change. If it takes less payroll in the succeeding year to provide a unit of net sales after inventory adjustment, that difference could be put into a pool at year end.

Other formulas could involve payroll to units of production, or payroll to sales less raw materials, or any of a myriad of ratios, depending upon the type of activity in which the corporation is engaged.

The key to the Scanlon Plan is that the employee has a direct feeling of participation in every unit of bottom-line measurement. The greater the employee's expertise at what he or she is expected to do on the job, the greater the reward over and beyond the norm. The bonus could be doled out on a monthly basis with a reserve to be paid at the end of the year for more immediate effort-to-result rewards.

Quite frequently, committees are involved in the Scanlon Plan to foster greater cooperation and understanding between employees and management, since improved production and greater sales efforts will result in larger bonuses for all.

One key value of the Scanlon Plan is that it provides an immediate award in line with results, complementing a plan such as an ESOP, in which results are generally on a long-range basis. Both are "piece-of-the-action" incentive plans, with great appeal to all levels of management and rank-and-file employees.

How to Design an Executive Incentive Program

The chief executive officer of a corporation has one of the most complicated of all activities. He or she must pull the strings governing all activities leading to the bottom line, including product determination, design, raw materials, manufacturing, marketing, pricing, personnel, and public relations. Any of these can involve a myriad of directions. The CEO must solve the problem by appointing decision makers, each being responsible for areas of decision making and implementation, and each reporting to a superior until the CEO reports to the directors and to such stockholders as may exist.

The simplest form of compensation is, of course, salary. Fringe benefits and perquisites average in excess of 35% of base salary. The top layer of super executives in major corporations receive nonvisible perquisites, plus bonuses that can go as high as 150% of base salary. Corporations must bear in mind reasonableness of compensation, which has proven to be quite subjective from the viewpoints of the IRS, the corporation, and the employees. Unreasonable compensation is treated as a dividend and, as such, is not deductible by the corporation and receives no earned income cap upon receipt by the employee.

Merit salary raises, while still in vogue for the lower echelons of white-collar and lower supervisory employees, are losing their appeal for the higher echelon executive. Merit increases subject the employee to the likelihood of the raise hinging upon personality, or whether there are conflicts with the individual who judges whether the merit increases are granted. For employees below the executive level, job description is becoming popular as a means of spelling automatic increases. An employee who graduates to the next higher category on the job description list is entitled to a specific and often publicized salary.

The real challenge comes in the design of an incentive package for those companies for which such incentive would make a difference in corporate earnings. Management by objective is fast becoming the new way of life in corporate compensation design.

In designing such a package, corporate objectives must be borne in mind. An incentive for an executive to attain a goal that is not in line with that of the company becomes counter-productive. The design of the executive inducement must keep this possibility in mind. Further, the compensation package must be tailor-made for each corporation. There is no standardization of compensation that will pass the test for every company.

In determining how to increase productivity, the corporation must bear in mind that no two executives are alike and that each is motivated in different ways. Certain proven incentives for some executives are not for others. Management should explore the differences before wasting a lot of time and money on the wrong concept. If, for example, executive Bill Jones is compelled to function 180 degrees off of his norm, he may well have an ulcer, a breakdown, or become a terminating executive. Executive Mary Smith, on the other hand, may blossom with the new responsibilities.

Beware of open-ended obligations. Be certain the incentive compensation does not:

• Run both parties into an unreasonable problem;

• Create too great a distinction between executives in terms of compensation; or

• Bankrupt the corporation.

Each increment of incentive compensation must be related to the additional increment of pretax earnings, which, without the incentive compensation, probably would not exist. Feasibility studies should be made to determine the cost, incremental pretax earnings, and effect on the financial statement under simulated production achievements by the executive or executives under consideration. The best plan is one that is easy to understand. It is free of ambiguities and is straightforward as to its reason for existence. It must be communicated in writing to the executives as well as to staff members who will be involved in administering the plan.

Counsel must pass judgment on the plan to avoid SEC problems or lawsuits. The accountant must review the impact the plan—or plans—might have on the financial statements.

Plans must be reviewed each year to see whether they are fulfilling their purpose and whether they are keeping the corporation in a competitive stance in terms of employee incentives. Compensation is more effective and generally less costly if the corporation beats the executive to the punch and anticipates the need for improvement before the executive is forced to request it. Things are never quite the same if the employee is put into that position.

The ESOP, as an incentive program, has a great deal going for it. It fulfills many of the corporation's nonaltruistic needs, such as increasing working capital and cash flow, while giving a beneficial interest to the employees on a long-term basis. In order to meet the costs of some of the compensation packages, the corporation might consider the ESOP as a means of reducing the aftertax cost by simply making cash contributions to the ESOP in an amount equal to those costs...thereby letting the tax savings reduce the net aftertax cash outlay to zero.

ESOPs afford those employees who like to invest their own funds an opportunity to do so. The plans may be designed so as to permit employees to make voluntary contributions to an ESOP with aftertax dollars. One's contributions must not exceed 10% of compensation. If the employees' contributions are invested in employer stock, the transaction will be considered a sale of stock to the employees. In this event, the stock will have to be registered on a Form S-8 under Section 2(3) of the Securities Act of 1933.

If the employees' voluntary contributions are invested in the stock of other companies, the transaction will be exempt from the 1933 Securities Act.

History of ESOPs

The modern ESOP parallels the theory first put forth by a prominent German economist, Johann Henrich Von Thunen, during the early days of the industrial revolution. Von Thunen put an ESOP of sorts into being when he set aside a share of his farm's profits for his employees.

He invested the profits in machinery that would enhance earnings. A portion of the profits was then put in each worker's name. Earnings that were invested in other than capital equipment spun off interest, which was allocated and distributed to the employees as a second income. The principal itself expanded and was distributed to the employee at retirement.

Von Thunen's concept was the antithesis of that set forth by his contemporary, Karl Marx, who felt that all capital should be owned by the government. Von Thunen wanted to spread the wealth among the people rather than let a handful of politicians control the productive capital and merely substitute the politicians for the few nonpoliticians who at that time owned the vast portion of the capital.

In 1920, contributions to defined-benefit pension plans were given favored tax treatment by Congress. Legislation was passed in 1921 marking the birth of profit-sharing and stock bonus plans. The Tax Revision Act of 1942 served as the catalyst to induce industry to install these various tax-sheltered retirement plans.

Revenue Ruling 46, enacted in 1953, permitted any qualified retirement plan to borrow money for the purpose of purchasing stock. One year later, the nation's first leveraged ESOP was instituted. This was the well-known Peninsula Newspaper, Inc. ESOP. The company's owner wished to retire and transfer ownership to the employees. This was accomplished by means of a bank loan to the ESOP, in which all employees participated. The experiment was eminently successful, and today the paper is thriving and owned by its employees.

In 1973, the Regional Rail Reorganization Act became law, introducing legislation permitting ESOPs as a vehicle to enable corporations to finance their capital requirements.

The Employee Retirement Income Security Act of 1974 (ERISA) detailed the workings of the ESOP concept and added a certain precision to its implementation...coupled with some confusion.

The Trade Act of 1974 then added incentives for communities feeling the impact of trade competition from abroad. It structured a $500,000,000 fund to be loaned in such situations, granting special favor to those companies having ESOPs.

The Tax Reduction Act of 1975 added impetus to the ESOP movement. Everything was "up" until proposed ESOP regulations were published on July 30, 1976, by the Internal Revenue Service and the Department of Labor. The proposed regulations reversed the positive direction that Congress had taken up to that time, including among other things the proviso that the voting rights of the stock be passed through to the ESOP participants. They also placed severe restrictions on the classes of stock to be held by the ESOP and eliminated the corporation's or ESOP's right of first refusal on distributed stock.

Then along came Section 803(h) of the Tax Reform Act of 1976, which included a statement to the effect that the earlier proposed regulations flew in the face of congressional intent that ESOPs are to be considered a technique of corporate finance. The Conference Committee then sent the drafters of the regulations back to the drawing board, marking the first time that Congress had ever slapped the wrists of those two austere agencies.

The proposed regulations were superseded by the final regulations on September 2, 1977, which turned the thesis of the proposed Regs around 180 degrees. The final Regs recognized the function of the ESOP as a financing device that can benefit employees as well as the corporation and its stockholders, negating the aforementioned provisions and reiterating congressional intent that the ESOP be treated as a valuable financial vehicle to create capital and to disseminate equity among the employees.

While the Revenue Act of 1978, enacted on November 9, 1978, created additional clarification as to ESOPs, this was more than offset by confusion. Among other things, it redefined ESOPs and the old Tax Reduction Act ESOPs (TRASOPs), providing that TRASOPs were to become known as ESOPs. "Leveraged ESOP" was the new term to denote what had been called an ESOP.

Practitioners largely ignored the change in the hope that corrective legislation would bring back the good old terms of former days. Their dream was partially realized with the passage of the Technical Corrections Act of 1979, which provided that a leveraged ESOP again became known as an ESOP. The "ESOP" under the '78 Act's definition of the old TRASOP was renamed a "tax credit employee stock ownership plan."

The Revenue Act of 1978 also introduced a requirement that the leveraged ESOP pass through the vote only on major corporate issues such as mergers or liquidations in those states where "more than a majority" of stockholders was required to vote on these decisions. Legislation was subsequently introduced to change this for the better.

"The Final and Temporary IRS Regulations on Requirements for Electing 11 Percent Investment Credit TRASOPs" were issued on January 19, 1979. Along with the aforementioned Technical Corrections Act of 1979, this further clarified and liberalized the tax-credit employee stock ownership plan.

At the end of 1980, the Miscellaneous Revenue Act of 1980 became law. One of the more important aspects of the law was the extension to stock bonus plans (essentially, nonleveraged ESOPs) of the right to make cash distributions to participants, subject to the participant's right to demand stock. This legislation, the first of the eighties, led to new bills by congressional proponents of ESOPs. It became apparent that the Reagan administration was off and running in the direction of ESOPs as a means of capital formation for private enterprise.

The Economic Recovery Tax Act of 1981 was positive for ESOPs. It provided for a payroll-based tax-credit ESOP to replace the capital-related investment tax credit TRASOP effective after 1982.

The Act also increased the allowable deductible contribution from 15% of covered payroll to 25% if used to repay ESOP loans after 1981. Contributions for servicing interest could be made without limit. Greater employer flexibility was assured by the addition of what amounts to a call on a participant's stock under certain circumstances. The put option period was also reduced.

The Deficit Reduction Act of 1984 was a bonanza for ESOPs. It provided for the tax-free rollover, which lets stockholders sell stock to an ESOP without incurring capital gains tax so long as the proceeds of the sale are reinvested in domestic stocks or bonds within one year and the ESOP owns 30% or more of the company. It also excludes from tax 50% of the interest income received by banks on insurance for ESOP loans. The Act made dividends payable to ESOPs tax deductible. ESOPs are permitted under the '84 Act to assume the estate tax liability of stockholders.

While legislation has become more stringent for other forms of qualified plans, it has been increasingly benign for ESOPs.

44

Things to Do in Connection With the Adoption and Maintenance of an ESOP

Good judgment dictates that a feasibility study be conducted to help the owners of a corporation determine scientifically whether an ESOP would fit their needs. A feasibility study should consist of:

☐ A preliminary valuation of the company's stock, assuming the stock is not publicly traded.

☐ A dilution study to determine the net dilutionary effect, if any, upon the holdings of existing shareholders.

☐ A liquidity study to determine the cash requirements for repurchasing the stock pursuant to a put. This is sometimes referred to as repurchase liability.

☐ A study to determine whether the ESOP should work in tandem with or replace an existing pension or profit-sharing plan, whether the present plan should be frozen and partially converted or fully converted, and how an ESOP would "mesh" with other fringe benefits.

If it is determined that an ESOP is in order, a board resolution will reflect this. The board will call for the design of a plan and trust document and the making of a contribution (presumably during the fiscal year), the communication of plan benefits to employees, the selection of an administrator and a trustee, and a full-blown valuation (assuming the company is privately held) by an independent appraisal firm. The corporation's accountant and attorney would be too close to the scene to be "arm's length."

The plan and trust should be presented to Internal Revenue Service for a letter of determination, booklets should be distributed to employees, and quite possibly employee meetings should be held to develop the greatest amount of public relations in connection with the ESOP's installation.

What Happens After the First Year?

An ESOP is part of the ongoing financial architecture of the corporation and should be used to solve many corporate and stockholder problems as well as serve as a marvelous fringe benefit. It is quite possible that it will be used in connection with acquiring other companies or possibly divesting oneself of unwanted subsidiaries. In any event, a liquidity study should be made on an annual basis to determine the emerging liabilities and uncover cash requirements in the event of death or turnover for exercising the put.

Updates of the stock valuation are quite inexpensive, generally amounting to approximately one-third of the first-year cost.

Annual administration fees are roughly equivalent to fees for administering profit-sharing plans. But it is important that the administrator be equipped with the computer software to keep track of the base cost of the stock as it is allocated to the participants' accounts and layer it year after year, including the base cost of forfeitures as of the time they were allocated to the accounts.

Constant overview of the plan and its performance is essential to the well-being of the ESOP. The administrator must also maintain a vigil as to changes that may occur from time to time in the area of legislation and legal interpretation.

The ESOP can prove to be a completely new and intriguing experience for a solid corporation that is well-suited to its adoption. It should not be installed for a marginal concern.

45

Employee Stock Ownership Plan Feasibility Checklist

Name of Corporation _____

Address _____

_____

Date of Incorporation _____ Fiscal Year Ends _____

Public? Yes _____ No _____ If Yes, What Exchange _____

Six Largest Stockholders:

	Stockholder	No. of Shares		Stockholder	No. of Shares
(1)	_____	_____	(4)	_____	_____
(2)	_____	_____	(5)	_____	_____
(3)	_____	_____	(6)	_____	_____

Corporation's Estimated Worth: $_____ .

	No. of Employees	Payroll
Nonunion	_____	$_____
Union	_____	$_____

(Attach detailed breakdown of employee data by subsidiary.)

Financial Summary for Preceding Three Years:

	Taxable Income	Taxes Paid
19____	$_____	$_____
19____	$_____	$_____
19____	$_____	$_____

Estimated Taxable Income for Current Year: $_____
(Attach financial statements for past three years.)

Projection for Next Three Years:

	Sales	Net Income
19____	$_____	$_____
19____	$_____	$_____
19____	$_____	$_____

Corporate Capitalization:

	Common Stock	Preferred Stock
Authorized	_____	_____
Outstanding	_____	_____

Long-Term Debt:

Maturity	Interest	Amount
_____	_____	_____
_____	_____	_____
_____	_____	_____

What Are the Objectives in Considering ESOP?

Check:

_____ Finance Debit	_____ Raise Capital
_____ Motivate Employees	_____ Convert Profit-Sharing Plan
_____ Create Market for Stock	_____ Other _____
_____ Increase Cash Flow	_____

(Attach copies of profit-sharing or pension plans, covered employee data, asset value, and annual contribution history since adoption.)

Corp, Inc., Feasibility Study

Table of Contents

EXHIBIT I
A CASE STUDY
CORP, INC., PROFILE

Date of Incorporation:	July 1, 1974
Fiscal Year End:	December 31
Nature of Activity	Manufacturer of small electric motors
Growth Pattern:	Average 10% annual increase in pretax net income last six years
Number of Employees:	Total number: 210 ESOP participants: 160 Union employees: none
ESOP Payroll:	$1,800,000
Existing Pension or Profit-Sharing Plans:	None
Current Year's Taxable Income:	$190,000
Public or Private Ownership:	Private
If Private, Names of Stockholders and Percentage Owned:	Mr. R. Corp _____ 80% Mrs. J. Proc _____ 20%

EXHIBIT II
CORP, INC.
FIVE-YEAR ESTIMATED PROJECTION:
PRETAX INCOME, ESOP PARTICIPANTS' PAYROLL,
AND CORPORATE CONTRIBUTIONS TO THE ESOP

(1) Fiscal Years Ending Dec. 31	(2) Pretax Income	(3) ESOP Participants' Payroll	(4) Corporate Contribution to ESOP
1985	$ 190,000	$ 1,800,000	$ 255,000
1986	200,000	1,900,000	200,000
1987	210,000	2,000,000	210,000
1988	220,000	2,100,000	220,000
1989	230,000	2,200,000	230,000
TOTALS	$1,050,000	$10,000,000	$1,115,000

EXHIBIT III
CORP, INC.
FIVE-YEAR CASH FLOW PROJECTION. ASSUMPTION: NO ESOP

Fiscal Yr. Ending Dec. 31	1985	1986	1987	1988	1989
Pretax Income	$190,000	$200,000	$210,000	$220,000	$230,000
Fed. & State Income Tax (A)	95,190	100,200	105,210	110,220	115,230
Cash Flow and Net Income	94,810	99,800	104,790	109,780	114,770

Aggregate Five-Year Cash Flow: $523,950

(A) Combined federal and state effective income tax rate assumed to be 50.1% for purpose of these calculations.

EXHIBIT IV
CORP, INC.
FIVE-YEAR CASH FLOW PROJECTION. ASSUMPTION: ESOP
ALL CONTRIBUTIONS IN STOCK

	Fiscal Yr. Ending Dec. 31	1985	1986	1987	1988	1989
(1)	Pretax Income	$190,000	$200,000	$210,000	$220,000	$230,000
(2)	Minus Stock Contributions to ESOP	225,000	200,000	210,000	220,000	230,000
(3)	Taxable Income	(65,000)	-0-	-0-	-0-	-0-
(4)	Income Tax	(32,565)	-0-	-0-	-0-	-0-
(5)	Net Aftertax Income	(32,435)	-0-	-0-	-0-	-0-
(6)	Cash Flow (A)	222,565	200,000	210,000	220,000	230,000

Aggregate Five-Year Cash Flow: $1,082,565

(A) Cash Flow = (1) minus (4)

EXHIBIT V
CORP, INC.
FIVE-YEAR CASH FLOW PROJECTION:
NO LOAN INVOLVED
ASSUMPTION: CORPORATE CONTRIBUTION OF CASH
AND STOCK TO ESOP

	Fiscal Yr. Ending Dec. 31	1985	1986	1987	1988	1989
(1)	Pretax Income	$190,000	$200,000	$210,000	$220,000	$230,000
(2)	Minus Contributions to ESOP					
	(a) Stock	127,245	99,800	104,790	109,780	115,770
	(b) Cash	127,755	100,200	105,210	110,220	114,230
	TOTAL	225,000	200,000	210,000	220,000	230,000
(3)	Taxable Income	(65,000)	-0-	-0-	-0-	-0-
(4)	Income Tax	(32,565)	-0-	-0-	-0-	-0-
(5)	Cash Flow (A)	94,810	99,800	104,790	109,780	115,770

Aggregate Five-Year Cash Flow: $524,950

(A) Cash Flow = (1) minus (2)(B) minus (4)

153

EXHIBIT VI
CORP, INC.
FIVE-YEAR CASH FLOW PROJECTION:
LOAN INVOLVED. NO ESOP

	Fiscal Yr. Ending Dec. 31	1985	1986	1987	1988	1989
(1)	Pretax Income	$190,000	$200,000	$210,000	$220,000	$230,000
(2)	Minus Interest on Loan	14,104	11,573	8,779	5,694	2,290
(3)	Adjusted Taxable Income	175,896	188,427	201,221	214,306	227,710
(4)	Income Tax	88,124	94,402	100,812	107,367	114,083
(5)	Payment Toward (A) Principal	24,384	26,915	29,709	32,794	36,198
(6)	Cash Flow (B)	63,388	67,110	70,700	74,145	77,429

(A) Corporation borrows $150,000 at 10%. Principal and interest paid off over five years by level quarterly payments of $9,622 per quarter.

(B) Cash Flow = (1) minus (2) minus (4) minus (5)

Aggregate Five-Year Cash Flow: $352,772

154

EXHIBIT VII
CORP, INC.
FIVE-YEAR CASH FLOW PROJECTION:
LOAN INVOLVED
ASSUMPTION: CORPORATE CONTRIBUTIONS OF CASH AND
STOCK TO ESOP

Fiscal Yr. Ending Dec. 31	1985	1986	1987	1988	1989
(1) Pretax Income	$190,000	$200,000	$210,000	$220,000	$230,000
(2) Minus Contributions to ESOP					
(a) Stock	127,245	99,800	104,790	109,780	114,770
(b) Cash for Note	38,488	38,488	38,488	38,488	38,488
(c) Cash for Liquidity	89,267	61,712	66,722	71,732	76,742
TOTAL	255,000	200,000	210,000	220,000	230,000
(3) Taxable Income	(65,000)	-0-	-0-	-0-	-0-
(4) Income Tax	(32,565)	-0-	-0-	-0-	-0-
(5) Cash Flow (A)	94,810	99,800	104,790	109,780	114,770

Aggregate Five-Year Cash Flow: $523,950

(A) Cash Flow = (1) minus (2)(b) minus (2)(c) minus (4)

CORP, INC., FEASIBILITY STUDY
SUMMARY

EXHIBIT III:
No ESOP—(no loan involved)
Five-year cash flow—$523,950

EXHIBIT IV:
ESOP—(no loan involved)
All corporate contributions to the ESOP are in the form of the corporation's own stock.
Five-year cash flow (with ESOP) $1,082,565
Five-year cash flow (no ESOP) 523,950

Difference .... $ 558,615

Observations: The corporate contributions to an ESOP have maximized cash flow, improving it by $558,615 over the five-year period as compared with the cash flow where no ESOP exists.

In addition, the employees enjoy a valuable fringe benefit.

EXHIBIT V:
ESOP—(no loan involved)
Unlike the preceding exhibit, the corporate contribution consists of a combination of its own stock as well as cash.

Five-year cash flow (cash and stock contributions) to an ESOP ... $524,950
Five-year cash flow (no ESOP) $523,950

Although the cash flow is not as great as in the preceding exhibit, the cash flow is almost the same when there is no ESOP. But, in addition, the ESOP provides a valuable fringe benefit to the employees.

Cash contributions amounting to $557,615 over the five-year period can be used for purposes including but not limited to:

(a) Buying stock from stockholders—creating a market.
(b) Purchasing insurance on the lives of stockholders to fund a buy-sell agreement.
(c) Retire debt.

EXHIBIT VI:
No ESOP—(loan involved)
This exhibit illustrates the effect of a $150,000 loan at 10% made directly to the corporation where no ESOP exists.

Five-year cash flow $352,772

EXHIBIT VII:

ESOP—(loan involved)

The aforementioned loan is made to and amortized by an ESOP. The corporation has made cash and stock contributions indicated in categories as follows:

(a) Stock.
(b) Cash for note retirement.
(c) Cash for liquidity.

The amount of stock contributed is designed to produce the same cash flow as that which is produced in the exhibit when no ESOP or loan is involved.

The cash for liquidity can be used to:

(a) Purchase stock from stockholders—creating a market.
(b) Purchase insurance to fund a buy-sell agreement between the stockholder and the ESOP.

Five-year cash flow $523,950

Observations: In addition to amortizing principal and interest, this exhibit demonstrates that cash can be provided to create a market for stockholders and provide for the estate planning liquidity needs with no change in cash flow. In addition to these obvious effects is the creation of a fine fringe benefit for employees.

RECOMMENDATION:

The implementation of an Employee Stock Ownership Plan is a viable concept for Corp, Inc.

Cash Flow:

The exhibits demonstrate that cash flow can be improved while providing the employees with a valuable fringe benefit. Fringe benefit stock valued at 15% of covered payroll can be contributed to the ESOP and apportioned in the trust for the benefit of the employees in accordance with a formula related to their compensation.

The value of the stock at the time it is contributed, over the five-year period, amounts to $1,115,000. This does not take into consideration any growth the stock might experience.

Tax Refund:

The corporation is eligible to receive a $32,565 tax refund by virtue of a 1980 contribution to the ESOP, which can amount to $255,000, exceeding the $190,000 pretax income by $65,000, thus putting the company in a loss position by that amount.

157

Liquid Asset and Cash Fund:

The illustration demonstrates that cash can be contributed in combination with stock, the sum in this instance amounting to $366,175. The cash can be used to:

(a) Purchase insurance to fund a buy-sell agreement between shareholders and the ESOP.
(b) Purchase stock directly from the shareholders.
(c) Make an acquisition.

Corporate Planning Flexibility:

(a) The corporation can adjust its taxable income and its cash flow.
(b) It can "cash out" minority stockholders.
(c) The company can refinance indebtedness.
(d) It can make acquisitions with pretax dollars.

Debt Reduction:

Servicing debt, using pretax dollars to liquidate principal and interest, is feasible as indicated in the exhibits.

New financing can be contemplated more readily where an ESOP exists.

It is therefore recommended that Corp, Inc., implement an ESOP prior to the end of the fiscal year.

Appendix

(1) SAMPLE ALLOCATION REPORT and PARTICIPATION STATEMENTS

(2) LEGISLATION, REGULATION and RULINGS AFFECTING ESOPs

(3) IRS FORMS REQUIRED FOR:
    (a) Original Plan Adoption or Amendment
    (b) Annual Administration
    (c) Plan Termination

Sample Allocation Report and Participation Statements*

*Courtesy R.K. Schaaf Associates, Incorporated

YOUR FAVORITE CORPORATION

EMPLOYEE STOCK OWNERSHIP PLAN

SAMPLE ALLOCATIONS REPORT FOR Y/E 12-31-84

YOUR FAVORITE CORPORATION EMPLOYEE STOCK OWNERSHIP PLAN   PAGE NO. 1
ALLOCATIONS REPORT FOR Y/E 12-31-84   VALUE PER SHARE LAST YEAR = $7.50 THIS YEAR =$10.00

NAME SOC.SEC.NO.	CODE	PARTICIPANT DATA	OTHER INV. ACCOUNT	SHS. IN CO. STOCK ACCT.	STOCK COST BASIS	YRS. SERV. ALLOC/COMP. PERC. VEST.

ALLEN, ROBERT
123-45-6789   A   12-10-43 (DOB)
12-31-83 BALANCES   02-15-83 (DOH) $ 0.00 $ 0.0000 $ 0.00
INTEREST EARNED   01-01-84 (DOP)   0.00   0.0000   0.00
CO.STOCK PURCHASES   -1,200.00   120.0000   1,200.00
V.I. DISTRIBUTIONS   -   - (DOT)   0.00   0.0000   0.00
FORFEITURES   132.42   12.1633   85.14   2
CO. CONTRIBUTIONS $8,000.00 (COMP)   1,200.00   0.0000   0.00   18.18%
12-31-84 BALANCES $ 132.42 $ 132.1633 $ 1,285.14   0%
        TOTAL VALUE OF ACCOUNTS IS $1,454.05   VESTED VALUE OF ACCOUNTS IS $0.00

BERMAN, LYNN WAS 'JONES' * T3-15-83,H5-18-83
234-56-7890   A   09-15-39 (DOB)
12-31-83 BALANCES   12-15-81 (DOH) $ 1,567.98 $ 134.7770 $ 943.44
INTEREST EARNED   01-01-82 (DOP)   149.37   0.0000   0.00
CO.STOCK PURCHASES   -1,500.00   150.0000   1,500.00
V.I. DISTRIBUTIONS   -   - (DOT)   0.00   0.0000   0.00
FORFEITURES   165.54   15.2041   106.43   3
CO. CONTRIBUTIONS $10,000.00 (COMP)   1,500.00   0.0000   0.00   18.18%
12-31-84 BALANCES $ 1,882.89 $ 299.9811 $ 2,549.87   10%
        TOTAL VALUE OF ACCOUNTS IS $4,882.70   VESTED VALUE OF ACCOUNTS IS $488.27

COLLINS, DONALD 10% V.I. PAID Y/E 84
345-67-8901   T   09-21-39 (DOB)
12-31-83 BALANCES   11-10-80 (DOH) $ 1,798.37 $ 141.3980 $ 989.79
INTEREST EARNED   01-01-81 (DOP)   0.00   0.0000   0.00
CO.STOCK PURCHASES   0.00   0.0000   0.00
V.I. DISTRIBUTIONS   02-15-84 (DOT)   -258.89   0.0000   0.00
FORFEITURES   -1,539.48   -141.3980   -989.79   3
CO. CONTRIBUTIONS $0.00 (COMP)   0.00   0.0000   0.00   0.00%
12-31-84 BALANCES $ 0.00 $ 0.0000 $ 0.00   0%
        TOTAL VALUE OF ACCOUNTS IS $0.00   VESTED VALUE OF ACCOUNTS IS $0.00

165

NAME SOC.SEC.NO. CODE	PARTICIPANT DATA	OTHER INV. ACCOUNT	SHS. IN CO. STOCK ACCT.	STOCK COST BASIS	YRS. SERV. ALLOC/COMP. PERC. VEST.
LEE, ROGER					
901-23-4567 A	11-29-35 (DOB)				
12-31-83 BALANCES	08-09-80 (DOH) $	4,957.15	369.8030 $	2,588.62	
INTEREST EARNED	01-01-81 (DOF)	472.23	0.0000	0.00	
CO.STOCK PURCHASES		-3,750.00	375.0000	3,750.00	
V.I. DISTRIBUTIONS	- - (DOT)	0.00	0.0000	0.00	
FORFEITURES		413.84	38.0102	266.07	4
CO. CONTRIBUTIONS	$25,000.00 (COMP)	3,750.00	0.0000	0.00	18.18%
12-31-84 BALANCES		5,843.22 $	782.8132 $	6,604.69	40%
TOTAL VALUE OF ACCOUNTS IS $13,671.35 VESTED VALUE OF ACCOUNTS IS $5,468.54					
SMITH, BERNARD OFFICER & SHAREHOLDER * REACHED NORMAL RETIREMENT AGE					
012-34-5678 AK	07-15-19 (DOB)				
12-31-83 BALANCES	01-05-76 (DOH) $	8,119.98	714.0220 $	4,998.15	
INTEREST EARNED	01-01-78 (DOF)	773.52	0.0000	0.00	
CO.STOCK PURCHASES		-7,500.00	750.0000	7,500.00	
V.I. DISTRIBUTIONS	- - (DOT)	0.00	0.0000	0.00	
FORFEITURES		827.68	76.0204	532.15	9
CO. CONTRIBUTIONS	$50,000.00 (COMP)	7,500.00	0.0000	0.00	18.18%
12-31-84 BALANCES		9,721.18 $	1,540.0424 $	13,030.30	100%
TOTAL VALUE OF ACCOUNTS IS $25,121.60 VESTED VALUE OF ACCOUNTS IS $25,121.60					
PLAN TOTAL					
12-31-83 BALANCES	(DOH) $	16,443.48	1,360.0000 $	9,520.00	
INTEREST EARNED	(DOF)	1,395.12	0.0000	0.00	
CO.STOCK PURCHASES		-13,950.00	1,395.0000	13,950.00	
V.I. DISTRIBUTIONS	(DOT)	-258.89	0.0000	0.00	
FORFEITURES		0.00	0.0000	0.00	0
CO. CONTRIBUTIONS	$93,000.00 (COMP)	13,950.00	0.0000	0.00	15.00%
12-31-84 BALANCES		17,579.71 $	2,755.0000 $	23,470.00	0%
TOTAL VALUE OF ACCOUNTS IS $45,129.71 VESTED VALUE OF ACCOUNTS IS $31,078.41					

TOTAL FORFEITURES ALLOCATED HERE $ 1,539.48   141.3980 $ 989.79

YOUR FAVORITE CORPORATION

EMPLOYEE STOCK OWNERSHIP PLAN

SAMPLE 12-31-84 PARTICIPANT DATA FILE LISTING

EMPLOYEE NO.	NAME SOC.SEC.NO.	PERC. VEST.	AC.YRS. CD.SERV.	DOB	DOH	DOP	DOT	COVERED COMPENSATION
	ALLEN, ROBERT							
15	123-45-6789	0	A 2	12-10-43	02-15-83	01-01-84		8,000.00
	BERMAN, LYNN			WAS 'JONES' * T3-15-83,H5-18-83				
11	234-56-7890	10	A 3	09-15-39	12-15-81	01-01-82		10,000.00
	COLLINS, DONALD			10% V.I. PAID Y/E 84				
7	345-67-8901	0	T 3	09-21-39	11-10-80	01-01-81	02-15-84	0.00
	LEE, ROGER							
5	901-23-4567	40	A 4	11-29-35	08-09-80	01-01-81		25,000.00
	SMITH, BERNARD			OFFICER & SHAREHOLDER * REACHED NORMAL RETIREMENT AGE				
1	012-34-5678	100	AK 9	07-15-19	01-05-76	01-01-78		50,000.00
	TOTAL							
0		0	0					93,000.00

YOUR FAVORITE CORPORATION

EMPLOYEE STOCK OWNERSHIP PLAN

SAMPLE DATA REQUEST REPORT FOR Y/E 12-31-85

```
     NAME      LAST YEAR'S   D.O.B.    MISC.PART.INFORMATION  COVERED   HOURS OF SERVICE
SOC.SEC.NO. AC.PERC.YEARS  D.O.H.    D.O.P.   D.O.T. /COMPENSATION/ 0 -/501-/1000/ OTHER DATA &
            CD.VEST.SERV.                              / 500/ 999/ +  / KEY EMPLOYEE INF.


ALLEN, ROBERT                12-10-43
123-45-6789 A    0%    2    02-15-83    01-01-84               $


BERMAN, LYNN                 09-15-39          WAS 'JONES' * T3-15-83,H5-18-83
234-56-7890 A    10%   3    12-15-81    01-01-82               $


COLLINS, DONALD              09-21-39          10% V.I. PAID Y/E 84
345-67-8901 T    0%    3    11-10-80    01-01-81  02-15-84     $


LEE, ROGER                   11-29-35
901-23-4567 A    40%   4    08-09-80    01-01-81               $


SMITH, BERNARD               07-15-19          OFFICER & SHAREHOLDER * REACHED NORMAL RETIREMENT AGE
012-34-5678 AK 100%   9    01-05-76    01-01-78               $                      / KEY EMPL.
```

*** LIST NEW PARTICIPANTS STARTING ON THE NEXT PAGE ***

YOUR FAVORITE CORPORATION EMPLOYEE STOCK OWNERSHIP PLAN
DATA REQUEST REPORT FOR YEAR ENDING 12-31-85 PAGE NO. 2

LIST NEW PARTICIPANTS BELOW - PLEASE REVIEW COVER LETTER AND INDICATE VESTING YEARS OF SERVICE
COMPLETED THROUGH PRIOR YEAR END & KEY EMPLOYEE STATUS. PLEASE CALL US IF YOU HAVE ANY QUESTIONS.

NAME   LAST YEAR'S   D.O.B.   MISC.PART.INFORMATION COVERED   HOURS OF SERVICE
SOC.SEC.NO. YRS.OF SERV.   D.O.H.   D.O.P.   D.O.T. /COMPENSATION/ 0 -/501-/1000/ OTHER DATA &
                                                        / 500/ 999/ + / KEY EMPLOYEE INF.

Y.OF S=/.../

Y.OF S=/.../

Y.OF S=/.../

Y.OF S=/.../

Y.OF S=/.../

Y.OF S=/.../

Y.OF S=/.../

Y.OF S=/.../

Y.OF S=/.../

174

YOUR FAVORITE CORPORATION

EMPLOYEE STOCK OWNERSHIP PLAN

PARTICIPATION STATEMENT

FOR BERNARD SMITH   FOR THE YEAR ENDING DECEMBER 31, 1984
==

YOUR ACCOUNTS

```
THE VALUE OF YOUR ACCOUNTS AS OF 12-31-83          $   13,475.15
CHANGE IN THE VALUE OF YOUR ACCOUNTS                    2,558.57
VESTED INTEREST DISTRIBUTIONS TO YOU                        0.00
FORFEITURES ALLOCATED TO YOUR ACCOUNTS                 1,587.88
THE COMPANY'S CONTRIBUTION FOR THE YEAR                7,500.00
                                                   ------------
THE VALUE OF YOUR ACCOUNTS AS OF 12-31-84          $   25,121.60
                                                   ============

YOUR VESTED PERCENTAGE AS OF 12-31-84                    100.00%
THE VESTED VALUE OF YOUR ACCOUNTS ON 12-31-84      $   25,121.60
                                                   ============
```

EACH SHARE OF THE 1,540.0424 SHARES OF THE COMPANY'S COMMON STOCK
ALLOCATED TO YOUR ACCOUNTS HAD AN APPRAISED VALUE OF $ 10.00 AS OF
12-31-84, AS COMPARED TO $ 7.50 AS OF 12-31-83. $ 9,721.18 WAS ALLO-
CATED TO YOUR OTHER INVESTMENTS ACCOUNT.

THE PLAN COMMITTEE MAY DIRECT THE   PLAN COMMITTEE
TRUSTEE TO USE ANY AVAILABLE FUNDS
IN THE TRUST TO BUY MORE SHARES OF
COMPANY STOCK, WHICH WILL THEN BE
ALLOCATED TO YOUR ACCOUNTS.   BY.......................

175

YOUR FAVORITE CORPORATION
EMPLOYEE STOCK OWNERSHIP PLAN
PARTICIPATION STATEMENT

FOR BERNARD SMITH   FOR THE YEAR ENDING DECEMBER 31, 1984
===

	EMPLOYEE STOCK OWNERSHIP PLAN ACCOUNTS	
	OTHER	COMPANY STOCK ACCOUNT *
	INVESTMENTS	IN DOLLARS	IN SHARES

YOUR ACCOUNT BALANCES AS OF 12-31-83	$8,119.98	$5,355.17 *	714.0220
YOUR SHARE OF PLAN EARNINGS	773.52	1,785.05 **	0.0000
YOUR SHARE OF COMPANY STOCK PURCHASES	-7,500.00	7,500.00	750.0000
VESTED INTEREST DISTRIBUTIONS TO YOU	0.00	0.00	0.0000
YOUR SHARE OF FORFEITURES	827.68	760.20	76.0204
THE COMPANY'S CONTRIBUTION FOR THE YEAR	7,500.00	0.00	0.0000
	============	============	============
YOUR ACCOUNT BALANCES AS OF 12-31-84	$9,721.18	$15,400.42	*1,540.0424
	============	============	============

TOTAL VALUE OF YOUR EMPLOYEE STOCK OWNERSHIP PLAN ACCOUNTS $25,121.60

            YOUR VESTED PERCENTAGE AS OF 12-31-84   100.00%

    THE VESTED VALUE OF YOUR PLAN ACCOUNTS AS OF 12-31-84 $25,121.60

* AS OF 12-31-83 THE VALUE OF THE COMPANY STOCK WAS $7.50 PER SHARE.
* AS OF 12-31-84 THE VALUE OF THE COMPANY STOCK WAS $10.00 PER SHARE.

** THIS AMOUNT REPRESENTS THE INCREASE IN THE VALUE
   OF COMPANY STOCK ALLOCATED TO YOUR ACCOUNT.

EMPLOYEE STOCK OWNERSHIP
PLAN COMMITTEE

By ....

176

YOUR FAVORITE CORPORATION

EMPLOYEE STOCK OWNERSHIP PLAN

PARTICIPATION STATEMENT

FOR BERNARD SMITH   FOR THE YEAR ENDING DECEMBER 31, 1984
==

	OTHER INVESTMENTS ACCOUNT	COMPANY STOCK ACCOUNT
THE BALANCES IN YOUR ACCOUNTS AS OF 12-31-83	$ 8,119.98	714.0220 SHARES
INTEREST EARNINGS ALLOCATED TO YOUR ACCOUNTS	773.52	0.0000
COMPANY STOCK PURCHASES ALLOCATED TO YOUR ACCOUNTS	-7,500.00	750.0000
VESTED INTEREST DISTRIBUTIONS PAID TO YOU	0.00	0.0000
FORFEITURES ALLOCATED TO YOUR ACCOUNTS	827.68	76.0204
THE COMPANY'S CONTRIBUTIONS FOR THE YEAR	7,500.00	0.0000
	------------	----------------
THE BALANCES IN YOUR ACCOUNTS AS OF 12-31-84	$ 9,721.18	1,540.0424 SHARES
	============	================

EACH SHARE OF THE COMPANY'S STOCK ALLOCATED TO YOUR ACCOUNT HAD AN APPRAISED
VALUE OF $10.00 AS OF 12-31-84, AS COMPARED TO $7.50 AS OF 12-31-83.

THE TOTAL VALUE OF YOUR EMPLOYEE STOCK OWNERSHIP PLAN ACCOUNTS WAS $25,121.60

                    YOUR VESTED PERCENTAGE AS OF 12-31-84 WAS   100.00%

          THE VESTED VALUE OF YOUR PLAN ACCOUNTS AS OF 12-31-84 WAS $25,121.60

YOUR VESTED INTEREST IS SUBJECT TO AUDIT UPON YOUR TERMINATION OF EMPLOYMENT.
THE PLAN COMMITTEE MAY DIRECT THE TRUSTEE TO USE ANY AMOUNTS IN YOUR OTHER
INVESTMENTS ACCOUNT TO PURCHASE COMPANY STOCK. ANY STOCK PURCHASED WILL BE
REFLECTED IN YOUR COMPANY STOCK ACCOUNT.

YOUR FAVORITE CORPORATION
EMPLOYEE STOCK OWNERSHIP PLAN
PARTICIPATION STATEMENT

FOR BERNARD SMITH   FOR THE YEAR ENDING DECEMBER 31, 1984
==

	OTHER INVESTMENTS ACCOUNT	COMPANY STOCK ACCOUNT
THE BALANCES IN YOUR ACCOUNTS AS OF 12-31-83	$ 8,119.98	714.0220 SHARES
INTEREST EARNINGS ALLOCATED TO YOUR ACCOUNTS	773.52	0.0000
COMPANY STOCK PURCHASES ALLOCATED TO YOUR ACCOUNTS	-7,500.00	750.0000
VESTED INTEREST DISTRIBUTIONS PAID TO YOU	0.00	0.0000
FORFEITURES ALLOCATED TO YOUR ACCOUNTS	827.68	76.0204
THE COMPANY'S CONTRIBUTIONS FOR THE YEAR	7,500.00	0.0000
THE BALANCES IN YOUR ACCOUNTS AS OF 12-31-84	$ 9,721.18	1,540.0424 SHARES

EACH SHARE OF THE COMPANY'S STOCK ALLOCATED TO YOUR ACCOUNT HAD AN APPRAISED
VALUE OF $10.00 AS OF 12-31-84, AS COMPARED TO $7.50 AS OF 12-31-83.

THE TOTAL VALUE OF YOUR EMPLOYEE STOCK OWNERSHIP PLAN ACCOUNTS WAS $25,121.60

          YOUR VESTED PERCENTAGE AS OF 12-31-84 WAS   100.00%

    THE VESTED VALUE OF YOUR PLAN ACCOUNTS AS OF 12-31-84 WAS $25,121.60

THE COMMITTEE MAY DIRECT THE TRUSTEE TO USE ANY   PLAN COMMITTEE
AMOUNTS IN YOUR OTHER INVESTMENTS ACCOUNT TO
PURCHASE COMPANY STOCK. ANY STOCK PURCHASED WILL
BE REFLECTED IN YOUR COMPANY STOCK ACCOUNT.
                                            BY_____

Legislation, Regulation
and Rulings Affecting ESOPs

Employee Retirement Income Security Act of 1974
Sections 406-08

PROHIBITED TRANSACTIONS

Sec. 406. (a) Except as provided in section 408:

(1) A fiduciary with respect to a plan shall not cause the plan to engage in a transaction, if he knows or should know that such transaction constitutes a direct or indirect—

(A) sale or exchange, or leasing, of any property between the plan and a party in interest;

(B) lending of money or other extension of credit between the plan and a party in interest;

(C) furnishing of goods, services, or facilities between the plan and a party in interest;

(D) transfer to, or use by or for the benefit of, a party in interest, of any assets of the plan; or

(E) acquisition, on behalf of the plan, of any employer security or employer real property in violation of section 407(a).

(2) No fiduciary who has authority or discretion to control or manage the assets of a plan shall permit the plan to hold any employer security or employer real property if he knows or should know that holding such security or real property violates section 407(a).

(b) A fiduciary with respect to a plan shall not—

(1) deal with the assets of the plan in his own interest or for his own account,

(2) in his individual or in any other capacity act in any transaction involving the plan on behalf of a party (or represent a party) whose interests are adverse to the interests of the plan or the interests of its participants or beneficiaries, or

(3) receive any consideration for his own personal account from any party dealing with such plan in connection with a transaction involving the assets of the plan.

(c) A transfer of real or personal property by a party in interest to a plan shall be treated as a sale or exchange if the property is subject to a mortgage or similar lien which the plan assumes or if it is subject to a mortgage or similar lien which a party-in-interest placed on the property within the 10-year period ending on the date of the transfer.

10 PERCENT LIMITATION WITH RESPECT TO ACQUISITION AND HOLDING OF EMPLOYER SECURITIES AND EMPLOYER REAL PROPERTY BY CERTAIN PLANS

Sec. 407. (a) Except as otherwise provided in this section and section 414:

(1) A plan may not acquire or hold—

(A) any employer security which is not a qualifying employer security, or

(B) any employer real property which is not qualifying employer real property.

(2) A plan may not acquire any qualifying employer security or qualifying employer real property, if immediately after such

acquisition the aggregate fair market value of employer securities and employer real property held by the plan exceeds 10 percent of the fair market value of the assets of the plan.

(3)(A) After December 31, 1984, a plan may not hold any qualifying employer securities or qualifying employer real property (or both) to the extent that the aggregate fair market value of such securities and property determined on December 31, 1984, exceeds 10 percent of the greater of—

(i) the fair market value of the assets of the plan, determined on December 31, 1984, or

(ii) the fair market value of the assets of the plan determined on January 1, 1975.

(B) Subparagraph (A) of this paragraph shall not apply to any plan which on any date after December 31, 1974; and before January 1, 1985, did not hold employer securities or employer real property (or both) the aggregate fair market value of which determined on such date exceeded 10 percent of the greater of

(i) the fair market value of the assets of the plan, determined on such date, or

(ii) the fair market value of the assets of the plan determined on January 1, 1975.

(4)(A) After December 31, 1979, a plan may not hold any employer securities or employer real property in excess of the amount specified in regulations under subparagraph (B). This subparagraph shall not apply to a plan after the earliest date after December 31, 1974, on which it complies with such regulations.

(B) Not later than December 31, 1976, the Secretary shall prescribe regulations which shall have the effect of requiring that a plan divest itself of 50 percent of the holdings of employer securities and employer real property which the plan would be required to divest before January 1, 1985, under paragraph (2) or subsection (c) (whichever is applicable).

(b)(1) Subsection (a) of this section shall not apply to any acquisition or holding of qualifying employer securities or qualifying employer real property by an eligible individual account plan.

(2) Cross References.—

(A) For exemption from diversification requirements for holding of qualifying employer securities and qualifying employer real property by eligible individual account plans, see section 404(a)(2).

(B) For exemption from prohibited transactions for certain acquisitions of qualifying employer securities and qualifying employer real property which are not in violation of 10 percent limitation, see section 408(e).

(C) For transitional rules respecting securities or real property subject to binding contracts in effect on June 30, 1974, see section 414(c).

(c)(1) A plan which makes the election, under paragraph (3) shall be treated as satisfying the requirement of subsection (a)(3) if and only if employer securities held on any date after December 31, 1974 and before January 1, 1985 have a fair market value, determined as of December 31, 1974, not in excess of 10 percent of the lesser of—

(A) the fair market value of the assets of the plan determined on such date (disregarding any portion of the fair market value of employer securities which is attributable to appreciation of such securities after December 31, 1974) but not less than the fair market value of plan assets on January 1, 1975, or

(B) an amount equal to the sum of (i) the total amount of the contributions to the plan received after December 31, 1974, and prior to such date, plus (ii) the fair market value of the assets of the plan, determined on January 1, 1975.

(2) For purposes of this subsection, in the case of an employer security held by a plan after January 1, 1975, the ownership of which is derived from ownership of employer securities held by the plan on January 1, 1975, or from the exercise of rights derived from such ownership, the value of such security held after January 1, 1975, shall be based on the value as of January 1, 1975, of the security from which ownership was derived. The Secretary shall prescribe regulations to carry out this paragraph.

(3) An election under this paragraph may not be made after December 31, 1975. Such an election shall be made in accordance with regulations prescribed by the Secretary, and shall be irrevocable. A plan may make an election under this paragraph only if on January 1, 1975, the plan holds no employer real property. After such election and before January 1, 1985 the plan may not acquire any employer real property.

(d) For purposes of this section—

(1) The term "employer security" means a security issued by an employer of employees covered by the plan, or by an affiliate of such employer. A contract to which section 408(b)(5) applies shall not be treated as a security for purposes of this section.

(2) The term "employer real property" means real property (and related personal property) which is leased to an employer of employees covered by the plan, or to an affiliate of such employer. For purposes of determining the time at which a plan acquires employer real property for purposes of this section, such property shall be deemed to be acquired by the plan on the date on which the plan acquires the property or on the date on which the lease to the employer (or affiliate) is entered into, whichever is later.

(3)(A) The term "eligible individual account plan" means an individual account plan which is (i) a profit-sharing, stock bonus, thrift, or savings plan; (ii) an employee stock ownership plan; or (iii) a money purchase plan which was in existence on the date of enactment of this Act and which on such date invested primarily in qualifying employer securities. Such term excludes an individual retirement account or annuity described in section 408 of the Internal Revenue Code of 1954.

(B) Notwithstanding subparagraph (A), a plan shall be treated as an eligible individual account plan with respect to the acquisition or holding of qualifying employer real property or qualifying employer securities only if such plan explicitly provides for acquisition and holding of qualifying employer securities or qualifying employer real property (as the case may be). In the case of a plan in existence on the date of enactment of this Act, this subparagraph shall not take effect until January 1, 1976.

(4) The term "qualifying employer real property" means parcels of employer real property—

   (A) if a substantial number of the parcels are dispersed geographically;

   (B) if each parcel of real property and the improvements thereon are suitable (or adaptable without excessive cost) for more than one use;

   (C) even if all of such real property is leased to one lessee (which may be an employer, or an affiliate of an employer); and

   (D) if the acquisition and retention of such property comply with the provisions of this part (other than section 404(a)(1)(B) to the extent it requires diversification, and sections 404(a)(1)(C), 406, and subsection (a) of this section).

(5) The term "qualifying employer security" means an employer security which is stock or a marketable obligation (as defined in subsection (e)).

(6) The term "employee stock ownership plan" means an individual account plan—

   (A) which is a stock bonus plan which is qualified, or a stock bonus plan and money purchase both of which are qualified, under section 401 of the Internal Revenue Code of 1954, and which is designed to invest primarily in qualifying employee securities, and

   (B) which meets such other requirements as the Secretary of the Treasury may prescribe by regulation.

(7) A corporation is an affiliate of an employer if it is a member of any controlled group of corporations (as defined in section 1563(a) of the Internal Revenue Code of 1954, except that "applicable percentage" shall be substituted for "80 percent" wherever the latter percentage appears in such section) of which the employer who maintains the plan is a member. For purposes of the preceding sentence, the term "applicable percentage" means 50 percent, or such lower percentage as the Secretary may prescribe by regulation. A person other than a corporation shall be treated as an affiliate of an employer to the extent provided in regulations of the Secretary. An employer which is a person other than a corporation shall be treated as affiliated with another person to the extent provided by regulations of the Secretary. Regulations under this paragraph shall be prescribed only after consultation and coordination with the Secretary of the Treasury.

(8) The Secretary may prescribe regulations specifying the extent to which conversions, splits, the exercise of rights, and similar transactions are not treated as acquisitions.

(e) For purposes of subsection (d)(5), the term "marketable obligation" means a bond, debenture, note, or certificate, or other evidence of indebtedness (hereinafter in this subsection referred to as "obligation") if—

   (1) such obligation is acquired—

      (A) on the market, either (i) at the price of the obligation prevailing on a national securities exchange which is registered with the Securities and Exchange Commission, or (ii) if the obligation is not traded on such a national securities exchange, at a price not less favorable to the plan than the offering price for the obligation as established by current bid and asked prices quoted by persons independent of the issuer;

(B) from an underwriter, at a price (i) not in excess of the public offering price for the obligation as set forth in a prospectus or offering circular filed with the Securities and Exchange Commission, and (ii) at which a substantial portion of the same issue is acquired by persons independent of the issuer; or

(C) directly from the issuer, at a price not less favorable to the plan than the price paid currently for a substantial portion of the same issue by persons independent of the issuer;

(2) immediately following acquisition of such obligation—

(A) not more than 25 percent of the aggregate amount of obligations issued in such issue and outstanding at the time of acquisition is held by the plan, and

(B) at least 50 percent of the aggregate amount referred to in subparagraph (A) is held by persons independent of the issuer; and

(3) immediately following acquisition of the obligation, not more than 25 percent of the assets of the plan is invested in obligations of the employer or an affiliate of the employer.

EXEMPTIONS FROM PROHIBITED TRANSACTIONS

Sec. 408. (a) The Secretary shall establish an exemption procedure for purposes of this subsection. Pursuant to such procedure, he may grant a conditional or unconditional exemption of any fiduciary or transaction, or class of fiduciaries or transactions, from all or part of the restrictions imposed by sections 406 and 407(a). Action under this subsection may be taken only after consultation and coordination with the Secretary of the Treasury. An exemption granted under this section shall not relieve a fiduciary from any other applicable provision of this Act. The Secretary may not grant an exemption under this subsection unless he finds that such exemption is—

(1) administratively feasible,

(2) in the interests of the plan and of its participants and beneficiaries, and

(3) protective of the rights of participants and beneficiaries of such plan.

Before granting an exemption under this subsection from section 406(a) or 407(a), the Secretary shall publish notice in the Federal Register of the pendency of the exemption, shall require that adequate notice be given to interested persons, and shall afford interested persons opportunity to present views. The Secretary may not grant an exemption under this subsection from section 406(b) unless he affords an opportunity for a hearing and makes a determination on the record with respect to the findings required by paragraphs (1), (2), and (3) of this subsection.

(b) The prohibitions provided in section 406 shall not apply to any of the following transactions:

(1) Any loans made by the plan to parties in interest who are participants or beneficiaries of the plan if such loans (A) are

available to all such participants and beneficiaries on a reasonably equivalent basis, (B) are not made available to highly compensated employees, officers, or shareholders in an amount greater than the amount made available to other employees, (C) are made in accordance with specific provisions regarding such loans set forth in the plan, (D) bear a reasonable rate of interest, and (E) are adequately secured.

(2) Contracting or making reasonable arrangements with a party in interest for office space, or legal, accounting, or other services necessary for the establishment or operation of the plan, if no more than reasonable compensation is paid therefor.

(3) A loan to an employee stock ownership plan (as defined in section 407(d)(6)), if—

    (A) such loan is primarily for the benefit of participants and beneficiaries of the plan, and

    (B) such loan is at an interest rate which is not in excess of a reasonable rate.

If the plan gives collateral to a party in interest for such loan, such collateral may consist only of qualifying employer securities (as defined in section 407(d)(5)).

(4) The investment of all or part of a plan's assets in deposits which bear a reasonable interest rate in a bank or similar financial institution supervised by the United States or a State, if such bank or other institution is a fiduciary of such plan and if—

    (A) the plan covers only employees of such bank or other institution and employees of affiliates of such bank or other institution, or

    (B) such investment is expressly authorized by a provision of the plan or by a fiduciary (other than such bank or institution or affiliate thereof) who is expressly empowered by the plan to so instruct the trustee with respect to such investment.

(5) Any contract for life insurance, health insurance, or annuities with one or more insurers which are qualified to do business in a State, if the plan pays no more than adequate consideration, and if each such insurer or insurers is—

    (A) the employer maintaining the plan, or

    (B) a party in interest which is wholly owned (directly or indirectly) by the employer maintaining the plan, or by any person which is a party in interest with respect to the plan, but only if the total premiums and annuity considerations written by such insurers for life insurance, health insurance, or annuities for all plans (and their employers) with respect to which such insurers are parties in interest (not including premiums or annuity considerations written by the employer maintaining the plan) do not exceed 5 percent of the total premiums and annuity considerations written for all lines of insurance in that year by such insurers (not including premiums or annuity considerations written by the employer maintaining the plan).

(6) The providing of any ancillary service by a bank or similar financial institution supervised by the United States or a State, if such bank or other institution is a fiduciary of such plan, and if—

186

(A) such bank or similar financial institution has adopted adequate internal safeguards which assure that the providing of such ancillary service is consistent with sound banking and financial practice, as determined by Federal or State supervisory authority, and

(B) the extent to which such ancillary service is provided is subject to specific guidelines issued by such bank or similar financial institution (as determined by the Secretary after consultation with Federal and State supervisory authority), and adherence to such guidelines would reasonably preclude such bank or similar financial institution from providing such ancillary service (i) in an excessive or unreasonable manner, and (ii) in a manner that would be inconsistent with the best interests of participants and beneficiaries of employee benefit plans.

Such ancillary services shall not be provided at more than reasonable compensation.

(7) The exercise of a privilege to convert securities, to the extent provided in regulations of the Secretary, but only if the plan receives no less than adequate consideration pursuant to such conversion.

(8) Any transaction between a plan and (i) a common or collective trust fund or pooled investment fund maintained by a party in interest which is a bank or trust company supervised by a State or Federal agency or (ii) a pooled investment fund of an insurance company qualified to do business in a State, if—

(A) the transaction is a sale or purchase of an interest in the fund,

(B) the bank, trust company, or insurance company receives not more than reasonable compensation, and

(C) such transaction is expressly permitted by the instrument under which the plan is maintained, or by a fiduciary (other than the bank, trust company, or insurance company, or an affiliate thereof) who has authority to manage and control the assets of the plan.

(9) The making by a fiduciary of a distribution of the assets of the plan in accordance with the terms of the plan if such assets are distributed in the same manner as provided under section 4044 of this Act (relating to allocation of assets).

(c) Nothing in section 406 shall be construed to prohibit any fiduciary from—

(1) receiving any benefit to which he may be entitled as a participant or beneficiary in the plan, so long as the benefit is computed and paid on a basis which is consistent with the terms of the plan as applied to all other participants and beneficiaries;

(2) receiving any reasonable compensation for services rendered, or for the reimbursement of expenses properly and actually incurred, in the performance of his duties with the plan; except that no person so serving who already receives full-time pay from an employer or an association of employers, whose employees are participants in the plan, or from an employee organization whose members are participants in such plan shall receive compensation from such plan, except for reimbursement of expenses properly and actually incurred; or

(3) serving as a fiduciary in addition to being an officer, employee, agent, or other representative of a party in interest.

(d) Section 407(b) and subsections (a), (b), (c), and (e) of this section shall not apply to any transaction in which a plan, directly or indirectly—

(1) lends any part of the corpus or income of the plan to;

(2) pays any compensation for personal services rendered to the plan to; or

(3) acquires for the plan any property from or sells any property to;

any person who is with respect to the plan an owner-employee (as defined in section 401(c)(3) of the Internal Revenue Code of 1954), a member of the family (as defined in section 267(c)(4) of such Code) of any such owner-employee, or a corporation controlled by any such owner-employee through the ownership, directly or indirectly, of 50 percent or more of the total combined voting power of all classes of stock entitled to vote or 50 percent or more of the total value of shares of all classes of stock of the corporation. For purposes of this subsection a shareholder employee (as defined in section 1379 of the Internal Revenue Code of 1954) and a participant or beneficiary of an individual retirement account, individual retirement annuity, or an individual retirement bond (as defined in section 408 or 409 of the Internal Revenue Code of 1954) and an employer or association of employers which establishes such an account or annuity under section 408(c) of such code shall be deemed to be an owner-employee.

(e) Sections 406 and 407 shall not apply to the acquisition or sale by a plan of qualifying employer securities (as defined in section 407 (d)(5)) or acquisition, sale or lease by a plan of qualifying employer real property (as defined in section 407(d)(4))—

(1) if such acquisition, sale, or lease is for adequate consideration (or in the case of a marketable obligation, at a price not less favorable to the plan than the price determined under Section 407(e)(1)),

(2) if no commission is charged with respect thereto, and

(3) if—

(A) the plan is an eligible individual account plan (as defined in section 407(d)(3)), or

(B) in the case of an acquisition or lease of qualifying employer real property by a plan which is not an eligible individual account plan, or of an acquisition of qualifying employer securities by such a plan, the lease or acquisition is not prohibited by section 407(a).

Internal Revenue Service
Department of the Treasury Regulations
September 2, 1977

Title 26—Internal Revenue

CHAPTER I—INTERNAL REVENUE SERV-
ICE, DEPARTMENT OF THE TREASURY

SUBCHAPTER D—MISCELLANEOUS EXCISE
TAXES

[T.D. 7506]

PART 54—PENSION, ETC. EXCISE TAX

Employee Stock Ownership Plans

AGENCY: Internal Revenue Service,
Treasury.

ACTION: Final regulations.

SUMMARY: This document provides
final regulations relating to employee
stock ownership plans ("ESOP's").
Changes in the applicable tax law were
made by the Employee Retirement Income Security Act of 1974 (ERISA). Together with temporary regulations published elsewhere in today's FEDERAL REG-
ISTER, these regulations are intended to
provide guidance for the public in complying with the law. They affect all employees who participate in ESOP's and
employers who establish ESOP's.

DATE: The regulations are generally
effective for plan years ending after
December 31, 1974.

FOR FURTHER INFORMATION CON-
TACT:

Thomas Rogan of the Legislation and
Regulations Division, Office of the
Chief Counsel, Internal Revenue Serv-
ice, 1111 Constitution Avenue NW.,
Washington, D.C. 20224 (Attention:
CC:LR:T) (202-566-3478).

SUPPLEMENTARY INFORMATION:

BACKGROUND

On July 30, 1976, the FEDERAL REGIS-
TER published proposed amendments to
the Income Tax Regulations (26 CFR
Part I) under section 301 of the Internal
Revenue Code of 1954 and to the Pen-
sion, etc. Excise Tax Regulations (26
CFR Part 54) under section 4975 (d)
(3), (e) (7), and (e) (8) of the Code (41
FR 31833). Similar Department of Labor
provisions appeared at the same time (41
FR 31870).

By a notice published in the FEDERAL
REGISTER on October 19, 1976, the public
was invited to comment orally or in writ-
ing not only upon issues addressed in the
proposed amendments, but also upon
issues addressed by section 803(h) of the
Tax Reform Act of 1976 (90 Stat. 1590)
and by the Conference Report of the
Committee of Conference on H.R. 10612
(H.R. Rep. No. 94-1515, 94th Cong., 2d
Sess., 539-542 (1976)), as both relate to
ESOP's.

A public hearing was held on November 12, 1976. After consideration of all
comments, some of the amendments are
adopted as revised by this Treasury decision. Others are revised and re-proposed elsewhere in today's FEDERAL REG-
ISTER. Also, temporary regulations paral-
lel to the re-proposed amendments are
adopted elsewhere in today's FEDERAL
REGISTER.

Both substantive and structural
changes are made in the proposed
amendments. Thus, the final regulations
differ considerably from the proposed
amendments. Certain provisions are
added. Others are restructured or deleted. However, many changes are designed solely to simplify the final regulations. Therefore, no substantive inference should be drawn solely from the fact
that a particular proposed amendment
is either deleted or restructured.

MAJOR SUBSTANTIVE DELETIONS

(1) TREATMENT OF SALE AS REDEMPTION

Many comments object to the proposed amendment under § 1.301-1(1).
The amendment would result in treating
some ESOP transactions as dividends
distributed by the employer to shareholders. Some of the comments question
the legal validity of this proposal, its
application solely to ESOP's, and its
failure to identify specific transactions
to which the proposal would apply. In
order that these comments may be considered further, this proposal is withdrawn. Guidance on this matter may be
expected within the context of shareholder transactions with employee plans
in general.

(2) SPECIAL REQUIREMENTS FOR USE OF LOAN PROCEEDS

Several comments suggest major revi-
sions to proposed § 54.4975-7(b) (2) (i)
(B) (2) *through* (5). These provisions relate to requirements with respect to voting stock; to non-voting common stock,
preferred stock or other equity securities;
to unrestricted dividend rights; and to
the overall limitation on employer securities (other than certain common stock
or convertible securities) acquired with
loan proceeds. The majority recommend
deletion. This document makes the deletion.

However, this deletion does not mean
that the Department of Labor and the
Internal Revenue Service are uncon-
cerned with the nature of securities acquired by an ESOP with the proceeds of
an exempt loan. The acquisition of securities by an ESOP will be judged by the

Department of Labor under the requirements of section 404(a)(1) of ERISA.

(3) PASS-THROUGH OF VOTING RIGHTS

The comments reflect a mixed reaction to the proposed amendment relating to the exercise of voting and other rights attributable to securities owned by an ESOP. Particularly, the comments focus on the provision requiring the pass-through of voting rights to participants with respect to allocated securities. Some comments favor the proposed amendments. Others suggest minor modifications. However, most of the comments object to the treatment of ESOP's differently in this respect from other qualified employee plans.

Because of these comments, the proposed § 54.4975-11(d) is withdrawn. The requirements generally applicable with respect to the exercise of rights under qualified employee plans apply to ESOP's.

MAJOR SUBSTANTIVE ADDITIONS

(1) RIGHTS OF FIRST REFUSAL

Section 54.4975-7(b)(9) is added under the final regulations to permit an ESOP to acquire employer securities that are subject to a right of first refusal.

Many comments stress the necessity of a right of first refusal to protect small, closely held corporations whose securities are not publicly traded from dilution of control, takeovers, by competitors, and inadvertent "going public". The final regulations reflect the comments by permitting a 14-day right of first refusal in favor of the employer, the ESOP, or both. However, the securities subject to a right of first refusal must not be publicly traded at the time the right is sought to be exercised. Also, the selling price and other terms of the purchase under a right of first refusal must not be less favorable to the seller of the security than the greater of the fair market value of the security or the purchase price and other terms offered by a third party making a good faith offer.

MAJOR REVISIONS

(1) DEFINITION OF "PUBLICLY TRADED"

In response to a number of comments, the concept of "publicly traded" is expanded under the final regulations to include securities quoted on a system sponsored by a registered national securities association. The primary effect of this change is to limit the extent to which a put option is required.

(2) SCOPE OF ESOP LOAN EXEMPTION

Many comments suggest that the proposed amendment limiting the scope of the ESOP loan exemption to the prohibitions of section 4975(c)(1)(A) through (D) is not supported by ERISA or its legislative history. The same criticism is made concerning the requirement that loans involving fiduciary self-dealing must be arranged and approved by an independent fiduciary.

Based upon a review of the comments and the legislative history, the scope of the ESOP loan exemption is expanded under the final regulations. The only prohibited transactions to which the exemption under section 4975(d)(3) does not apply are those arising under section 4975(c)(1)(F). relating to the receipt by a fiduciary of any consideration for his own personal account from a party dealing with a plan. Also. the independent fiduciary requirement is eliminated under the final regulations.

The ERISA Conference Report states that, because of potential problems with respect to ESOP loans by disqualified persons, "the conferees intend that all aspects of these transactions will be subject to special scrutiny by the Department of Labor and the Internal Revenue Service to ensure that they are primarily for the benefit of plan participants and beneficiaries" (H.R. Rep. No. 93-1280, 93d Cong., 2d Sess., 313 (1974)). The final regulations make it clear that the "special scrutiny" for ESOP transactions referred to by the conferees is not meant to require an administrative exemption for loans by fiduciaries. Rather, the language is interpreted as requiring the careful examination of these transactions to ensure that they are primarily for the benefit of participants and their beneficiaries and that they satisfy the requirements of section 404(a)(1) of ERISA.

(3) PRIMARY BENEFIT REQUIREMENT

The requirement that an ESOP loan be made primarily for the benefit of participants and beneficiaries of the plan is expressed with greater specificity under the final regulations. In response to comments requesting clarification of this provision, two tests are added under § 54.4975-7(b)(3) to illustrate how a determination can be made with respect to whether a transaction meets the primary benefit requirement. The first test, derived from the ERISA Conference Report, involves a determination based on the projected net effect of the loan on the ESOP over the duration of the transaction. (See ERISA Conference Report, p. 313.) The second test requires that the terms of an ESOP loan be at least as favorable as a comparable loan resulting from armslength negotiations involving independent parties.

(4) DEFAULT

The proposed amendment restricts the transfer of plan assets in the event of default to a failure to meet the loan payment schedule. As suggested in the comments, the final regulations are less restrictive. The limitation on the transfer of plan assets in the event of default applies only to loans in which the disqualified person extends credit in a form other than a guarantee.

(5) RELEASE FROM ENCUMBRANCE AND SUSPENSE ACCOUNT

The proposed amendments require securities to be released in at least equal annual amounts from encumbrance and from a suspense account. This rule is eliminated from the final regulations because, as pointed out in the comments, it is unnecessarily rigid. Instead, the final regulations now provide, as a general rule, for release of securities from encumbrance and the suspense account as principal and interest are paid. Also, an alternative rule now permits release from encumbrance and from the suspense account with reference to principal payments only. In the case of loans made after November 1, 1977, the alternative applies only to loans with a term of 10 years or less that require payments at a cumulative rate not less rapid than level annual payments. In these cases, interest payments will not be disregarded unless based on standard loan amortization tables.

The final regulations note that the release of securities in unequal annual amounts may reflect conditions causing plan disqualification if contributions are not substantial and recurring or if the limitations on annual additions under section 415 are exceeded.

(6) PUT OPTIONS

The comments address various aspects of the put option provision under the proposed amendments. Several comments express concern over the strain on an employer's cash supply that could result from the continuous exercise of put options by participants, unless installment payments were permissible. Others point out that under certain circumstances, the corporate laws of several states prohibit corporations from purchasing their own securities, and that certain corporations, e.g., banks, may be absolutely prohibited by law from issuing put options.

The final regulations relating to put options reflect many of these comments. Therefore, they differ considerably from the proposed amendments.

The final regulations address the problem that arises if an employer is prohibited by law from honoring a put option. In such cases, a third party other than the ESOP must be bound to honor the put option. They also make it clear that the ESOP must not be bound under any circumstances to honor a put option. However, it may be granted the option to assume the rights and obligations of the employer at the time that the put option is exercised.

The minimum duration of the put option is reduced to 15 months. However, if, for example, the employer or a designated third party is prohibited by law from honoring a put option, the 15-month period runs only when the legal restriction ceases to apply. Also, a security not subject to a put option when distributed must be subject to the requirements for put options if, for example, it ceases to be publicly traded within 15 months after distribution.

Other new put option provisions include a limitation on the number of years over which periodic payments under a put option may be spread and a prohibition of certain payment restrictions. Also, the scope of the put option requirement is expanded to include publicly traded securities that are not freely tradable because of certain restrictions.

(7) SPECIAL RULES FOR CERTAIN EXEMPT LOANS

A number of comments indicate the need to permit retroactive amendment of certain ESOP loans to prevent inadvertent prohibited transactions in loan agreements consummated in good faith before the publication of the final regulations. In light of these comments, the proposed amendments are modified to provide transitional relief.

The regulations provide special rules for loans entered into before January 1, 1976. These loans are not subject to the requirements relating to puts, calls or other options, or buy-sell or similar arrangements; liability of ESOP's; default; release from encumbrance; rights of first refusal; put options; and other loan terms. They are subject to the remaining provisions of the regulation because these provisions could be reasonably anticipated by reading the statutory provisions relating to ESOP's.

Other special rules apply more restrictively to loans made between January 1, 1976, and November 1, 1977. These additional restrictions embody provisions contained in Technical Information Release 1413, guidelines relating to ESOP's, published on November 4, 1975 (1975–50 I.R.B. 16). However, these special rules would allow an ESOP loan made during this period to be exempt for the entire loan period even though the loan fails to satisfy the three additional provisions under the special rules for release from encumbrance or the provisions relating to rights of first refusal and default.

In addition, a loan may be retroactively amended under the final regulations to comply with the default and put option provisions. Under the special rule for put options, a security distributed without a put option will satisfy the final regulations as of the date of distribution if by November 1, 1977 the security becomes subject to a put option satisfying the regulations. The 15-month period for the duration of the put option begins with the date on which the security becomes subject to the put option.

(8) TRANSITIONAL RULES FOR PLANS

The comments also note that transitional rules are lacking under the proposed amendments for plan qualification as an ESOP. This relief is available under the final regulations for ESOP's established before November 1. 1977 if they are amended by December 31. 1977. to satisfy the final regulations.

(9) PURCHASE OF LIFE INSURANCE

Many comments criticize the limitation in the proposed amendments on the purchase of life insurance policies with ESOP assets that are not the proceeds of an exempt loan. That limitation is deleted. Thus, in general, the rules applicable to purchases of life insurance by qualified plans apply to ESOP's. However. the rule of the proposed amendments restricting the use of exempt loan proceeds by an ESOP is unchanged. Thus. an ESOP loan is not exempt if life insurance policies are acquired with the loan proceeds.

(10) VALUATION

Many comments urge deletion of the requirement that an annual certificate of value must be provided in certain situations. The final regulations delete this requirement. They also add the requirement that any determination of value must be made in good faith. In the case of a transaction involving a plan and a disqualified person, this determination must be made as of the date of the transaction. In all other cases, it must be made as of the most recent valuation date under the plan.

An independent appraisal is recognized as a good faith determination of value. However, in the case of a transaction between a plan and a disqualified person, a determination based only on an independent appraisal may not be conclusive.

(11) QUALIFYING EMPLOYER SECURITY

The term "other equity security" is included in the definition of "qualifying employer security" under the Code but not under section 407(d)(5) of ERISA. The proposed amendments are silent on this difference. One comment suggests that this difference is of substantive significance. Since insufficient justification is offered in support of this suggestion, no change is made.

GUIDELINES SUPERSEDED

Questions and answers relating to ESOP's were published in Technical Information Release (TIR) 1413 on November 4. 1975, as guidelines pending the issuance of regulations. The regulations under this Treasury decision supersede the following of those questions and answers in so far as they apply to ESOP's:

(1) G-1, relating to definition of ESOP;

(2) F-3, relating to rights of first refusal;

(3) F-4, relating to call options;

(4) F-5, relating to buy-sell arrangements with shareholders;

(5) F-6, to the extent that the first paragraph of the answer applies to section 4975(e)(7)(A). relating to the funding of ESOP's;

(6) F-9, relating to incidental life insurance; and

(7) F-10, relating to loans to ESOP's.

DRAFTING INFORMATION

The principal author of this regulation was Thomas Rogan of the Legislation and Regulations Division of the Office of Chief Counsel, Internal Revenue Service. However, personnel from other offices of the Internal Revenue Service, Treasury Department. and Department of Labor participated in developing the regulation, both on matters of substance and style.

ADOPTION OF AMENDMENTS TO THE REGULATIONS

Accordingly, 26 CFR Part 54 is amended as follows:

Paragraph 1. There is inserted in the appropriate place the following new section:

§ 54.4975-7 Other statutory exemptions.

(a) [Reserved].

(b) *Loans to employee stock ownership plans—*

(1) *Definitions.* When used in this paragraph (b) and § 54.4975-11, the terms listed below have the following meanings:

(i) *ESOP.* The term "ESOP" refers to an employee stock ownership plan that meets the requirements of section 4975 (e) (7) and § 54.4975-11. It is not synonymous with "stock bonus plan." A stock bonus plan must, however, be an ESOP to engage in an exempt loan. The qualification of an ESOP under section 401 (a) and § 54.4975-11 will not be adversely affected merely because it engages in a non-exempt loan.

(ii) *Loan.* The term "loan" refers to a loan made to an ESOP by a disqualified person or a loan to an ESOP which is guaranteed by a disqualified person. It includes a direct loan of cash, a purchase-money transaction, and an assumption of the obligation of an ESOP. "Guarantee" includes an unsecured guarantee and the use of assets of a disqualified person as collateral for a loan, even though the use of assets may not be a guarantee under applicable state law. An amendment of a loan in order to qualify as an exempt loan is not a refinancing of the loan or the making of another loan.

(iii) *Exempt loan.* The term "exempt loan" refers to a loan that satisfies the provisions of this paragraph (b). A "non-exempt loan" is one that fails to satisfy such provisions.

(iv) *Publicly traded.* The term "publicly traded" refers to a security that is listed on a national securities exchange registered under section 6 of the Securities Exchange Act of 1934 (15 U.S.C. 78*l*) or that is quoted on a system sponsored by a national securities association registered under section 15A(b) of the Securities Exchange Act (15 U.S.C. 78o).

(v) *Qualifying employer security.* The term "qualifying employer security" refers to a security described in § 54.4975-12.

(2) *Statutory exemption.*—(i) *Scope.* Section 4975(d)(3) provides an exemption from the excise tax imposed under section 4975 (a) and (b) by reason of section 4975(c)(1) (A) through (E). Section 4975(d)(3) does not provide an exemption from the imposition of such tax by reason of section 4975(c) (1)(F), relating to fiduciaries receiving consideration for their own personal account from any party dealing with a plan in connection with a transaction involving the income or assets of the plan.

(ii) *Special scrutiny of transaction.* The exemption under section 4975(d) (3) includes within its scope certain transactions in which the potential for self-dealing by fiduciaries exists and in which the interests of fiduciaries may conflict with the interests of participants. To guard against those potential abuses, the Internal Revenue Service will subject these transactions to special scrutiny to ensure that they are primarily for the benefit of participants and their beneficiaries. Although the transactions need not be arranged and approved by an independent fiduciary, fiduciaries are cautioned to exercise scrupulously their discretion in approving them. For example, fiduciaries should be prepared to demonstrate compliance with the net effect test and the arm's-length standard under paragraph (b) (3) (ii) and (iii) of this section. Also, fiduciaries should determine that the transaction is truly arranged primarily in the interest of participants and their beneficiaries rather than, for example, in the interest of certain selling shareholders.

(3) *Primary benefit requirement.*—(i) *In general.* An exempt loan must be primarily for the benefit of the ESOP participants and their beneficiaries. All the surrounding facts and circumstances, including those described in paragraph (b)(3) (ii) and (iii) of this section, will be considered in determining whether the loan satisfies this requirement. However, no loan will satisfy the requirement unless it satisfies the requirements of paragraphm (b) (4), (5), and (6) of this section.

(ii) *Net effect on plan assets.* At the time that a loan is made, the interest rate for the loan and the price of securities to be acquired with the loan proceeds should not be such that plan assets might be drained off.

(iii) *Arm's-length standard.* The terms of a loan, whether or not between in-dependent parties, must, at the same time the loan is made, be at least as favorable to the ESOP as the terms of a comparable loan resulting from arm's-length negotiations between independent parties.

(4) *Use of loan proceeds.* The proceeds of an exempt loan must be used within a reasonable time after their receipt by the borrowing ESOP only for any or all of the following purposes:

(i) To acquire qualifying employer securities.

(ii) To repay such loan.

(iii) To repay a prior exempt loan. A new loan, the proceeds of which are so used, must satisfy the provisions of this paragraph (b).

Except as provided in paragraph (b) (9) and (10) of this section or as otherwise required by applicable law, no security acquired with the proceeds of an exempt loan may be subject to a put, call, or other option, or buy-sell or similar arrangement while held by and when distributed from a plan, whether or not the plan is then an ESOP.

(5) *Liability and collateral of ESOP for loan.* An exempt loan must be without recourse against the ESOP. Furthermore, the only assets of the ESOP that may be given as collateral on an exempt loan are qualifying employer securities of two classes: those acquired with the proceeds of the loan and those that were used as collateral on a prior exempt loan repaid with the proceeds of the current exempt loan. No person entitled to payment under the exempt loan shall have any right to assets of the ESOP other than:

(i) Collateral given for the loan,

(ii) Contributions (other than contributions of employer securities) that are made under an ESOP to meet its obligations under the loan, and

(iii) Earnings attributable to such collateral and the investment of such contributions.

The payments made with respect to an exempt loan by ESOP during a plan year must not exceed an amount equal to the sum of such contributions and earnings received during or prior to the year less such payments in prior years. Such contributions and earnings must be accounted for separately in the books of account of the ESOP until the loan is repaid.

(6) *Default.* In the event of default upon an exempt loan, the value of plan assets transferred in satisfaction of the loan must not exceed the amount of default. If the lender is a disqualified person, a loan must provide for a transfer of plan assets upon default only upon and to the extent of the failure of the plan to meet the payment schedule of the loan. For purposes of this subparagraph (6), the making of a guarantee does not make a person a lender.

(7) *Reasonable rate of interest.* The

interest rate of a loan must not be in excess of a reasonable rate of interest. All relevant factors will be considered in determining a reasonable rate of interest, including the amount and duration of the loan, the security and guarantee (if any) involved, the credit standing of the ESOP and the guarantor (if any), and the interest rate prevailing for comparable loans. When these factors are considered, a variable interest rate may be reasonable.

(8) *Release from encumbrance*—(i) *General rule.* In general, an exempt loan must provide for the release from encumbrance under this subdivision (i) of plan assets used as collateral for the loan. For each plan year during the duration of the loan, the number of securities released must equal the number of encumbered securities held immediately before release for the current plan year multiplied by a fraction. The numerator of the fraction is the amount of principal and interest paid for the year. The denominator of the fraction is the sum of the numerator plus the principal and interest to be paid for all future years. See § 54.4975-7(b)(8)(iv). The number of future years under the loan must be definitely ascertainable and must be determined without taking into account any possible extensions or renewal periods. If the interest rate under the loan is variable, the interest to be paid in future years must be computed by using the interest rate applicable as of the end of the plan year. If collateral includes more than one class of securities, the number of securities of each class to be released for a plan year must be determined by applying the same fraction to each class.

(ii) *Special rule.* A loan will not fail to be exempt merely because the number of securities to be released from encumbrance is determined solely with reference to principal payments. However, if release is determined with reference to principal payments only, the following three additional rules apply. The first rule is that the loan must provide for annual payments of principal and interest at a cumulative rate that is not less rapid at any time than level annual payments of such amounts for 10 years. The second rule is that interest included in any payment is disregarded only to the extent that it would be determined to be interest under standard loan amortization tables. The third rule is that this subdivision (ii) is not applicable from the time that, by reason of a renewal, extension, or refinancing, the sum of the expired duration of the exempt loan, the renewal period, the extension period, and the duration of a new exempt loan exceeds 10 years.

(iii) *Caution against plan disqualification.* Under an exempt loan, the number of securities released from encumbrance may vary from year to year. The release

of securities depends upon certain employer contributions and earnings under the ESOP. Under § 54.4975-11(d)(2) actual allocations to participants' accounts are based upon assets withdrawn from the suspense account. Nevertheless, for purposes of applying the limitations under section 415 to these allocations, under § 54.4975-11(a)(8)(ii) contributions used by the ESOP to pay the loan are treated as annual additions to participants' accounts. Therefore, particular caution must be exercised to avoid exceeding the maximum annual additions under section 415. At the same time, release from encumbrance in annual varying numbers may reflect a failure on the part of the employer to make substantial and recurring contributions to the ESOP which will lead to loss of qualification under section 401(a). The Internal Revenue Service will observe closely the operation of ESOP's that release encumbered securities in varying annual amounts, particularly those that provide for the deferral of loan payments or for balloon payments.

(iv) *Illustration.* The general rule under paragraph (b)(8)(i) of this section operates as illustrated in the following example:

Example. Corporation X establishes an ESOP that borrows $750,000 from a bank. X guarantees the loan, which is for 15 years at 5% interest and is payable in level annual amounts of $72,256.72. Total payments on the loan are $1,083,850.80. The ESOP uses the entire loan proceeds to acquire 15,000 shares of X stock which is used as collateral for the loan. The number of securities to be released for the first year is 1,000 shares, i.e., 15,000 shares × $72,256.72/$1,083,850.80 = 15,000 shares x 1/15. The number of securities to be released for the second year is 1,000 shares, i.e., 14,000 shares × $72,256.72/$1,011,594.08 = 14,000 shares × 1/14. If all loan payments are made as originally scheduled, the number of securities released in each succeeding year of the loan will also be 1,000.

(9) *Right of first refusal.* Qualifying employer securities acquired with proceeds of an exempt loan may, but need not, be subject to a right of first refusal. However, any such right must meet the requirements of this subparagraph (9). Securities subject to such right must be stock or an equity security, or a debt security convertible into stock or an equity security. Also, the securities must not be publicly traded at the time the right may be exercised. The right of first refusal must be in favor of the employer, the ESOP, or both in any order of priority. The selling price and other terms under the right must not be less favorable to the seller than the greater of the value of the security determined under § 54.4975-11(d)(5), or the purchase price and other terms offered by a buyer, other than the employer or the ESOP, making a good faith offer to purchase the security. The right of first re-

fusal must lapse no later than 14 days after the security holder gives written notice to the holder of the right that an offer by a third party to purchase the security has been received.

(10) *Put option.* A qualifying employer security acquired with the proceeds of an exempt loan by an ESOP after September 30, 1976, must be subject to a put option if it is not publicly traded when distributed or if it is subject to a trading limitation when distributed. For purposes of this sumfparagraph (10), a "trading limitation" on a security is a restcition under any Federal or state securities law, any regulation thereunder, or an agreement, not prohibited by this paragraph (b), affecting the security which would make the security not as freely tradable as one not subject to such restriction. The put option must be exercisable only by a participant, by the participant's donees, or by a person (including an estate or its distributee) to whom the security passes by reason of a participant's death. (Under this subparagraph (10), "participant" means a participant and beneficiaries of the participant under the ESOP.) The put option must permit a participant to put the security to the employer. Under no circumstances may the put option bind the ESOP. However, it may grant the ESOP an option to assume the rights and obligations of the employer at the time that the put option is exercised. If it is known at the time a loan is made that Federal or state law will be violated by the employer's honoring such put option, the put option must permit the security to be put, in a manner consistent with such law, to a third party (e.g., an affiliate of the employer or a shareholder other than the ESOP) that has substantial net worth at the time the loan is made and whose net worth is reasonably expected to remain substantial.

(11) *Duration of put option—(i) General rule.* A put option must be exercisable at least during a 15-month period which begins on the date the security subject to the put option is distributed by the ESOP.

(ii) *Special rule.* In the case of a security that is publicly traded without restriction when distributed but ceases to be so traded within 15 months after distribution, the employer must notify each security holder in writing on or before the tenth day after the date the security ceases to be so traded that for the remainder of the 15-month period the security is subject to a put option. The number of days between such tenth day and the date on which notice is actually given, if later than the tenth day, must be added to the duration of the put option. The notice must inform distributees of the terms of the put options that they are to hold. Such terms must satisfy the requirements of paragraph (b) (10) through (12) of this section.

(12) *Other put option provisions.—(i) Manner of exercise.* A put option is exercised by the holder notifying the employer in writing that the put option is being exercised.

(ii) *Time excluded from duration of put option.* The period during which a put option is exercisable does not include any time when a distributee is unable to exercise it because the party bound by the put option is prohibited from honoring it by applicable Federal or state law.

(iii) *Price.* The price at which a put option must be exercisable is the value of the security, determined under § 54.4975-11(d)(5).

(iv) *Payment terms.* The provisions for payment under a put option must be reasonable. The deferral of payment is reasonable if adequate security and a reasonable interest rate are provided for any credit extended and if the cumulative payments at any time are no less than the aggregate of reasonable periodic payments as of such time. Periodic payments are reasonable if annual installments, beginning with 30 days after the date the put option is exercised, are substantially equal. Generally, the payment period may not end more than 5 years after the date the put option is exercised. However, it may be extended to a date no later than the earlier of 10 years from the date the put option is exercised or the date the proceeds of the loan used by the ESOP to acquire the security subject to the put option are entirely repaid.

(v) *Payment restrictions.* Payment under a put option may be restricted by the terms of a loan, including one used to acquire a security subject to a put option made before November 1, 1977. Otherwise, payment under a put option must not be restricted by the provisions of a loan or any other arrangement, including the terms of the employer's articles of incorporation, unless so required by applicable state law.

(13) *Other terms of loan.* An exempt loan must be for a specific term. Such loan may not be payable at the demand of any person, except in the case of default.

(14) *Status of plan as ESOP.* To be exempt, a loan must be made to a plan that is an ESOP at the time of such loan. However, a loan to a plan formally designated as an ESOP at the time of the loan that fails to be an ESOP because it does not comply with section 401(a) of the Code or § 54.4975-11 will be exempt as of the time of such loan if the plan is amended retroactively under section 401(b) or § 54.4975-11(a)(4).

(15) *Special rules for certain loans.—(i) Loans made before January 1, 1976.* A loan made before January 1, 1976, or made afterwards under a binding agreement in effect on January 1, 1976 (or under renewals permitted by the terms of the agreement on that date) is exempt for the entire period of the loan if it otherwise satisfies the provisions

of this paragraph (b) for such period, even though it does not satisfy the following provisions of this section: the last sentence of paragraph (b)(4) and all of paragraph (b) (5), (6), (8) (i) and (ii), and (9) through (13), inclusive.

(ii) *Loans made after December 31, 1975, but before November 1, 1977.* A loan made after December 31, 1975, but before November 1, 1977 or made afterwards under a binding agreement in effect on November 1, 1977 (or under renewals permitted by the terms of the agreement on that date) is exempt for the entire period of the loan if it otherwise satisfies the provisions of this paragraph (b) for such period even though it does not satisfy the following provisions of this section: paragraph (b) (6) and (9) and the three additional rules listed in paragraph (b) (8) (ii).

(iii) *Release rule.* Notwithstanding paragraph (b)(15) (i) and (ii) of this section, if the proceeds of a loan are used to acquire securities after November 1, 1977, the loan must comply by such date with the provisions of paragraph (b)(8) of this section.

(iv) *Default rule.* Notwithstanding paragraph (b)(15) (i) and (ii) of this section, a loan by a disqualified person other than a guarantor must meet the requirements of paragraph (b)(6) of this section. A loan will meet these requirements if it is retroactively amended before November 1, 1977 to meet these requirements.

(v) *Put option rule.* With respect to a security distributed before November 1, 1977, the put option provisions of paragraph (b) (10), (11), and (12) of this section will be deemed satisfied as of the date the security is distributed if by December 31, 1977, the security is subject to a put option satisfying such provisions. For purposes of satisfying such provisions, the security will be deemed distributed on the date the put option is issued. However, the put option provisions need not be satisfied with respect to a security that is not owned on November 1, 1977, by a person in whose hands a put option must be exercisable.

Par. 2. There are inserted in the appropriate place the following new sections:

§ 54.4975–11 "ESOP" requirements.

(a) *In general.*—(1) *Type of plan.* To be an "ESOP" (employee stock ownership plan), a plan described in section 4975(e)(7)(A) must meet the requirements of this section. See section 4975 (e)(7)(B).

(2) *Designation as ESOP.* To be an ESOP, a plan must be formally designated as such in the plan document.

(3) *Non-terminable provisions.* [Reserved]

(4) *Retroactive amendment.* A plan meets the requirements of this section as of the date that it is designated as an

ESOP if it is amended retroactively to meet, and in fact does meet, such requirements at any of the following times:

(i) 12 months after the date on which the plan is designated as an ESOP;

(ii) 90 days after a determination letter is issued with respect to the qualification of the plan as an ESOP under this section, but only if the determination is requested by the time in paragraph (a) (4)(i) of this section; or

(iii) A later date approved by the district director.

(5) *Addition to other plan.* An ESOP may form a portion of a plan the balance of which includes a qualified pension, profit-sharing, or stock bonus plan which is not an ESOP. A reference to an ESOP includes an ESOP that forms a portion of another plan.

(6) *Conversion of existing plan to an ESOP.* If an existing pension, profit-sharing, or stock bonus plan is converted into an ESOP, the requirements of section 404 of the Employee Retirement Income Security Act of 1974 (ERISA) (88 Stat. 877), relating to fiduciary duties, and section 401(a) of the Code, relating to requirements for plans established for the exclusive benefit of employees, apply to such conversion. A conversion may constitute a termination of an existing plan. For definition of a termination, see the regulations under section 411(d) (3) of the Code and section 4041(f) of ERISA.

(7) *Certain arrangements barred.*—(i) *Buy-sell agreements.* An arrangement involving an ESOP that creates a put option must not provide for the issuance of put options other than as provided under § 54.4975–7(b) (10), (11) and (12). Also, an ESOP must not otherwise obligate itself to acquire securities from a particular security holder at an indefinite time determined upon the happening of an event such as the death of the holder.

(ii) *Integrated plans.* [Reserved]

(8) *Effect of certain ESOP provisions on section 401 (a) status.*—(i) *Exempt loan requirements.* An ESOP will not fail to meet the requirements of section 401 (a)(2) merely because it gives plan assets as collateral for an exempt loan under § 54.4975–7(b)(5) or uses plan assets under § 54.49757(b)(6) to repay an exempt loan in the event of default.

(ii) *Individual annual contribution limitation.* An ESOP will not fail to meet the requirements of section 401(a)(16) merely because annual additions under section 415(c) are calculated with respect to employer contributions used to repay an exempt loan rather than with respect to securities allocated to participants.

(iii) *Income pass-through.* [Reserved]

(9) *Transitional rules for ESOP's established before November 1, 1977.* A plan established before November 1, 1977 that otherwise satisfies the provisions of

this section constitutes an ESOP if it is amended by December 31, 1977, to comply from November 1, 1977 with this section even though before November 1, 1977 the plan did not satisfy paragraphs (c) and (d) (2), (4), and (5) of this section.

(10) *Additional transitional rules.* [Reserved].

(b) *Plan designed to invest primarily in qualifying employer securities.* A plan constitutes an ESOP only if the plan specifically states that it is designed to invest primarily in qualifying employer securities. Thus, a stock bonus plan or a money purchase pension plan constituting an ESOP may invest part of its assets in other than qualifying employer securities. Such plan will be treated the same as other stock bonus plans or money purchase pension plans qualified under section 401a with respect to those investments.

(c) *Suspense account.* All assets acquired by an ESOP with the proceeds of an exempt loan under section 4975 (d) (3) must be added to and maintained in a suspense account. They are to be withdrawn from the suspense account by applying § 54.4975–7(b) (8) and (15) as if all securities in the suspense account were encumbered. Such assets acquired before November 1, 1977, must be withdrawn by applying § 54.4975–7(b) (8) or the provision of the loan that controls release from encumbrance. Assets in such suspense accounts are assets of the ESOP. Thus, for example, such assets are subject to section 401(a) (2).

(d) *Allocations to accounts of participants—*(1) *In general.* Except as provided in this section, amounts contributed to an ESOP must be allocated as provided under § 1.401–1(b) (ii) and (iii) of this chapter, and securities acquired by an ESOP must be accounted for as provided under § 1.402(a)–1(b) (2) (ii) of this chapter.

(2) *Assets withdrawn from suspense account.* As of the end of each plan year, the ESOP must consistently allocate to the participants' accounts non-monetary units representing participants' interests in assets withdrawn from the suspense account.

(3) *Income.* Income with respect to securities acquired with the proceeds of an exempt loan must be allocated as income of the plan except to the extent that the ESOP provides for the use of income from such securities to repay the loan.

(4) *Forfeitures.* If a portion of a participant's account is forfeited, qualifying employer securities allocated under paragraph (d) (2) of this section must be forfeited only after other assets. If interests in more than one class of qualifying employer securities have been allocated to the participant's account, the participant must be treated as forfeiting the same proportion of each such class.

(5) *Valuation.* For purposes of § 54.4975–7(b) (9) and (12) and this section, valuations must be made in good faith and based on all relevant factors for determining the fair market value of securities. In the case of a transaction between a plan and a disqualified person, value must be determined as of the date of the transaction. For all other purposes under this subparagraph (5), value must be determined as of the most recent valuation date under the plan. An independent appraisal will not in itself be a good faith determination of value in the case of a transaction between a plan and a disqualified person. However, in other cases, a determination of fair market value based on at least an annual appraisal independently arrived at by a person who customarily makes such appraisals and who is independent of any party to a transaction under § 54.4975–7(b) (9) and (12) will be deemed to be a good faith determination of value.

(e) *Multiple plans.—*(1) *General rule.* An ESOP may not be considered together with another plan for purposes of applying section 401(a) (4) and (5) or section 410(b) unless:

(i) The ESOP and such other plan exist on November 1, 1977, or

(ii) Paragraph (e) (2) of this section is satisfied.

(2) *Special rule for combined ESOP's.* [Reserved]

(f) *Distribution.—*(1) *In general.* Except as provided in paragraph (f) (2) and (3) of this section, with respect to distributions, a portion of an ESOP consisting of a stock bonus plan or a money purchase pension plan is not to be distinguished from other such plans under section 401(a). Thus, for example, benefits distributable from the portion of an ESOP consisting of a stock bonus plan are distributable only in stock of the employer. Also, benefits distributable from the money-purchase portion of the ESOP may be, but are not required to be, distributable in qualifying employer securities.

(2) *Exempt loan proceeds.* If securities acquired with the proceeds of an exempt loan available for distribution consist of more than one class, a distributee must receive substantially the same proportion of each such class. However, as indicated in paragraph (f) (1) of this section, benefits distributable from the portion of an ESOP consisting of a stock bonus plan are distributable only in stock of the employer.

(3) *Income.* [Reserved]

§ 54.4975–12 Definition of the term "qualifying employer security".

(a) *In general.* For purposes of section 4975(e) (8) and this section, the term "qualifying employer security" means an employer security which is:

(1) Stock or otherwise an equity security, or

(2) A bond, debenture, note, or certificate or other evidence of indebtedness which is described in paragraphs (1), (2), and (3) of section 503(e).

(b) *Special rule.* In determining whether a bond, debenture, note, or certificate or other evidence of indebtedness is described in paragraphs (1), (2), and (3) of section 503(e), any organization described in section 401(a) shall be treated as an organization subject to the provisions of section 503.

(Secs. 4975(e)(7) and 7805, Revenue Code of 1954 (88 Stat. 976, 68A Stat. 917; 26 U.S.C. 4975(e)(7), 7805).)

JEROME KURTZ,
*Commissioner
of Internal Revenue.*

Approved: August 26, 1977.

LAURENCE N. WOODWORTH,
*Assistant Secretary of the
Treasury.*

[FR Doc. 77-25696 Filed 8-30-77:2:52 pm]

Revenue Procedure 77-30

26 CFR 601.201: *Rulings and determination letters.*
(Also Part I, Sections 301, 302, 1001; 1.301-1, 1.302-1).

Rev. Proc. 77-30

SECTION 1. PURPOSE.

The purpose of this Revenue Procedure is to set forth the circumstances under which the Internal Revenue Service will issue an advance ruling that a proposed sale of employer stock to a related qualified defined contribution employee plan of deferred compensation will be a sale of the stock rather than a distribution of property, taxable under section 301 of the Internal Revenue Code of 1954 to the selling shareholder.

SEC. 2. BACKGROUND.

The operating rules published in this Revenue Procedure are intended only to assist taxpayers and their representatives in preparing ruling requests. These operating rules do not define, as a matter of law, the circumstances under which a sale of stock can be treated as a corporate distribution of property under section 301 of the Code.

A requested ruling under this Revenue Procedure will usually be issued if the operating rules in Section 4 of this Revenue Procedure are complied with and if all other pertinent provisions of the Internal Revenue Code, Income Tax Regulations, Revenue Procedures, and Revenue Rulings are complied with.

The authority and general procedures of the National Office and the Offices of the District Directors of the Internal Revenue Service for the issuance of advance rulings and determination letters are outlined in Rev. Proc. 72-3, 1972-1 C.B. 698, and section 601.201 of the Statement of Procedural Rules (26 CFR section 601.201 (1977)). See also Rev. Proc. 72-9, 1972-1 C.B. 718. Careful attention to all of the requirements of these documents will also serve to minimize delays in processing requests for rulings.

SEC. 3. DEFINITION OF TERMS

For purposes of this Revenue Procedure only, the following definitions shall apply:

.01 The "employer" is the corporation that is maintaining the related qualified defined contribution employee plan of deferred compensation to which employer stock is to be sold.

.02 A "related qualified defined contribution employee plan of deferred compensation" is a defined contribution plan that is maintained by the employer for the exclusive benefit of the employer's employees and is qualified under section 401(a) of the Code.

.03 "Covered compensation" of an employee is the employee's compensation upon which allocations of employer contributions to the employee's account are based.

.04 The "account balance" of an employee consists of the amounts contributed to the employee's account in the plan and the employee's allocable share of forfeitures, income. and gains, less the employee's allocable share of expenses and losses.

.05 "Related persons" are the spouse, parents, grandparents, children, and grandchildren of the selling shareholder.

SEC. 4. OPERATING RULES.

A ruling will usually be issued that a proposed sale of employer stock to a related qualified defined contribution employee plan of deferred compensation will be a sale of the stock, rather than a distribution of property, taxable to the selling shareholder under section 301 of the Code, if the following conditions are satisfied:

.01 The combined beneficial interest in the employee plan of the selling shareholder and all related persons does not exceed 20 percent. This requirement will not be satisfied if: (1) the combined covered compensation of the selling shareholder and related persons exceeds 20 percent of total covered compensation under the plan; (2) the total of the account balances (vested and nonvested) of the selling shareholder and related persons exceeds 20 percent of the total of all employee account balances (vested and nonvested) in the plan; or (3) the combined interest (vested and nonvested) of the selling shareholder and related persons in any separately managed fund or account within the plan exceeds 20 percent of the total net assets in that fund or account.

.02 Any restrictions on disposition of the employer stock held by the employee plan and on employer stock received by employees from the employee plan (other than restrictions imposed by Federal or state securities laws) are no more onerous than the disposition restrictions on at least a majority of the shares of employer stock held by other shareholders of the employer.

.03 It is represented that there is no plan, intention or understanding for the employer to redeem any of the stock from the employee plan.

Sec. 5. Inquiries.

Inquiries about this Revenue Procedure should refer to its number and should be addressed to the Assistant Commissioner (Technical), Attention: Washington, D. C. 20224.

[4830-01-M]

Title 26—Internal Revenue

CHAPTER I—INTERNAL REVENUE SERVICE, DEPARTMENT OF THE TREASURY

SUBCHAPTER D—MISCELLANEOUS EXCISE TAX

[T.D. 7571]

PART 54—PENSION EXCISE TAX REGULATIONS

PART 141—TEMPORARY EXCISE TAX REGULATIONS UNDER THE EMPLOYEE RETIREMENT INCOME SECURITY ACT OF 1974

Employee Stock Ownership Plans

AGENCY: Internal Revenue Service, Treasury.

ACTION: Publication of full text of final regulations.

SUMMARY: This document sets forth the full text of previously adopted final regulations (43 FR 53718), November 17, 1978, FR Doc. 78-32151 relating to employee stock ownership plans.

DATE: The regulations are generally effective for plan years ending after December 31, 1974.

FOR FURTHER INFORMATION CONTACT:

Thomas Rogan of the Employee Plans and Exempt Organizations Division, Office of the Chief Counsel, Internal Revenue Service, 1111 Constitution Avenue, N.W., Washington, D.C. 20224 (Attention: CC:EE), 202-566-3589, not a toll-free number.

SUPPLEMENTARY INFORMATION:

BACKGROUND

On September 2, 1977, the FEDERAL REGISTER (42 FR 44396) published proposed amendments to the Pension Excise Tax Regulations (26 CFR Part 54). These proposed amendments were adopted as temporary regulations in a Treasury decision published in the same issue of the FEDERAL REGISTER (42 FR 44394). After consideration of all written comments received regarding the proposed amendments, those amendments were adopted, as revised, by Treasury Decision 7571, published in the FEDERAL REGISTER for November 17, 1978 (43 FR 53718). Treasury Decision 7571 also superseded the related temporary regulations.

However, Treasury Decision 7571 as published in the FEDERAL REGISTER contained only the changes to the notice of proposed rulemaking published on September 2, 1977, rather than the full text of the final regulations. This document sets forth the full text of the final regulations.

DRAFTING INFORMATION

The principal author of this regulation was Thomas Rogan of the Employee Plans and Exempt Organizations Division of the Office of the Chief Counsel, Internal Revenue Service. However, personnel from other offices of the Internal Revenue Service and Treasury Department participated in developing the regulation, both on matters of substance and style.

Accordingly, the full text of the final regulations adopted by Treasury Decision 7571 is as follows:

GEORGE H. JELLY,
Director, Employee Plans and Exempt Organizations Division.

26 CFR is amended as follows:

1. In Part 54, § 54.4975-11 is amended by—

a. Revising paragraph (a)(3), (7)(ii), (8)(iii), and (10),

b. Adding a new sentence at the end of paragraph (d)(3),

c. Revising paragraph (e)(2), and

d. Revising paragraph (f)(3).

These revised and added provisions read as follows:

§ 54.4975-11 "ESOP" requirements.

(a) In general. * * *

(3) *Continuing loan provisions under plan*—(i) *Creation of protections and rights.* The terms of an ESOP must formally provide participants with certain protections and rights with respect to plan assets acquired with the proceeds of an exempt loan. These protections and rights are those referred to in the third sentence of § 54.4975-7(b)(4), relating to put, call, or other options and to buy-sell or sim-

ilar arrangements, and in § 54.4975-7(b)(10), (11), and (12), relating to put options.

(ii) *"Nonterminable" protections and rights.* The terms of an ESOP must also formally provide that these protections and rights are nonterminable. Thus, if a plan holds or has distributed securities acquired with the proceeds of an exempt loan and either the loan is repaid or the plan ceases to be an ESOP, these protections and rights must continue to exist under the terms of the plan. However, the protections and rights will not fail to be nonterminable merely because they are not exercisable under § 54.4975-7(b)(11) and (12)(ii). For example, if, after a plan ceases to be an ESOP, securities acquired with the proceeds of an exempt loan cease to be publicly traded, the 15-month period prescribed by § 54.4975-7(b)(11) includes the time when the securities are publicly traded.

(iii) *No incorporation by reference of protections and rights.* The formal requirements of paragraph (a)(3)(i) and (ii) of this section must be set forth in the plan. Mere reference to the third sentence of § 54.4975-7(b)(4) and to the provisions of § 54.4975-7(b)(10), (11), and (12) is not sufficient.

(iv) *Certain remedial amendments.* Notwithstanding the limits under paragraph (a)(4) and (10) of this section on the retroactive effect of plan amendments, a remedial plan amendment adopted before December 31, 1979, to meet the requirements of paragraph (a)(3)(i) and (ii) of this section is retroactively effective as of the later of the date on which the plan was designated as an ESOP or November 1, 1977.

* * * * *

(7) *Certain arrangements barred.* * * *

(ii) *Integrated plans.* A plan designated as an ESOP after November 1, 1977, must not be integrated directly or indirectly with contributions or benefits under title II of the Social Security Act or any other State or Federal Law. ESOP's established and integrated before such date may remain integrated. However, such plans must not be amended to increase the integration level or the integration percentage. Such plans may in operation continue to increase the level of integration if under the plan such increase is limited by reference to a criterion existing apart from the plan.

(8) *Effect of certain ESOP provisions on section 401(a) status.* * * *

(iii) *Income pass-through.* An ESOP

will not fail to meet the requirements of section 401(a) merely because it provides for the current payment of income under paragraph (f)(3) of this section.

* * * * *

(10) *Additional transitional rules.* Notwithstanding paragraph (a)(9) of this section, a plan established before November 1, 1977, that otherwise satisfies the provisions of this section constitutes an ESOP if by December 31, 1977, it is amended to comply from November 1, 1977, with this section even though before such date the plan did not satisfy the following provisions of this section:

(i) Paragraph (a) (3) and (8) (iii);
(ii) The last sentence of paragraph (d)(3); and
(iii) Paragraph (f)(3).

* * * * *

(d) *Allocations to accounts of participants.* * * *
(3) *Income.* * * * Certain income may be distributed currently under paragraph (f)(3) of this section.

* * * * *

(e) *Multiple plans* * * *
(2) *Special rule for combined ESOP's.* Two or more ESOP's, one or more of which does not exist on November 1, 1977, may be considered together for purposes of applying section 401(a) (4) and (5) or section 410(b) only if the proportion of qualifying employer securities to total plan assets is substantially the same for each ESOP and—
(i) The qualifying employer securities held by all ESOP's are all of the same class; or
(ii) The ratios of each class held to all such securities held is substantially the same for each plan.
(3) *Amended coverage, contribution, or benefit structure.* For purposes of paragraph (e)(1)(i) of this section, if the coverage, contribution, or benefit structure of a plan that exists on November 1, 1977 is amended after that date, as of the effective date of the amendment, the plan is no longer considered to be a plan that exists on November 1, 1977.
(f) *Distribution.* * * *
(3) *Income.* Income paid with respect to qualifying employer securities acquired by an ESOP in taxable years beginning after December 31, 1974, may be distributed at any time after receipt by the plan to participants on whose behalf such securities have been allocated. However, under an ESOP that is a stock bonus plan, income held by the plan for a 2-year

202

period or longer must be distributed under the general rules described in paragraph (f)(1) of this section. (See the last sentence of section 803(h). Tax Reform Act of 1976.)

* * * * *

§ 141.4975-11 [Deleted]

2. Part 141 is amended by deleting § 141.4975-11.

[FR Doc. 79-698 Filed 1-8-79: 8:45 am]

Excerpts From
Revenue Act of 1978

PART II—EMPLOYEE STOCK OWNERSHIP PLANS
SEC. 141. ESOPS.

(a) IN GENERAL.—Subpart A of part I of subchapter D of chapter 1 (relating to general rule for pension, profit-sharing, stock bonus plans, etc.) is amended by adding at the end thereof the following new section:

SEC. 409A. QUALIFICATIONS FOR ESOPS.

"(a) ESOP DEFINED.—Except as otherwise provided in this title, for purposes of this title, the term 'ESOP' means a defined contribution plan which—

"(1) meets the requirements of section 401(a),

"(2) is designed to invest primarily in employer securities, and

"(3) meets the requirements of subsections (b), (c), (d), (e), (f), (g), and (h) of this section.

"(b) REQUIRED ALLOCATION OF EMPLOYER SECURITIES.—

"(1) IN GENERAL.—A plan meets the requirements of this subsection if—

"(A) the plan provides for the allocation for the plan year of all employer securities transferred to it or purchased by it (because of the requirements of section 48(n)(1)(A)) to the accounts of all participants who are entitled to share in such allocation, and

"(B) for the plan year the allocation to each participant so entitled is an amount which bears substantially the same proportion to the amount of all such securities allocated to all such participants in the plan for that year as the amount of compensation paid to such participant during that year bears to the compensation paid to all such participants during that year.

"(2) COMPENSATION IN EXCESS OF $100,000 DISREGARDED.—For purposes of paragraph (1), compensation of any participant in excess of the first $100,000 per year shall be disregarded.

"(3) DETERMINATION OF COMPENSATION.—For purposes of this subsection, the amount of compensation paid to a participant for any period is the amount of such participant's compensation (within the meaning of section 415(c)(3)) for such period.

"(4) SUSPENSION OF ALLOCATION IN CERTAIN CASES.—Notwithstanding paragraph (1), the allocation to the account of any participant which is attributable to the basic ESOP credit may be extended over whatever period may be necessary to comply with the requirements of section 415.

"(c) PARTICIPANTS MUST HAVE NONFORFEITABLE RIGHTS.—A plan meets the requirements, of this subsection only if it provides that each participant has a nonforfeitable right to any employer security allocated to his account.

"(d) EMPLOYER SECURITIES MUST STAY IN THE PLAN.—A plan meets the requirements of this subsection only if it provides that no employer security allocated to a participant's account under subsection (b) may be distributed from that account before the end of the 84th month beginning after the month in which the security is allocated to the account. To the extent provided in the plan, the preceding sentence shall not apply in the case of separation from service, death, or disability.

"(e) VOTING RIGHTS.—

"(1) IN GENERAL.—A plan meets the requirements of this subsection if it meets the requirements of paragraph (2) or (3), whichever is applicable.

"(2) REQUIREMENTS WHERE EMPLOYER HAS A REGISTRATION-TYPE CLASS OF SECURITIES.—If the employer has a registration-type class of securities, the plan meets the requirements of this paragraph only if each participant in the plan is entitled to direct the plan as to the manner in which employer securities which are entitled to vote and are allocated to the account of such participant are to be voted.

"(3) REQUIREMENT FOR OTHER EMPLOYERS.—If the employer does not have a registration-type class of securities, the plan meets the requirements of this paragraph only if each participant in the plan is entitled to direct the plan as to the manner in which voting rights under employer securities which are allocated to the account of such participants are to be exercised with respect to a corporate matter which (by law or charter) must be decided by more than a majority vote of outstanding common shares voted.

"(4) REGISTRATION-TYPE CLASS OF SECURITIES DEFINED.—For purposes of this subsection, the term 'registration-type class of securities' means—

"(A) a class of securities required to be registered under section 12 of the Securities Exchange Act of 1934, and

"(B) a class of securities which would be required to be so registered except for the exemption from registration provided in subsection (g)(2)(H) of such section 12.

"(f) PLAN MUST BE ESTABLISHED BEFORE EMPLOYER'S DUE DATE.—

"(1) IN GENERAL.—A plan meets the requirements of this subsection for a plan year only if it is established on or before the due date for the filing of the employer's tax return for the taxable year (including any extensions of such date) in which or with which the plan year ends.

"(2) SPECIAL RULE FOR FIRST YEAR.—A plan which otherwise meets the requirements of this section shall not be considered to have failed to meet the requirements of section 401(a) merely because it was not established by the close of the first taxable year of the employer for which an ESOP credit is claimed by the employer.

"(g) TRANSFERRED AMOUNTS MUST STAY IN PLAN EVEN THOUGH INVESTMENT CREDIT IS REDETERMINED OR RECAPTURED.—A plan meets the requirement of this subsection only if it provides that amounts which are transferred to the plan (because of the requirements of section 48(n)(1)) shall remain in the plan (and, if allocated under the plan, shall remain so allocated) even though part or all of the ESOP credit is recaptured or redetermined.

"(h) RIGHT TO DEMAND EMPLOYER SECURITIES; PUT OPTION.—

"(1) IN GENERAL.—A plan meets the requirements of this subsection if a participant who is entitled to a distribution from the plan—

"(A) has a right to demand that his benefits be distributed in the form of employer securities, and

"(B) if the employer securities are not

204

readily tradable on an established market, has a right to require that the employer repurchase employer securities under a fair valuation formula.

"(2) PLAN MAY DISTRIBUTE CASH IN CERTAIN CASES.—A plan which otherwise meets the requirements of this section shall not be considered to have failed to meet the requirements of section 401(a) merely because under the plan the benefits may be distributed in cash or in the form of employer securities.

"(i) REIMBURSEMENT FOR EXPENSES OF ESTABLISHING AND ADMINISTERING PLAN.—A plan which otherwise meets the requirements of this section shall not be treated as failing to meet such requirements merely because it provides that—

"(1) EXPENSES OF ESTABLISHING PLAN.—As reimbursement for the expenses of establishing the plan, the employer may withhold from amounts due the plan for the taxable year for which the plan is established (or the plan may pay) so much of the amounts paid or incurred in connection with the establishment of the plan as does not exceed the sum of—

"(A) 10 percent of the first $100,000 which the employer is required to transfer to the plan for that taxable year under section 48(n)(1), and

"(B) 5 percent of any amount so required to be transferred in excess of the first $100,000; and

"(2) ADMINISTRATIVE EXPENSES.—As reimbursement for the expenses of administering the plan, the employer may withhold from amounts due the plan (or the plan may pay) so much of the amounts paid or incurred during the taxable year as expenses of administering the plan as does not exceed the lesser of—

"(A) the sum of—

"(i) 10 percent of the first $100,000 of the dividends paid to the plan with respect to stock of the employer during the plan year ending with or within the employer's taxable year, and

"(ii) 5 percent of the amount of such dividends in excess of $100,000 or

"(B) $100,000.

"(j) CONDITIONAL CONTRIBUTIONS TO THE PLAN.—A plan which otherwise meets the requirements of this section shall not be treated as failing to satisfy such requirements (or as failing to satisfy the requirements of section 401(a) of this title or of section 403(c)(1) of the Employee Retirement Income Security Act of 1974) merely because of the return of a contribution (or a provision permitting such a return) if—

"(1) the contribution to the plan is conditioned on a determination by the Secretary that such plan meets the requirements of this section,

"(2) the application for a determination described in paragraph (1) is filed with the Secretary not later than 90 days after the date on which an ESOP credit is claimed, and

"(3) the contribution is returned within 1 year after the date on which the Secretary issues notice to the employer that such plan does not satisfy the requirements of this section.

"(k) REQUIREMENTS RELATING TO CERTAIN WITHDRAWALS.—Notwithstanding any other law or rule of law—

"(1) the withdrawal from a plan which otherwise meets the requirements of this section by the employer of an amount contributed for purposes of the matching ESOP

credit shall not be considered to make the benefits forfeitable, and

"(2) the plan shall not, by reason of such withdrawal, fail to be for the exclusive benefit of participants or their beneficiaries, if the withdrawn amounts were not matched by employee contributions or were in excess of the limitations of section 415. Any withdrawal described in the preceding sentence shall not be considered to violate the provisions of section 403(c)(1) of the Employee Retirement Income Security Act of 1974:

"(l) EMPLOYER SECURITIES DEFINED.—For purposes of this section—

"(1) IN GENERAL.—The term 'employer securities' means common stock issued by the employer (or by a corporation which is a member of the same controlled group) which is readily tradable on an established securities market.

"(2) SPECIAL RULE WHERE THERE IS NO READILY TRADABLE COMMON STOCK.—If there is no common stock which meets the requirements of paragraph (1), the term 'employer securities' means common stock issued by the employer (or by a corporation which is a member of the same controlled group) having a combination of voting power and dividend rights equal to or in excess of—

"(A) that class of common stock of the employer (or of any other such corporation) having the greatest voting power, and

"(B) that class of stock of the employer (or of any other such corporation) having the greatest dividend rights.

"(3) PREFERRED STOCK MAY BE ISSUED IN CERTAIN CASES.—Noncallable preferred stock shall be treated as meeting the requirements of paragraph (1) if such stock is convertible at any time into stock which meets the requirements of paragraph (1) and if such conversion is at a conversion price which (as of the date of the acquisition by the ESOP) is reasonable.

"(4) CONTROLLED GROUP OF CORPORATIONS DEFINED.—

"(A) IN GENERAL.—For purposes of this subsection, the term 'controlled group of corporations' has the meaning given to such term by section 1563(a) (determined without regard to subsections (a)(4) and (e)(3)(C) of section 1563).

"(B) COMMON PARENT MAY OWN ONLY 50 PERCENT OF FIRST TIER SUBSIDIARY.—For purposes of subparagraph (A), if the common parent owns directly stock possessing at least 50 percent of the voting power of all classes of stock and at least 50 percent of each class of nonvoting stock in a first tier subsidiary, such subsidiary (and all other corporations below it in the chain which would meet the 80 percent test of section 1563(a) if the first tier subsidiary were the common parent) shall be treated as includible corporations.

"(m) CONTRIBUTIONS OF STOCK OF CONTROLLING CORPORATION.—If the stock of a corporation which controls another corporation or which controls a corporation controlled by such other corporation is contributed to an ESOP of the controlled corporation, then no gain or loss shall be recognized, because of that contribution, to the controlled corporation. For purposes of this subsection, the term 'control' has the same meaning as that term has in section 368(c).

"(n) CROSS REFERENCES.—

"(1) For requirements for allowance of ESOP credit, see section 48(n).

"(2) For assessable penalties for failure to meet requirements of this section, or for failure to make contributions required with respect to the allowance of an ESOP credit, see section 6699."

(b) AMENDMENT OF INVESTMENT CREDIT RULES.—Section 48 (relating to definitions and special rules) is amended by redesignating subsection (n) as subsection (p) and by inserting after subsection (m) the following new subsections:

"(n) REQUIREMENTS FOR ALLOWANCE OF ESOP PERCENTAGE.—

"(1) IN GENERAL.—

"(A) BASIC ESOP PERCENTAGE.—The basic ESOP percentage shall not apply to any taxpayer for any taxable year unless the taxpayer on his return for such taxable year agrees, as a condition for the allowance of such percentage—

"(i) to make transfers of employer securities to an ESOP maintained by the taxpayer having an aggregate value equal to 1 percent of the amount of the qualified investment (as determined under subsections (c) and (d) of section 46) for the taxable year, and

"(ii) to make such transfers at the times prescribed in subparagraph (C).

"(B) MATCHING ESOP PERCENTAGE.—The matching ESOP percentage shall not apply to any taxpayer for any taxable year unless the basic ESOP percentage applies to such taxpayer for such taxable year, and the taxpayer on his return for such taxable year agrees, as a condition for the allowance of the matching ESOP percentage—

"(i) to make transfers of employer securities to an ESOP maintained by the taxpayer having an aggregate value equal to the sum of the qualified matching employee contributions made to such ESOP for the taxable year, and

"(ii) to make such transfers at the times prescribed in subparagraph (C).

"(C) TIMES FOR MAKING TRANSFERS.—The aggregate of the transfers required under subparagraph (A) and (B) shall be made—

"(i) to the extent allocable to that portion of the ESOP credit allowed for the taxable year or allowed as a carryback to a preceding taxable year, not later than 30 days after the due date (including extensions) for filing the return for the taxable year, or

"(ii) to the extent allocable to that portion of the ESOP credit which is allowed as a carryover in a succeeding taxable year, not later than 30 days after the due date (including extensions) for filing the return for such succeeding taxable year.

The Secretary may by regulations provide that transfers may be made later than the times prescribed in the preceding sentence where the amount of any credit or carryover or carryback for any taxable year exceeds the amount shown on the return for the taxable year.

"(D) ORDERING RULES.—For purposes of subparagraph (C), the portion of the ESOP credit allowed for the current year or as a carryover or carryback shall be determined—

"(i) first by treating the credit or carryover or carryback as attributable to the regular percentage,

"(ii) second by treating the portion (not allocated under clause (i)) of such credit or carryover or carryback as attributable to the basic ESOP percentage, and

"(iii) finally by treating the portion (not allocated under clause (i) or (ii)) as attributable to the matching ESOP percentage.

"(2) QUALIFIED MATCHING EMPLOYEE CONTRIBUTION DEFINED.—

"(A) IN GENERAL.—For purposes of this subsection, the term 'qualified matching employee contribution' means, with respect to any taxable year, any contribution made by an employee to an ESOP maintained by the taxpayer if—

"(i) each employee who is entitled to an allocation of employer securities transferred to the ESOP under paragraph (1)(A) is entitled to make such a contribution,

"(ii) the contribution is designated by the employee as a contribution intended to be taken into account under this paragraph for the taxable year,

"(iii) the contribution is paid in cash to the employer or plan administrator not later than 24 months after the close of the taxable year, and is invested forthwith in employer securities, and

"(iv) the ESOP meets the requirements of subparagraph (B).

"(B) PLAN REQUIREMENTS.—For purposes of subparagraph (A), the ESOP meets the requirements of this subparagraph if—

"(i) participation in the ESOP is not required as a condition of employment and the ESOP does not require matching employee contributions as a condition of participation in the ESOP,

"(ii) employee contributions under the ESOP meet the requirements of section 401 (a)(4), and

"(iii) the ESOP provides for allocation of all employer securities transferred to it or purchased by it (because of the requirements of paragraph (1)(B) to the account of each participant in an amount equal to such participant's matching employee contributions for the year.

"(3) CERTAIN CONTRIBUTIONS OF CASH TREATED AS CONTRIBUTIONS OF EMPLOYER SECURITIES.—For purposes of this subsection, a transfer of cash shall be treated as a transfer of employer securities if the cash is, under the ESOP, used within 30 days to purchase employer securities.

"(4) ADJUSTMENTS IF ESOP CREDIT RECAPTURED.—If any portion of the ESOP credit is recaptured under section 47 of the ESOP credit is reduced by a final determination—

"(A) the employer may reduce the amount required to be transferred to the ESOP under paragraph (1) for the current taxable year or any succeeding taxable year by an amount equal to such portion (or reduction), or

"(B) notwithstanding the provisions of paragraph (5) and to the extent not taken into account under subparagraph (A), the employer may deduct an amount equal to such portion (or reduction), subject to the limitation of section 404.

"(5) DISALLOWANCE OF DEDUCTION.—No deduction shall be allowed under section 162, 212, or 404 for amounts required to be transferred to an ESOP under this subsection.

"(6) DEFINITIONS.—For purposes of this subsection—

"(A) EMPLOYEE SECURITIES.—The term 'employer securities' has the meaning given to such term by section 409A(1).

"(B) VALUE.—The term 'value' means—

"(i) in the case of securities listed on a national exchange, the average of closing prices of such securities for the 20 consecutive trading days immediately preceding the due date for filing the return for the taxable year (determined with regard to extensions), or

"(ii) in the case of securities not listed on a national exchange, and fair market value as determined in good faith and in accordance with regulations prescribed by the Secretary.

"(o) CERTAIN CREDITS DEFINED.—For purpose of this title—

"(1) REGULAR INVESTMENT CREDIT.—The term 'regular investment credit' means that portion of the credit allowable by section 38 which is attributable to the regular percentage.

"(2) ENERGY INVESTMENT CREDIT.—The term 'energy investment credit' means that portion of the credit allowable by section 38 which is attributable to the energy percentage.

"(3) ESOP CREDIT.—The term 'ESOP credit' means the sum of—

"(A) the basic ESOP credit, and

"(B) the matching ESOP credit.

"(4) BASIC ESOP CREDIT.—The term 'basic ESOP credit' means that portion of the credit allowable by section 38 which is attributable to the basic ESOP percentage.

"(5) MATCHING ESOP CREDIT.—The term 'matching ESOP credit' means that portion of the credit allowable by section 38 which is attributable to the matching ESOP.

"(6) BASIC ESOP PERCENTAGE.—The term 'basic ESOP percentage' means the 1-percent ESOP percentage set forth in section 46(a)(2)(E)(i).

"(7) MATCHING ESOP PERCENTAGE.—The term 'matching ESOP percentage' means the additional ESOP percentage (not to exceed ½ of 1 percent) set forth in section 46(a)(2)(E)(ii)."

(c) ASSESSABLE PENALTIES.—

(1) IN GENERAL.—Subchapter B of chapter 68 (relating to assessable penalties) is amended by adding at the end thereof the following new section:

"SEC. 6699. ASSESSABLE PENALTIES RELATING TO ESOP.

"(a) IN GENERAL.—If a taxpayer who has claimed an ESOP credit for any taxable year—

"(1) fails to satisfy any requirement provided by section 409A, or

"(2) fails to make any contribution which is required under section 48(n) within the period required for making such contribution.

the taxpayer shall pay a penalty in an amount equal to the amount involved in such failure.

"(b) NO PENALTY WHERE THERE IS TIMELY CORRECTION OF FAILURE.—Subsection (a) shall not apply with respect to any failure if the employer corrects such failure (as determined by the Secretary) within 90 days after the Secretary notifies him of such failure.

"(c) AMOUNT INVOLVED DEFINED.—

"(1) IN GENERAL.—For purposes of this section, the term 'amount involved' means an amount determined by the Secretary.

"(2) MAXIMUM AND MINIMUM AMOUNT.—The amount determined under paragraph (1)—

"(A) shall not exceed the amount determined by mutliplying the qualified investment of the employer for the taxable year to which the failure relates by the ESOP percentage claimed by the employer for such year, and

"(B) shall not be less than the product of one-half of 1 percent of the amount referred to in subparagraph (A), multiplied by the number of months (or parts thereof) during which such failure continues."

(2) CLERICAL AMENDMENT.—The table of sections for such subchapter B is amended by adding at the end thereof the following new item:

"Sec. 6699. Assessable penalties relating to ESOP."

(d) REGULAR TAX DEDUCTION FOR PURPOSES OF THE MINIMUM TAX DETERMINED WITHOUT REGARD TO ESOP PERCENTAGE.—Subsection (c) of section 56 (defining regular tax deduction) is amended by adding at the end thereof the following new sentence: "For purposes of the preceding sentence, the amount of the credit allowable under section 38 shall be determined without regard to the ESOP percentage set forth in section 46(a)(2)(E)."

(e) ESOP CREDIT EXTENDED FOR 3 YEARS.—Subparagraph (E) of section 46(a)(2) (relating to amount of business investment credit for current taxable year) is amended by striking out "and ending on December 31, 1980," each place it appears and inserting in lieu thereof "December 31, 1983"

(f) TECHNICAL AND CONFORMING AMENDMENTS.—

(1) Subsections (d), (e), and (f) of section 301 of the Tax Reduction Act of 1975 are hereby repealed.

(2) Subparagraph (E) of section 46(a)(2) is amended—

(A) by striking out "section 301(e) of the Tax Reduction Act of 1975" and inserting in lieu thereof "section 48(n)(1)(B)", and

(B) by striking out "section 301(d) of the Tax Reduction Act of 1975" and inserting in lieu thereof "section 409A".

(3) Paragraph (21) of section 401(a) is amended to read as follows:

"(21) A trust forming part of an ESOP shall not fail to be considered a permanent program merely because employer contributions under the plan are determined solely by reference to the amount of credit which would be allowable under section 46(a) if the employer made the transfer described in section 48(n)(1)."

(4) The last sentence of section 1504(a) (defining affiliated group) is amended to read as follows:

"As used in this subsection, the term 'stock' does not include nonvoting stock which is limited and preferred as to dividends, employer securities (within the meaning for section 409A(l) while such securities are held under an ESOP, or qualifying employer securities (within the meaning of section 4975(e)(8)) while such securities are held under a leveraged employee stock ownership plan which meets the requirements of section 4975(s)(7)."

(5) Paragraph (7) of section 4975(e) (defining employee stock ownership plan) is amended—

(A) by striking out "EMPLOYEE" in the paragraph heading and inserting in lieu thereof "LEVERAGED EMPLOYEE", and

(B) by striking out "employee" in the text and inserting in lieu thereof "leveraged employee", and

(C) by adding at the end thereof the following new sentence:

"A plan shall not be treated as a leveraged employee stock ownership plan unless it meets the requirements of subsections (e) and (h) of section 409A."

207

(6) Paragraph (3) of section 4975(d) is amended by striking out "employee" and inserting in lieu thereof "leveraged employee".

(7) Subparagraph (B) of section 415(c)(6) is amended by striking out clauses (i) and (ii) and inserting in lieu thereof the following:

"(i) the term 'employee stock ownership plan' means a leveraged employee stock ownership plan (within the meaning of section 4975(e)(7)) or an ESOP,

"(ii) the term 'employer securities has the meaning given to such term by section 409A.".

(8) The table of sections for part I of subchapter D of chapter 1 is amended by inserting after the item relating to section 409 the following new item:

"Sec. 409A. Qualification for ESOPs."

(9) Section 404(a)(2) and section 805(d) are each amended by striking out "and (20)" and inserting in lieu thereof "(20), and (22)"

(g) EFFECTIVE DATES.—

(1) IN GENERAL.—The amendments made by this section other than by subsection (f) (3) shall apply with respect to qualified investment for taxable years beginning after December 31, 1978. The amendment made by subsection (f)(7) shall apply to years beginning after December 31, 1978.

(2) RETROACTIVE APPLICATION OF AMENDMENT MADE BY SUBSECTION (d).—In determining the regular tax deduction under section 6 of the Internal Revenue Code of 1954 for any taxable year beginning before January 1, 1979, the amount of the credit allowable under section 38 shall be determined without regard to section 46(a)(2)(B) of such Code (as in effect before the enactment of the Energy Tax Act of 1978).

SEC. 142. CERTAIN LUMP SUM DISTRIBUTIONS EXCLUDED FROM GROSS ESTATE WHERE RECIPIENT ELECTS NOT TO APPLY 10-YEAR AVERAGING.

(a) IN GENERAL.—Subsection (c) of section 2039 (relating to rexemption of annuities under certain trusts and plans) is amended by striking out "(other than a lump sum distribution described in section 402(e)(4), de-

termined without regard to the next to the last sentence of section 402(e)(4)(A))" and inserting in lieu thereof "(other than an amount described in subsection (f))".

(b) DEFINITIONS.—Section 2039 is amended by adding at the end thereof the following new subsection:

"(f) LUMP SUM DISTRIBUTIONS.—

"(1) IN GENERAL.—An amount is described in this subsection if it is a lump sum distribution described in section 402(e)(4) (determined without regard to the next to the last sentence of section 402(e)(4)(A))

"(2) EXCEPTION WHERE RECIPIENT ELECTS NOT TO TAKE 10-YEAR AVERAGING.—A lump sum distribution described in paragraph (1) shall be treated as not described in this subsection if the recipient elects irrevocably (at such time and in such manner as the Secretary may by regulations prescribe) to treat the distribution as taxable under section 402(a) without the application of paragraph (2) thereof."

(c) EFFECTIIVE DATE.—The amendments made by this section shall apply with respect to the estates of decedents dying after December 31, 1978.

SEC. 143. QUALIFIED PLANS REQUIRED TO PASS THROUGH VOTING RIGHTS ON EMPLOYEE SECURITIES.

(a) IN GENERAL.—Subsection (a) of section 401 (relating to qualified pension, profit-sharing, and stock bonus plans) is amended by inserting after paragraph (21) the following new paragraph:

"(22) If a defined contributions plan—

"(A) is established by an employer whose stock is not publicly traded, and

"(B) after acquiring securities of the employer, more than 10 percent of the total assets of the plan in securities of the employer,

any trust forming part of such plan shall not constitute a qualified trust under this section unless the plan meets the requirements of subsection (e) of section 409A."

(b) EFFECTIVE DATE.—The amendment made by subsection (a) shall apply to acquisitions of securities after December 31, 1979.

ESOP Unrelated Business Taxable Income

Revenue Ruling 79-122

This provision is part of Rev. Rul. 79-122.

Section 512.—Unrelated Business Taxable Income

26 CFR 1.512(b)-1: Exceptions, additions, and limitations.
(Also Sections 401, 511. 513, 514, 4975; 1.401-1, 1.511-2, 1.513-1, 1.514(b)-1, 54.4975-11.)

Leveraged ESOP; unrelated income; debt-financed securities. Employer securities purchased with borrowed funds by a qualified trust forming part of a leveraged employee stock ownership plan that satisfies the requirements of section 4975(e)(7) of the Code are not debt-financed property within the meaning of section 514(b), and dividends and interest earned on such securities are not unrelated business taxable income to the trust; Rev. Ruls. 71-311 and 74-197 distinguished.

Rev. Rul. 79-122

Advice has been requested whether "unrelated business taxable income" within the meaning of section 512 of the Internal Revenue Code of 1954 results from the payment of dividends or interest on employer securities purchased with funds borrowed by a trust forming part of a leveraged employee stock ownership plan (ESOP) that satisfies the requirements of sections 401(a) and 4975(e)(7) of the Code.

Section 511(a) of the Code imposes a tax on the unrelated business taxable income (as defined in section 512) of every organization described in sections 401(a) and 501(a) and certain other organizations. Section 512(a)(1) defines the term "unrelated business taxable income" as the gross income derived by any organization from any unrelated trade or business (as defined in section 513) regularly carried on by it, less the deductions allowed by Chapter 1 of the Code which are directly connected with the carrying on of such trade or business, both computed with the modifications provided in section 512(b).

Section 512(b)(1) of the Code excludes from the term "unrelated business taxable income" all dividends, interest, and annuities, and all deductions directly connected with such income. However, section 512(b)(4) provides that, notwithstanding these exclusions, in the case of debt-financed property (as defined in section 514) there shall be included, as an item of gross income derived from an unrelated trade or business, the amount ascertained under section 514(a)(1) (relating to the percentage of the income from debt-financed property that is taken into account), and there shall be allowed, as a deduction, the amount ascertained under section 514(a)(2) (relating to the percentage of deductions taken into account with respect to debt-financed property).

Section 514(b)(1) of the Code defines "debt-financed property" as any property that is held to produce income and with respect to which there is an acquisition indebtedness (as defined in section 514(c)) at any time during the taxable year (or, if the property was disposed of during the taxable year, with respect to which there was an acquisition indebtedness at any time during the 12-month period ending with the date of such disposition). Section 514(c) provides in part that "acquisition indebtedness" means with respect to any debt-financed property, the unpaid amount of the indebtedness incurred by the organization in acquiring, or improving such property. However, section 514(c)(4) provides that the term "acquisition indebtedness" does not include indebtedness the incurrence of which is inherent in the performance or exercise of the purpose or function constituting the basis of the organization's exemption. Furthermore, section 514(b)(1)(A)(i) excludes from debt-financed property any property substantially all the use of which is substantially related (aside from the need of the organization for income or funds) to the exercise or performance by such organization of its charitable, educational, or other purpose or function constituting the basis for its exemption under section 501. Section 1.514(b)-1(b)(1)(i) of the Income Tax Regulations refers to section 1.513-1 for principles applicable in determining whether there is a substantial relationship to the exempt purpose of the organization.

Section 1.513-1(d)(2) of the regulations states that a trade or business is "related" to exempt purposes, in the relevant sense, only where the conduct of the business activities has causal relationship to the achievement of exempt purposes (other than through the production of income) ; and it is "substantially related," for purposes of section 513, only if the causal relationship is a substantial one.

Rev. Rul. 71-311, 1971-2 C.B. 184, explains that an employees' trust forming part of a plan qualified under section 401(a) of the Code is subject to tax on unrelated business taxable income under section 511 and, in this connection, refers to sections 512(b)(4) and 514, regarding the inclusion of certain debt-financed income in unrelated business taxable income.

Rev. Rul. 74-197, 1974-1 C.B. 143, explains that the exceptions contained in either section 514(b)(1)(A)(i) of the Code or section 514(c)(4) do not apply to investment borrowing of an exempt employees pension trust that is maintained for the purpose of paying definitely determinable benefits to its participants or their beneficiaries, as described in section 1.401-1(a)(2)(i) of the regulations. Because the purpose of such a trust is to receive the contributions of the employer, the employees or both, and to use the contributions and increments thereon

to provide pension benefits to the employee participants at retirement, the indebtedness was an acquisition indebtedness as defined in section 514(c) and the property acquired with the borrowed funds is not substantially related (aside from the need of the trust for funds) to the exercise or performance by the trust of its exempt purpose or function. Accordingly, the exempt trust's investment activity could result in unrelated business taxable income within the meaning of section 512.

Section 4975(e)(7) of the Code provides that the term "leveraged employee stock ownership plan" means a defined contribution plan (A) which is a stock bonus plan which is qualified, or a stock bonus and a money purchase plan both of which are qualified under section 401(a), and which are designed to invest primarily in qualifying employer securities; and (B) which is otherwise defined in regulations prescribed by the Secretary or his delegate. Under a leveraged ESOP an employee stock ownership trust generally acquires stock of the employer with the proceeds of a loan made to it by a financial institution. Frequently, the loan is guaranteed by the employer. The employer's contributions to the employees' trust are applied to retire the loan.

An ESOP is a technique of corporate finance designed to build beneficial equity ownership of shares in the employer corporation into its employees substantially in proportion to their relative income without requiring any cash outlay on their part, any reduction in pay or other employee benefits, or the surrender of any rights on the part of the employees. S. Rep. No. 94-938, 1976-3 C.B. (Vol. 3) 49, 218. Congress _ intended to encourage ESOP's as a method of strengthening the free private enterprise system that would solve the dual problems of securing capital funds for necessary capital growth and of bringing about stock ownership by all corporate employees.

210

The Tax Reform Act of 1976, section 803(h), 1976-3 C.B. (Vol. 1) 1, 66. Therefore, a leveraged ESOP's capital growth and stock ownership objectives are to be considered part of its exempt function under section 401(a) of the Code and borrowing to purchase employer securities is an integral part of accomplishing these objectives.

Because the indebtedness incurred by a leveraged ESOP to purchase employer securities is inherent in the performance or exercise of the purpose or function constituting the basis of the ESOP's exemption, such borrowing is not "acquisition indebtedness" within the meaning of section 514(a) of the Code. Furthermore, the employer securities that are purchased by a leveraged ESOP are substantially related to the exercise or performance by the ESOP of the purpose or function constituting the basis of the ESOP's exemption as described in section 514 (b)(1)(A)(i).

Accordingly, the employer securities purchased by a leveraged ESOP with borrowed funds are not "debt-financed property" within the meaning of section 514(b) of the Code and the dividends and interest thereon will not be "unrelated business taxable income" within the meaning of section 512. This situation is distinguishable from a situation in which a pension or profit sharing plan that satisfies the requirements of section 401(a) borrows money to purchase securities of the employer; in the latter situation the exempt trusts' borrowing to purchase employer securities could result in unrelated business taxable income within the meaning of section 512.

Rev. Rul. 71-311 and Rev. Rul. 74-197 are distinguished.

Miscellaneous Revenue Act of 1980

Be it enacted by the Senate and House of Representatives of the United States of America in Congress assembled,

SECTION 1. SHORT TITLE; AMENDMENT OF 1954 CODE.

(a) SHORT TITLE.—This Act may be cited as the "Miscellaneous Revenue Act of 1980."

(b) AMENDMENT OF 1954 CODE.—Except as otherwise expressly provided, whenever in this Act an amendment or repeal is expressed in terms of an amendment to, or repeal of, a section or other provision, the reference shall be considered to be made to a section or other provision of the Internal Revenue Code of 1954.

Subtitle B—Amendments Relating to Employee Stock Ownership Plans

SEC. 221. CASH DISTRIBUTION OPTION AND PUT OPTION FOR STOCK BONUS PLANS.

(a) IN GENERAL.—Subsection (a) of section 401 (relating to requirements for qualification) is amended by inserting immediately before the last sentence thereof the following new paragraph:

> "(23) A stock bonus plan which otherwise meets the requirements of this section shall not be considered to fail to meet the requirements of this section because it provides a cash distribution option to participants if that option meets the requirements of section 409A(h)(2)."

(b) EFFECTIVE DATE.—The amendment made by subsection (a) shall apply with respect to plan years beginning after December 31, 1980.

SEC. 222. LIMITATION ON ANNUAL ADDITIONS TO PARTICIPANT ACCOUNTS UNDER EMPLOYEE STOCK OWNERSHIP PLANS.

(a) IN GENERAL.—Subparagraph (A) of section 415(c)(6) (relating to special limitation for employee stock ownership plan) is amended by inserting, "or purchased with cash contributed," after "contributed."

(b) EFFECTIVE DATE.—The amendment made by subsection (a) shall apply with respect to years beginning after December 31, 1980.

SEC. 223. VALUATION OF EMPLOYER SECURITIES IN TAX CREDIT EMPLOYEE STOCK OWNERSHIP PLANS.

(a) IN GENERAL.—Clause (i) of section 48(n)(6)(B) (defining value for employer securities) is amended by striking out "the due date for filing the return for the taxable year (determined with regard to extensions)" and inserting in lieu thereof "the date on which the securities are contributed to the plan."

(b) EFFECTIVE DATE.—The amendments made by subsection (a) shall apply with respect to taxable years beginning after December 31, 1980.

SEC. 224. PARTICIPATION OF SUBSIDIARY CORPORATION IN TAX CREDIT EMPLOYEE STOCK OWNERSHIP PLAN.

(a) IN GENERAL.—Paragraph (4) of section 409A(1) (defining controlled group of corporations) is amended—

(1) by striking out the caption and inserting in lieu thereof "(4) APPLICATION TO CONTROLLED GROUP OF CORPORA-TIONS.—,"

(2) by striking out "COMMON PARENT MAY OWN ONLY" in the caption of subparagraph (B) and inserting in lieu thereof "WHERE COMMON PARENT OWNS AT LEAST," and

(3) by adding at the end thereof the following new subparagraph:

"(C) WHERE COMMON PARENT OWNS 100 PERCENT OF FIRST TIER SUBSIDIARY.—For purposes of subparagraph (A), if the common parent owns directly stock possessing all of the voting power of all classes of stock and all of the nonvoting stock, in a first tier subsidiary, and if the first tier subsidiary owns directly stock possessing at least 50 percent of the voting power of all classes of stock, and at least 50 percent of each class of nonvoting stock, in a second tier subsidiary of the common parent, such second tier subsidiary [and all other corporations below it in the chain which would meet the 80 percent test of section 1563(a) if the second tier subsidiary were the common parent] shall be treated as includible corporations."

(b) EFFECTIVE DATE.—The amendment made by subsection (a) shall apply with respect to qualified investment for taxable years beginning after December 31, 1978.

SEC. 225. PARTICIPATION RULES FOR TAX CREDIT EMPLOYEE STOCK OWNERSHIP PLAN WHICH IS ONLY EMPLOYER-PROVIDED ALTERNATIVE TO INDIVIDUAL RETIREMENT SAVINGS.

(a) IN GENERAL.—Subsection (b) of section 410 (relating to eligibility) is amended—

(1) by redesignating paragraph (2) as (3),

(2) by striking out "paragraph (1)" in paragraph (3) (as so redesignated) and inserting in lieu thereof "paragraphs (1) and (2)," and

(3) by inserting after paragraph (1) the following new paragraph:

"(2) SPECIAL RULE FOR CERTAIN PLANS.—A trust which is part of a tax credit employees stock ownership plan which is the only plan of an employer intended to qualify under section 401(a) shall not be treated as not a qualified trust under section 401(a) solely because it fails to meet the requirements of paragraph (1) if—

"(A) it benefits 50 percent or more of all the employees who are eligible under the plan (excluding employees who have not satisfied the minimum age and service requirements, if any, prescribed by the plan as a condition of participation), and

"(B) the sum of the amounts allocated to each participant's account for the year does not exceed 2 percent of the compensation of that participant for the year."

(b) CONFORMING AMENDMENTS.—

(1) The last sentence of section 401(a)(4) is amended by striking out "section 410(b)(2)(A)" and inserting in lieu thereof "section 410(b)(3)(A)."

(2) Subparagraph (B) of section 401(d)(3) is amended—

(A) by striking out "section 410(b)(2)(A)" and inserting in lieu thereof "section 410(b)(3)(A)," and

(B) by striking out "section 410(b)(2)(C)" and inserting in lieu thereof "section 410(b)(3)(C)."

(3) The last sentence of section 408(k)(2) is amended by striking out "section 410(b)(2)" and inserting in lieu thereof "section 410(b)(3)."

(4) Clause (i) of section 408(k)(3)(B) is amended by striking out "section 410(b)(2)" and inserting in lieu thereof "section 410(b)(3)."

(c) EFFECTIVE DATE.—The amendments made by this section shall apply with respect to plan years beginning after December 31, 1980.

EXCERPTS FROM
ECONOMIC RECOVERY TAX ACT OF 1981

Subtitle D—Employee Stock Ownership Provisions

SEC. 331. PAYROLL-BASED CREDIT FOR ESTABLISHING EMPLOYEE STOCK OWNERSHIP PLAN.

(a) IN GENERAL.—Subpart A of part IV of subchapter A of chapter 1 (relating to credits allowed), as amended by section 221 of this Act, is further amended by inserting immediately after section 44F the following new section:

"SEC. 44G. EMPLOYEE STOCK OWNERSHIP CREDIT.

"(a) GENERAL RULE.—

"(1) CREDIT ALLOWED.—In the case of a corporation which elects to have this section apply for the taxable year and which meets the requirements of subsection (c)(1), there is allowed as a credit against the tax imposed by this chapter for the taxable year an amount equal to the amount of the credit determined under paragraph (2) for such taxable year.

"(2) DETERMINATION OF AMOUNT.—

"(A) IN GENERAL.—The amount of the credit determined under this paragraph for the taxable year shall be equal to the lesser of—

"(i) the aggregate value of employer securities transferred by the corporation for the taxable year to a tax credit employee stock ownership plan maintained by the corporation, or

"(ii) the applicable percentage of the amount of the aggregate compensation (within the meaning of section 415(c)(3)) paid or accrued during the taxable year to all employees under a tax credit employee stock ownership plan.

"(B) APPLICABLE PERCENTAGE.—For purposes of applying subparagraph (A)(ii), the applicable percentage shall be determined in accordance with the following table:

"For aggregate compensation paid or accrued during a portion of the taxable year occurring in calendar year:	The applicable percentage is:
1983	0.5
1984	0.5
1985	0.75
1986	0.75
1987	0.75
1988 or thereafter	0

"(b) LIMITATION BASED ON AMOUNT OF TAX.—

"(1) LIABILITY FOR TAX.—

"(A) IN GENERAL.—The credit allowed by subsection (a) for any taxable year shall not exceed an amount equal to the sum of—

"(i) so much of the liability for tax for the taxable year as does not exceed $25,000, plus

"(ii) 90 percent of so much of the liability for tax for the taxable year as exceeds $25,000.

"(B) LIABILITY FOR TAX DEFINED.—For purposes of this paragraph, the term 'liability for tax' means the tax imposed by this chapter for the taxable year, reduced by the sum of the credits allowed under a section of this subpart having a lower number designation than this section, other

than credits allowable by sections 31, 39, and 43. For purposes of the preceding sentence, the term 'tax imposed by this chapter' shall not include any tax treated as not imposed by this chapter under the last sentence of section 53(a).

"(C) CONTROLLED GROUPS.—In the case of a controlled group of corporations, the $25,000 amount specified in subparagraph (A) shall be reduced for each component member of such group by apportioning $25,000 among the component members of such group in such manner as the Secretary shall by regulations prescribe. For purposes of the preceding sentence, the term 'controlled group of corporations' has the meaning assigned to such term by section 1563(a) (determined without regard to subsections (a)(4) and (e)(3)(C) of such section).

"(2) CARRYBACK AND CARRYOVER OF UNUSED CREDIT.—

"(A) ALLOWANCE OF CREDIT.—If the amount of the credit determined under this section for any taxable year exceeds the limitation provided under paragraph (1)(A) for such taxable year (hereinafter in this paragraph referred to as the 'unused credit year'), such excess shall be—

"(i) an employee stock ownership credit carryback to each of the 3 taxable years preceding the unused credit year, and

"(ii) an employee stock ownership credit carryover to each of the 15 taxable years following the unused credit year,

and shall be added to the amount allowable as a credit by this section for such years. If any portion of such excess is a carryback to a taxable year ending before January 1, 1983, this section shall be deemed to have been in effect for such taxable year for purposes of allowing such carryback as a credit under this section. The entire amount of the unused credit for an unused credit year shall be carried to the earliest of the 18 taxable years to which (by reason of clauses (i) and (ii)) such credit may be carried, and then to each of the other 17 taxable years to the extent that, because of the limitation contained in subparagraph (B), such unused credit may not be added for a prior taxable year to which such unused credit may be carried.

"(B) LIMITATION.—The amount of the unused credit which may be added under subparagraph (A) for any preceding or succeeding taxable year shall not exceed the amount by which the limitation provided under paragraph (1)(A) for such taxable year exceeds the sum of—

"(i) the credit allowable under this section for such taxable year, and

"(ii) the amounts which, by reason of this paragraph, are added to the amount allowable for such taxable year and which are attributable to taxable years preceding the unused credit year.

"(3) CERTAIN REGULATED COMPANIES.—No credit shall be allowed under this section to a taxpayer if—

"(A) the taxpayer's cost of service for ratemaking purposes or in its regulated books of account is reduced by reason of any portion of such credit which results from the transfer of employer securities or cash to a tax credit employee stock ownership plan which meets the requirements of section 409A;

216

"(B) the base to which the taxpayer's rate of return for ratemaking purposes is applied is reduced by reason of any portion of such credit which results from a transfer described in subparagraph (A) to such employee stock ownership plan; or

"(C) any portion of the amount of such credit which results from a transfer described in subparagraph (A) to such employee stock ownership plan is treated for ratemaking purposes in any way other than as though it had been contributed by the taxpayer's common shareholders.

"(c) DEFINITIONS AND SPECIAL RULES.—

"(1) REQUIREMENTS FOR CORPORATION.—A corporation meets the requirements of this paragraph if it—

"(A) establishes a plan—

"(i) which meets the requirements of section 409A, and

"(ii) under which no more than one-third of the employer contributions for the taxable year are allocated to the group of employees consisting of—

"(I) officers,

"(II) shareholders owning more than 10 percent of the employer's stock (within the meaning of section 415(c)(6)(B)(iv)), or

"(III) employees described in section 415(c)(6)(B)(iii), and

"(B) agrees, as a condition for the allowance of the credit allowed by this subsection—

"(i) to make transfers of employer securities to a tax credit employee stock ownership plan maintained by the corporation having an aggregate value of not more than the applicable percentage for the taxable year (determined under subsection (a)(2)) of the amount of the aggregate compensation (within the meaning of section 415(c)(3)) paid or accrued by the corporation during the taxable year, and

"(ii) to make such transfers at the times prescribed in paragraph (2).

"(2) TIMES FOR MAKING TRANSFERS.—The transfers required under paragraph (1)(B) shall be made not later than 30 days after the due date (including extensions) for filing the return for the taxable year.

"(3) ADJUSTMENTS TO CREDIT.—If the credit allowed under this section is reduced by a final determination, the employer may reduce the amount required to be transferred to the tax credit employee stock ownership plan under paragraph (1)(B) for the taxable year in which the final determination occurs or any succeeding taxable year by an amount equal to such reduction to the extent such reduction is not taken into account in any deduction allowed under section 404(i)(2).

"(4) CERTAIN CONTRIBUTIONS OF CASH TREATED AS CONTRIBUTIONS OF EMPLOYER SECURITIES.—For purposes of this section, a transfer of cash shall be treated as a transfer of employer securities if the cash is, under the tax credit employee stock ownership plan, used within 30 days to purchase employer securities.

"(5) DISALLOWANCE OF DEDUCTION.—Except as provided in section 404(i), no deduction shall be allowed under section 162, 212, or 404 for amounts required to be transferred to a tax credit employee stock ownership plan under this section.

"(6) EMPLOYER SECURITIES.—For purposes of this section, the

term 'employer securities' has the meaning given such term in section 409A(1).

"(7) VALUE.—For purposes of this section, the term 'value' means—

"(A) in the case of securities listed on a national exchange, the average of closing prices of such securities for the 20 consecutive trading days immediately preceding the date on which the securities are contributed to the plan, or

"(B) in the case of securities not listed on a national exchange, the fair market value as determined in good faith and in accordance with regulations prescribed by the Secretary.".

(b) DEDUCTIBILITY OF UNUSED PORTIONS OF THE CREDIT.—Section 404 is amended by adding at the end thereof the following new subsection:

"(i) DEDUCTIBILITY OF UNUSED PORTIONS OF EMPLOYEE STOCK OWNERSHIP CREDIT.—

"(1) UNUSED CREDIT CARRYOVERS.—There shall be allowed as a deduction (without regard to any limitations provided under this section) for the last taxable year to which an unused employee stock ownership credit carryover (within the meaning of section 44G(b)(2)(A)) may be carried, an amount equal to the portion of such unused credit carryover which expires at the close of such taxable year.

"(2) REDUCTIONS IN CREDIT.—There shall be allowed as a deduction (subject to the limitations provided under this section) an amount equal to any reduction of the credit allowed under section 44G resulting from a final determination of such credit to the extent such reduction is not taken into account in section 44G(c)(3).".

(c) CONFORMING AMENDMENTS.—

(1) Section 409A (relating to qualifications for tax credit employee stock ownership plans) is amended—

(A) by inserting "or 44G(c)(1)(B)" after "section 48(n)(1)(A)" in subsection (b)(1)(A),

(B) by inserting "or the credit allowed under section 44G (relating to the employee stock ownership credit)" after "basic employee plan credit" in subsection (b)(4),

(C) by inserting "or 44G(c)(1)(B)" after "section 48(n)(1)" in subsection (g),

(D) by inserting "or the credit allowed under section 44G (relating to employee stock ownership credit)" after "employee plan credit" in subsection (g),

(E) by inserting "or 44G(c)(1)(B)" after "section 48(n)(1)" in subsection (i)(1)(A),

(F) by inserting "section 44G(c)(1)(B), or" after "required under" in subsection (m),

(G) by inserting "or employee stock ownership credit" after "employee plan credit" in subsection (n)(2), and

(H) by adding at the end of subsection (n) the following new paragraph:

"(3) For requirements for allowance of an employee stock ownership credit, see section 44G.".

(2) Subsection (c) of section 56 (relating to regular tax deductions defined)·is amended by striking out "and 43" and inserting in lieu thereof "43, and 44G".

(3) Subsection (a) of section 6699 (relating to assessable penalties relating to tax credit employee stock ownership plan) is amended—

218

(A) by inserting "or a credit allowable under section 44G (relating to the employee stock ownership credit)" after "employee plan credit",

(B) by striking out "section 409A, or" in paragraph (1) and inserting in lieu thereof "section 409A with respect to a qualified investment made before January 1, 1983,",

(C) by inserting after paragraph (2) the following new paragraphs:

"(3) fails to satisfy any requirement provided under section 409A with respect to a credit claimed under section 44G in taxable years ending after December 31, 1982, or

"(4) fails to make any contribution which is required under section 44G(c)(1)(B) within the period required for making such contribution,".

(4) Paragraph (2) of section 6699 is amended to read as follows:

"(2) MAXIMUM AND MINIMUM AMOUNT.—

"(A) The amount determined under paragraph (1) with respect to a failure described in paragraph (1) or (2) of subsection (a)—

"(i) shall not exceed the amount of the employee plan credit claimed by the employer to which such failure relates, and

"(ii) shall not be less than the product of one-half of 1 percent of the amount referred to in subparagraph (A), multiplied by the number of months (or parts thereof) during which such failure continues.

"(B) The amount determined under paragraph (1) with respect to a failure described in paragraph (3) or (4) of subsection (a)—

"(i) shall not exceed the amount of the credit claimed by the employer under section 44G to which such failure relates, and

"(ii) shall not be less than the product of one-half of 1 percent of the amount referred to in subparagraph (A), multiplied by the number of months (or parts thereof) during which such failure continues."

(d) TECHNICAL AMENDMENTS RELATED TO CARRYOVER AND CARRYBACK OF CREDITS.—

(1) CARRYOVER OF CREDIT.—

(A) Subparagraph (A) of section 55(c)(4) (relating to credits), as amended by this Act, is amended by inserting "44G(b)(1)," before "53(b)".

(B) Subsection (c) of section 381 (relating to items of the distributor or transferor corporation), as amended by this Act, is amended by adding at the end thereof the following new paragraph:

"(29) CREDIT UNDER SECTION 44G.—The acquiring corporation shall take into account (to the extent proper to carry out the purposes of this section and section 44G, and under such regulations as may be prescribed by the Secretary) the items required to be taken into account for purposes of section 44G in respect of the distributor or transferor corporation."

(C) Section 383 (relating to special limitations on unused investment credits, work incentive program credits, new employee credits, alcohol fuel credits, foreign taxes, and capital losses), as in effect for taxable years beginning with and after the first taxable year to which the amendments made by the Tax Reform Act of 1976 apply, is amended—

(i) by inserting "to any unused credit of the corpora-tion under section 44G(b)(2)," after "44F(g)(2),", and

(ii) by inserting "EMPLOYEE STOCK OWNERSHIP CRED-ITS," after "RESEARCH CREDITS," in the section heading.

(D) Section 383 (as in effect on the day before the date of the enactment of the Tax Reform Act of 1976) is amended—

(i) by inserting "to any unused credit of the corpora-tion which could otherwise be carried forward under section 44G(b)(2)," after "44F(g)(2),", and

(ii) by inserting "EMPLOYEE STOCK OWNERSHIP CRED-ITS," after "RESEARCH CREDITS," in the section heading.

(E) The Table of sections for part V of subchapter C of chapter 1 is amended by inserting "employee stock owner-ship credits," after "research credits," in the item relating to section 383.

(2) CARRYBACK OF CREDIT.—

(A) Subparagraph (C) of section 6511(d)(4) (defining credit carryback), as amended by this Act, is amended by striking out "and research credit carryback" and inserting in lieu thereof "research credit carryback, and employee stock own-ership credit carryback".

(B) Section 6411 (relating to quick refunds in respect of tentative carryback adjustments), as amended by this Act, is amended—

(i) by striking out "or unused research credit" each place it appears and inserting in lieu thereof "unused research credit, or unused employee stock ownership credit";

(ii) by inserting "by an employee stock ownership credit carryback provided by section 44G(b)(2)" after "by a research and experimental credit carryback pro-vided in section 44F(g)(2), in the first sentence of sub-section (a);

(iii) by striking out "or a research credit carryback from" each place it appears and inserting in lieu there-of "a research credit carryback, or employee stock own-ership credit carryback from"; and

(iv) by striking out "new employee credit carryback)" in the second sentence of subsection (a) and inserting in lieu thereof "new employee credit carryback, or, in the case of an employee stock ownership credit carryback, to an investment credit carryback, a new employee credit carryback or a research and experimental credit carryback)".

(e) OTHER TECHNICAL AND CLERICAL AMENDMENTS.—

(1) Subsection (b) of section 6096 (relating to designation of income tax payments to Presidential Election Campaign Fund), as amended by this Act, is amended by striking out "and 44F" and inserting in lieu thereof "44F, and 44G".

(2) The table of sections for subpart A of part IV of sub-chapter A of chapter 1 is amended by inserting after the item relating to section 44F the following new item:

"Sec. 44G. Employee stock ownership credit."

(f) EFFECTIVE DATE.—

(1) The amendments made by subsection (a) shall apply to ag-gregate compensation (within the meaning of section 415(c)(3) of the Internal Revenue Code of 1954), paid or accrued after De-cember 31, 1982, in taxable years ending after such date.

220

(2) The amendments made by subsections (b) and (c) shall apply to taxable years ending after December 31, 1982.

SEC. 332. TERMINATION OF THE PORTION OF THE INVESTMENT CREDIT AT-TRIBUTABLE TO EMPLOYEE PLAN PERCENTAGE.

(a) IN GENERAL.—Subparagraph (E) of section 46(a)(2) (relating to employee plan percentage) is amended—

(1) by striking out "December 31, 1983" in clauses (i) and (ii) and inserting in lieu thereof "December 31, 1982",

(2) by striking out "and" at the end of clause (i),

(3) by striking out the period at the end of clause (ii) and inserting in lieu thereof ", and", and

(4) by inserting after clause (ii) the following new clause:

"(iii) with respect to any period·beginning after December 31, 1982, zero.".

(b) TECHNICAL AMENDMENT.—Clause (i) of section 48(n)(1)(A) (relating to requirements for allowance of employee plan percentage) is amended by striking out "equal to" and inserting in lieu thereof "which does not exceed".

(c) EFFECTIVE DATES.—

(1) The amendments made by subsection (a) shall be effective on the date of enactment of this Act.

(2) The amendment made by subsection (b) shall apply to qualified investments made after December 31, 1981.

SEC. 333. TAX TREATMENT OF CONTRIBUTIONS ATTRIBUTABLE TO PRINCI-PAL AND INTEREST PAYMENTS IN CONNECTION WITH AN EM-PLOYEE STOCK OWNERSHIP PLAN.

(a) DEDUCTIBILITY.—Section 404(a) (relating to deductions for employer contributions to an employees' trust) is amended by adding at the end thereof the following new paragraph:

"(10) CERTAIN CONTRIBUTIONS TO EMPLOYEE STOCK OWNER-SHIP PLANS.—

"(A) PRINCIPAL PAYMENTS.—Notwithstanding the provi-sions of paragraphs (3) and (7), if contributions are paid into a trust which forms a part of an employee stock owner-ship plan (as described in section 4975(e)(7)), and such con-tributions are, on or before the time prescribed in para-graph (6), applied by the plan to the repayment of the prin-cipal of a loan incurred for the purpose of acquiring quali-fying employer securities (as described in section 4975(e)(8)), such contributions shall be deductible under this para-graph for the taxable year determined under paragraph (6). The amount deductible under this paragraph shall not, however, exceed 25 percent of the compensation otherwise paid or accrued during the taxable year to the employees under such employee stock ownership plan. Any amount paid into such trust in any taxable year in excess of the amount deductible under this paragraph shall be deduct-ible in the succeeding taxable years in order of time to the extent of the difference between the amount paid and de-ductible in each such succeeding year and the maximum amount deductible for such year under the preceding sen-tence.

"(B) INTEREST PAYMENT.—Notwithstanding the provi-sions of paragraphs (3) and (7), if contributions are made to an employee stock ownership plan (described in subpara-graph (A)) and such contributions are applied by the plan to the repayment of interest on a loan incurred for the pur-pose of acquiring qualifying employer securities (as de-scribed in subparagraph (A)), such contributions shall be

deductible for the taxable year with respect to which such contributions are made as determined under paragraph (6).".

(b) EXCLUSION FROM LIMITATION ON ANNUAL ADDITIONS.—

(1) IN GENERAL.—Section 415(c)(6) (relating to limitations on benefits and contributions made under qualified plans) is amended by adding at the end thereof the following new subparagraph:

"(C) In the case of an employee stock ownership plan (as described in section 4975(e)(7)), under which no more than one-third of the employer contributions for a year which are deductible under paragraph (10) of section 404(a) are allocated to the group of employees consisting of officers, shareholders owning more than 10 percent of the employer's stock (determined under subparagraph (B)(iv)), or employees described in subparagraph (B)(iii), the limitations imposed by this section shall not apply to—

"(i) forfeitures of employer securities under an employee stock ownership plan (as described in section 4975(e)(7)) if such securities were acquired with the proceeds of a loan (as described in section 404(a)(10)(A)), or

"(ii) employer contributions to such an employee stock ownership plan which are deductible under section 404(a)(10)(B) and charged against the participant's account.".

(2) EFFECTIVE DATE.—The amendment made by this subsection shall apply to years beginning after December 31, 1981.

SEC. 334. CASH DISTRIBUTIONS FROM AN EMPLOYEE STOCK OWNERSHIP PLAN.

Section 409A(h)(2) (relating to right to demand employer securities) is amended—

(1) by adding at the end thereof the following new sentence: "In the case of an employer whose charter or bylaws restrict the ownership of substantially all outstanding employer securities to employees or to a trust described in section 401(a), a plan which otherwise meets the requirements of this subsection or section 4975(e)(7) shall not be considered to have failed to meet the requirements of section 401(a) merely because it does not permit a participant to exercise the right described in paragraph (1)(A) if such plan provides that participants entitled to a distribution from the plan shall have a right to receive such distribution in cash."; and

(2) by striking out "this section" in the first sentence thereof and inserting in lieu thereof "this subsection".

SEC. 335. PUT OPTION FOR STOCK BONUS PLANS.

Section 401(a)(23) (relating to cash distribution option for stock bonus plans) is amended by striking out "409A(h)(2)" and inserting in lieu thereof "409A(h), except that in applying section 409A(h) for purposes of this paragraph, the term 'employer securities' shall include any securities of the employer held by the plan".

SEC. 336. PUT OPTION REQUIREMENTS FOR BANKS; PUT OPTION PERIOD.

Section 409A(h) (relating to put options for employee stock ownership plans) is amended by adding at the end thereof the following new paragraphs:

"(3) SPECIAL RULE FOR BANKS.—In the case of a plan established and maintained by a bank (as defined in section 581) which is prohibited by law from redeeming or purchasing its own securities, the requirements of paragraph (1)(B) shall not apply if the plan provides that participants entitled to a distri-

222

bution from the plan shall have a right to receive a distribution in cash.

"(4) PUT OPTION PERIOD.—An employer shall be deemed to satisfy the requirements of paragraph (1)(B) if it provides a put option for a period of at least 60 days following the date of distribution of stock of the employer and, if the put option is not exercised within such 60-day period, for an additional period of at least 60 days in the following plan year (as provided in regulations promulgated by the Secretary).".

SEC. 337. DISTRIBUTION OF EMPLOYER SECURITIES FROM A TAX CREDIT EMPLOYEE STOCK OWNERSHIP PLAN IN THE CASE OF A SALE OF EMPLOYER ASSETS OR STOCK.

(a) IN GENERAL.—Section 409A(d) (relating to distribution of employer securities) is amended by striking out the last sentence thereof and inserting in lieu thereof the following: "To the extent provided in the plan, the preceding sentence shall not apply in the case of—

"(1) death, disability, or separation from service;

"(2) a transfer of a participant to the employment of an acquiring employer from the employment of the selling corporation in the case of—

"(A) a sale to the acquiring employer of substantially all of the assets used by the selling corporation in a trade or business conducted by the selling corporation, or

"(B) the sale of substantially all of the stock of a subsidiary of the employer, or

"(3) with respect to the stock of a selling corporation, a disposition of such selling corporation's interest in a subsidiary when the participant continues employment with such subsidiary.".

(b) EFFECTIVE DATE.—The amendments made by this section shall apply to distributions described in section 409A(d) of the Internal Revenue Code of 1954 (or any corresponding provision of prior law) made after March 29, 1975.

SEC. 338. PASS THROUGH OF VOTING RIGHTS ON EMPLOYER SECURITIES.

(a) IN GENERAL.—Paragraph (22) of section 401(a) (relating to qualified pension, profit-sharing, and stock bonus plans) is amended to read as follows:

"(22) if a defined contribution plan (other than a profit-sharing plan)—

"(A) is established by an employer whose stock is not publicly traded, and

"(B) after acquiring securities of the employer, more than 10 percent of the total assets of the plan are securities of the employer,

any trust forming part of such plan shall not constitute a qualified trust under this section unless the plan meets the requirements of subsection (e) of section 409A."

(b) EFFECTIVE DATE.—The amendment made by this section shall apply to acquisitions of securities after December 31, 1979.

SEC. 339. EFFECTIVE DATE.

Except as otherwise provided, the amendments made by this subtitle shall apply to taxable years beginning after December 31, 1981.

ESOP Provisions of
the Internal Revenue Code
as Added or Amended by
the Tax Reform Act of 1984

CODE SEC. *41.* EMPLOYEE STOCK OWNERSHIP CREDIT.

(a) GENERAL RULE.—

(1) Amount of Credit.—In the case of a corporation which elects to have this section apply for the taxable year and which meets the requirements of subsection (c)(1), for purposes of section 38, the amount of the employee stock ownership credit determined under this section for the taxable year is an amount equal to the amount of the credit determined under paragraph (2) for such taxable year.

(2) Determination of Amount.—

*   *   *

(B Applicable Percentage.—For purposes of applying subparagraph (A)(ii), the applicable percentage shall be determined in accordance with the following table:

For aggregate compensation paid or accrued during a portion of the taxable year occurring in calendar year:	*The applicable percentage is:*
1983, 1984, 1985, 1986, or 1987	*0.5*
1988 or thereafter	*0.*

(b) CERTAIN UNREGULATED COMPANIES.—No credit attributable to compensation taken into account for the ratemaking purposes involved shall be determined under this section with respect to a taxpayer if—

(1) the taxpayer's cost of service for ratemaking purposes or in its regulated books of account is reduced by reason of any portion of such credit which results from the transfer of employer securities or cash to a tax credit employee stock ownership plan which meets the requirements of section 409;

(2) the base to which the taxpayer's rate of return for ratemaking purposes is applied is reduced by reason of any portion of such credit which results from a transfer described in paragraph (1) to such employee stock ownership plan; or

(3) any portion of the amount of such credit which results from a transfer described in paragraph (1) to such employee stock ownership plan is treated for ratemaking purposes in any way other than as though it had been contributed by the taxpayer's common shareholders.

Under regulations prescribed by the Secretary, rules similar to the rules of paragraphs (4) and (7) of section 46(f) shall apply for purposes of the preceding sentence.

(c) DEFINITIONS AND SPECIAL RULES.—

(1) Requirements for Corporation.—A corporation meets the requirements of this paragraph if it—

(A) establishes a plan—

(i) which meets the requirements of *section 409,* and

*   *   *

(3) Adjustments to Credit.—If *the credit determined under this section* is reduced by a final determination, the employer may reduce the amount required to be transferred to the tax credit employee stock ownership plan under paragraph (1)(B) for the taxable year in which the final determination occurs or to any succeeding taxable year by an amount equal to such reduction to the extent such reduction is not taken into account in any deduction allowed under section 404(i)(2).

*   *   *

(6) Employer Securities.—For purposes of this section, the term "employer securities" has the meaning given such term in *section 409(l).*

*   *   *

CODE SEC. 116. PARTIAL EXCLUSION OF DIVIDENDS RECEIVED BY INDIVIDUALS.

*   *   *

(e) DIVIDENDS FROM EMPLOYEE STOCK OWNERSHIP PLANS.—Subsection (a) shall not apply to any dividend described in section 404(k).

227

CODE SEC. 133. INTEREST ON CERTAIN LOANS USED TO ACQUIRE EMPLOYER SECURITIES.

(a) IN GENERAL.—Gross income does not include 50 percent of the interest received by—

(1) a bank (within the meaning of section 581),

(2) an insurance company to which subchapter L applies, or

(3) a corporation actively engaged in the business of lending money,
with respect to a securities acquisition loan.

(b) SECURITIES ACQUISITION LOAN.—

(1) In General.—For purposes of this section, the term "securities acquisition loan" means any loan to a corporation, or to an employee stock ownership plan, to the extent that the proceeds are used to acquire employer securities (within the meaning of section 409(l)) for the plan.

(2) Loans Between Related Persons.—The term "securities acquisition loan" shall not include—

(A) any loan made between corporations which are members of the same controlled group of corporations, or

(B) any loan made between an employee stock ownership plan and any person that is—

(i) the employer of any employees who are covered by the plan; or

(ii) a member of a controlled group of corporations which includes such employer.

(3) Controlled Group of Corporations.—For purposes of this paragraph, the term "controlled group of corporations" has the meaning given such term by section 409(l)(4).

(c) EMPLOYEE STOCK OWNERSHIP PLAN.—For purposes of this section, the term "employee stock ownership plan" has the meaning given to such term by section 4975(e)(7).

CODE SEC. 404. DEDUCTION FOR CONTRIBUTIONS OF AN EMPLOYER TO AN EMPLOYEES' TRUST OR ANNUITY PLAN AND COMPENSATION UNDER A DEFERRED-PAYMENT PLAN.

(a) GENERAL RULE.—* * *

(9) Certain Contributions to Employee Stock Ownership Plans.—

* * *

(i) DEDUCTIBILITY OF UNUSED PORTIONS OF EMPLOYEE STOCK OWNERSHIP CREDIT.—
(1) Unused Credit Carryovers.—If any portion of the employee stock ownership credit determined under section 41 for any taxable year has not, after the application of section 38(c), been allowed under section 38 for any taxable year, such portion shall be allowed as a deduction (without regard to any limitations provided under this section) for the last taxable year to which such portion could have been allowed as a credit under section 39.

(2) Reductions in Credit.—There shall be allowed as a deduction (subject to the limitations provided under this section) an amount equal to any reduction of the credit allowed under section 41 resulting from a final determination of such credit to the extent such reduction is not taken into account under section 41(c)(3).

(j) SPECIAL RULES RELATING TO APPLICATION WITH SECTION 415.—

* * *

(k) DIVIDENDS PAID DEDUCTIONS.—In addition to the deductions provided under subsection (a), there shall be allowed as a deduction to a corporation the amount of any dividend paid in cash by such corporation during the taxable year with respect to the stock of such corporation if—
(1) such stock is held on the record date for the dividend by a tax credit employee stock ownership plan (as defined in section 409) or an employee stock ownership plan (as defined in section 4975(e)(7)) which is maintained by such corporation or by any other corporation that is a member of a controlled group of corporations (within the meaning of section 409(1)(4)) that includes such corporation, and

(2) in accordance with the plan provisions—

(A) the dividend is paid in cash to the participants in the plan, or

(B) the dividend is paid to the plan and is distributed in cash to participants in the plan not later than 90 days after the close of the plan year in which paid.

CODE SEC. 1016. ADJUSTMENTS TO BASIS.

(a) GENERAL RULE.—Proper adjustment in respect of the property shall in all cases be made—

* * *

(27) in the case of qualified replacement property, the acquisition of which resulted under section 1042 in the nonrecognition of any part of the gain realized on the sale or exchange of any property, to the extent provided in section 1042(c).

(b) SUBSTITUTED BASIS.—Whenever it appears that the basis of property in the hands of the taxpayer is a substituted basis, then the adjustments provided in subsection (a) shall be made after first making in respect of such substituted basis proper adjustments of a similar nature in respect of the period during which the property was held by the transferor, donor, or grantor, or during which the other property was held by the person for whom the basis is to be determined. A similar rule shall be applied in the case of a series of substituted bases.

* * *

CODE SEC. 1042. SALES OF STOCK TO STOCK OWNERSHIP PLANS OR CERTAIN COOPERATIVES.

(a) NONRECOGNITION OF GAIN.—If—

(1) the taxpayer elects the application of this section with respect to any sale of qualified securities,

(2) the taxpayer purchases qualified replacement property within the replacement period, and

(3) the requirements of subsection (b) are met with respect to such sale, then the gain (if any) on such sale shall be recognized only to the extent that the amount realized on such sale exceeds the cost to the taxpayer of such qualified replacement property.

(b) REQUIREMENTS TO QUALIFY FOR NONRECOGNITION.—A sale of qualified securities meets the requirements of this subsection if—

(1) Sale of Employee Organizations.—The qualified securities are sold to—

(A) an employee stock ownership plan (as defined in section 4975(e)(7)), or

(B) an eligible worker-owned cooperative.

(2) Employees Must Own 30 Percent of Stock After Sale.—The plan or cooperative referred to in paragraph (1) owns, immediately after the sale, at least 30 percent of the total value of the employer securities (within the meaning of section 409(l)) outstanding as of such time.

(3) Plan Maintained for Benefit of Employees.—No portion of the assets of the plan or cooperative attributable to employer securities (within the meaning of section 409(l)) acquire by the plan or cooperative described in paragraph (1) accrue under such plan, or are allocated by such cooperative, for the benefit of—

(A) the taxpayer,

(B) any person who is a member of the family of the taxpayer (within the meaning of section 267(c)(4)), or

(C) any other person who owns (after application of section 318(a)) more than 25 percent in value of any class of outstanding employer securities.

(4) Written Statement Required.—

(A) In General.—The taxpayer files with the Secretary the written statement described in subparagraph (B).

(B) Statement.—A statement is described in this subparagraph if it is a verified written statement of—

(i) the employer whose employees are covered by the plan described in paragraph (l), or

(ii) any authorized officer of the cooperative described in paragraph (l), consenting to the application of section 4978(a) with respect to such employer or cooperative.

(c) DEFINITIONS; SPECIAL RULES.—For purposes of this section.-

(1) Qualified Securities.—The term "qualified securities" means employer securities (as defined in section 409(l)) which—

(A) are issued by a domestic corporation that has no securities outstanding that are readily tradable on an established securities market,

(B) at the time of the sale described in subsection (a)(1), have been held by the taxpayer for more than 1 year, and

(C) were not received by the taxpayer in—

(i) a distribution from a plan described in section 401(a), or

(ii) a transfer pursuant to an option or other right to acquire stock to which section 83, 422, 422A, 423, or 424 applies.

(2) Eligible Worker-Owned Cooperative.—The term "eligible worker-owned cooperative" means any organization—

(A) to which part I of subchapter T applies,

(B) a majority of the membership of which is composed of employees of such organization,

(C) a majority of the voting stock of which is owned by members,

(D) a majority of the board of directors of which is elected by the members on the basis of 1 person 1 vote, and

(E) a majority of the allocated earnings and losses of which are allocated to members on the basis of—

(i) patronage,

(ii) capital contributions, or

(iii) some combination of clauses (i) and (ii).

(3) Replacement Period.—The term "replacement period" means the period which begins 3 months before the date on which the sale of qualified securities occurs and which ends 12 months after the date of such sale.

(4) Qualified Replacement Property.—The term "qualified replacement property" means any securities (as defined in section 165(g)(2)) issued by a domestic corporation which does not, for the taxable year in which such stock is issued, have passive investment income (as defined in section 1362(d)(3)(D)) that exceeds 25 percent of the gross receipts of such corporation for such taxable year.

(5) Securities Acquired by Underwriter.—No acquisition of securities by an underwriter in the ordinary course of his trade or business as an underwriter, whether or not guaranteed, shall be treated as a sale for purposes of subsection (a).

(6) Time for Filing Election.—An election under subsection (a) shall be filed not later than the last day prescribed by law (including extensions thereof) for filing the return of tax imposed by this chapter for the taxable year in which the sale occurs.

(d) BASIS OF QUALIFIED REPLACEMENT PROPERTY.—The basis of the taxpayer in qualified replacement property purchased by the taxpayer during the replacement period shall be reduced by the amount of gain not recognized by reason of such purchase and the application of subsection (a). If more than one item of qualified replacement property is purchased, the basis of each of such items shall be reduced by an amount determined by multiplying the total gain not recognized by reason of such purchase and the application of subsection (a) by a fraction—

(1) the numerator of which is the cost of such item of property, and

(2) the denominator of which is the total cost of all such items of property.

(e) STATUTE OF LIMITATIONS.—If any gain is realized by the taxpayer on the sale or exchange of any qualified securities and there is in effect an election under subsection (a) with respect to such gain, then—

(1) the statutory period for the assessment of any deficiency with respect to such gain shall not expire before the expiration of 3 years from the date the Secretary is notified by the taxpayer (in such manner as the Secretary may by regulations prescribe) of—

(A) the taxpayer's cost of purchasing qualified replacement property which the taxpayer claims results in nonrecognition of any part of such gain,

(B) the taxpayer's intention not to purchase qualified replacement property within the replacement period, or

(C) a failure to make such purchase within the replacement period, and

(2) such deficiency may be assessed before the expiration of such 3-year period notwithstanding the provisions of any other law or rule of law which would otherwise prevent such assessment.

CODE SEC. 1223. HOLDING PERIOD OF PROPERTY.

For purposes of this subtitle—

* * *

(13) In determining the period for which the taxpayer has held qualified replacement property within the meaning of section 1042(b)) the acquisition of which resulted under section 1042 in the nonrecognition of any part of the gain realized on the sale of qualified securities (within the meaning of section 1042(b)), there shall be included the period for which such qualified securities had been held by the taxpayer.

(14) Cross References.—

(A) For special holding period provision relating to certain partnership distributions, see section 735(b).

(B) For special holding period provision relating to distributions of appreciated property to corporations, see section 301(e).

CODE SEC. 2210. LIABILITY FOR PAYMENT IN CASE OF TRANSFER OF EMPLOYER SECURITIES TO AN EMPLOYEE STOCK OWNERSHIP PLAN OR A WORKER-OWNED COOPERATIVE.

(a) IN GENERAL.—If—

(1) employer securities—

(A) are acquired from the decedent by an employee stock ownership plan or by an eligible worker-owned cooperative from any decedent,

(B) pass from the decedent to such a plan or cooperative, or

(C) are transferred by the executor to such a plan or cooperative, and

(2) the executor elects the application of this section and files the agreements described in subsection (e) before the due date (including extensions) for filing the return of tax imposed by section 2001,

then the executor is relieved of liability for payment of that portion of the tax imposed by section 2001 which such employee stock ownership plan or cooperative is required to pay under subsection (b).

(b) PAYMENT OF TAX BY EMPLOYEE STOCK OWNERSHIP PLAN OR COOPERATIVE.—

(1) In General.—An employee stock ownership plan or eligible worker-owned cooperative—

(A) which has acquired employer securities from the decedent, or to which such securities have passed from the decedent or been transferred by the executor, and

(B) with respect to which an agreement described in subsection (e)(1) is in effect, shall pay that portion of the tax imposed by section 2001 with respect to the taxable estate of the decedent which is described in paragraph (2).

(2) Amount of Tax to Be Paid.—The portion of the tax imposed by section 2001 with respect to the taxable estate of the decedent that is referred to in paragrah (1) is equal to the lesser of—

(A) the value of the employer securities described in subsection (a)(1) which is included in the gross estate of the decedent, or

(B) the tax imposed by section 2001 with respect to such taxable estate reduced by the sum of the credits allowable against such tax.

(c) INSTALLMENT PAYMENTS.—

(1) In General.—If—

(A) the executor of the estate of the decedent (without regard to this section) elects to have the provisions of section 6166 (relating to extensions of time for payment of estate tax where estate consists largely of interest in closely held business) apply to payment of that portion of the tax imposed by section 2001 wih respect to such estate which is attributable to employer securities, and

(B) the plan administrator or the cooperative provides to the executor the agreement described in subsection (e)(1),

then the plan administrator or the cooperative may elect, before the due date (including extensions) for filing the return of such tax, to pay all or part of the tax described in subsection (b)(2) in installments under the provisions of section 6166.

(2) Interest on Installments.—In determining the 4-percent portion for purposes of section 6601(j)—

    (A) the portion of the tax imposed by section 2001 with respect to an estate for which the executor is liable, and

    (B) the portion of such tax which an employer stock ownership plan or an eligible worker-owned cooperative is liable,

shall be aggregated.

(d) GUARANTEE OF PAYMENTS.—Any employer—

(1) whose employees are covered by an employee stock ownership plan, and

(2) who has entered into an agreement described in subsection (e)(2) which is in effect, shall guarantee (in such manner as the Secretary may prescribe) the payment of any amount such plan is required to pay under subsection (b), including any interest payable under section 6601 which is attributable to such amount.

(e) AGREEMENTS.—The agreements described in this subsection are as follows:

(1) A written agreement signed by the plan administrator, or by an authorized officer of the eligible worker-owned cooperative, consenting to the application of subsection (b) to such plan or cooperative.

(2) A written agreement signed by the employer whose employees are covered by the plan described in subsection (b) consenting to the application of subsection (d).

(f) EXEMPTION FROM TAX ON PROHIBITED TRANSACTIONS.—The assumption under this section by an employee stock ownership plan of any portion of the liability for the tax imposed by section 2001 shall be treated as a loan described in section 4975(d)(3).

(g) DEFINITIONS.—For purposes of this section—

(1) Employer Securities.—The term "employer securities" has the meaning given such term by section 409(l).

(2) Employee Stock Ownership Plan.—The term "employee stock ownership plan" has the meaning given such term by section 4975(e)(7).

(3) Eligible Worker-Owned Cooperative.—The term "eligible worker-owned cooperative" has the meaning given to such term by section 1041(b)(2).

(4) Plan Administrator.—The term "plan administrator" has the meaning given such term by section 414(g).

CODE SEC. 4978. TAX ON CERTAIN DISPOSITIONS BY EMPLOYEE STOCK OWNERSHIP PLANS AND CERTAIN COOPERATIVES.

(a) TAX ON DISPOSITIONS OF SECURITIES TO WHICH SECTION 1042 APPLIES BEFORE CLOSE OF MINIMUM HOLDING PERIOD. If, during the 3-year period after the date on which the employee stock ownership plan or eligible worker-owned cooperative acquired any qualified securities in a sale to which section 1042 applied, such plan or cooperative disposes of any qualified securities and—

(1) the total number of shares held by such plan or cooperative after such disposition is less than the total number of employer securities held immediately after such sale, or

(2) except to the extent provided in regulations, the value of qualified securities held by such plan or cooperative after such disposition is less than 30 percent of the total value of all employer securities as of such disposition,

there is hereby imposed a tax on the disposition equal to the amount determined under subsection (b).

(b) AMOUNT OF TAX.—

(1) In General.—The amount of the tax imposed by paragraph (1) shall be equal to 10 percent of the amount realized on the disposition.

(2) Limitation.—The amount realized taken into account under paragraph (1) shall not exceed that portion allocable to qualified securities acquired in the sale to which section 1042 applied (determined as if such securities were disposed of before any other securities).

(3) Distributions to Employees.—The amount realized on any distribution to an employee for less than fair market value shall be determined as if the qualified security had been sold to the employee at fair market value.

(c) LIABILITY FOR PAYMENT OF TAXES.—The tax imposed by this subsection shall be paid by—

(1) the employer, or

(2) the eligible worker-owned cooperative, that made the written statement described in section 1042(a)(2)(B).

(d) SECTION NOT TO APPLY TO CERTAIN DISPOSITIONS.—

(1) Certain Distributions to Employees.—This section shall not apply with respect to any distribution of qualified securities (or sale of such securities) which is made by reason of—

(A) the death of the employee,

(B) the retirement of the employee after the employee has attained 59½ years of age,

(C) the disability of the employee (within the meaning of section 72(m)(5)), or

(D) the separation of the employee from service for any period which results in a 1-year break in service (within the meaning of section 411(a)(6)(A)).

(2) Certain Reorganizations.—In the case of any exchange of qualified securities in any reorganization described in section 368(a)(1) for stock of another corporation, such exchange shall not be treated as a disposition for purposes of this section.

(e) DEFINITIONS AND SPECIAL RULES.—For purposes of this section—

(1) Employee Stock Ownership Plan.—The term "employee stock ownership plan" has the meaning given to such term by section 4975(e)(7).

(2) Qualified Securities.—The term "qualified securities" has the meaning given to such term by section 1042(b)(1).

(3) Eligible Worker-Owned Cooperative.—The term "eligible worker-owned cooperative" has the meaning given to such term by section 1042(b)(1).

(4) Disposition.—The term "disposition" includes any distribution.

(5) Employer Securities.—The term "employer securities" has the meaning given to such term by section 409(l).

CODE SEC. 6018. ESTATE TAX RETURNS.

*   *   *

(c) ELECTION UNDER SECTION 2210.—In all cases in which subsection (a) requires the filing of a return, if an executor elects the applications of section 2210—

(1) Return by Executor.—The return which the executor is required to file under the provisions of subsection (a) shall be made with respect to that portion of estate tax imposed by subtitle B which the executor is required to pay.

(2) Return by Plan Administrator.—The plan administrator of an employee stock ownership plan or the eligible worker-owned cooperative, as the case may be, shall make a return with respect to that portion of the tax imposed by section 2001 which such plan or cooperative is required to pay under section 2210(b).

Original Plan Adoption
or Amendment

Forms required for submission to IRS for procuring a Letter of Determination in connection with the original implementation of an ESOP and for amendments.

Form **SS-4**

(Rev. 9–82)
Department of the Treasury
Internal Revenue Service

Application for Employer Identification Number

**(For use by employers and others as explained in the instructions.
Please read the instructions before completing this form.)
For Paperwork Reduction Act Notice, see page 2.**

OMB No. 1545–0003   Expires 9–30–85

1 Name (True name and not trade name. If partnership, see page 4.)	**2** Social security no., if sole proprietor	**3** Ending month of accounting year

4 Trade name, if any, of business (if different from item 1)

5 General partner's name, if partnership; principal officer's name, if corporation; or grantor's name, if trust

6 Address of principal place of business (Number and street)

7 Mailing address, if different

8 City, State, and ZIP code

9 County of principal business location

10 Type of organization
☐ Individual ☐ Trust ☐ Partnership ☐ Other (specify)
☐ Governmental ☐ Nonprofit organization ☐ Corporation

11 Date you acquired or started this business (Mo., day, year)

12 Reason for applying
☐ Started new business ☐ Purchased going business ☐ Other (specify)

13 First date you paid or will pay wages for this business (Mo., day, year)

14 Nature of principal business activity (See instructions on page 4.)

15 Do you operate more than one place of business?   ☐ Yes ☐ No

16 Peak number of employees expected in next 12 months (If none, enter "0") ▶
Nonagricultural	Agricultural	Household

17 If nature of business is manufacturing, state principal product and raw material used.

18 To whom do you sell most of your products or services?
☐ Business establishments (wholesale) ☐ General public (retail) ☐ Other (specify)

19 Have you ever applied for an identification number for this or any other business? ☐ Yes ☐ No

If "Yes," enter name and trade name. Also enter approx. date, ▶ city, and State where you applied and previous number if known.

Under penalties of perjury, I declare that I have examined this application, and to the best of my knowledge and belief it is true, correct, and complete.

Signature and Title ▶   Date ▶

Telephone number (include area code)

Please leave blank ▶	Geo.	Ind.	Class	Size	Reas. for appl.	**Part I**

237

General Instructions

Paperwork Reduction Act Notice.—We ask for this information to carry out the Internal Revenue laws of the United States. We need it to ensure that you are complying with these laws. You are required to give us this information.

Purpose.—Use this form to apply for an employer identification number (EIN). Return both parts of this form to the Internal Revenue Service. You will receive your EIN in the mail.

Who must file.—You must file this form if you have not obtained an EIN before and:

(a) You pay wages to one or more employees; or

(b) You are required to have an EIN to use on any return, statement, or other document, even if you are not an employer.

Trusts, estates, corporations, partnerships, or nonprofit organizations (churches, clubs, etc.) must use EINs even if they have no employees.

Individuals who file Schedules C or F (Form 1040) must use EINs if they are required to file excise, employment, or alcohol, tobacco, or firearms returns.

File only one Form SS–4, regardless of the number of businesses operated or the number of trade names a business operates under. However, each corporation of an affiliated group must file a separate application.

If you have become the new owner of an existing business, you cannot use the EIN of the old owner. If you already have an EIN, use that number. If you do not have an EIN, apply for one on this form.

If you have incorporated a sole proprietorship or formed a partnership, you must get a new EIN for the corporation or partnership.

If you do not have a number by the time a return is due, write "Applied for" and the date you applied in the space shown for the number. If you do not have a number by the time a tax deposit is due, send your payment to the Internal Revenue Service Center where you file your returns. Make it payable to IRS and show on it your name (as shown on Form SS–4), address, kind of tax, period covered, and date you applied for an EIN.

For more information about EINs, see Publication 583, Information for Business Taxpayers.

When to file.—File early enough to allow time for us to process Form SS–4 and send you an EIN before you need the number for a return or deposit. (If possible, file 4 weeks before you will need the number.) See "Where to file" on page 4.

Specific Instructions

Most lines on this form are self-explanatory. The instructions that follow are for those lines that may not be.

Lines 1, 2, 4, and 5.

Sole proprietors.—On line 1, enter your first name, middle initial, and last name. On line 2, enter your social security number and, if you have a trade name for business purposes, enter it on line 4.

Partnerships.—On line 1, enter the legal name of the partnership as it appears in the partnership agreement. On line 4, enter the trade name, if any, and on line 5, enter the first name, middle initial, and last name of a general partner. A general partner should sign this form.

Corporations.—On line 1, enter the corporate name as set forth in the corporation's charter or other legal document creating it. On line 4, enter the trade name, if any, and on line 5, enter the first name, middle initial, and last name of a principal officer. A principal officer should sign this form.

Trusts.—On line 1, enter the name of the trust. On line 4, enter the name of the trustee and on line 5, enter the first name, middle initial, and last name of the grantor. The trustee should sign this form. (See the instruction for line 11.)

Estates of a decedent, insolvent, etc.—On line 1, enter the name of the estate. On line 4, enter the first name, middle initial, and last name of the administrator or other fiduciary. The administrator or other fiduciary should sign this form. (See the instruction for line 11.)

Line 3.—If you have not yet established an accounting year, write "not established" on line 3 and notify your IRS Service Center when you establish an accounting year. (Be sure to include your employer identification number when you write.)

Line 10.—Note the following before you check:

Governmental.—This box is for an organization that is a State, county, school district, municipality, etc., or one that is related to such entities, such as a county hospital or city library.

Nonprofit organization (other than governmental).—This box is for religious, charitable, scientific, literary, educational, humane, or fraternal, etc., organizations. Generally, a nonprofit organization must apply to IRS for an exemption from Federal income tax. Details on how to apply are in IRS Publication 557, Tax-Exempt Status for Your Organization.

Line 11.—For trusts, enter the date the trust was legally created.

For estates, enter the date of death of the decedent whose name appears on line 1.

Line 14.—Describe the principal business engaged in. See the examples that follow.

(a) Governmental.—State the type of governmental organization (whether it is a State, county, school district, municipality, etc.) or its relationship to such entities (for example, a county hospital, city library, etc.).

(b) Nonprofit (other than governmental).—State whether it is organized for religious, charitable, scientific, literary, educational, or humane purposes, and state the principal activity (for example, religious organization—hospital; charitable organization—home for the aged; etc.).

(c) Mining and quarrying.—State the process and the principal product (for example, mining bituminous coal, contract drilling for oil, quarrying dimension stone, etc.).

(d) Contract construction.—State whether it is general contracting or special trade contracting, and show the type of work normally performed (for example, general contractor for residential buildings, electrical subcontractor, etc.).

(e) Trade.—State the type of sale and the principal line of goods sold (for example, wholesale dairy products, manufacturer's representative for mining machinery, retail hardware, etc.).

(f) Manufacturing.—State the type of establishment operated (for example, sawmill, vegetable cannery, etc.). On line 17 state the principal product manufactured and the raw material used.

(g) Other activities.—State the exact type of business operated (for example, advertising agency, farm, labor union, real estate agency, steam laundry, rental of coin-operated vending machines, investment club, etc.).

Where to file.—

If your principal business, office or agency, or legal residence in the case of an individual, is located in:	File with the Internal Revenue Service Center at:
New Jersey, New York City and counties of Nassau, Rockland, Suffolk, and Westchester	Holtsville, NY 00501
New York (all other counties), Connecticut, Maine, Massachusetts, New Hampshire, Rhode Island, Vermont	Andover, MA 05501
District of Columbia, Delaware, Maryland, Pennsylvania	Philadelphia, PA 19255
Alabama, Florida, Georgia, Mississippi, South Carolina	Atlanta, GA 31101
Michigan, Ohio	Cincinnati, OH 45999
Arkansas, Kansas, Louisiana, New Mexico, Oklahoma, Texas	Austin, TX 73301
Alaska, Arizona, Colorado, Idaho, Minnesota, Montana, Nebraska, Nevada, North Dakota, Oregon, South Dakota, Utah, Washington, Wyoming	Ogden, UT 84201
Illinois, Iowa, Missouri, Wisconsin	Kansas City, MO 64999
California, Hawaii	Fresno, CA 93888
Indiana, Kentucky, North Carolina, Tennessee, Virginia, West Virginia	Memphis, TN 37501

If you have no legal residence, principal place of business, or principal office or agency in any Internal Revenue district, file your return with the Internal Revenue Service Center, Philadelphia, PA 19255.

Please sign and date this application.

☆ U.S. GOVERNMENT PRINTING OFFICE : 1982—O–363–459

Form **4461**
(December 1968)

Department of the Treasury
Internal Revenue Service

Sponsor Application
Approval of Master or Prototype Plan
(Form of Plan under Section 401(a) of the Internal
Revenue Code and related Trust under Section 501(a) of the Internal Revenue Code)

NOTE: Form 3672 must be used for plans covering self-employed individuals.

1. Approval requested— ☐ Initial ☐ Amendment

2. Name and address (*Including ZIP code*) of sponsoring organization	3. Employer identification number of sponsor

4. Type of organization

☐ Bank ☐ Insurance company ☐ Regulated investment company ☐ Trade or professional association

5. Name and address (*Including ZIP code*) of funding organization, if master plan	6. Employer identification number of organization

7. Form of plan	8. Name of plan
☐ Standardization form plan ☐ Variable form plan	

9. If pension or annuity plan, indicate type of plan

Unit-benefit	Fixed-benefit	Flat-benefit	Money-purchase	Other (*Specify*)
☐	☐	☐	☐	☐

10. If profit-sharing plan, indicate type of contribution formula	11. Is plan indicated in item 9 or 10 integrated with social security
☐ Definite ☐ None	☐ Yes ☐ No

12. Funding medium

☐ Trust ☐ Custodial account ☐ Group annuity contract ☐ Individual contracts ☐ Other (*Specify*)

13. Attach copy of plan, trust agreement, amendments, and related documents unless previously submitted and furnish a brief description of the following provisions and indicate the article or section where such provisions are contained.

Item	Description	Article or Section
Eligibility Requirements (a) Length of service		
(b) Age (*Minimum and maximum*)		
(c) Job class (*Salaried, hourly-paid, etc.*)		
(d) Other:		
Contribution Formula (e) Employer		
(f) Employee: (1) ☐ Required		
(2) ☐ Voluntary		
Allocation Formula		
Benefit Formula (g) Normal retirement		
(h) Early retirement		
(i) Disability retirement		
(j) Death: (1) Before retirement		
(2) After retirement		
(k) Other:		

(*Continued on reverse*)

Under penalties of perjury, I declare that I have examined this application, including accompanying statements, and to the best of my knowledge and belief it is true, correct, and complete.

-------------------------------- -------------------------------- --------------------------------
(Signature) (Title) (Date)

239

Item	Description	Article or Section
Vesting Provisions		
Age and Service Requirement for Benefits		
(l) Normal retirement		
(m) Early retirement		
(n) Disability retirement		
(o) Other:		

14. Indicate the article or section of the plan or trust where the following provisions are contained.

Item	Article or Section	Item	Article or Section
(a) Definition of compensation		(g) Separate administration of each employer's fund	
(b) Provision for amendment		(1) Disposition of forfeitures	
(c) Provision for termination of employer participation		(2) Disposition of dividends and other credits	
(d) Limitation of benefits in event of early termination of pension plan		(3) Exclusion of employer whose plan fails to meet requirements of Sec. 401(a) of the Code	
(e) Nontransferability of annuity contracts		(h) Prohibition against reversion	
(f) Vesting upon termination of plan or upon complete discontinuance of contributions		(i) Annual valuation of assets	

15. Additional Information Required if Trustee is Designated in Item 5

(a) Name of Trust

(b) Month accounting period of trust ends *(Circle one number)*

1   2   3   4   5   6   7   8   9   10   11   12

General Instructions

A. Who may file.—Trade or professional associations, banks, insurance companies, or regulated investment companies.

B. What to file.—This application is to be used for initial approval and amendment of the form of a master or prototype pension, annuity, or profit-sharing plan, that does not include self-employed individuals.

C. Where to file.—Commissioner of Internal Revenue, Washington, D.C. 20224, Attention: T:MS:PT.

D. Type of plan.—A "master plan" is a form of plan in which the funding organization is designated by the sponsor and a "prototype plan" is a form of plan in which the funding organization is designated by the adopting employer. A "standardized form plan" is either a master or prototype plan that is adopted by employers without change. Such a plan must contain restrictive provisions relating to the trustee, coverage, vesting, and contribution formula, if a profit-sharing plan. A "variable form plan" is either a master or prototype plan that permits an employer to select various options such as contributions, benefits, vesting, and employee coverage. The options must be set forth in the body of the plan or in a separate document.

E. Signature.—The application must be signed by either the president, vice-president or other principal officer who is authorized to sign.

Specific Instructions

1. If the request relates to initial approval, check the appropriate box at the top of the form, attach a copy of the plan, trust agreement, and specimen insurance contracts if applicable, and indicate the Article or Section containing the provisions described in Item 13. Give a brief description of the provisions using attachments, if necessary.

2. If the request relates to an amendment of a plan previously approved as to form, complete this application in detail and attach a copy of the amendment and a summary of the changes. If written consent of participating employers is required to amend the plan, attach a statement evidencing their consent.

3. If the request relates to a trusteed master plan, show the name and address of the trustee in Item 5. In addition show the name of the trust and circle in Item 15 the month the accounting period of the trust ends. A custodial account is treated as a trust.

☆ ☆ ☆ ☆ U.S. GOVERNMENT PRINTING OFFICE : 1968—O-322-295

Form 4461 (12–68)

Supplemental Application Form for Approval of Employee Benefit Plans Under TEFRA

▶ **For Paperwork Reduction Act Notice, see the Instructions for Form 5300.**

Caution: *This supplemental application must be submitted with all Form 5300, 5301, 5303, 5307, and 6406 determination requests including requests by adopters of Master or Prototype plans of Self-Employed Individuals.*

1(a) Name of plan sponsor (employer if single employer)	**1(b)** Employer Identification Number
Address (number and street)	
City or town, State and ZIP code	

Answer items 2 through 6 either by checking "N/A" if the item does not apply, or by entering the Article or Section and Page Number of the plan where the provision is found.	N/A	Article or Section and Page Number
2 Does the plan provide for maximum limitation under section 415 as amended by TEFRA?		
3(a) Does the plan provide a method for determining whether it is top-heavy within the meaning of section 416?		
(b) Does the plan contain provisions that become effective automatically if the plan becomes top-heavy?		
(c) If (b) is "Yes," do they include:	/////////	/////////
(I) A vesting provision under section 416(b)?		
(II) A minimum benefit under section 416(c)?		
(III) The compensation limit under section 416(d)?		
(d) Does the plan define the following terms:	/////////	/////////
(I) Key employee?		
(II) Accrued benefit for section 416 purposes?		
(III) Required aggregation group?		
(Iv) Top-heavy group?		
4(a) Are distributions of benefits to key employees who are participants in a top-heay plan required to begin not later than the tax year in which they reach age 70½?		
(b) Are distributions of benefits to employees other than key employees who are participants in a top-heavy plan required to begin not later than the later of the end of the tax year in which they reach age 70½ or retirement?		
(c) Does the plan require the entire interest of the participant to be distributed over the life of the participant, or the participant and the participant's spouse, or over the life expectancy or joint life and last survivor expectancy of the participant and his or her spouse?.		
(d) Does the plan provide that a participant's interest must be distributed within 5 years after the participant's death, or the death of the participant's spouse, if applicable?		
5 If this is an integrated defined contribution plan, does the contribution rate satisfy section 401(l)?		
6 Does the employer receive services from any leased employees within the meaning of section 414(n)?		
If "Yes," are the leased employees included as employees in the employee data given for the plan?		

Reminder: *If this request relates to the adoption of Master or Prototype or field prototype plan, you must attach the latest opinion or notification letter issued to the sponsor. If this request relates to an amendment of an individually designed plan you must attach a copy of the latest determination letter.*

Schedule T (Form 5300) (1-84)

Instructions

(Section references are to the Internal Revenue Code unless otherwise noted.)

Purpose of Form.—Schedule T(Form 5300) is used by applicants for a favorable determination letter on the qualified status of certain retirement plans to provide information under the Tax Equity and Fiscal Responsibility Act of 1982 (TEFRA). It must be attached to Forms 5300, 5301, 5303, 5307, and 6406 in order for those applications to be considered complete.

1(a).—Enter the name, address and EIN of the plan sponsor as shown on the Form 5300, 5301, 5303, 5307, or 6406 to which this schedule is attached.

2.—TEFRA decreased the maximum dollar limitations applicable to qualified defined contribution and defined benefit plans. These new limits apply to limitation years ending after July 1, 1982, for plans not in existence on that date; and apply to limitation years beginning after December 31, 1982, for all other plans. Plans may continue to have "Cost of Living" language even though no adjustments will be made with respect to any calendar year beginning before 1986. See T-1 of Notice 83-10, 1983-1 C.B. 536.

3(a).—A qualified plan must contain some mechanism by which the plan administrator can implement the section 416 minimum requirements if the plan becomes top-heavy. A defined benefit plan is top-heavy when the ratio of the present value of accrued benefits for key employees to the present value of accrued benefits for all employees (including beneficiaries) exceeds 60%. A defined contribution plan is top-heavy when the ratio of accounts for key employees to the accounts for all employees (including beneficiaries but excluding former key employees) exceeds 60%. All distributions that were made during the 5-year period ending on the most recent determination date must be taken into account. Also, employee contributions, whether mandatory or voluntary, must be taken into account except for deductible employee contributions. See section 416.

If the employer maintains other qualified plans (including a Simplified Employee Plan), benefits from all plans in the required aggregation group must be taken into account for determining the top-heavy ratio.

(b).—The plan must contain provisions that are effective in any plan year in which the plan is top-heavy. The con-tributions must satisfy the vesting requirement of section 416(b), the minimum benefit provision of section 416(c), the compensation limits of section 416(d), and the adjustment to section 415 limits in section 416(h). The plan must also preclude any change in the plan's benefit structure (including vesting) resulting from a change in the plan's top-heavy status from violating section 411(a)(10).

Note: *A plan is not required to contain section 416 provisions if the plan contains a single benefit structure that satisfies the requirements of sections 416(b), (c), and (d). Also, collectively-bargained plans with no key employees, or plans that will never have a key employee need not contain top-heavy provisions.*

4(a) and 4(b).—See section 401(a)(9)(A)(i).

4(c) and 4(d).—See section 401(a)(9)(B).

A qualified plan must provide that if an employee dies before the entire distribution has been completed or, if distributions have started to the surviving spouse and the spouse dies before distributions are completed, the entire interest, or the remaining part of the interest if distributions have already started, will be distributed within five years after the employee's death (or the death of the surviving spouse).

5.—The rate of contributions in excess of the integration level may not exceed the rate of contributions below the integration level by more than the applicable tax rate under section 3111(a) at the beginning of the plan year.

6.—Section 414(n) (added by TEFRA section 248) deals with persons who are the employees of an employee leasing organization, but who perform services during the course of their employment for a separate trade or business (a recipient organization). Such leased employees are to be considered employees of the recipient organization at certain times and for certain qualification requirements unless the leasing organization adopts and maintains the type of qualified plan specified in section 414(n).

Section 414(n) provides a safe harbor for a recipient organization if the leasing organization maintains a qualified, nonintegrated, money purchase pension plan that provides for immediate participation, full and immediate vesting, and an annual contribution of 7½% of compensation. If these requirements are met, the leased employee does not have to be counted for any purpose pertaining to the qualified plans of the recipient organization.

☆U.S. Government Printing Office: 1984—421-108/288

Form **5301**	**Application for**	OMB No. 1545–0197

Form 5301
(Rev. Dec. 1982)

Department of the Treasury
Internal Revenue Service

Application for
Determination for Defined Contribution Plan
For Profit-sharing, Stock Bonus and Money Purchase Plans
(Under sections 401(a), 401(k), and 501(a) of the Internal Revenue Code)

OMB No. 1545–0197
Expires 12–31–85

For IRS Use Only
File
folder
number ▶

▶ **Church and Governmental Plans.**—All items need not be completed. See instruction B. "What to File."

CAUTION: *Before submitting this application, be sure that all line items (other than exceptions indicated above) are complete (enter N/A if an item does not apply). Also be sure all information requested in the form or instructions is included, and the application is signed by the employer, plan administrator or authorized representative. Failure to meet these requirements may result in a request for the missing information or return of the application for completion, in which event there will be a delay in processing your application.*

1 (a) Name of plan sponsor (employer if single employer plan)

1 (b) Employer identification no.

Address (number and street)

1 (c) Employer's tax year ends
Month   Day   Year 19

City or town, State and ZIP code

Telephone number
(   )

2 Person to be contacted if more information is needed (If same as 1(a) enter "same as 1(a)"). (See Specific Instructions.)

Name

Telephone number
(   )

Address

3 (a) Determination requested for (check applicable box(es)): See Instruction B. "What to File."
- *(i)* ☐ Initial qualification—Date plan signed _____ Date plan effective _____
- *(ii)* ☐ Amendment after initial qualification—Date amendment signed _____ Date amendment effective _____
- *(iii)* ☐ Affiliated service group status (section 414(m))   Date effective _____
- *(iv)* ☐ Partial termination   Date effective _____

(b) Enter IRS file folder number shown on the last determination letter issued to the plan sponsor _____

(c) Is this application also expected to satisfy the notice requirement for this plan for merger, consolidation, or transfer of plan assets or liabilities involving another plan? See specific instructions . . . . ☐ Yes ☐ No

(d) Were employees who are interested parties given the required notification of the filing of this application? . ☐ Yes ☐ No

(e) Is this plan or trust currently under examination or is any issue related to this plan or trust currently pending before the Internal Revenue Service, the Department of Labor, the Pension Benefit Guaranty Corporation, or any court? . . ☐ Yes ☐ No
If "Yes," attach explanation.

(f) Does your plan contain cash or deferred arrangements described in section 401(k)? . . . . ☐ Yes ☐ No
If "Yes," is a determination also requested on the qualification of those provisions? (See instruction B.) . . ☐ Yes ☐ No

4 (a) Name of plan

(b) Plan number ▶ _____
(c) Plan year ends ▶ _____
(d) Is this a Keogh (H.R. 10) plan? . . . . ☐ Yes ☐ No
(e) If "Yes," is an owner-employee in the plan? ☐ Yes ☐ No

5 Other qualified plans—Enter for each other qualified plan you maintain (do not include plans that were established under union-negotiated agreements that involved other employers):
(a) Name of plan ▶ _____
(b) Type of plan ▶ _____
(c) Rate of employer contribution ▶ _____
(d) Allocation formula ▶ _____
(e) Benefit formula or monthly benefit ▶ _____
(f) Number of participants ▶ _____

6 Type of entity (check only one box):
(a) ☐ Corporation   **(b)** ☐ Subchapter S corporation   **(c)** ☐ Sole proprietor   **(d)** ☐ Partnership
(e) ☐ Tax exempt organization   **(f)** ☐ Church   **(g)** ☐ Governmental organization
(h) ☐ Other (specify) ▶

7 (a) If this is an adoption of a district-approved pattern plan, enter name of the plan ▶

(b) Notification letter no.

8 Type of plan: **(a)** ☐ Profit-sharing   **(b)** ☐ Stock bonus   **(c)** ☐ Money purchase   **(d)** ☐ Target benefit
(e) ☐ Other (specify) ▶

Under penalties of perjury, I declare that I have examined this application, including accompanying statements, and to the best of my knowledge and belief it is true, correct, and complete.

Signature _____   Title _____   Date _____

For Paperwork Reduction Act Notice, see page 1 of the instructions.

363–450–1

(Section references are to the Internal Revenue Code, unless otherwise specified)

Where applicable, indicate the article or section and page number of the plan or trust where the following provisions are contained. If not applicable, enter N/A.

		Section and Page Number

9 (a) General eligibility requirements:
  (i) ☐ All employees *(ii)* ☐ Hourly rate employees only *(iii)* ☐ Salaried employees only
  (iv) ☐ Other (specify) ▶ -------------------
  (v) Length of service (number of years) ▶ -------------------
  (vi) Minimum age (specify) ▶ -------------------
  (vii) Maximum age (specify) ▶ -------------------
(b) Does any plan amendment since the last determination letter change the method of crediting service for eligibility? . . . . ☐ Yes ☐ No

	Yes	No	Not Certain
10 Participation (see specific instructions):			
(a) *(i)* Is the employer a member of an affiliated service group? . . . . If your answer is "No," go to 10(b).	▨	▨	▨
(ii) Did a prior ruling letter rule on what organizations were members of the employer's affiliated service group or did the employer receive a determination letter that considered the effect of section 414(m) on this plan?			
(iii) If (ii) is "Yes," have the facts on which that letter was based materially changed? . . .			
(b) Is the employer a member of a controlled group of corporations or a group of trades or businesses under common control?			

	Number

11 Coverage of plan at (give date) .... (attach Form(s) 5302—see instructions)
(If the employer is a member of an affiliated service group, a controlled group of corporations, or a group of trades or businesses under common control, employees of all members of the group must be considered in completing the following schedule.) If your plan contains cash or deferred arrangements described in section 401(k) see the specific instructions for line 11.

		Number
(a) Total employed (see specific instructions) (include all self-employed individuals)		
(b) Statutory exclusions under this plan (do not count an employee more than once)		
(i) Minimum age or years of service required		
(ii) Employees included in collective bargaining.		
(iii) Other (specify)		
(c) Total statutory exclusions under this plan (add (b)(i) through (iii))		
(d) Employees not excluded under the statute (subtract (c) from (a))		
(e) Other employees ineligible under terms of this plan (Do not count an employee included in (b))		
(f) Employees eligible to participate (subtract (e) from (d))		
(g) Number of employees participating in this plan		
(h) Percent of nonexcluded employees who are participating (divide (g) by (d))	% ▨	
Complete (i) only if (h) is less than 70% and complete (j) only if (i) is 70% or more.		
(i) Percent of nonexcluded employees who are eligible to participate (divide (f) by (d))	%	▨
(j) Percent of eligible employees who are participating (divide (g) by (f))	%	
If (h) and (i) are less than 70% or (j) is less than 80%, see specific instructions and attach schedule of information.	▨	
(k) Total number of participants (include certain retired and terminated employees (see specific instructions)) .		
(l) Has a plan amendment since the last determination letter resulted in exclusion of previously covered employees? ☐ Yes ☐ No		▨

	Yes	No	Section and Page Number
12 Does the plan define the following terms—			
(a) Compensation (earned income if applicable)?			
(b) Break in service?			
(c) Hour of service (under Department of Labor Regulations)?			
(d) Joint and survivor annuity?			
(e) Normal retirement age?			
(f) Year of service?			
(g) Entry date?			
13 (a) Employee contributions:			
(i) Does the plan allow voluntary deductible employee contributions?			
(ii) If "Yes," are the voluntary deductible employee contributions appropriately limited? . .			
(iii) Are voluntary nondeductible contributions limited for all qualified plans to 10% or less of compensation?			
(iv) Are employee contributions nonforfeitable?			

363–450–1

13 *(Continued)*

  (b) Employer contributions:

    (i) Profit-sharing or stock bonus plan contributions are determined under:

      ☐ A definite formula　　　　☐ An indefinite formula　　　☐ Both

    (ii) Profit-sharing or stock bonus plan contributions are limited to:

      ☐ Current earnings　　　　☐ Accumulated earnings　　　☐ Combination

    (iii) Money purchase—Enter rate of contribution ▶ --

    (iv) State target benefit formula, if applicable ▶

	Yes	No	Section and Page Number

14 Integration:

Is this plan integrated with social security or railroad retirement? . . . .

If "Yes" and this is a target benefit plan, attach a schedule of compliance with Rev. Rul. 71–446 (see specific instructions).

15 Vesting:

  (a) Are years of service with other members of a controlled group of corporations, trades, or businesses under common control, or an affiliated service group counted for vesting and eligibility to participate? . . . .

  (b) Are employee's rights to normal retirement benefits nonforfeitable on reaching normal retirement age as defined in section 411(a)(8)? . . . .

  (c) Does any amendment to the plan decrease any participant's accrued benefit? . . . .

  (d) Does any amendment to the plan directly or indirectly affect the computation of the nonforfeitable percentage of a participant's accrued benefit? . . . .

  (e) Does the plan preclude forfeiture of an employee's vested benefits for cause? . . . . . .

  (f) Check the appropriate box to indicate the vesting provisions of the plan:

    (i) ☐ Full and immediate.

    (ii) ☐ Full vesting after 10 years of service; i.e., no vesting for the first 9 years, 100% after 10 years (section 411(a)(2)(A)).

    (iii) ☐ 5- to 15-year vesting (section 411(a)(2)(B)).

    (iv) ☐ Rule of 45 (section 411(a)(2)(C)).

    (v) ☐ 4/40 vesting (Rev. Procs. 75–49 and 76–11).

    (vi) ☐ 10% vesting for each year of service (not to exceed 100%).

    (vii) ☐ 100% vesting within 5 years after contributions are made (class year plans only).

    (viii) ☐ Other (specify—see specific instructions and attach schedule).

16 Administration: **(a)** Type of funding entity:

    (i) ☐ Trust (benefits provided in whole from trust funds)

    (ii) ☐ Custodial account described in section 410(f) and not included in (iv) below

    (iii) ☐ Trust or arrangement providing benefits partially through insurance and/or annuity contracts

    (iv) ☐ Trust or arrangement providing benefits exclusively through insurance and/or annuity contracts

    (v) ☐ Other (specify) ▶ --

	Yes	No

  (b) Does the trust agreement prohibit reversion of funds to the employer? (Rev. Rul. 77–200) . .

  (c) Specify the limits placed on the purchase of insurance contracts, if any:

    (i) Ordinary life ▶ ---

    (ii) Term insurance ▶ ---

    (iii) Other (specify) ▶ ---

  (d) If the trustees may earmark specific investments, including insurance contracts, are such investments subject to the employee's consent, or purchased ratably when employee consent is not required? . . . .

  (e) Are loans to participants limited to their vested interests? . . . .

17 Requirements for benefits—distributions—allocations:

  (a) Normal retirement age is ▶ ---------------

  (b) Early retirement age is ▶ ----------------- Years of service/participation required ▶ ----------------

  (c) Does the plan provide for payment of benefits according to section 401(a)(14)? . . . .

  (d) Distribution of account balances may be made in:

    (i) ☐ Lump sum　　　*(ii)* ☐ Annuity contracts

    (iii) ☐ Substantially equal annual installments—not more than ▶-------------- years

    (iv) ☐ Other (specify) ▶

  (e) If distributions are made in installments, they are credited with:

    (i) ☐ Fund earnings

    (ii) ☐ Interest at a rate of ▶--------------% per year

    (iii) ☐ Other (specify ▶

363–450–2

	Yes	No	Section and Page Number
17 *(Continued):*			
(f) Does the plan comply with the payment of benefits provisions of section 401(a)(11)? . . .			
(g) If this is a stock bonus plan, are distributions made in employer stock?			
(h) If this is a pension plan, does it permit distribution only on death, disability, plan termination, or termination of employment?			
(i) If this is a profit-sharing or stock bonus plan, what other events permit distributions? _____ _____	////	////	
(j) If participants may withdraw their mandatory contributions or earnings, may withdrawal be made without forfeiting vested benefits based on employer contributions?	////	////	
(k) Are contributions allocated on the basis of total compensation? . . . . If "No," see specific instructions and attach schedule.	////	////	
(l) Are forfeitures allocated, in case of a profit-sharing or stock bonus plan, on basis of total compensation? If "No," explain how they are allocated	////	////	
(m) Are trust earnings and losses allocated on the basis of account balances? . . . . If "No," explain how they are allocated.	////	////	
(n) For target benefit or other money purchase plan, are forfeitures applied to reduce employer contributions?	////	////	
(o) Does the plan provide for maximum limitation under section 415?			
(p) Does the plan prohibit the assignment or alienation of benefits?			
(q) Does the plan meet the requirements of section 401(a)(12)?			
(r) Are trust assets valued at fair market value?			
(s) Are trust assets valued at least annually on a specified date? If "No," explain			
18 Termination of plan or trust:	////	////	
(a) Are the participants' rights to benefits under the plan nonforfeitable (to the extent funded) upon termination of partial termination of the plan?	////	////	
(b) Are employees' rights under the plan nonforfeitable on complete discontinuance of contributions under a profit-sharing or stock bonus plan?			
19 This section applies to Keogh (HR. 10) plans only:	////	////	
(a) Do owner-employees have the option to participate?			
(b) Does the plan prohibit distribution of benefits to owner-employees before age 59½, except for disability and plan termination?			
(c) Does the plan prohibit excess contributions for self-employed individuals?			
(d) Are distributions of benefits to owner-employees required to start not later than age 70½? . .			
(e) Are the self-employed individual participants covered only under this plan?			
(f) Does the plan prohibit the allocation of forfeitures to self-employed individuals?			

	Yes	No
20 Plans other than pattern plans:		
a. For a request on initial qualification are the following attached:		
(i) Copies of all instruments constituting the plan?		
(ii) Copies of trust indentures, group annuity contracts, or custodial agreements?		
b. For a request on the effect of an amendment after initial qualification, are the following attached:		
(i) A copy of the plan amendment(s)?		
(ii) A description of the amendment(s) covering the changes to the plan sections?		
(iii) An explanation of the plan sections before the amendment?		
(iv) An explanation of the effect of the amendment(s) on the provisions of the plan sections?		
c. For a request on the qualification of the entire plan as amended after initial qualification, are the following attached:		
(i) A copy of the plan incorporating all amendments made to the date of the application?		
(ii) A statement indicating the copy of the plan is complete in all respects and a determination letter is being requested on the qualification of the entire plan?		
(iii) A copy of trust indentures, group annuity contracts, or custodial agreements, if there has been any change since copies were last furnished to IRS?		
21 Pattern plans (For a notification letter, see Rev. Proc. 76–15 and Information Release 1653):		
a. For adoption of a pattern plan, are the following attached:		
(i) A copy of the notification letter sent to the sponsor or law firm?		
(ii) A certification that the notification letter has not been withdrawn and is still in effect with respect to the plan being submitted, and that such plan has not changed in any way?		
(iii) On initial qualification, a complete plan and trust or custodial account?		
(iv) For an amendment, a description of the amendment and an explanation of the provisions before and after the amendment?		

BEFORE SUBMITTING THIS APPLICATION, SEE THE PROCEDURAL REQUIREMENTS CHECKLIST IN THE SPECIFIC INSTRUCTIONS.

☆U.S. Government Printing Office: 1984–421-108/301   363–450-1

Employee Census

▶ **Attach to application for determination—defined benefit and defined contribution plans.** (Round off to nearest dollar)

OMB No. 1545-0416

This Form is N⸱⸱ ⸱pen to Public Inspection

Schedule of 25 highest paid participating employees for 12-month period ended ▶

Name of employer

Employer identification number

Line no.	Participant's last name and initials (See instructions) (a)	Check		Age (d)	Years of service (e)	Annual Nondeferred Compensation			Employee contributions under the plan (i)	Defined Benefit		Defined Contribution				
		Officer, shareholder or self-employed (b)	Percent of voting stock or business owned (c)			Used in computing benefits or employee's share of contributions (f)	Excluded (g)	Total (h)		Annual benefit expected under this plan (j)	Annual benefit under each other qualified defined benefit plan of deferred compensation (k)	Employer contribution allocated (l)	Number of units, if any (m)	Forfeitures allocated in the year (n)	Amount allocated under each other defined contribution plan of deferred compensation (o)
1															
2															
3															
4															
5															
6															
7															
8															
9															
10															
11															
12															
13															
14															
15															
16															
17															
18															
19															
20															
21															
22															
23															
24															
25															

Total for above . . . .

Totals for all others (specify number ▶ ( )

Total for all participants . . . .

For Paperwork Reduction Act Notice, see back of this form.

See instructions on the back of this form.

Form **5302** (Rev. 11-83)

General Information

(Section references are to the Internal Revenue Code unless otherwise noted specified.)

Paperwork Reduction Act Notice.— We ask for the information to carry out the Internal Revenue laws of the United States. We need it to determine whether taxpayers meet the legal requirements for plan approval. If you want to have your plan approved by IRS, you are required to give us this information.

Purpose of Form.—This schedule is to be used by the Internal Revenue Service in its analysis of an application for determination as to whether a plan of deferred compensation qualifies under section 401(a) and 401(k), if applicable.

Public Inspection.—Section 6104(a)(1)(B) provides, generally, that applications filed for the qualification of a pension, profit-sharing or stock bonus plan, will be open to public inspection. However, section 6104(a)(1)(C) provides that information concerning the compensation of any participant will not be open to public inspection. Consequently, the information contained in this schedule will not be open to public inspection, including inspection by plan participants and other employees of the employer who established the plan.

General Instructions

Prepare the employee census for a current 12-month period. Generally the 12 month period should be the employer's tax year, a calendar year, or the plan year. If the actual information is not available, compensation, contributions, etc., may be projected for a 12-month period. However, such projection must be clearly identified.

Who Must File.—Every employer or plan administrator who files an application for determination for a defined benefit or a defined contribution plan is required to attach this schedule, complete in all details.

For collectively bargained plans a Form 5302 is required only if the plan covers employees of the representative labor union(s) or of any plan(s) for union members, and if so, a separate Form 5302 is required for each such union or plan. For a plan, other than a collectively bargained plan, maintained by more than one employer (where all employers in each affiliated service group, controlled group of corporations, or group of trades or businesses under common control are considered one employer) a separate Form 5302 is required for each such employer.

Specific Instructions

Column (a), first list any participant who at any time during the 5-year period prior to the start of the current 12-month period owned directly or indirectly 10% or more of the voting stock or 10% or more of the business. Next list the remaining participants in order of current compensation (see Note 2 and instructions for column (h)) starting with the highest paid, followed by the next highest paid and so on. If there are fewer than 25 participants, list all the participants. Otherwise, only the first 25 who fall under the priorities listed above need be listed on lines 1 through 25.

Note 1: *For purposes of this form, "participant" means any employee who satisfies the participation requirements prescribed by the plan.*

Column (b), enter a check mark or an "X" to indicate that a participant is either an officer, a shareholder or self-employed. If a participant is none of the above enter N/A in this column for that participant.

Column (c), (i) enter the percentage of voting stock owned by a participant. For example, participant "P" owns 200 shares of voting stock of the employer's 5,000 shares outstanding. The percentage is 4% (200 ÷ 5,000). If a participant owns only nonvoting stock of the employer, make no entry in this column.

(ii) if an unincorporated business enter the percentage of the business owned by the participant.

If a participant owns neither of the above enter N/A.

Column (d), enter the attained age of each participant as of the end of the year for which this schedule applies. For example, if a participant's 47th birthday was on January 7, 1983, and the schedule covers the calendar year 1983, enter 47 for that participant.

Column (e), enter the number of full years of service each participant has been employed by the employer, and any prior employer if such employment is recognized for plan purposes.

Column (f), enter the amount of each participant's compensation that is recognized for plan purposes in computing the benefit (for a defined benefit plan) or in computing the amount of employer contribution that is allocated to the account of each participant (for a defined contribution plan). Do not include any portion of the employer contributions to this or any other qualified plan as compensation for any participant.

Column (g), enter the amount of compensation that is not recognized for

purposes of column (f). For example, if a participant received $12,500 compensation for the year, $1,000 of which was a bonus and the plan does not recognize bonuses for plan purposes, enter $11,500 in column (f) and $1,000 in column (g).

Note 2: *"Compensation" for purposes of column (h) is defined as all amounts (including bonuses and overtime) paid to the participant for services rendered the employer. Do not enter employer contributions made to this or any other qualified plan.*

Column (h), enter the total amount of compensation for the year for each participant. The amount entered in this column will be the sum of the amounts entered in columns (f) and (g) for each participant.

Column (i), enter the total amount of mandatory and voluntary contributions made by each participant. If the plan does not provide for employee contributions of any kind, enter "N/A."

Column (j), enter the amount of benefit each participant may expect to receive at normal retirement age based on current information, assuming no future compensation increases. For example, under a 30% benefit plan, a participant whose benefit is based on annual compensation of $10,000 may expect an annual benefit of $3,000 ($10,000 × 30%) at retirement. In this case enter $3,000.

Column (k), enter the amount of benefit each participant may expect to receive under other qualified defined benefit plan(s) of deferred compensation of the employer.

Column (l), enter the amount of the employer's contribution that is allocated to the account of each participant.

Column (m), enter the number of units, if any, used to determine the amount of the employer contribution that is allocated to each participant.

Column (n), enter the amount of the forfeitures that is allocated to each participant, unless forfeitures are allocated to reduce employer contributions.

Column (o), enter the portion of the employer's contribution that is attributable to the cost for providing each participant's benefits under all defined contribution plans of the employer other than this plan.

Caution: *Before submitting this schedule, be sure that all relevant items are complete. Failure to meet this requirement may result in a request for the missing information or return of the schedule for completion, in which event there will be a delay in processing your application.*

☆U.S. Government Printing Office: 1984—421-108/10040

Form **5307**

(Rev. August 1979)

Department of the Treasury
Internal Revenue Service

Short Form Application for
Determination for Employee Benefit Plan
(Other than Plans that Include Self-employed Individuals)
(Under sections 401(a) and 501(a) of the Internal Revenue Code)

For IRS Use Only

File
folder
number ▶

▶ Please complete every item on this form. If an item does not apply, enter N/A.

1 (a) Name, address and ZIP code of employer

....

....

| Telephone number ▶ ( ) |

(b) Name, address and ZIP code of plan administrator, if other than employer

.. ..

....

| Telephone number ▶ ( ) |

2 (a) Employer's identification number

(b) Employer's tax year ends

3 Administrator's identification number

(c) Name, address and phone number of person to be contacted if more information is needed:

Name ▶ .... Telephone number ▶ ( ) ....

Address ▶ ....

4 Determination requested for:

(a) *(i)* ☐ Initial qualification—date plan adopted ▶ ....

(ii) ☐ Amendment—date adopted ▶ ....

(iii) If (ii) is checked, enter file folder number ▶ ....

(b) Were employees who are interested parties given the required notification of the filing of this application? . ☐ **Yes** ☐ **No**

5 Check appropriate box to indicate the type of plan entity:

(a) ☐ Single-employer plan

(b) ☐ Plan of controlled group of corporations
or of common control employers

(c) ☐ Multiple-employer plan

(d) ☐ Church

(e) ☐ Governmental organization

(f) ☐ Other (specify) ▶ ....

6 (a) Name of plan

(b) Plan number ▶ ....

(c) Plan year ends ▶

7 (a) This is a:

(i) ☐ Master or prototype plan

(ii) ☐ Field prototype plan

(iii) ☐ Other (see instructions)

(b) Letter serial number or notification letter number

8 (a) Defined benefit plan—Indicate whether:

(i) ☐ Unit benefit

(ii) ☐ Fixed benefit

(iii) ☐ Flat benefit

(iv) ☐ Other (specify) ▶ ....

(b) Defined contribution plan—Indicate whether:

(i) ☐ Profit-sharing

(ii) ☐ Money purchase

(iii) ☐ Stock bonus

(iv) ☐ Target benefit

(c) *(i)* If 8(a) (i), (ii), (iii), or (iv) is checked, is this a defined benefit plan covered under the Pension Benefit Guaranty Corporation termination insurance program?
☐ Yes ☐ No ☐ Not determined

(ii) If 4(a) (ii) and 8(b) (i), (ii), (iii), or (iv) are checked, was the plan covered by the termination insurance program prior to the amendment? ☐ Yes ☐ No

9 Effective date of plan

10 Effective date of amendment

11 Date plan was communicated to employees ▶ ....

How communicated ▶

12 Integration:

Is this plan integrated with Social Security or Railroad Retirement? . . . . ☐ **Yes** ☐ **No**

13 Type of funding entity:

(a) ☐ Trust

(b) ☐ Custodial account

(c) ☐ Non-trusteed

(d) ☐ Trust with insurance contracts

14 (a) Does plan provide for maximum limitation under section 415? . . . . ☐ **Yes** ☐ **No**

(b) Do you maintain any other qualified plan(s)? . . . . ☐ **Yes** ☐ **No**

Under penalties of perjury, I declare that I have examined this application, including accompanying statements, and to the best of my knowledge and belief it is true, correct and complete.

Signature ▶ _____ Title ▶ _____ Date ▶ _____

Signature ▶ _____ Title ▶ _____ Date ▶ _____

Form **5307** (Rev. 8–79)

15 Is any issue relating to this plan or trust currently pending before the Internal Revenue Service, the Department of Labor, the Pension Benefit Guaranty Corporation or any Court? . . . . ☐ **Yes** ☐ **No**
If "Yes," attach explanation.

16 Coverage of plan at (give date) ▶ ---

	Number
(a) Total employed	
(b) Exclusions under plan (do not count an employee more than once):	
(i) Minimum age (specify) ▶................................. Years of service (specify) ▶....................	
(ii) Employees included in collective bargaining	
(iii) Nonresident aliens who receive no earned income from United States sources	
(c) Total exclusions, sum of (b)(i) through (iii)	
(d) Employees not excluded under the statute, (a) minus (c)	
(e) Ineligible under plan because of (do not count an employee included in (b)):	
(i) Minimum pay (specify) ▶ --	
(ii) Hourly-paid	
(iii) Maximum age (specify) ▶--	
(iv) Other (specify) ▶--	
(f) Employees ineligible, sum of (e)(i) through (iv)	
(g) Employees eligible to participate, line (d) minus line (f)	
(h) Number of employees participating in plan	

(i) Percent of nonexcluded employees who are participating, (h) divided by (d) . . . . . ⎰_____ %
Complete (j) only if (i) is less than 70% and complete (k) only if (j) is 70% or more.

(j) Percent of nonexcluded employees who are eligible to participate, (g) divided by (d) . . _____ %

(k) Percent of eligible employees who are participating, (h) divided by (g) . . . . . . ⎱_____ %
If (i) and (j) are less than 70% or (k) is less than 80%, see instructions.
(l) Total number of participants, include certain retired and terminated employees (see instructions) . .

17 Vesting—Check the appropriate box to indicate the vesting provisions of the plan:
(a) ☐ Full and immediate
(b) ☐ Full vesting after 10 years of service (see instructions)
(c) ☐ 5- to 15-year vesting, i.e., 25% after 5 years of service, 5% additional for each of the next 5 years, then 10% additional for each of the next 5 years (see instructions)
(d) ☐ Rule of 45 (see section 411(a)(2)(C)) (see instructions)
(e) ☐ For each year of employment, commencing with the 4th such year, vesting not less than 40% after 4 years of service, 5% additional for each of the next 2 years, and 10% additional for each of the next 5 years
(f) ☐ Other (specify and see instructions) ▶ . . . .

18 Complete only for a plan of more than one employer:

	Number
(a) Total number of participants (include certain retired and terminated employees)	
(b) Participants whose benefits or accounts are fully vested	
(c) Number of contributing employers	

Form 5309
(Rev. December 1982)

Department of the Treasury
Internal Revenue Service

Application for Determination of Employee Stock Ownership Plan

(Under section 409A or 4975(e)(7) of the Internal Revenue Code)

File with Form 5301, 5303 or 5307, whichever applies

OMB No. 1545-0284
Expires 9-30-85

For IRS Use Only

File folder
number ▶

1 Name, address and ZIP code of employer	2 Employer's identification number
	3 Date plan was adopted
Telephone number ▶ ( )	Mo. Day Yr.

4 This application is for (complete one):

(a) ☐ A tax credit employee stock ownership plan under section 409A

(b) ☐ An employee stock ownership plan under section 4975(e)(7)

5 Type of plan:

(a) ☐ Profit-sharing

(b) ☐ Stock bonus

(c) ☐ Money purchase

(d) ☐ Money purchase and stock bonus

Indicate the section and page number in the plan document where the following provisions will be found.	Section and Page Number

6 Complete the following for all plans:

(a) **Plan is designed to invest primarily in employer securities** . . . .

(b) **Each participant must be entitled to direct the plan to vote the allocated securities as required in section 409A(e)** . . . .

(c) **A participant entitled to a distribution from the plan has a right to demand the distribution in employer securities and, if the securities are not readily marketable, the employer will repurchase the securities under a fair valuation formula** . . . .

7 Only plans applying under section 409A complete the following:

(a) **All employer securities transferred to or purchased by the plan because of the requirements of section 48(n)(1)(A) or 44G(c)(1)(B) shall be allocated for the plan year to the accounts of all participants who are entitled to share in these allocations** . . . .

(b) **The allocation to each participant of the employer securities transferred or purchased because of section 48(n)(1)(A) or 44G(c)(1)(B) is in substantially the same proportion as each employee's compensation is to the total compensation of all participants. For this allocation, compensation of any participant in excess of the first $100,000 per year shall be disregarded** . . . .

(c) **No allocated securities as described in section 409A(d) may be distributed to any participant before the end of the 84th month after the month of allocation of such securities except for separation from service, death, disability, or as otherwise stated in section 409A(d)** . . . .

(d) **The right of all participants to the securities allocated to them must be nonforfeitable** . . . .

(e) **If any part of the employee plan credit or employee stock ownership credit is recaptured or redetermined, amounts transferred to the plan because of the requirements of section 48(n)(1) or 44G(c)(1)(B) shall remain in the plan and, if allocated, shall remain allocated** . . . .

8 Only plans applying under section 4975(e)(7) complete the following:

(a) **Plan is designated as an employee stock ownership plan within the meaning of section 4975(e)(7)** . . .

(b) **The establishment and maintenance of a suspense account as required under regulations section 54.4975-11(c)** . . . .

(c) **Participants' rights to plan assets acquired by use of the exempt loan are protected as specified in regulations section 54.4975-11(a)(3)(i) and (ii)** . . . .

Under penalties of perjury, I declare that I have examined this application, including accompanying statements, and to the best of my knowledge and belief it is true, correct and complete.

Signature ▶ _____   Title ▶ _____   Date ▶ _____

For Paperwork Reduction Act Notice, see back of form.

Form **5309** (Rev. 12-82)

Instructions

(Section references are to the Internal Revenue Code.)

General Information

Use this form to apply for a determination letter for either a Tax Credit Employee Stock Ownership Plan that meets the requirements of section 409A, or an Employee Stock Ownership Plan (ESOP) that meets the requirements of section 4975(e)(7). Use the form in conjunction with Form 5301, 5303, or 5307, whichever applies.

The plan you establish must be designed to invest primarily in employer securities. For a definition of employer securities as it pertains to your plan, see section 409A(l) or section 4975(e)(8). Also see regulations section 1.46–8(d) for the formal plan requirements.

Paperwork Reduction Act Notice.—The Paperwork Reduction Act of 1980 says that we must tell you why we are collecting this information, how it is to be used, and whether your response is voluntary, required to obtain a benefit, or mandatory. The information is used to determine whether you meet the legal requirements for the plan approval you request. Your filing of this information is only required if you wish IRS to determine if your plan qualifies under section 409A or 4975(e)(7).

General Instructions

A. Who May File

1. Any corporate employer who elects to have the section 44G, employee stock ownership credit apply and establishes a plan intended to meet the requirements under section 409A.

2. Any corporate employer who has established an ESOP intended to meet the requirements under section 4975(e)(7).

☆ U.S. Government Printing Office: 1982—381-108/40

B. What to File

1. For initial determination or amendment of a plan intended to meet the requirements under section 409A or 4975(e)(7), file Forms 5309 and 5301, 5303 or 5307 plus a copy of all documents and statements required by those forms.

2. To amend a plan previously qualified under section 401(a) so that it also meets the requirements of section 409A or 4975(e)(7), submit completed Forms 5309 and 5301, 5303 or 5307 plus all the documents and statements required by those forms.

C. How to File

Attach the completed Form 5309 to Form 5301, 5303 or 5307 (whichever applies) and file with that form.

D. Signature

The application must be signed by the principal officer authorized to sign.

Form **6406** (Rev. Oct. 1984) Department of the Treasury Internal Revenue Service	**Short Form Application for Determination for Amendment of Employee Benefit Plan** (Under sections 401(a) and 501(a) of the Internal Revenue Code)	OMB No. 1545-0229 Expires 7-31-87 **For IRS Use Only** File folder number ▶

The following MUST be submitted with this form:

- A copy of the plan amendments
- A description of the amendment covering the changes to the plan sections
- An explanation of the plan sections before the amendment
- An explanation of the effects of the amendment on the provisions of the plan sections

▶ **Please complete every item on this form. If an item does not apply, enter N/A.**

1 (a) Name, address and ZIP code of employer

(b) Employer's identification number

(c) Employer's tax year ends

Telephone number ▶ (   )

2 Check the applicable box to indicate the application form you filed for your last determination letter.
Form ☐ 5300   ☐ 5301   ☐ 5303   ☐ 5307

3 Has the adopting employer terminated or adopted any plans since receiving the last determination letter for this plan? . . . . ☐ Yes   ☐ No
If "Yes," see instructions.

4 (a) Determination requested for amendment:
    (i) Effective date of plan ▶ _____ *(ii)* Effective date of amendment ▶ _____
    (iii) Enter file folder number ▶ _____
(b) Were employees who are interested parties given the required notification of the filing of this application?   ☐ Yes   ☐ No

5 Type of employer, check appropriate box:
(a) ☐ Corporation   **(d)** ☐ Partnership
(b) ☐ S corporation   **(e)** ☐ Tax exempt organization
(c) ☐ Sole proprietor

6 Check appropriate box to indicate the type of plan entity: **(c)** ☐ Multi-employer plan
(a) ☐ Single-employer plan   **(d)** ☐ Other multiple-employer plan
(b) ☐ Plan of controlled group of corporations, of   **(e)** ☐ Church
    common control employers or of an affiliated   **(f)** ☐ Governmental
    service group   **(g)** ☐ Other (specify) ▶ _____

7 (a) Name of plan   **(b)** Plan number _____ **(c)** Plan year ends _____

    (d) Is this a Keogh (H.R. 10) plan? . . . . ☐ Yes   ☐ No

8 (a) This is a: **(b)** Most recent IRS letter serial number or notification letter number
    (i) ☐ Master or prototype plan   *(iv)* ☐ Basic plan
    (ii) ☐ Field prototype plan   *(v)* ☐ Not applicable
    (iii) ☐ District—approved pattern plan

9 (a) Defined benefit plan—Indicate whether: *(iii)* ☐ Flat benefit
    (i) ☐ Unit benefit   *(iv)* ☐ Other (specify) ▶ _____
    (ii) ☐ Fixed benefit

    (b) Defined contribution plan—Indicate whether:
    (i) ☐ Profit-sharing   *(iii)* ☐ Stock bonus
    (ii) ☐ Money purchase   *(iv)* ☐ Target benefit

    (c) Type of funding entity:
    (i) ☐ Trust   *(iii)* ☐ Non-trusteed
    (ii) ☐ Custodial account   *(iv)* ☐ Trust with insurance contracts

10 Integration:
Is this plan integrated with Social Security or Railroad Retirement? . . . . ☐ Yes   ☐ No

11 Is any issue relating to this plan or trust currently pending before the Internal Revenue Service, the Department of Labor, the Pension Benefit Guaranty Corporation or any Court? . . . . ☐ Yes   ☐ No
If "Yes," attach explanation.

Under penalties of perjury, I declare that I have examined this application, including accompanying statements, and to the best of my knowledge and belief it is true, correct and complete.

Signature ▶ _____ Title ▶ _____ Date ▶ _____

Signature ▶ _____ Title ▶ _____ Date ▶ _____

For Paperwork Reduction Act Notice, see page 1 of the instructions for this form.

253

12 **(a)** Did the amendment change the eligibility requirements of the plan? . . . . ☐ **Yes** ☐ **No**
    If "Yes," complete item 13 below. If "No," complete only 13(a), (h) and (l).

   (b) Did the amendment change the vesting provisions of the plan? . . . . ☐ **Yes** ☐ **No**
    If "Yes," complete item 14 below.

	Number
13 Coverage of plan at (give date) .... Enter here the number of self-employed individuals ▶	
(a) Total employed (if a Keogh plan, include all self-employed individuals)	
(b) Exclusions under plan (do not count an employee more than once):	
(i) Minimum age (specify) ▶	
(ii) Years of service (specify) ▶	
(iii) Employees included in collective bargaining	
(iv) Non-resident aliens who receive no earned income from United States sources	
(c) Total exclusions (add (b)(i) through (iv))	
(d) Employees not excluded under the statute, (a) minus (c)	
(e) Ineligible under plan because of (do not count an employee included in (b)):	
(i) Minimum pay (specify) ▶	
(ii) Hourly-paid	
(iii) Maximum age (specify) ▶	
(iv) Other (specify) ▶	
(f) Employees ineligible (add (e)(i) through (iv))	
(g) Employees eligible to participate ((d) minus (f))	
(h) Number of employees participating in plan	
(i) Percent of nonexcluded employees who are participating (divide (h) by (d)) . . . . ___% Complete (j) only if (i) is less than 70% and complete (k) only if (j) is 70% or more.	
(j) Percent of nonexcluded employees who are eligible to participate (divide (g) by (d)) . ___%	
(k) Percent of eligible employees who are participating (divide (h) by (g)) . . . . . . ___% If (i) and (j) are less than 70% or (k) is less than 80%, see instructions.	
(l) Total number of participants; include certain retired and terminated employees (see instructions) . .	

14 Vesting—Check the appropriate box to indicate the vesting provisions of the plan:
   (a) ☐ Full and immediate
   (b) ☐ Full vesting after 10 years of service (-0-% years 1 through 10, 100% after 10 years)
   (c) ☐ 5- to 15-year vesting, i.e., 25% after 5 years of service, 5% additional for each of the next 5 years,
        then 10% additional for each of the next 5 years (see instructions)
   (d) ☐ Rule of 45 (see section 411(a)(2)(C))
   (e) ☐ For each year of employment, commencing with the 4th such year, vesting not less than 40% after
        4 years of service, 5% additional for each of the next 2 years, and 10% additional for each of the
        next 5 years
   (f) ☐ Other (specify and see instructions) ▶ ....

Annual Administration

Forms to be submitted annually in connection with plan administration.

Form **941E**
(Rev. January 1985)
Department of the Treasury
Internal Revenue Service

Quarterly Return of Withheld Federal Income Tax

▶ **For Paperwork Reduction Act Notice, see page 2.**
Please type or print

Your name, address, employer identification number, and calendar quarter of return. (If not correct, please change.) ▶	Name	Date quarter ended
	Address and ZIP code	Employer identification number

OMB No. 1545-0029
Expires 12-31-85

T
FF
FD
FP
I
T

If address is different from prior return, check here ▶ ☐

If you are not liable for returns in the future, write "FINAL" ▶   Date final wages paid . . . . ▶

Complete For First Quarter Only

1	Number of employees (except household) employed in the pay period that includes March 12th ▶	1
2	Total wages and tips subject to withholding, plus other compensation . . . . ▶	2
3	Total income tax withheld from wages, tips, pensions, annuities, sick pay, gambling, etc. . . . ▶	3
4	Adjustment of withheld income tax for preceding quarters of calendar year . . . . . . ▶	4
5	Adjusted total of income tax withheld . . . . ▶	5
6	Backup withholding . . . . ▶	6
7	Adjustment of backup withholding tax for preceding quarters of calendar year . . . . . . ▶	7
8	Adjusted total of backup withholding . . . . ▶	8
9	Total taxes (add lines 5 and 8) . . . . ▶	9
10	Advance earned income credit (EIC) payments, if any (see instructions) . . . . ▶	10
11	Net taxes (subtract line 10 from line 9). **This must equal line IV below** (plus line IV of Schedule A (Form 941) if you have treated backup withholding as a separate liability.) . . . . ▶	11
12	Total deposits for quarter, including overpayment applied from prior quarter, from your records . ▶	12
13	Undeposited taxes due (subtract line 12 from line 11). Enter here and pay to IRS . . . . . . ▶	13
14	If line 12 is more than line 11, enter overpayment here ▶ $ _____ and check if to be:	14

☐ Applied to next return or   ☐ Refunded.

Record of Federal Tax Liability (Complete if line 11 is $500 or more)

See the instructions under rule 4 for details before checking these boxes.
Check only if you made eighth-monthly deposits using the 95% rule ▶ ☐   Check only if you are a first time 3-banking-day depositor ▶ ☐

Date wages paid		First month of quarter		Second month of quarter		Third month of quarter
		Tax liability (*Do not show Federal tax deposits here.*)				
1st through 3rd	A		I		Q	
4th through 7th	B		J		R	
8th through 11th	C		K		S	
12th through 15th	D		L		T	
16th through 19th	E		M		U	
20th through 22nd	F		N		V	
23rd through 25th	G		O		W	
26th through the last	H		P		X	
Total liability for month	I		II		III	

IV Total for quarter (add lines **I, II,** and **III**) . . . . ▶

Under penalties of perjury, I declare that I have examined this return, including accompanying schedules and statements, and to the best of my knowledge and belief it is true, correct, and complete.

Signature ▶   Title ▶   Date ▶

Please file this form with your Internal Revenue Service Center (see instructions on "Where to File").   Form **941E** (Rev. 1-85)

Highlights

Paperwork Reduction Act Notice.—We ask for this information to carry out the Internal Revenue laws of the United States. We need it to ensure that taxpayers are complying with these laws and to allow us to figure and collect the right amount of tax. You are required to give us this information.

Backup Withholding.— Payers must generally withhold 20% of taxable interest, dividend, and certain other payments if payees fail to furnish payers with the correct taxpayer identification number. There are other circumstances where the payer is also required to withhold. This withholding is referred to as backup withholding. Please see **Form W-9, Payer's Request for Taxpayer Identification Number and Certification,** and the **1985 Instructions for Form 1099 Series, 1098, 5498, and 1096,** for more details.

Report backup withholding amounts on line 6, Backup withholding, on the same 941E you use for reporting income tax withholding. For tax deposit purposes, see Completing the Record of Federal Tax Liability on page 4.

Forms W-4.—Send in each quarter with Form 941E copies of any Forms W-4 received during this quarter from employees (1) claiming more than 14 withholding allowances or (2) claiming exemption from income tax withholding if their wages are expected to usually exceed $200 a week. Include on each copy your name, address, and employer identification number. Do not send copies for employees who no longer work for you at the end of the quarter. For details, see **Circular E,** Employer's Tax Guide.

You may send in copies to your Internal Revenue Service Center more often than quarterly if you like. If you do so, include a cover letter giving your name, address, and employer identification number. In certain cases, IRS may notify you in writing that you must submit specified Forms W-4 more frequently to your District Director separate from your Form 941E.

If you want to use magnetic media to transmit W-4 data to the IRS, see Revenue Procedure 80-8 in Cumulative Bulletin 1980-1, page 592.

Base withholding on the Forms W-4 that you sent in unless IRS notifies you in writing to do otherwise.

Circular E explains the rules for withholding, paying, depositing, and reporting Federal income tax, social security taxes, and Federal unemployment (FUTA) tax on wages and fringe benefits. Circular A, Agricultural Employer's Tax Guide, explains the rules for employers who have farmworkers. These rules are different, so please ask for this circular if you have farmworkers. You can get these circulars free from IRS offices.

General Instructions

Purpose of Form.—Use this form to report the income tax you withheld from wages, tips, pensions, annuities, third-party sick pay, supplemental unemployment compensation benefits, certain gambling winnings, and backup withholding.

If you pay wages taxable under the Federal Insurance Contributions Act (FICA), file **Form 941,** Employer's Quarterly Federal Tax Return, not Form 941E.

Who Must File.—Employers who report only backup withholding and withheld income tax should use this form. These include State and local governments, payers of supplemental unemployment compensation benefits, certain churches and church-controlled organizations, and certain payers of annuities and sick pay. State and local governments should deposit withheld income tax and file Form 941E with IRS, but they should send social security payments and reports to their State agency.

Example. A, an insurance company, makes annuity payments under contracts bought by individuals. A has employees whose wages are subject to social security taxes. A must file Form 941 and combine the income tax withheld from annuities with the income tax withheld from A's employees' wages.

When to File.—File a return for the first quarter you are required to withhold income tax and for each quarter thereafter.

Due Dates for Returns

Quarter	Ending	Due Date
Jan.-Feb.-Mar.	March 31	April 30
Apr.-May-June	June 30	July 31
July-Aug.-Sept.	Sept. 30	Oct. 31
Oct.-Nov.-Dec.	Dec. 31	Jan. 31

If you deposited all taxes when due for a quarter, you have 10 more days after the above due date to file. For example, your return for the quarter that ends on March 31 would be due by May 10 instead of April 30.

After you file your first return, we will send you a form every 3 months. We will print on it your name, address, employer identification number (EIN), and date the quarter ends. Please use this form. If you don't have a form, get one from an IRS office in time to file the return when due. If you use a form that is not preaddressed, please list your name and EIN exactly as shown on your last return. Also show the date the quarter ends.

If you temporarily stop paying wages or your work is seasonal, file a return for each quarter. Do this even though you have no tax to report. But if you go out of business or stop paying wages, file a final return. Be sure to fill in the entries above line 1.

Where to File.—

If your legal residence, principal place of business, office, or agency is located in	File with the Internal Revenue Service Center at
New Jersey, New York City and counties of Nassau, Rockland, Suffolk, and Westchester	Holtsville, NY 00501
New York (all other counties), Connecticut, Maine, Massachusetts, New Hampshire, Rhode Island, Vermont	Andover, MA 05501
Delaware, District of Columbia, Maryland, Pennsylvania	Philadelphia, PA 19255
Alabama, Florida, Georgia, Mississippi, South Carolina	Atlanta, GA 31101
Michigan, Ohio	Cincinnati, OH 45999
Arkansas, Kansas, Louisiana, New Mexico, Oklahoma, Texas	Austin, TX 73301
Alaska, Arizona, Colorado, Idaho, Minnesota, Montana, Nebraska, Nevada, North Dakota, Oregon, South Dakota, Utah, Washington, Wyoming	Ogden, UT 84201
Illinois, Iowa, Missouri, Wisconsin	Kansas City, MO 64999
California, Hawaii	Fresno, CA 93888
Indiana, Kentucky, North Carolina, Tennessee, Virginia, West Virginia	Memphis, TN 37501
If you have no legal residence or principal place of business in any State	Philadelphia, PA 19255

Employer Identification Number (EIN).—If you have not asked for a number, apply for one on **Form SS-4,** Application for Employer Identification Number. You can get this form from IRS or Social Security Administration (SSA) offices. If you do not have a number by the time a return is due, write "Applied for" and the date you applied in the space shown for the number. For more information concerning an EIN, see **Publication 583,** Information for Business Taxpayers. If you took over a business, please do not use the old owner's number.

Penalties and Interest.—There are penalties for filing a return late and paying or depositing tax late, unless there is reasonable cause. If you are late, please attach an explanation to your return.

The law also provides a penalty of 25% of the overstatement if, without reasonable cause, you overstate the amount you deposited.

There are also penalties for willful failure to file returns and pay taxes when due, collect tax, furnish statements to employees, or keep records, and for filing false or fraudulent returns or submitting bad checks.

In some cases, an officer or responsible employee of a corporation or a member or responsible employee of a partnership may be liable for payment of the withheld tax.

Interest is charged on tax paid late at the rate set by law.

You can avoid penalties and interest by filing correct returns on time and by paying any tax due with the returns.

Specific Instructions

Line 1. Number of employees.—Complete for the January-March calendar quarter only. Do not include household employees, persons who receive no pay during the pay period, pensioners, or members of the Armed Forces. If you have only household employees in the pay period, enter zero on this line.

Line 2.—Enter the total of all wages you paid, tips reported to you, and other compensation you paid to your employees, even if you do not have to withhold income tax on it. Do not include annuities, third-party sick pay, supplemental unemployment compensation benefits, or gambling winnings, even if you withheld income tax on them.

Line 3.—Enter the total income tax you withheld on wages, tips, annuities, sick pay, supplemental unemployment compensation benefits, and gambling winnings on line 3.

Line 4. Adjustment of withheld income tax.—Use line 4 to correct errors in income tax withheld from wages paid in earlier quarters of the same calendar year. Explain any amount on Form 941c or attach a statement that shows: *(a)* what the error was; *(b)* ending date of each quarter in which the error was made; *(c)* the amount of the error for each quarter; *(d)* the quarter in which you found the error; and *(e)* how you and your employee(s) have settled any overcollection or undercollection.

Do not use this line to adjust income tax withholding for earlier years.

Line 5. Adjusted total of income tax withheld.—Add line 4 to line 3 if you are reporting additional withheld income tax for an earlier quarter in this calendar year. Subtract line 4 from line 3 if you are reducing the amount of withheld income tax reported for an earlier quarter during this calendar year.

Line 6. Backup withholding.—Enter the income tax you withheld as backup withholding on line 6.

Line 7. Adjustment of backup withholding.—Use line 7 to correct errors on backup withholding tax.

Line 10. Advance EIC payments, if any.—Enter the total advance earned income credit (EIC) payments made during the quarter.

Line 11. Net tax.—Subtract line 10 from line 9 and enter the result. If line 10 is more than line 9, enter the result in brackets.

(Continued on page 4)

Form **941E**
(Rev. January 1985)
Department of the Treasury
Internal Revenue Service

Quarterly Return of Withheld Federal Income Tax
▶ **For Paperwork Reduction Act Notice, see page 2.**
Please Type Or Print

OMB No. 1545-0029
Expires 12-31-85

Type or print in this space your name, address, and employer identification number as shown on original.

Return for calendar quarter ending
(Enter month and year as on original)

YOUR COPY

If you are not liable for returns in the future, write "FINAL." ▶   Date final wages paid . . . . ▶

Complete For First Quarter Only

1	Number of employees (except household) employed in the pay period that includes March 12th ▶	1
2	Total wages and tips subject to withholding, plus other compensation . . . . ▶	2
3	Total income tax withheld from wages, tips, pensions, annuities, sick pay, gambling, etc. . . . ▶	3
4	Adjustment of withheld income tax for preceding quarters of calendar year . . . . ▶	4
5	Adjusted total of income tax withheld . . . . ▶	5
6	Backup withholding . . . . ▶	6
7	Adjustment of backup withholding tax for preceding quarters of calendar year	7
8	Adjusted total of backup withholding . . . . ▶	8
9	Total taxes (add lines 5 and 8) . . . . ▶	9
10	Advance earned income credit (EIC) payments, if any (see instructions) . . . . ▶	10
11	Net taxes (subtract line 10 from line 9). **This must equal line IV below** (plus line IV of Schedule A (Form 941) if you have treated backup withholding as a separate liability.) . . . . . . ▶	11
12	Total deposits for quarter, including overpayment applied from prior quarter, from your records ▶	12
13	Undeposited taxes due (subtract line 12 from line 11). Enter here and pay to IRS . . . . ▶	13
14	If line 12 is more than line 11, enter overpayment here ▶ $ _____ and check if to be:	14

☐ Applied to next return or   ☐ Refunded.

Record of Federal Tax Liability (Complete if line 11 is $500 or more)

See the instructions under rule 4 for details before checking these boxes.
Check only if you made eighth-monthly deposits using the 95% rule ▶ ☐   Check only if you are a first time 3-banking-day depositor ▶ ☐

Date wages paid		First month of quarter		Second month of quarter		Third month of quarter
1st through 3rd	A		I		Q	
4th through 7th	B		J		R	
8th through 11th	C		K		S	
12th through 15th	D		L		T	
16th through 19th	E		M		U	
20th through 22nd	F		N		V	
23rd through 25th	G		O		W	
26th through the last	H		P		X	
Total liability for month	I		II		III	

IV Total for quarter (add lines *I*, *II*, and *III*) . . . . ▶

Under penalties of perjury, I declare that I have examined this return, including accompanying schedules and statements, and to the best of my knowledge and belief it is true, correct, and complete.

Signature ▶   Title ▶   Date ▶

Important.—Keep this copy and a copy of each related schedule or statement.   Form **941E** (Rev. 1-85)

259

Line 12. Total deposits for the quarter.—
Enter the total deposits for the quarter including any overpayment applied from the previous quarter.

Line 13. Undeposited tax due.—If you deposited all tax when due, any balance on this line will be less than $500.

Line 14. Overpayment.—If you deposited more than the correct amount for a quarter, you can have the overpayment refunded or applied to your next return.

Completing the Record of Federal Tax Liability

For tax deposit purposes, you can either combine backup withholding with other taxes reported on Form 941E and deposit the combined total, or you can treat backup withholding as a separate tax and deposit it separately following the same deposit rules used for social security and withheld income taxes.

If you treat backup withholding as a separate tax, show the backup withholding amounts for deposit purposes on **Schedule A (Form 941),** Record of Federal Backup Withholding Tax Liability, and when depositing these taxes, mark the "Sched. A" entry on the deposit coupon. Schedule A (Form 941) must be attached to Form 941E.

If your taxes for the quarter (line 11) are less than $500, you do not have to complete the Record of Federal Tax Liability. You may pay the taxes with Form 941E or deposit them by the due date of the return.

If your taxes for the quarter are $500 or more, you **must** complete the Record of Federal Tax Liability.

Each month is divided into eight deposit periods that end on the 3rd, 7th, 11th, 15th, 19th, 22nd, 25th, and last day of the month as shown in the Record. If your taxes for every month are less than $3,000, you can show them on the Total lines (I, II, and III) and skip the other lines. If your taxes for any month are $3,000 or more, find the eighth-monthly period(s) during the quarter in which you had a payday. Make entries only on the lines next to these periods. (For example, if you pay wages on the 1st and 15th of each month, complete lines A, D, I, L, Q, T, and the monthly Total lines.)

Enter your tax liability (income tax withheld minus any Advance Earned Income Credit payments) for each eighth-monthly period during which you had a payday.

The total of the Tax liability column (line IV) (plus Line IV of Schedule A if you have treated backup withholding as a separate liability) must equal Net taxes (line 11). Otherwise, you may be charged a penalty, based on your average tax liability, for not making deposits of taxes.

Taxpayers who willfully claim credit on line 12 for deposits not made are subject to fines and other criminal penalties.

How to Make Deposits.—In general, you must deposit backup withholding and withheld income tax with an authorized financial institution or a Federal Reserve bank or branch that serves your area. Use **Form 8109,** Federal Tax Deposit Coupon, which must be included with each deposit, to indicate the type of tax being deposited. To avoid a possible penalty, do not mail your deposit directly to IRS. Records of your deposits will be sent to IRS for crediting to your business accounts.

If you hand-deliver your deposit to an authorized depositary on the due date, be sure to deliver it before the depositary closes its business day.

There will no longer be periodic mailouts of Federal tax deposit forms. If you need additional coupons, use the FTD Reorder Form (**Form 8109A**) included in the coupon book. If you do not have a coupon book, please request one from your IRS district office. There are 15 coupons and a reorder form in each book and the coupons can be used to deposit any type of tax for any tax year. Please see the instructions in the front of the coupon book for additional information.

Rules When Your Deposits Are Due

The amount of taxes you owe determines the frequency of deposits. You owe these taxes when you pay the wages, not when your payroll period ends. The rules and examples below tell you how often to deposit taxes.

(1) Less than $500 at the end of a quarter.—If at the end of the quarter your total undeposited taxes for the quarter are less than $500, you do not have to deposit the taxes. You may pay the taxes to IRS with Form 941E, or you may deposit them by the end of the next month.

(2) Less than $500 at the end of any month.—If at the end of any month your total undeposited taxes are less than $500, you do not have to make a deposit. You may carry the taxes over to the following month within the quarter. (See Example A.)

(3) $500 or more but less than $3,000 at the end of any month.—If at the end of any month your total undeposited taxes are $500 or more but less than $3,000, you must deposit the taxes within 15 days after the end of the month.

Exception: If this occurs at the end of a month in which you made a deposit of $3,000 or more, see Examples D and E.

(4) $3,000 or more at the end of any eighth-monthly period.—If at the end of any eighth-monthly period your total undeposited taxes are $3,000 or more, deposit the taxes within 3 banking days after the end of the eighth-monthly period. (See Examples B, C, D and E.) Do not count as banking days local holidays observed by authorized financial institutions, Saturdays, Sundays, and legal holidays.

Note: *Deposits of $20,000 or more which are made by taxpayers required to deposit taxes more than once a month, must be received by the due date to be timely. See Circular E for details.*

You will be considered to meet rule 4 if:

• You deposit at least 95% of the tax liability for the eighth-monthly period within 3 banking days after the end of the period; and

You deposit any underpayment as follows:

• If the eighth-monthly period is in the first or second month of the quarter, you deposit the underpayment with the first deposit that is required to be made after the 15th of the following month.

• If the eighth-monthly period is in the last month of the quarter, you deposit any underpayment of $500 or more by the due date of the return. (Any underpayment less than $500 can be paid with Form 941E as explained in rule 1.)

Only check the first box at the top of the Record of Federal Tax Liability if you are making deposits using the 95% rule.

Examples

Example A.—The taxes on wages paid in October are $450, and the taxes on wages paid in November are $550. No deposit is required for October (because of rule 2), but add the $450 to the $550 for November and deposit the total ($1,000) by December 15 (as required by rule 3).

Example B.—The taxes on wages paid from the 1st through the 3rd of the month are $3,500. Deposit these taxes within 3 banking days after the 3rd of the month (as required by rule 4).

Example C.—The taxes on wages paid from the 4th through the 7th of a month are $2,500 and the taxes on wages paid from the 8th through the 11th are $2,000. A separate deposit is not required for the $2,500, but add it to the $2,000 and deposit the total ($4,500) within 3 banking days after the 11th of the month (as required by rule 4).

Example D.—The taxes on wages paid from the 23rd through the 25th of January are $3,500. Deposit these taxes within 3 banking days after the 25th of the month (as required by rule 4). The taxes on wages paid from the 26th through the end of January are $2,500. Since a deposit was already made for an eighth-monthly period during the month, a separate deposit is not required for the $2,500 (because of the exception to rule 3). Carry the $2,500 over and add it to the taxes on wages paid in February. Then follow rules 3 and 4 to determine when the next deposit is required. (However, if this occurs in the last month of a quarter, deposit any balance due of $500 or more but less than $3,000 by the end of the next month.)

Example E.—Wages are paid on Wednesday for the prior week. In the first quarter paydays are on January 2, 9, 16, 23, and 30; February 6, 13, 20, and 27; and March 6, 13, 20, and 27. Taxes are $1,050 for each payday.

Enter $1,050 on lines A, C, E, G, H, J, L, N, P, R, T, V, and X. Enter $5,250 on Total line I; $4,200 on lines II and III; and $13,650 on line IV.

You must make a deposit within 3 banking days of January 19, February 7, February 28, and March 22 because undeposited taxes reached at least $3,000 for the eighth-monthly periods ending on those dates.

The undeposited taxes at the end of January of $2,100 (for paydays on the 23rd and 30th) may be carried over to February because of the exception to rule 3 as explained in Example D. At the end of February, there is no carryover since the undeposited taxes are $3,150 and must be deposited within 3 banking days. At the end of March, the undeposited taxes of $1,050 (for the payday on the 27th) must be deposited by April 30 (because of the exception to rule 3 for the last month of a quarter as explained in Example D).

Exception to rule 4.—If this is the first time you are required to make a deposit within 3 banking days after the end of an eighth-monthly period, you may deposit the taxes by the 15th day of the next month (instead of within 3 banking days after the eighth-monthly period) if you meet all of the following conditions:

• You were not required to deposit taxes for any eighth-monthly period during the last 4 quarters.

• You were not required to deposit taxes for any eighth-monthly period during earlier months of this quarter.

• Your total undeposited taxes at the end of any eighth-monthly period during this month are less than $10,000.

Check the second box at the top of the Record of Federal Tax Liability only if you qualify for this exception to rule 4 and attach a statement showing your net taxes for each of the last 4 calendar quarters.

Signature.—Be sure to sign the return.

☆U.S. Government Printing Office: 1985—461-495/10146

Form **5308**
(Rev. November 1984)
Department of the Treasury
Internal Revenue Service

Request for Change in Plan/Trust Year

(Under Code Section 412(c)(5))
This Form Replaces Form 1128 for Employee Plans

OMB No. 1545-0201
Expires 7-31-87

To be Filed in Duplicate

Please type or print

Name of employer (or plan administrator if a multiple employer plan)	Employer identification number
Address (number and street) of employer (or plan administrator if a multiple employer plan)	Check one or both: Change in plan year . . . . . . ▶
City or town, State and ZIP code	Change in trust year . . . . . . ▶

1 Name of plan and/or trust

2 Plan number (enter each digit in a separate block) . . . ▶

3 Present plan and/or trust year ends

4 Permission is requested to change to a plan and/or trust year ending

5 The above change will require a return for a short period
Beginning ___ 19___   Ending ___ 19___

6 Return for short period will be filed with the Internal Revenue Service Center at

7 Date of latest IRS determination letter (or opinion letter if the plan is an HR-10 Master or Prototype Plan)

8 Area code and telephone number

9 State the reasons for requesting the change. (Attach a separate sheet if more space is needed.)

10 Is the plan a profit-sharing, stock bonus, insurance contract (described in section 412(i)), governmental, or a church plan (described in section 414(e))? . . . . ☐ **Yes** ☐ **No**
If "Yes," see instructions, Who Must File.

11 Enter the unrelated business taxable income* (or loss) of the trust for the 3 tax years immediately before the short period and for the short period. If necessary, estimate the amount for the short period.

3rd preceding year	2nd preceding year	1st preceding year	Short period

*See section 511 and the instructions on the back of this form.

12 Has the plan and/or trust year previously been changed? . . . . ☐ **Yes** ☐ **No**
If "Yes," give date, reason for prior change, and beginning and end of the prior short period ▶ _____

Signature

Under penalties of perjury, I declare that I have examined this application (including any accompanying schedules and statements), and to the best of my knowledge and belief it is true, correct, and complete.

Official's signature	Title	Date

Make NO Entries Below—For Internal Revenue Service Use ONLY

▶ Approval Action

Based solely on the information furnished in this application, the requested change in the plan and/or trust year indicated above is approved and may be made subject to conditions 1 through 5 listed on the back of this form.

Chief, Employee Plans Rulings and Qualifications Branch	Date

Person to contact ▶
Phone ▶
Symbols ▶
Internal Revenue Service
Washington, DC 20224

▶ Disapproval Action

This application cannot be approved for the following reason:
☐ Not timely filed.
☐ Other ▶ _____
_____

Chief, Employee Plans Rulings and Qualifications Branch	Date

Person to contact ▶
Phone ▶
Symbols ▶
Internal Revenue Service
Washington, DC 20224

For Paperwork Reduction Act Notice, see back of form.

Form **5308** (Rev. 11-84)

Instructions

(Section references are to the Internal Revenue Code.)

Paperwork Reduction Act Notice

The Paperwork Reduction Act of 1980 says that we must tell you why we are collecting this information, how it is to be used, and whether your response is voluntary, required to obtain a benefit, or mandatory. We ask for the information to carry out the Internal Revenue Laws of the United States. We need it to determine if you may change your plan or trust year. You are required to give us this information.

Who Must File

Employers or plan administrators must file Form 5308 to change their plan years under section 412(c)(5) or trust years for trusts related to the plans, under section 442.

If you file Form 5308, you may not change the plan or trust year until IRS approves the change. Rev. Procs. 76-9, 1976-1 C.B. 547, and 76-10, 1976-1 C.B. 548, do not apply to employee plans.

Note: The change in plan or trust year does not affect the limitation year or definition of year of service contained in the plan unless other appropriate action is taken.

You do not need to file Form 5308 to change the plan year of a profit-sharing plan, stock bonus plan, insurance contract (described in section 412(i), governmental plan, or church plan (described in section 414(e)). However, you must file Form 5308 to change the trust year related to these plans.

Conditions That Apply to the Change

1. You must make the change by filing an annual return for the short period by the last day of the 7th month after the end of the short period.

2. You must file annual returns for later years based on a full 12-month period ending on the last day of the new plan and/or trust year.

3. The plan or trust must keep its qualified status for the short period required to make the change, as well as for the tax year immediately before the short period.

4. If you file Form 5308 before the end of the short period, the amount of unrelated business taxable income from the time of filing to the end of the short period must not differ from the amount shown on line 11. (See instructions regarding unrelated business taxable income.)

5. If the plan or trust contains provisions that conflict with the approved change, you must make appropriate amendments.

Plan and Trust Year Changes

If you are changing both the plan year and the trust year, and the two currently have different years, or different years are desired, you must make each request on a separate Form 5308.

Reason for Requesting the Change

A change in plan or trust year will be approved only if there is a substantial business reason for requesting the change. In determining whether a substantial business purpose has been established for making the requested change, consideration will be given to all facts and circumstances relating to the change, including whether the change is being made merely to delay the effective date of any tax statute. Furthermore, a substantial business purpose cannot be established if change would create a substantial distortion of income. The business reason must be specifically stated on line 9. Not establishing a substantial business reason is grounds for denying the change.

Unrelated Business Taxable Income

An exempt trust may have unrelated business taxable income under section 511. If the plan is not funded by a trust or if the trust has no unrelated business taxable income, enter "None" on line 11. If you file Form 5308 before the end of the short period, the amount of unrelated business taxable income from the time of filing to the end of the short period must match the amount you enter on line 11. If it does not, you must submit a new request on Form 5308. (Since an inaccurate estimate of unrelated business taxable income during the short period will require a new application, it is advisable to file Form 5308 after the end of the short period, if the trust might have unrelated business taxable income during that period.)

Time and Place for Filing

File this form **in duplicate** with the Commissioner of Internal Revenue, Washington, DC 20224, Attention: OP:E:EP:RQ, by the 15th day of the second calendar month after the end of the short period required to make the change.

On each attachment show the plan's or trust's name, identifying number, and address. Also show the date, and the fact that it is an attachment to Form 5308.

If an agent is making an application on behalf of a taxpayer, a power of attorney must be included specifically authorizing the agent to represent the taxpayer. **Form 2848**, Power of Attorney And Declaration of Representative, may be used for this purpose.

Information Requested

You must furnish all of the applicable information requested. Otherwise, your request may not be approved.

Signature

An application for a single employer plan must be signed by the employer. An application for a plan of more than one employer must be signed by the plan administrator.

Change in Funding Methods

Do not file Form 5308 to change your plan's funding method. See Rev. Proc. 78-37, 1978-2 C.B. 540.

☆ U.S. Government Printing Office: 1984—461-495/10059

Form **5330**
(Rev. May 1984)

Department of the Treasury
Internal Revenue Service

Return of Initial Excise Taxes
Related to Pension and Profit-Sharing Plans

(Under sections 4971, 4973(a)(2) and 4975 of the Internal Revenue Code)

OMB No. 1545-0575

For tax year beginning _____ , 19____ and ending _____ , 19____

Name (see general instructions)	Check applicable box and enter number:
	☐ Employer identification number **OR**
Address (number and street)	☐ Social security number
	(see general instructions)
City or town, State and ZIP code	

Name and address of employer whose plan was involved in the prohibited transaction	Employer identification number
	Plan year ending
Name of plan	Plan number

Part I — Taxes on Failure to Meet Minimum Funding Standards

1	Accumulated funding deficiency in the plan's minimum funding standard account (see specific instructions) . .	
2	Accumulated funding deficiency in the plan's alternative minimum funding standard account (see specific instructions)	
3	Tax due—5% of line 1 or 5% of line 2 (see instructions). Enter here and on line 14 . . . . ▶	

Part II — Tax on Excess Contributions to 403(b)(7)(A) Custodial Accounts

4	Total amount contributed for current year, less rollovers identified in section 4973(c)(1)	
5	Amount excludable from gross income under section 403(b) (see instructions)	
6	Current year excess contributions (line 4 less line 5, but not less than zero)	
7	Prior year excess contributions not previously eliminated—if zero proceed to line 11	
8	Contribution credit (if line 5 exceeds line 4, enter the excess, otherwise enter zero)	
9	Total of all prior years' distributions out of the account included in your gross income under section 72(e) and not previously used to reduce excess contributions	
10	Adjusted prior years' excess contributions (line 7 less the total of lines 8 and 9)	
11	Taxable excess contributions (line 6 plus line 10)	
12	Excess contributions tax—Enter the lesser of 6% of line 11 or 6% of the value of your account as of the last day of the year. Enter here and on line 15 . . . . ▶	

Part III — Tax on Prohibited Transactions

13 (a) Transaction number	a. Date of transaction (see instructions)	b. Description of prohibited transaction	c. Amount involved in prohibited transaction (see instructions)	d. Initial tax on prohibited transaction (5% of column c) (see instructions)
(i)				
(ii)				
(iii)				

(b) Tax due—Add amounts in column d. Enter here and on line 16 . . . . ▶

Please Sign Here

Under penalties of perjury, I declare that I have examined this return, including accompanying schedules and statements, and to the best of my knowledge and belief, it is true, correct, and complete. Declaration of preparer (other than taxpayer) is based on all information of which preparer has any knowledge.

▶ _____ Your signature ▶ _____ Date

Paid Preparer's Use Only

Preparer's signature ▶	▶ _____ Date
Firm's name (or yours, if self-employed) and address ▶	

For Paperwork Reduction Act Notice, see page 1 of the instructions.

Form **5330** (Rev. 5-84)

Part IV	Summary of Taxes Due

14 Tax on failure to meet minimum funding standard (from line 3) . . . . _____

15 Tax on excess contributions to 403(b)(7)(A) custodial accounts (from line 12) . . . . _____

16 Tax on prohibited transactions (from line 13(b)) . . . . _____

17 **(a)** Total tax (add lines 14, 15 and 16) . . . . _____

     (b) Enter amount of tax paid upon filing of Form 5558, if applicable   . . . . _____

     (c) Total tax due (subtract line 17(b) from line 17(a)). Pay in full with return. (Make checks or money orders payable to Internal Revenue Service) . . . . ▶ _____

18 Are you electing to be taxed on a prohibited transaction which occurred prior to January 1, 1975, so that your plan and trust will retain its exempt status? . . . . □ **Yes**   □ **No**

19 Have you corrected any of the prohibited transactions which you are reporting on this return? . . . . □ **Yes**   □ **No** If "Yes," complete Part VI.

Part V	Schedule of Other Participating Disqualified Persons

20

a. Name and address of disqualified person	b. Transaction number from Part III	c. Employer identification number or social security number
(i)		
(ii)		
(iii)		

Part VI	Description and Documentation of Correction

21

a. Transaction number from Part III	b. Nature of correction	c. Date of correction

☆U.S. Government Printing Office: 1984—421-108/307

264

Instructions for Form 5330

(Revised May 1984)

Return of Initial Excise Taxes Related to Pension and Profit-Sharing Plans

(Section references are to the Internal Revenue Code of 1954 unless otherwise specified.)

General Information

Paperwork Reduction Act Notice

The Paperwork Reduction Act of 1980 says we must tell you why we are collecting this information, how we will use it, and whether you have to give it to us. We ask for the information to carry out the Internal Revenue laws of the United States. We need it to ensure that you are complying with these laws and to allow us to figure and collect the right amount of tax. You are required to give us this information.

Purpose

This return is to be used to report the tax on (i) a minimum funding deficiency (section 4971); (ii) excess contributions to a section 403(b)(7)(A) custodial account (section 4973(a)); and (iii) a prohibited transaction occurring after December 31, 1974 (section 4975).

This return is also to be used to make the election under section 2003(c)(1)(B) of the Employee Retirement Income Security Act of 1974 (ERISA). This election allows a disqualified person to elect to pay the section 4975 tax on a prohibited transaction which took place prior to January 1, 1975, in order to avoid loss of the exempt status by a trust.

NOTE: *Excess contributions tax on Keogh (H.R.-10) Plans for tax years beginning before 1/1/84 should be reported on Form 5330 (Rev. December 1981).*

Who Must File

A Form 5330 must be filed by:

(1) any employer who fails to meet the minimum funding standards under section 412 (for liability for tax in case of an employer who is a party to a collective bargaining agreement see section 413(b)(6)); or

(2) any individual with respect to whom there has been made an excess contribution to a 403(b)(7)(A) custodial account and which excess has not been eliminated as specified in section 4973(c)(2)(A) and (B); or

(3) any disqualified person who participates in a prohibited transaction (other than a fiduciary acting only as such or an individual (or his beneficiary) who engages in a prohibited transaction with respect to his individual retirement account) for each tax year or part thereof in the "taxable period" applicable to such prohibited transaction.

The payment of tax and filing of Form 5330 is required for each year in which you fail to meet the minimum funding standards under section 412 or contribute an excess amount to your 403(b)(7)(A) custodial account . The payment of tax and filing of Form 5330 is also required for each year (or part thereof) in the "taxable period" applicable to a prohibited transaction and ends with the earliest of: (i) the date correction is completed, (ii) the date of mailing of a notice of deficiency, or (iii) the date on which the tax under section 4975(a) is assessed.

Definitions

A. Plan.—For purposes of these definitions, the term "plan" means a trust described in section 401(a) which forms part of a plan, or a plan described in section 403(a) or 405(a), which trust or plan is exempt from tax under section 501(a), an individual retirement account described in section 408(a), an individual retirement annuity described in section 408(b) or a retirement bond described in section 409. For purposes of the tax on minimum funding deficiencies and prohibited transactions, a trust, plan, account, annuity or bond which, at any time, has been determined by the Internal Revenue Service to be a trust, plan, account, annuity or bond as described in the preceding sentence is a plan subject to these taxes.

A trust described in section 501(c)(22) is considered a plan for purposes of prohibited transactions.

B. Disqualified Person.—A "disqualified person" is any person who is:

(1) a fiduciary;

(2) a person providing services to the plan;

(3) an employer, any of whose employees are covered by the plan;

(4) an employee organization, any of whose members are covered by the plan;

(5) an owner, direct or indirect, of 50% or more of—(a) the combined voting power of all classes of stock entitled to vote, or the total value of shares of all classes of stock of a corporation, (b) the capital interest or the profits interest of a partnership, or (c) the beneficial interest of a trust or unincorporated enterprise, which is an employer or an employee organization described in (3) or (4);

(6) a member of the family of any individual described in (1), (2), (3), or (5) (member of a family is the spouse, ancestor, lineal descendant, and any spouse of a lineal descendant);

(7) a corporation, partnership, or trust or estate of which (or in which) 50% or more of the interest described in (5)(a), (b), and (c) is owned directly or indirectly, or held by persons described in (1), (2), (3), (4), or (5);

(8) an officer, director (or an individual having powers or responsibilities similar to those of officers or directors), a 10% or more shareholder, or highly compensated employee (earning 10% or more of the yearly wages of an employer) of a person described in (3), (4), (5), or (7);

(9) a 10% or more (in capital or profits) partner or joint venturer of a person described in (3), (4), (5), or (7); or

(10) any disqualified person, as described in (1) through (9) above, who is a disqualified person with respect to any plan to which a section 501(c)(22) trust is permitted to make payments under section 4223 of ERISA.

C. Prohibited Transaction.—Means any direct or indirect:

(1) (a) sale or exchange, or leasing, of any property between a plan and a disqualified person;

(b) transfer of real or personal property by a disqualified person to a plan where the property is subject to a mortgage or similar lien placed on the property by the disqualified person within 10 years prior to the transfer, or the property transferred is subject to a mortgage or similar lien which the plan assumes;

(2) lending of money or other extension of credit between a plan and a disqualified person;

(3) furnishing of goods, services, or facilities between a plan and a disqualified person;

(4) transfer to, or use by or for the benefit of, a disqualified person of income or assets of a plan;

(5) act by a disqualified person who is a fiduciary whereby he (she) deals with the income or assets of a plan in his (her) own account; or

(6) receipt of any consideration for his (her) own personal account by any disqualified person who is a fiduciary from any party dealing with the plan connected with a transaction involving the income or assets of the plan.

D. Exemptions.—See section 4975(d) for specific exemptions to prohibited transactions.

In addition, section 2003(c)(2) of ERISA contains rules which delay the application of section 4975 for certain arrangements in effect on June 30, 1974. Furthermore, certain other transactions or classes of transactions have been exempted pursuant to section 4975(c)(2).

General Instructions

A. When and Where to File.—

(1) For taxes due other than tax resulting from an election to be taxed under section 2003(c)(1)(B) of ERISA, this return is to be filed on or before the last day of the seventh month after the end of the taxable year of the employer or other person who must file this return. However, you may be granted an extension of time to file this return if the request is made in writing on or before the due date for filing this return. Form 5558, Application for Extension of Time to File Certain Employee Plan Returns, may be used to request this extension. Such extension shall not exceed six months.

(2) For tax due resulting from an election to be taxed under section 2003(c)(1)(B) of ERISA, this return is to be filed prior to 120 days after the date of notification, under section 1.503(a)-1(c) of the income tax regulations, that the trust shall not be exempt from taxation under section 501(a) because it engaged in a pre-1975 prohibited transaction.

Note: *If contributions are made to your plan within 8½ months after the plan year ended, you automatically have an extension until that time for filing Form 5330 and paying the 5% tax on any funding deficiency (see section 412(c)(10)). If the contributions are not made within the 8½-month period, the Form 5330 is due at the normal time, 7 months after the employer's tax year ended.*

This return should be filed with the Internal Revenue Service Center where you filed your income tax return.

B. Name, Address, etc.—The name of the employer or the name of the individual on whom the tax is imposed should appear on the line designated on page 1. If an employer is filing this return, the employer's identification number should be entered to the right of the name in the space indicated. If an individual (other than a sole proprietor filing as an employer) is filing this return, the individual's social security number should be entered to the right of the name in the space indicated.

C. Signature of Preparer.—If someone fills out your return and does not charge you, that person should not sign your return. For example, your regular full-time employee or your partner in business does not have to sign. (This example is not all inclusive.)

Generally, anyone who is paid to prepare your return must sign your return and fill in the other blanks in the Paid Preparer Use Only area of your return.

Reminders

Penalties and Interest

A. Interest.—Interest will be charged on taxes not paid on or before their due date, even if an extension of time to file is granted.

B. Late Filing of Return.—The law provides a penalty of from 5 percent to 25 percent of the tax due for filing late unless you can show reasonable cause for the delay. If you file a return late, attach an explanation to your return.

C. Late Payment of Tax.—The penalty for not paying tax when due is ½ of 1 percent of the unpaid amount for each month or part of a month it remains unpaid. The maximum penalty is 25 percent of the unpaid amount. The penalty applies to any unpaid tax shown on a return. It also applies to any additional tax shown on a bill if it is not paid within 10 days from the date of the bill. The penalty is in addition to the applicable interest charge on late payments.

Specific Instructions

Part I

If your plan has an accumulated funding deficiency as defined in section 412 (section 418B if this is a multiemployer plan in reorganization), complete lines 1 and 3. Complete line 2 only if the alternative minimum funding standards account is used. (See Schedule B (Form 5500) and Form 5500, Form 5500-C, or Form 5500-R, whichever is applicable.) Enter 5% of line 1 on line 3; or, if line 2 applies, enter the lesser of 5% of line 1 or 5% of line 2, on line 3.

Part II

Line 5.—The amount excludable for your taxable year is the lesser of:

(a) The exclusion allowance which is the excess of: (i) 20% of your compensation includible in gross income (do not include any amount contributed by your employer for your annuity) from your employer, multiplied by the number of years of service as of the end of your taxable year for which you are computing this exclusion allowance over,(ii) the aggregate of the amounts which have been contributed by your employer and excludable from your gross income in prior years; or

(b) The annual employer contribution limitation. Since tax-sheltered annuities are considered defined contribution plans, the limitation is the lesser of:

(1) $30,000 or

(2) 25% of the employee's compensation for the year.

If you are an employee of an educational institution, hospital, or home health service agency, you may elect alternative limitations under section 415(c)(4)(A), (B) or (C).

Part III

Note: *Section 141.4975-13 of the Temporary Excise Tax Regulations provides that, until superseded by permanent regulations under section 4975(f), the definitions of "amount involved," and "correction" found in section 53.4941(e)-1 of the Foundation Excise Tax Regulations will be controlling.*

Line 13(a), Column a.—List all prohibited transactions that took place during the current taxable year. Also list all prohibited transactions that took place in prior years unless either the transaction was corrected in a prior tax year or the section 4975(a) tax was assessed in the prior tax year.

Remember, transactions involving the use of money (loans, etc.) or other property (rent, etc.) will be treated as giving rise to a new prohibited transaction on the first day of each succeeding taxable year or portion of a succeeding taxable year which is within the "taxable period."

Column c. *Amount involved in prohibited transaction.*—The "amount involved" with respect to a prohibited transaction means the greater of the amount of money and fair market value of the other property given, or the amount of money and the fair market value of the other property received, except that, in the case of services described in section 4975(d)(2) and (10) the amount involved shall be only the excess compensation. Fair market value shall be determined as of the date on which the prohibited transaction occurs. Where the use of money or other property is involved, the amount involved shall be the greater of the amount paid for such use or the fair market value of such use for the period for which the money or other property is used. Further, transactions involving the use of money or other property will be treated as giving rise to a prohibited transaction occurring on the date of the actual transaction plus a new prohibited transaction on the first day of each succeeding taxable year or

portion of a succeeding taxable year which is within the "taxable period." The "taxable period" is the period of time beginning with the date of the prohibited transaction and ending with the earliest of: (i) the date correction is completed, (ii) the date of the mailing of a notice of deficiency, or (iii) the date on which the tax under section 4975(a) is assessed. See instruction for line 20 for the definition of "correction."

Example: *A disqualified person borrows money from a plan. The fair market value of the actual interest on the loan is $1,000 per month. The loan was made on July 1, 1981, and repaid on December 31, 1982 (date correction is completed). The disqualified person's tax year is the calendar year. The disqualified person files a Form 5330 for the tax years 1981 and 1982 on July 31, 1982 (date tax was assessed), and July 31, 1983, respectively.*

From the above facts the "taxable period" for the first prohibited transaction runs from July 1, 1981 (date of loan), through July 31, 1982 (date tax was assessed). The "taxable period" for the second prohibited transaction runs from January 1, 1982,

through December 31, 1982 (date of correction).

The disqualified person files a Form 5330 for 1981 on July 31, 1982, paying the tax due on the first prohibited transaction which occurred on July 1, 1981. The amount involved to be reported on the Form 5330 filed for 1981 is $6,000 (6 months X $1,000). The amount involved in the second prohibited transaction, which is deemed to have occurred on January 1, 1982, is $12,000 (12 months X $1,000). The taxable period for the second prohibited transaction runs from January 1, 1982, through December 31, 1982, when correction took place.

Since the taxable period of the first prohibited transaction ended July 31, 1982, and the taxable period of the second prohibited transaction ended December 31, 1982, at least part of the year 1982 is in both taxable periods. Therefore, the amount reported on Form 5330 filed for 1982 would include both the first prohibited transaction of July 1, 1981, $6,000, and the second prohibited transaction of January 1, 1982, $12,000. Therefore, item 13 of Form 5330 would be completed in the following manner:

For 1981

PART III.—Tax on Prohibited Transactions

13(a) Transaction number	a. Date of transaction (see instructions)	b. Description of prohibited transaction	c. Amount involved in prohibited transaction (see instructions)	d. Initial tax on prohibited transaction (5% of column c) (see instructions)
(i)	7-1-81	Loan	$6,000	$300
(ii)				
(iii)				
(b) Tax due—Add amounts in column d. Enter here and on line 16 . . . . ▶				$300

For 1982

PART III.—Tax on Prohibited Transactions

13(a) Transaction number	a. Date of transaction (see instructions)	b. Description of prohibited transaction	c. Amount involved in prohibited transaction (see instructions)	d. Initial tax on prohibited transaction (5% of column c) (see instructions)
(i)	7-1-81	Loan	$6,000	$300
(ii)	1-1-82	Loan	12,000	600
(iii)				
(b) Tax due—Add amounts in column d. Enter here and on line 16 . . . . ▶				$900

Part IV

Line 19.—If you are electing as provided under section 2003(c)(1)(B) of ERISA to have section 4975 apply to a prohibited transaction which occurred prior to January 1, 1975, check "Yes."

Line 20.—In order to avoid liability for additional taxes and penalties under section 4975, and in some cases further initial taxes, the prohibited transaction must be corrected within the taxable period. The term "corrected" is defined as undoing the prohibited transaction to the extent possible, but in any case placing the plan in a financial position not worse than that in which it would be if the disqualified person were acting under the highest fiduciary standards.

If at the time this return is filed the prohibited transaction giving rise to the liability for tax under section 4975 has been corrected, the answer to line 20 should be "Yes." Also, Part VI should be completed for each correction, giving the following information:(a) the number of the transaction from Part III; (b) the nature of the correction; and (c) the date of the correction.

Part V

Where more than one disqualified person participates in the same prohibited transaction, the name, address and the social security number or employer identification number of each participant other than the participant who is filing this return must be listed on this schedule.

☆ U.S. Government Printing Office: 1984—421-108/308

Form **5500**

Department of the Treasury
Internal Revenue Service

Department of Labor
Pension and Welfare Benefit Programs

Pension Benefit Guaranty Corporation

Annual Return/Report of Employee Benefit Plan
(With 100 or more participants)

This form is required to be filed under sections 104 and 4065 of the
Employee Retirement Income Security Act of 1974 and sections 6057(b)
and 6058(a) of the Internal Revenue Code, referred to as the Code.

▶ For Paperwork Reduction Act Notice, see page 1 of the instructions.

OMB No. 1210-0016

1984

This Form is Open
to Public Inspection

For the calendar plan year 1984 or fiscal plan year beginning _____ , 1984, and ending _____ , 19 __ .

Type or print in ink all entries on the form, schedules, and attachments. If an item does not apply, enter "N/A." File the originals.

This return/report is: *(i)* ☐ the return/report filed for the plan's first year; *(ii)* ☐ an amended return/report; or
(iii) ☐ the final return/report filed for the plan.

▶ Caution: A penalty of $25 a day for the late or incomplete filing of this return/report will be assessed unless reasonable cause is established—see General Instruction F.

▶ Welfare benefit plans with 100 or more participants, complete only items 1 through 11, 13 through 16 and item 22.

▶ Keogh (H.R. 10) plans must check the box in item 5(a)(iii).

▶ If you have been granted an extension of time to file this form, you must attach a copy of the approved extension to this form.

Use IRS label. Otherwise, please print or type.	**1 (a)** Name of plan sponsor (employer if for a single employer plan)	**1 (b)** Employer identification number
	Address (number and street)	**1 (c)** Telephone number of sponsor ( )
	City or town, State and ZIP code	**1 (d)** If plan year changed since last return/report, check here. ▶ ☐

2 (a) Name of plan administrator (if same as plan sponsor enter "Same")

1 (e) Business code number ▶

Address (number and street)

2 (b) Administrator's employer identification no.

City or town, State and ZIP code

2 (c) Telephone number of administrator ( )

3 Is the name, address and identification number of the plan sponsor and/or plan administrator the same as they appeared on the last return/report filed for this plan? ☐ Yes ☐ No. If "No," enter the information from the last return/report in (a) and/or (b).
(a) Sponsor ▶ _____ EIN _____
(b) Administrator ▶ _____ EIN _____
(c) If (a) indicates a change in the sponsor's name and EIN, is this a change in sponsorship only? (See specific instructions for definition of sponsorship.) ☐ Yes ☐ No

4 Check appropriate box to indicate the type of plan entity (check only one box):
(a) ☐ Single-employer plan   (c) ☐ Multiemployer plan   (e) ☐ Multiple-employer plan (other)
(b) ☐ Plan of controlled group of corporations or common control employers   (d) ☐ Multiple-employer-collectively-bargained plan   (f) ☐ Group insurance arrangement (of welfare plans)

5 (a) *(i)* Name of plan ▶ _____

5 (b) Effective date of plan

(ii) ☐ Check if name of plan changed since last return/report
(iii) ☐ Check this box if this is a Keogh (H.R. 10) plan.

5 (c) Enter three-digit plan number ▶

6 Check at least one item in (a) or (b) and applicable items in (c):
(a) Welfare benefit plan (Plan numbers 501 through 999):   *(i)* ☐ Health insurance   *(ii)* ☐ Life insurance
     (iii) ☐ Supplemental unemployment   *(iv)* ☐ Other (specify) ▶ _____
(b) Pension benefit plan (Plan numbers 001 through 500):
   (i) Defined benefit plan—(Indicate type of defined benefit plan below):
     (A) ☐ Fixed benefit   (B) ☐ Unit benefit   (C) ☐ Flat benefit   (D) ☐ Other (specify) ▶ _____
   (ii) Defined contribution plan—(indicate type of defined contribution plan below):
     (A) ☐ Profit-sharing   (B) ☐ Stock bonus   (C) ☐ Target benefit   (D) ☐ Other money purchase
     (E) ☐ Other (specify) ▶ _____
   (iii) ☐ Defined benefit plan with benefits based partly on balance of separate account of participant (Code section 414(k))
   (iv) ☐ Annuity arrangement of a certain exempt organization (Code section 403(b)(1))
   (v) ☐ Custodial account for regulated investment company stock (Code section 403(b)(7))
   (vi) ☐ Pension plan utilizing individual retirement accounts or annuities (described in Code section 408) as the sole funding vehicle for providing benefits
   (vii) ☐ Other (specify) ▶

Under penalties of perjury and other penalties set forth in the instructions, I declare that I have examined this return/report, including accompanying schedules and statements, and to the best of my knowledge and belief, it is true, correct, and complete.

Date ▶ _____ Signature of employer/plan sponsor ▶ _____

Date ▶ _____ Signature of plan administrator ▶ _____

6 (c) Other plan features: *(i)* ☐ Thrift-savings   *(ii)* ☐ Participant-directed account plan

       (iii) ☐ Pension plan maintained outside the United States   *(iv)* ☐ Master trust (see instructions) ▶ - - - - - - - - - - - - - -

		Yes	No
(d) Single-employer plans enter the tax year end of the employer in which this plan year ends . . ▶ Month _____ Day _____ Year _____			
(e) Is this a pension plan of an affiliated service group?			
(f) Does this plan contain a cash or deferred arrangement described in Code section 401(k)?			

7 Number of participants as of the end of the plan year (welfare plans complete only (a)(iv), (b), (c) and (d)):

   (a) Active participants: *(i)*   Number fully vested .

                      (ii)   Number partially vested . . . .

                      (iii)   Number nonvested . . . .

                      (iv)   Total . . . .

   (b) Retired or separated participants receiving benefits . . . .

   (c) Retired or separated participants entitled to future benefits . . . .

   (d) Subtotal (add (a)(iv), (b) and (c)) . . . .

   (e) Deceased participants whose beneficiaries are receiving or are entitled to receive benefits . . . .

   (f) Total (add (d) and (e)) . . . .

	Yes	No
(g) *(i)* Was any participant(s) separated from service with a deferred vested benefit for which a Schedule SSA (Form 5500) is required to be attached to this form?		
(ii) If "Yes," enter the number of separated participants required to be reported ▶		

8 Plan amendment information (welfare plans do not complete (b)(ii)):

   (a) Was any amendment to this plan adopted in this plan year? . . . .

   (b) If "Yes," *(i)* And if any amendments have resulted in a change in the information contained in a summary plan description or previously furnished summary description of modifications—

           (A) Have summary descriptions of the change(s) been sent to participants? . . . .

           (B) Have summary descriptions of the change(s) been filed with DOL? . . . .

        (ii) Does any amendment result in the reduction of the accrued benefit of any participant under the plan? .

   (c) Enter the date the most recent amendment was adopted . . . . ▶ Month _____ Day _____ Year _____

   (d) *(i)* Has a summary plan description been filed with DOL for this plan? . . . .

       (ii) If (i) is "Yes," what was the employer identification number and the plan number used to identify it?

       Employer identification number ▶   Plan number ▶

9 Plan termination information (welfare plans complete only (a), (b), (c) and (f)):

   (a) Was this plan terminated during this plan year or any prior plan year? . . . . If "Yes," enter year ▶ _____

   (b) Were all plan assets either distributed to participants or beneficiaries, transferred to another plan, or brought under the control of PBGC?

   (c) Was a resolution to terminate this plan adopted during this plan year or any prior plan year? . . . . .

   (d) If (a) or (c) is "Yes," have you received a favorable determination letter from IRS for the termination? . . . . .

   (e) If (d) is "No," has a determination letter been requested from IRS? . . . .

   (f) If (a) or (c) is "Yes," have participants and beneficiaries been notified of the termination or the proposed termination?

   (g) If (a) is "Yes," and the plan is covered by PBGC, is the plan continuing to file a PBGC Form 1 and pay premiums until the end of the plan year in which assets are distributed or brought under the control of PBGC? . . . .

10 (a) In this plan year, was this plan merged or consolidated into another plan, or were assets or liabilities transferred to another plan? . . . .

If "Yes," identify other plan(s):

	(c) Employer identification number(s)	**(d)** Plan number(s)
(b) Name of plan(s) ▶ - - - - - - - - - - - - - - - - -	- - - - - - - - - - -	- - - - - - - -
- -	- - - - - - - - - - -	- - - - - - - -

   (e) Has Form 5310 been filed? . . . . ☐ **Yes** ☐ **No**

11 Indicate funding arrangement: **(a)** ☐ Trust (benefits provided in whole from trust funds)

   (b) ☐ Trust or arrangement providing benefits partially through insurance and/or annuity contracts

   (c) ☐ Trust or arrangement providing benefits exclusively through insurance and/or annuity contracts

   (d) ☐ Custodial account described in Code section 401(f) and not included in (c) above

   (e) ☐ Other (specify) ▶ -

   (f) If (b) or (c) is checked, enter the number of Schedules A (Form 5500) which are attached . . . . ▶

12 (a) Has the plan used the services of a contract administrator (see instructions)? . . . . ☐ **Yes** ☐ **No**

     If "Yes," you must complete line (1) of the schedule below.

   (b) Did any other person who rendered services to the plan receive, directly or indirectly, compensation from the plan in the plan year? . ☐ **Yes** ☐ **No**

     If "Yes," furnish the following information starting on line (2):

a. Name	**b.** Employer identification number (see instructions)	**c.** Official plan position	**d.** Relationship to employer, employee organization, or person known to be a party-in-interest	**e.** Gross salary or allowances paid by plan	**f.** Fees and commissions paid by plan	**g.** Nature of service code (see instructions)
(1)		Contract admin.				13
(2)						
(3)						

13   Plan assets and liabilities at the beginning and the end of the plan year (list all assets and liabilities at current value). A fully insured welfare plan or a pension plan with no trust and which is funded entirely by allocated insurance contracts which fully guarantee the amount of benefit payments should check the box and not complete the rest of this item ▶ . . . . □

Note: *Include all plan assets and liabilities of a trust or separately maintained fund. (If more than one trust/fund, report on a combined basis.) Include all insurance values except for the value of that portion of an allocated insurance contract which fully guarantees the amount of benefit payments. Round off amounts to the nearest dollar. Trusts with no assets at the beginning and the end of the plan year enter zero on line 13(h).*

Assets	a. Beginning of year	b. End of year
(a) Cash: *(i)* On hand		
(ii) In bank: (A) Certificate of deposit		
(B) Other interest bearing		
(C) Noninterest bearing		
(iii) Total cash (add (i) and (ii))		
(b) Receivables: *(i)* Employer contributions . . .		
(ii) Employee contributions		
(iii) Other		
(iv) Reserve for doubtful accounts		
(v) Net receivables (subtract (iv) from the total of (i),(ii) and (iii))		
(c) General investments other than party-in-interest investments:	///////////	///////////
(i) U.S. Government securities (A) Long term		
(B) Short term		
(ii) State and municipal securities		
(iii) Corporate debt instruments: (A) Long term		
(B) Short term		
(iv) Corporate stocks: (A) Preferred		
(B) Common		
(v) Shares of a registered investment company .		
(vi) Real estate		
(vii) Mortgages		
(viii) Loans other than mortgages		
(ix) Value of interest in pooled fund(s)		
(x) Value of interest in master trust		
(xi) Other investments		
(xii) Total general investments (add (i) through (xi))		
(d) Party-in-interest investments:	///////////	///////////
(i) Corporate debt instruments		
(ii) Corporate stocks: (A) Preferred		
(B) Common		
(iii) Real estate		
(iv) Mortgages		
(v) Loans other than mortgages		
(vi) Other investments		
(vii) Total party-in-interest investments (add (i) through (vi))		
(e) Buildings and other depreciable property used in plan operation	///////////	///////////
(f) Value of unallocated insurance contracts (other than pooled separate accounts):	///////////	///////////
(i) Separate accounts		
(ii) Other		
(iii) Total (add (i) and (ii))		
(g) Other assets		
(h) Total assets (add (a)(iii), (b)(v), (c)(xii), (d)(vii), (e), (f)(iii) and (g))		
Liabilities	///////////	///////////
(i) Payables: *(i)* Plan claims		
(ii) Other payables		
(iii) Total payables (add (i) and (ii))		
(j) Acquisition indebtedness		
(k) Other liabilities		
(l) Total liabilities (add (i), (j), and (k))		
(m) Net assets (subtract (l) from (h))		
(n) During the plan year what were the:	///////////	
(i) Total costs of acquisitions for common stock?		
(ii) Total proceeds from dispositions of common stock?		

14 Plan income, expenses and changes in net assets for the plan year.

Note: *Include all income and expenses of a trust(s) or separately maintained fund(s) including any payments made for allocated insurance contracts. Round off amounts to nearest dollar.*

Income	a. Amount	b. Total
(a) Contributions received or receivable in cash from—		
(i) Employer(s) (including contributions on behalf of self-employed individuals) . .		
(ii) Employees		
(iii) Others		
(b) Noncash contributions (specify nature and by whom made) ▶		
(c) Total contributions (add total of (a)(iii) and (b))		
(d) Earnings from investments—		
(i) Interest		
(ii) Dividends		
(iii) Rents		
(iv) Royalties		
(e) Net realized gain (loss) on sale or exchange of assets—		
(i) Aggregate proceeds		
(ii) Aggregate costs		
(f) Other income (specify) ▶		
(g) Total income (add (c) through (f))		

Expenses	a. Amount	b. Total
(h) Distribution of benefits and payments to provide benefits—		
(i) Directly to participants or their beneficiaries		
(ii) To insurance carrier or similar organization for provision of benefits		
(iii) To other organizations or individuals providing welfare benefits		
(i) Interest expense		
(j) Administrative expenses—		
(i) Salaries and allowances		
(ii) Fees and commissions		
(iii) Insurance premiums for Pension Benefit Guaranty Corporation		
(iv) Insurance premiums for fiduciary insurance other than bonding		
(v) Other administrative expenses.		
(k) Other expenses (specify) ▶		
(l) Total expenses (add (h) through (k))		
(m) Net income (expenses) (subtract (l) from (g))		

(n) Changes in net assets —	a. Amount	b. Total
(i) Unrealized appreciation (depreciation) of assets		
(ii) Net investment gain (or loss) from all master trust investment accounts . . .		
(iii) Other changes (specify) ▶		
(o) Net increase (decrease) in net assets for the year (add (m) and (n))		
(p) Net assets at beginning of year (line 13(m), column a).		
(q) Net assets at end of year (add (o) and (p)) (equals line 13(m), column b)		

15 All plans complete (a). Plans funded with insurance policies or annuity contracts also complete (b) and (c):

		Yes	No
(a)	Since the end of the plan year covered by the last return/report has there been a termination in the appointment of any trustee, accountant, insurance carrier, enrolled actuary, administrator, investment manager or custodian?		
	If "Yes," explain and include the name, position, address and telephone number of the person whose appointment has been terminated ▶		
(b)	Have any insurance policies or annuities been replaced during this plan year?		
	If "Yes," explain the reason for the replacement ▶		

(c) At any time during the plan year was the plan funded with:
(i) ☐ Individual policies or annuities, *(ii)* ☐ Group policies or annuities, or *(iii)* ☐ Both.

		Yes	No

16 Bonding:

(a) Was the plan insured by a fidelity bond against losses through fraud or dishonesty? . . . .

If "Yes," complete (b) through (f); if "No," only complete (g).

(b) Indicate the number of plans covered by this bond ▶ ....

(c) Enter the maximum amount of loss recoverable ▶ ....

(d) Enter the name of the surety company ▶ ....

....

(e) Does the plan, or a known party-in-interest with respect to the plan, have any control or significant financial interest, direct or indirect, in the surety company or its agents or brokers? . . . .

(f) In the current plan year was any loss to the plan caused by the fraud or dishonesty of any plan official or employee of the plan or of other person handling funds of the plan? . . . .

If "Yes," see Specific Instructions.

(g) If the plan is not insured by a fidelity bond, explain why not ▶ ....

....

17 Information about employees of employer at end of the plan year.

(a) Does the plan satisfy the percentage tests of Code section 410(b)(1)(A)? If "No," complete only (b) below and see Specific Instructions . . . .

(b) Total number of employees . . . .

(c) Number of employees excluded under the plan because of:

    (i) Minimum age or years of service . . . .

    (ii) Employees on whose behalf retirement benefits were the subject of collective bargaining . . .

    (iii) Nonresident aliens who receive no earned income from United States sources . . . . . .

    (iv) Total excluded (add (i), (ii) and (iii)) . . . .

(d) Total number of employees not excluded (subtract (c)(iv) from (b)) . . . .

(e) Employees ineligible (specify reason) ▶ ....

(f) Employees eligible to participate (subtract (e) from (d)) . . . .

(g) Employees eligible but not participating . . . .

(h) Employees participating (subtract (g) from (f)) . . . .

		Yes	No

18 Is this plan an adoption of any of the plans below? (If "Yes," check appropriate box and enter IRS serial number):

(a) ☐ Master/prototype, **(b)** ☐ Field prototype, **(c)** ☐ Pattern, **(d)** ☐ Model plan, or **(e)** ☐ Bond purchase plan . .

Enter the four or eight-digit IRS serial number (see instructions) ▶

19 (a) Is it intended that this plan qualify under Code section 401(a) or 405? . . . .

(b) Have you requested or received a determination letter from the IRS for this plan? . . . .

(c) Is this a plan with Employee Stock Ownership Plan features? . . . .

    (i) If "Yes," was a current appraisal of the value of the stock made immediately before any contribution of stock or the purchase of the stock by the trust for the plan year covered by this return/report? . . . .

    (ii) If (i) is "Yes," was the appraisal made by an unrelated third party? . . . .

20 (a) If plan is integrated, check appropriate box:

    (i) ☐ Social security   (ii) ☐ Railroad retirement   (iii) ☐ Other

(b) Does the employer/sponsor listed in item 1(a) of this form maintain other qualified pension benefit plans? . . . .

If "Yes," list the number of plans including this plan ▶

21 (a) If this is a defined benefit plan, is it subject to the minimum funding standards for this plan year? . . . .

If "Yes," attach Schedule B (Form 5500).

(b) If this is a defined contribution plan, i.e., money purchase or target benefit, is it subject to the minimum funding standards? (If a waiver was granted, see instructions.) . . . .

If "Yes," complete (i), (ii) and (iii) below:

    (i) Amount of employer contribution required for the plan year under Code section 412 . . . . . .

    (ii) Amount of contribution paid by the employer for the plan year . . . .

    Enter date of last payment by employer . . . . . ▶ Month _____ Day _____ Year _____

    (iii) If (i) is greater than (ii), subtract (ii) from (i) and enter the funding deficiency here; otherwise enter zero. (If you have a funding deficiency, file Form 5330.) . . . .

		Yes	No

22 Answer questions (a), (b), and (c) relating to the plan year. If (a)(i), (ii), (iii), (iv) or (v) is checked "Yes," schedules of those items in the format set forth in the instructions are required to be attached to this form.

(a) *(i)* Did the plan have assets held for investment? . . . .

    (ii) Did any non-exempt transaction involving plan assets involve a party known to be a party-in-interest? . . . .

    (iii) Were any loans by the plan or fixed income obligations due the plan in default as of the close of the plan year or classified during the year as uncollectable? . . . .

	Yes	No
22 *(Continued)*		
(iv) Were any leases to which the plan was a party in default or classified during the year as uncollectable?		
(v) Were any plan transactions or series of transactions in excess of 3% of the current value of plan assets? . . .		

(b) The accountant's opinion is *(i)* ☐ Required, or *(ii)* ☐ Not required

(c) If the accountant's opinion is required, attach it to this form and check the appropriate box. This opinion is:

    (i) ☐ Unqualified

    (ii) ☐ Qualified

    (iii) ☐ Adverse

    (iv) ☐ Other (explain) ▶

23 (a) Is the plan covered under the Pension Benefit Guaranty Corporation termination
insurance program? . . . . ☐ **Yes** ☐ **No** ☐ **Not determined**

(b) If (a) is "Yes," or "Not determined," enter the employer identification number and the plan number used to identify it.

Employer identification number ▶   Plan number ▶

	Yes	No
24 (a) Is this plan a top-heavy plan within the meaning of Code section 416 for this plan year?	//////	//////
(b) If (a) is "Yes," complete (i), (ii) and (iii) below:		
(i) Has the plan complied with the vesting requirements of Code section 416(b)?		
(ii) Has the plan complied with the minimum benefit requirements of Code section 416(c)?		
(iii) Has the plan complied with the limitation on compensation of Code section 416(d)?		
25 Have any individuals performed services as a leased employee for this employer or for any other employer who is aggregated with this employer under section 414(b), (c), or (m)? . . . . If "Yes," see instructions for completing item 17.	//////	//////

✿ U.S. GOVERNMENT PRINTING OFFICE: 1985-423-261 E.I. 43-0787287

SCHEDULE A
(Form 5500)
Department of the Treasury
Internal Revenue Service

Department of Labor
Pension and Welfare Benefit Programs

Pension Benefit Guaranty Corporation

Insurance Information

This schedule is required to be filed under section 104 of the
Employee Retirement Income Security Act of 1974.

▶ **File as an Attachment to Forms 5500, 5500-C, or 5500-R**

OMB No. 1210-0016

19**84**

**This Form Is
Open to Public
Inspection**

For calendar year 1984 or fiscal plan year beginning _____ , 1984 and ending _____ , 19___

▶ **Part I must be completed for all plans required to file this schedule.**
▶ **Part II must be completed for all insured pension plans.**
▶ **Part III must be completed for all insured welfare plans.**

▶ **Enter master trust name in place of "sponsor" and specify investment account in place of "plan" if filing for a master trust.**

Name of plan sponsor as shown on line 1(a) of Form 5500, 5500-C, or 5500-R

Employer identification number

Name of plan

Enter three digit
plan number ▶

Part I — Summary of All Insurance Contracts Included in Parts II and III
Group all contracts in the same manner as in Parts II and III.

1 Check appropriate box: **(a)** ☐ Welfare plan **(b)** ☐ Pension plan **(c)** ☐ Combination pension and welfare plan

2 Coverage:

(a) Name of insurance carrier	(b) Contract or identification number	(c) Approximate number of persons covered at end of policy or contract year	Policy or contract year	
			(d) From	(e) To

3 Insurance fees and commissions paid to agents and brokers:

(a) Contract or identification number	(b) Name and address of the agents or brokers to whom commissions or fees were paid	(c) Amount of commissions paid	(d) Fees paid	
			Amount	Purpose
Total				

4 Premiums due and unpaid at end of the plan year ▶ $ _____ , contract or identification number ▶

Part II — Insured Pension Plans
Provide information for each contract on a separate Part II. Where individual contracts are provided, the entire group of such individual contracts with each carrier may be treated as a unit for purposes of this report.

▶ Contract or identification number ▶

5 Contracts with allocated funds, for example, individual policies or group deferred annuity contracts:
- **(a)** State the basis of premium rates ▶ _____
- **(b)** Total premiums paid to carrier . . . .
- **(c)** If the carrier, service or other organization incurred any specific costs in connection with the acquisition or retention of the contract or policy, other than reported in 3 above, enter amount . . . .
  Specify nature of costs ▶

6 Contracts with unallocated funds, for example, deposit administration or immediate participation guarantee contracts. Do not include portions of these contracts maintained in separate accounts:
- **(a)** Balance at the end of the previous policy year . . . .
- **(b)** Additions: *(i)* Contributions deposited during year . . . .
  - *(ii)* Dividends and credits . . . .
  - *(iii)* Interest credited during the year . . . .
  - *(iv)* Transferred from separate account . . . .
  - *(v)* Other (specify) ▶ _____
  - *(vi)* Total additions . . . .
- **(c)** Total of balance and additions, add (a) and (b)(vi) . . . .
- **(d)** Deductions:
  - *(i)* Disbursed from fund to pay benefits or purchase annuities during year.
  - *(ii)* Administration charge made by carrier . . . .
  - *(iii)* Transferred to separate account . . . .
  - *(iv)* Other (specify) ▶ _____
  - *(v)* Total deductions. . . . .
- **(e)** Balance at end of current policy year, subtract (d)(v) from (c) . . . .

7 Separate accounts: Current value of plan's interest in separate accounts at year end . . . .

For Paperwork Reduction Act Notice, see page 1 of the instructions for Form 5500.

Schedule A (Form 5500) 1984

Part III	**Insured Welfare Plans**

Provide information for each contract on a separate Part III. If more than one contract covers the same group of employees of the same employer(s) or members of the same employee organization(s), the information may be combined for reporting purposes if such contracts are experience-rated as a unit. Where individual contracts are provided, the entire group of such individual contracts with each carrier may be treated as a unit for purposes of this report.

8 (a) Contract or identification number	**(b)** Type of benefit	**(c)** List gross premium for each contract	**(d)** Premium rate or subscription charge

9 Experience rated contracts:**(a)** Premiums: *(i)* Amount received . . . .

　　(ii)　Increase (decrease) in amount due but unpaid . . . .

　　(iii)　Increase (decrease) in unearned premium reserve . . . .

　　(iv)　Premiums earned, add (i) and (ii), and subtract (iii) . . . .

(b) Benefit charges: *(i)* Claims paid . . . .

　　(ii)　Increase (decrease) in claim reserves . . . .

　　(iii)　Incurred claims, add (i) and (ii) . . . .

　　(iv)　Claims charged . . . .

(c) Remainder of premium: *(i)* Retention charges (on an accrual basis)—(A) Commissions .

　　(B)　Administrative service or other fees . . . .

　　(C)　Other specific acquisition costs . . . .

　　(D)　Other expenses . . . .

　　(E)　Taxes . . . .

　　(F)　Charges for risks or contingencies . . . .

　　(G)　Other retention charges . . . .

　　(H)　Total retention . . . .

　　(ii) Dividends or retroactive rate refunds. (These amounts were ☐ paid in cash or ☐ credited.) . . . .

(d) Status of policyholder reserves at end of year: *(i)* Amount held to provide benefits after retirement . . . .

　　(ii)　Claim reserves . . . .

　　(iii)　Other reserves . . . .

(e) Dividends or retroactive rate refunds due (do not include amount entered in (c)(ii)) . . . . . .

10 Non experience rated contracts: (a) Total premiums or subscription charges paid to carrier . . . .

(b) If the carrier, service or other organization incurred any specific costs in connection with the acquisition or retention of the contract or policy, other than reported in 3 above, report amount . . . .

Specify nature of costs ▶ --

If additional space is required for any item, attach additional sheets the same size as this form.

General Instructions

This schedule must be attached to Form 5500, 5500-C, or 5500-R for every defined benefit, defined contribution and welfare benefit plan where any benefits under the plan are provided by an insurance company, insurance service or other similar organization.

Exception: Schedule A (Form 5500) is not needed if the plan covers only (1) an individual (or an individual and spouse) who wholly owns a trade or business, whether incorporated or unincorporated, or (2) a partner in a partnership or a partner and spouse.

Plans Participating in Master Trust(s).—For insurance or annuity contracts that are held in a master trust and owned jointly by two or more plans participating in a master trust, a single Schedule A (Form 5500) for each contract must be included in the information relating to the master trust which is filed with DOL. The individual plans need not file the Schedule A (Form 5500) but must treat unallocated funds or any interest in a separate account held in a master trust as part of an investment account for purposes of their annual report. (See the return/report master trust filing instructions.)

Specific Instructions

(References are to the line items on the form.)

Include only contracts with policy or contract years ending with or within the plan year. Data on Schedule A (Form 5500) should be reported only for such policy or contract years. Exception: If the insurance company maintains records on the basis of a plan year rather than policy or contract year, data on Schedule A (Form 5500) may be reported for the plan year.

Include only the contracts issued to the plan for which this return/report is being filed.

2(c).—Since the plan coverage may fluctuate during the year, the number of persons entered should be that which the administrator determines will most reasonably reflect the number covered by the plan at the end of the policy or contract year.

Where contracts covering individual employees are grouped, entries should be determined as of the end of the plan year.

2(d) and (e).—Enter the beginning and ending dates of the policy year for each contract listed under column (b). Where separate contracts covering individual employees are grouped, enter "N/A" in column (d).

3.—All sales commissions are to be reported in column (c) regardless of the identity of the

recipient. Override commissions, salaries, bonuses, etc., paid to a general agent or manager for managing an agency, or for performing other administrative functions, are not to be reported. Fees to be reported in column (d) represent payments by insurance carriers to agents and brokers for items other than commissions (e.g., service fees, consulting fees and finders fees). Fees paid by insurance carriers to persons other than agents and brokers should be reported in Parts II and III on Schedule A (Form 5500) as acquisition costs, administrative charges, etc., as appropriate. For plans with 100 or more participants, fees paid by employee benefit plans to agents, brokers and other persons are to be reported in item 12, Form 5500.

5(a).—The rate information called for here may be furnished by attachment of appropriate schedules of current rates filed with appropriate State insurance departments or by a statement as to the basis of the rates.

6.—Show deposit fund amounts rather than experience credit records when both are maintained.

8(d).—The rate information called for here may be furnished by attachment of appropriate schedules of current rates or by a statement as to the basis of the rates.

✿ U.S. GOVERNMENT PRINTING OFFICE: 1985-423-263 E.I. 43-0787287

SCHEDULE P
(Form 5500)

Department of the Treasury
Internal Revenue Service

Annual Return of Fiduciary
of Employee Benefit Trust

▶ File as an attachment to Form 5500, 5500-C, or 5500-R.

OMB No. 1210-0016

1984

For trust calendar year 1984 or fiscal year beginning _____ , 1984, and ending _____ , 19 ____ .

Please type or print

1 (a) Name of trustee or custodian

(b) Address (number and street)

(c) City or town, State and ZIP code

2 Name of trust

3 Name of plan if different from name of trust

4 Have you furnished the participating employee benefit plan(s) with the trust financial information required to be reported by the plan(s) on their Forms 5500, or 5500-C? . . . . ☐ **Yes** ☐ **No**

5 Enter the plan sponsor's employer identification number as shown on the form to which this schedule is attached . . . . ▶

Under penalties of perjury, I declare that I have examined this schedule, and to the best of my knowledge and belief it is true, correct, and complete.

Date ▶ _____   Signature of fiduciary ▶ _____

Instructions

(Section references are to the Internal Revenue Code .)

A. Purpose of Form

You may use this schedule to satisfy the requirements under section 6033(a) for an annual information return from every section 401(a) organization exempt from tax under section 501(a).

The filing of this form will also start the running of the statute of limitations under section 6501(a) for any trust described in section 401(a) which is exempt from tax under section 501(a).

B. Who May File

(1) Every trustee of a trust described in section 401(a) which was created as part of an employee benefit plan.

(2) Every custodian of a custodial account described in section 401(f).

C. How to File

File Schedule P (Form 5500) for the trust year ending with or within any participating plan's plan year as an attachment to the Form 5500, 5500-C, or 5500-R filed by the plan for that plan year.

Schedule P (Form 5500) may be filed only as an attachment to a Form 5500, 5500-C, or 5500-R. A separately filed Schedule P (Form 5500) will not be accepted.

If the trust or custodial account is used by more than one plan, file only one Schedule P (Form 5500). It must be filed as an attachment to one of the participating plan's returns/reports. If a plan uses more than one trust or custodial account for its funds, file one Schedule P (Form 5500) for each trust or custodial account.

D. Signature

The fiduciary (trustee or custodian) must sign this schedule. If there is more than one fiduciary, one of them, authorized by the others, may sign.

E. Other Returns and Forms that May be Required

(1) Form 990-T.—For trusts described in section 401(a), a tax is imposed on income derived from business that is unrelated to the purpose for which the trust received a tax exemption. Report such income and tax on Form 990-T, Exempt Organization Business Income Tax Return. (See sections 511 through 514 and related regulations.)

(2) Forms W-2P and 1099-R.—If you made payments or distributions to individual beneficiaries of a plan, report these payments on Forms W-2P or 1099-R. (See sections 6041 and 6047 and related regulations.)

(3) Forms 941 or 941E.—If you made payments of distributions to individual beneficiaries of a plan, you are required to withhold income tax from those payments, unless the payee elects not to have the tax withheld. Report this withholding on Form 941 or 941E. (See Forms 941 or 941E and Circular E, Publication 15.)

For the Paperwork Reduction Act Notice, see page 1 of the Form 5500 instructions.

Schedule P (Form 5500) 1984

★U.S.GPO:1985-0-423-266 ★ E.I. 430814328

SCHEDULE SSA
(Form 5500)

Department of the Treasury
Internal Revenue Service

Annual Registration Statement Identifying Separated Participants With Deferred Vested Benefits

Under Section 6057(a) of the Internal Revenue Code
▶ File as an attachment to Form 5500, 5500–C, or 5500–R.
▶ For the Paperwork Reduction Act Notice, see page 1 of the Form 5500 instructions.

OMB No. 1210-0016

19**84**

This Form Is NOT
Open to Public
Inspection

For the calendar year 1984 or fiscal plan year beginning _____ , 1984 and ending _____ , 19 ___

▶ This form must be filed for each plan year in which one or more participants with deferred vested benefit rights separated from the service covered by the plan. See instructions on when to report a separated employee.

1 (a) Name of sponsor (employer if for a single employer plan)

Address (number and street)

City or town, State and ZIP code

1 (b) Sponsor's employer identification number

1 (c) Is this a plan to which more than one employer contributes? . . ☐ Yes ☐ No

2 (a) Name of plan administrator (if other than sponsor)

Address (number and street)

City or town, State or ZIP code

2 (b) Administrator's employer identification no.

3 (a) Name of plan

3 (b) Plan number ▶

4 Have you notified each separated participant of his or her deferred benefit? . . . . ☐ Yes ☐ No

5 Separated participants with deferred vested benefits (if additional space is required, see instruction, What to File):

(a) Social Security Number	(b) Name of participant	Enter code for nature and form of benefit		Amount of vested benefit			(h) Plan year in which participant separated
		(c) Type of annuity	(d) Payment frequency	(e) Defined benefit plan—periodic payment	Defined contribution plan		
					(f) Units or shares	(g) Total value of account	

The Following Information Is Optional (See Specific Instruction 6)

6 Use this item to report (i) separated participants with deferred vested benefits who were previously reported on Schedule SSA (Form 5500) and who have received part or all of their vested benefits or who have forfeited their benefits during the plan year for which this form is being filed, and (ii) to delete participants erroneously reported on a prior Schedule SSA (Form 5500):

Note: *Participants listed in this item because they have received part of their vested benefits must also be reported in item 5 above listing their remaining vested benefits.*

(a) Social Security Number	(b) Name of participant	Enter code for nature and form of benefit		Amount of vested benefit			(h) Plan year in which participant separated
		(c) Type of annuity	(d) Payment frequency	(e) Defined benefit plan—periodic payment	Defined contribution plan		
					(f) Units or shares	(g) Total value of account	

Under penalties of perjury, I declare that I have examined this report and to the best of my knowledge and belief, it is true, correct and complete.

....
Date   **Signature of plan administrator**

General Instructions

Note: *Please type or print all information and submit original copy only.*

Who Must File.—The plan administrator must file this form for any plan year for which a separated plan participant is reported under "When to Report a Separated Participant" below.

What to File.—File this schedule and complete all items. If you need more space, use additional copies of Schedule SSA, completing only items 1, 3, 5, and 6 of the additional copies.

A machine-generated computer listing showing the information required in items 5 and 6 may be submitted in lieu of completing items 5 and 6 on the schedule. Complete items 1 through 4 on Schedule SSA and enter in items 5 and 6 a statement that a list is attached. On each page of the computer list, enter the name of the sponsor, the EIN, the plan name and the plan number. The list must be in the same format as items 5 and 6.

How to File.—File as an attachment to Form 5500, 5500-C, or 5500-R.

When to Report a Separated Participant.—

In general, *for a plan to which only one employer contributes,* a participant must be reported on Schedule SSA if:

(1) the participant separates from service covered by the plan in a plan year beginning after December 31, 1975, and

(2) the participant is entitled to a deferred vested benefit under the plan.

The separated participant must be reported no later than on the Schedule SSA filed for the plan year following the plan year in which separation occurred. The participant may be reported earlier (i.e., on the Schedule SSA filed for the plan year in which separation occurred).

However, a participant is not required to be reported on Schedule SSA if before the date the Schedule SSA is required to be filed (including any extension of time for filing) the participant:

(1) is paid some or all of the deferred vested retirement benefit,

(2) returns to service covered by the plan, or

(3) forfeits all of the deferred vested retirement benefit.

In general, *for a plan to which more than one employer contributes,* a participant must be reported on Schedule SSA if:

(1) the participant incurs two successive one-year breaks in service (as defined in the plan for vesting purposes) in service computation periods beginning after December 31, 1974, and

(2) the participant is (or may be) entitled to a deferred vested benefit under the plan.

The participant must be reported no later than on the Schedule SSA filed for the plan year in which the participant completed the second of the two consecutive one-year breaks in service. The participant may be reported earlier (i.e., on the Schedule SSA filed for the plan year in which he or she separated from service or completed the first one-year break in service).

However, a participant is not required to be reported on Schedule SSA if before the date the Schedule SSA is required to be filed (including any extension of time for filing) the participant:

(1) is paid some or all of the deferred vested retirement benefit,

(2) accrues additional retirement benefits under the plan, or

(3) forfeits all of the deferred vested retirement benefit.

Cessation of Payment of Benefits.—As described above in "When to Report a Separated Participant" a participant is not required to be reported on Schedule SSA if before the date the Schedule SSA is required to be filed, some of the deferred vested benefit to which the participant is entitled is paid to the participant. If payment of the deferred vested benefit ceases before all of the benefit is paid to the participant, the benefit to which the participant remains entitled must be reported on the Schedule SSA filed for the plan year following the last plan year within which any of the benefit was paid to the participant. However, a participant is not required to be reported on Schedule SSA on account of a cessation of payment of benefits if before the date the schedule is required to be filed (including any extension of time for filing) the participant:

(1) returns to service covered by the plan,

(2) accrues additional retirement benefits under the plan, or

(3) forfeits the remaining benefit.

Separation of a Re-employed Employee.— The deferred vested benefit reported on the current Schedule SSA for a re-employed employee who is again separated from service must include only the benefit not previously reported in or for prior years. Generally, the benefit to be shown on the current filing will be the benefit earned during the re-employment period.

Caution: A penalty may be assessed if Schedule SSA (Form 5500) is not filed timely.

Specific Instructions

4. Check "Yes" if you have complied with the requirements of Code section 6057(e). The notification to each participant must include the information set forth on this schedule and the information with respect to any contributions made by the participant and not withdrawn by the end of the plan year. Any benefits that are forfeitable if the participant dies before a certain date must be shown on the statement.

5(a). Please be careful to enter the exact social security number of each participant listed.

If the participant is a foreign national employed outside of the United States who does not have a social security number, enter the participant's nationality.

5(b). Enter each participant's name exactly as it appears on the participant's social security card or the employer's payroll records for purposes of reporting to the Social Security Administration.

5(c). From the following list select the code that describes the type of annuity that will be provided for the participant. The type of annuity to be entered is the type that normally accrues under the plan at the time of the participant's separation from service covered by the plan (or for a plan to which more than one employer contributes at the time the participant incurs the second consecutive one-year break in service under the plan).

A A single sum

B Annuity payable over fixed number of years

C Life annuity

D Life annuity with period certain

E Cash refund life annuity

F Modified cash refund life annuity

G Joint and last survivor life annuity

M Other

5(d). From the following list select the code that describes the benefit payment frequency during a 12-month period.

A Lump sum

B Annually

C Semi-annually

D Quarterly

E Monthly

M Other

5(e). For a defined benefit plan, enter the amount of the periodic payment that a participant would normally be entitled to receive under 5(c), commencing at normal retirement age. However, if it is more expedient to show the amount of periodic payment the participant would be entitled to receive at early retirement date, enter that amount.

For a plan to which more than one employer contributes, if the amount of the periodic payment cannot be accurately determined because the plan administrator does not maintain complete records of covered service, enter an estimated amount and add the letter "X" in column 5(c) in addition to the annuity code to indicate that it is an estimate. If, from records maintained by the plan administrator it cannot be determined whether the participant is entitled to any deferred vested benefit, but there is reason to believe he or she may be entitled, leave column 5(e) blank and enter "Y" in column 5(c) in addition to the annuity code.

5(f). For a defined contribution plan, if the plan states that a participant's share of the fund will be determined on the basis of units, enter the number of units credited to the participant.

If, under the plan, participation is determined on the basis of shares of stock of the employer, enter the number of shares and add the letter "S" to indicate shares. A number without the "S" will be interpreted to mean units.

5(g). For defined contribution plans, enter the value of the participant's account at the time of separation.

6. If, after a participant has been reported on Schedule SSA, the participant:

(1) is paid some or all of the deferred vested retirement benefit, or

(2) forfeits all of the deferred vested retirement benefit,

the plan administrator may, at its option, request that the participant's deferred vested benefit be deleted from Social Security Administration records. Information reported in item 6, columns (a) through (g), is to be the exact information previously reported on Schedule SSA for the participant.

If this option is chosen because the participant is paid some of the deferred vested benefit, the reporting requirements described in "Cessation of Payment of Benefits" above apply if payment of the benefit ceases before all of the benefit is paid to the participant.

Also, if a person was erroneously reported on a prior Schedule SSA, use item 6 to delete this information from Social Security Administration records.

Signature.—This form must be signed by the plan administrator. If more than one Schedule SSA is filed for one plan, only page one should be signed.

Form **5500-C**	**Return/Report of Employee Benefit Plan**	OMB No. 1210-0016

Form **5500-C**

Department of the Treasury
Internal Revenue Service

Department of Labor
Pension and Welfare Benefit Programs

Pension Benefit Guaranty Corporation

Return/Report of Employee Benefit Plan

(With fewer than 100 participants)

This form is required to be filed under sections 104 and 4065 of the Employee Retirement Income Security Act of 1974 and sections 6057(b) and 6058(a) of the Internal Revenue Code, referred to as the Code.

OMB No. 1210-0016

1984

This Form is Open to Public Inspection

For the calendar plan year 1984 or fiscal plan year beginning _____ , 1984, and ending _____ , 19____ .

Type or print in ink all entries on the form, schedules, and attachments. If an item does not apply, enter "N/A." File the originals.

This return/report is: (i) ☐ the return/report filed for the plan's first plan year; (ii) ☐ an amended return/report; or (iii) ☐ the final return/report filed for the plan.

▶ **Caution:** A penalty of $25 a day for the late or incomplete filing of this return/report will be assessed unless reasonable cause is established.
▶ Welfare benefit plans required to file this form do not complete items 7(b), 12, and 24 through 30.
   Certain welfare benefit plans are not required to file this form—see instructions.
▶ Keogh (HR 10) plans must check the box in item 5(a)(iii).
▶ Check here ▶ ☐ and do NOT complete items 6(c)(iv), 8(b) and (d); 9(c), 12, 13, 17, 18, 20, 21, 22, 23, 27, and 30 if this return/report is for a pension benefit plan that covers only an individual who wholly owns a trade or business, whether incorporated or unincorporated.
▶ If you have been granted an extension of time to file this form, you must attach a copy of the approved extension to this form.

Use IRS label. Otherwise, please print or type.	**1 (a)** Name of plan sponsor (employer, if for a single employer plan)	**1 (b)** Employer identification number
	Address (number and street)	**1 (c)** Telephone number of sponsor ( )
	City or town, State and ZIP code	**1 (d)** If plan year changed since last return/report, check here ▶ ☐
2 (a)	Name of plan administrator (if same as plan sponsor enter "Same")	**1 (e)** Business code number
	Address (number and street)	**2 (b)** Administrator's employer identification no.
	City or town, State and ZIP code	**2 (c)** Telephone number of administrator ( )

3 Is the name, address and identification number of plan sponsor and/or plan administrator the same as they appeared on the last return/report filed for this plan? ☐ Yes ☐ No. If "No," enter the information from the last return/report in (a) and/or (b).

(a) Sponsor ▶ _____ EIN _____

(b) Administrator ▶ _____ EIN _____

(c) If (a) indicates a change in the sponsor's name and EIN, is this a change in sponsorship only? (See specific instructions for definition of sponsorship.)
   ☐ Yes ☐ No

4 Check box to indicate the type of plan entity (check only one box):
   (a) ☐ Single-employer plan
   (b) ☐ Plan of controlled group of corporations or common control employers
   (c) ☐ Multiemployer plan
   (d) ☐ Multiple-employer-collectively-bargained plan
   (e) ☐ Multiple-employer plan (other)

5 (a) (i) Name of plan ▶ _____
   (ii) ☐ Check if name of plan changed since the last return/report.
   (iii) ☐ Check this box if this is a Keogh (HR10) plan.

5 (b) Effective date of plan

5 (c) Enter three-digit plan number ▶

6 Check at least one item in (a) or (b) and applicable items in (c): **(a)** Welfare benefit plan (Plan numbers 501 through 999):
   (i) ☐ Health insurance   (ii) ☐ Life insurance   (iii) ☐ Supplemental unemployment
   (iv) ☐ Other (specify) ▶ _____

   (b) Pension benefit plan (Plan numbers 001 through 500): (i) Defined benefit plan—(indicate type of defined benefit plan below):
      (A) ☐ Fixed benefit   (B) ☐ Unit benefit   (C) ☐ Flat benefit   (D) ☐ Other (specify) ▶ _____

   (ii) Defined contribution plan—(Indicate type of defined contribution plan below):
      (A) ☐ Profit-sharing   (B) ☐ Stock bonus   (C) ☐ Target benefit   (D) ☐ Other money purchase
      (E) ☐ Other (specify) ▶ _____

   (iii) ☐ Defined benefit plan with benefits based partly on balance of separate account of participant (Code section 414(k))
   (iv) ☐ Annuity arrangement of a certain exempt organization (Code section 403(b)(1))
   (v) ☐ Custodial account for regulated investment company stock (Code section 403(b)(7))
   (vi) ☐ Pension plan utilizing individual retirement accounts or annuities (described in Code section 408) as the sole funding vehicle for providing benefits
   (vii) ☐ Other (specify) ▶

Under penalties of perjury and other penalties set forth in the instructions, I declare that I have examined this return/report, including accompanying schedules and statements, and to the best of my knowledge and belief it is true, correct, and complete.

Date ▶ _____ Signature of employer/plan sponsor ▶ _____

Date ▶ _____ Signature of plan administrator ▶ _____

For Paperwork Reduction Act Notice, see page 1 of the Instructions.

Form **5500-C** (1984)

281

6 (c) Other plan features: *(i)* ☐ Thrift-savings   *(ii)* ☐ Participant-directed account plan

(iii) ☐ Pension plan maintained outside the United States (see instructions) *(iv)* ☐ Master trust (see instructions) ▶ ....

	Yes	No
(d) Single employer plans enter the tax year end of the employer in which this plan year ends ▶ Month...... Day....... Year.......		
(e) Is this a pension plan of an affiliated service group?		
(f) Does this plan contain a cash or deferred arrangement described in Code section 401(k)?		

7 (a) Total participants *(i)* Beginning of plan year ▶ .... *(ii)* End of plan year ▶ ....

(b) *(i)* Was any pension benefit plan participant(s) separated from service with a deferred vested benefit for which a Schedule SSA (Form 5500) is required to be attached?

(ii) If "Yes," enter the number of separated participants required to be reported .... ▶

8 Plan amendment information (welfare plans do NOT complete (b)(ii)):

(a) Were any plan amendments to this plan adopted since the end of the plan year covered by the last return/report Form 5500, 5500-C or 5500-K which was filed for this plan (or during this plan year if this is the initial return/report)?

(b) If "Yes," *(i)* And if any amendments have resulted in a change in the information contained in a summary plan description or previously furnished summary description of modifications:

(A) Have summary descriptions of the changes been sent to participants?

(B) Have summary descriptions of the changes been filed with DOL?

(ii) Does any such amendment result in the reduction of the accrued benefit of any participant under the plan?

(c) Enter the date the most recent amendment was adopted ...... ▶ Month .... Day .... Year ....

(d) *(i)* Has a summary plan description been filed with DOL for this plan?

(ii) If (i) is "Yes," what was the employer identification number and the plan number used to identify it?
Employer identification number ▶   Plan number ▶

9 Plan termination information:

(a) Was this plan terminated during this plan year or any prior plan year? If "Yes," enter year ▶ ....

(b) If "Yes," were all trust assets either distributed to participants or beneficiaries, transferred to another plan or brought under the control of PBGC?

(c) If (a) is "Yes," and the plan is covered by PBGC, is the plan continuing to file a PBGC Form 1 and pay premiums until the end of the plan year in which assets are distributed or brought under the control of PBGC?

10 (a) Was this plan merged or consolidated into another plan, or were assets or liabilities transferred to another plan since the end of the plan year covered by the last return/report Form 5500, 5500-C or 5500-K which was filed for this plan (or during this plan year if this is the initial return/report)?

If "Yes," identify the other plan(s):   **(c)** Employer identification number(s)   **(d)** Plan number(s)

(b) Name of plan(s) ▶

(e) Has Form 5310 been filed? ☐ Yes ☐ No

11 Indicate funding arrangement:

(a) ☐ Trust **(b)** ☐ Fully insured **(c)** ☐ Combination **(d)** ☐ Other (specify) ▶ ....

(e) If (b) or (c) is checked, enter the number of Schedules A (Form 5500) which are attached ...... ▶

12 (a) Is the plan covered under the Pension Benefit Guaranty Corporation termination insurance program? ☐ Yes ☐ No ☐ Not determined

(b) If (a) is "Yes," or "Not determined," enter the employer identification number and the plan number used to identify it.
Employer identification number ▶   Plan number ▶

13 Complete both (a) and (b):

	Yes	No
(a) Is the plan insured by a fidelity bond?		
(i) If "Yes," enter name of surety company ▶		
(ii) Amount of bond coverage ▶		
(b) Was any loss discovered since the last return/report Form 5500, 5500-C or 5500-K was filed for this plan (or during this plan year if this is the initial return/report)?		

14 (a) If this is a defined benefit plan, is it subject to the minimum funding standards for this plan year?
If "Yes," attach Schedule B (Form 5500).

(b) If this is a defined contribution plan, i.e., money purchase or target benefit, is it subject to the minimum funding standards (if a waiver was granted, see instructions)?

If "Yes," complete (i), (ii) and (iii) below:

(i) Amount of employer contribution required for the plan year .... $

(ii) Amount of contribution paid by the employer for the plan year .... $

Enter date of last payment by employer ▶ Month .... Day .... Year ....

(iii) If (i) is greater than (ii) subtract (ii) from (i) and enter the funding deficiency here. Otherwise enter zero. (If you have a funding deficiency, file Form 5330.) .... $

15　Plan assets and liabilities at the beginning and end of the current plan year (list all assets and liabilities at current value). A fully insured welfare plan or a pension plan with no trust and which is funded entirely by allocated insurance contracts which fully guarantee the amount of benefit payments should check the box and not complete the rest of this item　. . . . . ▶ ☐

Note: *Include all plan assets and liabilities of a trust or separately maintained fund. If more than one trust/fund, report on a combined basis. Include all insurance values except for the value of that portion of an allocated insurance contract which fully guarantees the amount of benefit payments. Round off amounts to nearest dollar. If you have no assets to report enter ''-0-'' on line 15(f).*

Assets	a. Beginning of year	b. End of year
(a)　Cash— *(i)* Interest bearing		
(ii)　Non-interest bearing		
(iii)　Total cash		
(b)　Receivables.		
(c)　Investments—		
(i)　　Government securities		
(ii)　　Pooled funds/mutual funds		
(iii)　Corporate (debt and equity instruments). . .		
(iv)　Value of interest in master trust		
(v)　　Real estate and mortgages		
(vi)　Other		
(vii)　Total investments		
(d)　Building and other depreciable property used in plan operation		
(e)　Unallocated insurance contracts		
(f)　Other assets		
(g)　Total assets (add (a)(iii); (b); (c)(vii); (d); (e) and (f)).		
Liabilities and Net Assets		
(h)　Payables		
(i)　Acquisition indebtedness		
(j)　Other liabilities		
(k)　Total liabilities (add (h) through (j))		
(l)　Net assets (subtract (k) from (g)).		

16　Plan income, expenses and changes in net assets during the plan year. Include all income and expenses of a trust(s) or separately maintained fund(s), including any payments made for allocated insurance contracts. Round off amounts to nearest dollar.

	a. Amount	b. Total
(a)　Contributions received or receivable in cash from:		
(i)　Employer(s) (including contributions on behalf of self-employed individuals)		
(ii)　Employees		
(iii)　Others		
(b)　Noncash contributions		
(c)　Earnings from investments (interest, dividends, rents, royalties).		
(d)　Net realized gain (loss) on sale or exchange of assets		
(e)　Other income (specify) ▶ _____		
(f)　Total income (add (a) through (e))		
(g)　Distribution of benefits and payments to provide benefits:		
(i)　Directly to participants or their beneficiaries.		
(ii)　To insurance carrier or similar organization for provision of benefits (including prepaid medical plans)		
(iii)　To other organizations or individuals providing welfare benefits.		
(h)　Interest expense		
(i)　Administrative expenses (salaries, fees, commissions, insurance premiums).		
(j)　Other expenses (specify) ▶ _____		
(k)　Total expenses (add (g) through (j))		
(l)　Net income (subtract (k) from (f))		
(m)　Changes in net assets: (i) Unrealized appreciation (depreciation) of assets		
(ii)　Net investment gain (or loss) from all master trust investment accounts . . .		
(iii)　Other changes (specify) ▶ _____		
(n)　Net increase (decrease) in net assets for the year (add (l) and (m))		
(o)　Net assets at beginning of year (line 15(k), column a)		
(p)　Net assets at end of year (add (n) and (o)) (equals line 15(k), column b). . . .		

17 As of the end of the plan year:

		Yes	No
(a)	What percentage of plan assets are loaned to a party-in-interest?		%
(b)	What percentage of plan assets are invested in securities issued by a party-in-interest?		%
(c)	What percentage of plan assets are invested in real estate which is leased by a party-in-interest?		%

18 Since the end of the plan year covered by the last return/report Form 5500, 5500-C or 5500-K which was filed for this plan (or during this plan year if this is the initial return/report):

(a) Has there been a termination in the appointment of any trustee, accountant, insurance carrier, enrolled actuary, administrator, investment manager or custodian? . . . .

If "Yes," explain and include the name, position, address and telephone number of the person whose appointment has been terminated ▶ _____

_____

(b) Has the plan used the services of a contract administrator? . . . .

If "Yes," enter the contract administrator's name and employer identification number (see instructions)▶ _____

_____

(c) Indicate the amount of the plan's administrative expenses for the:

(i) Preceding year ▶ $ _____, *(ii)* Second preceding year ▶ $ _____

(d) Have any insurance policies or annuities been replaced? . . . .

(e) Was the plan funded with: *(i)* ☐ Individual policies or annuities *(ii)* ☐ Group policies or annuities *(iii)* ☐ Both

19 Since the end of the plan year covered by the last return/report Form 5500, 5500-C or 5500-K which was filed for this plan (or during this plan year if this is the initial return/report):

(a) Other than transactions described in the exceptions outlined in the instructions, were there any transactions, directly or indirectly, between the plan and a party-in-interest? . . . .

If "Yes," see specific instructions.

(b) Has the plan granted an extension on any loan for which, before the granting of an extension, it has not received all the principal and interest payments due under the terms of the loan? . . . .

(c) Has the plan granted an extension of time or renewal for the payment of any obligation owed to it which amounts to more than 10% of the plan assets? . . . .

20 As of the end of any plan year since the end of the plan year covered by the last return/report, Form 5500, 5500-C or 5500-K which was filed for this plan (or as of the end of this plan year if this is the initial return/report):

(a) Did the plan have investments of the type reportable under item 15(c)(vii) or (ix) which in the aggregate in either category exceeded 15% of plan assets? . . . .

(b) Did the plan have loans outstanding or investments in a single enterprise (other than the United States Government) which exceeded 15% of plan assets?. . . . .

21 During the plan year covered by this return:

(a) Did the plan acquire any qualifying employer security or qualifying employer real property, when immediately after such acquisition the aggregate fair market value of employer securities and employer real property held by the plan exceeded 10% of the fair market value of the plan assets? . . . .

(b) Did the plan acquire any qualifying employer security or qualifying employer real property, when immediately after such acquisition the aggregate fair market value of employer securities and employer real property held by the plan exceeded 10% of the fair market value of the plan assets? · · · · · · · · · · · · · · · · ·

(c) Has any plan fiduciary had either a financial interest worth more than $1,000 in any party providing services to the plan or received anything of value from any party providing services to the plan? . . . .

(d) Has any employer owed the plan contributions which were more than three months past due under the terms of the plan? . .

(e) Were any loans by the plan or fixed income obligations due the plan in default as of the close of the plan year, or classified as uncollectable? . . . .

(f) Were any leases to which the plan was a party in default or classified as uncollectable? . . . .

22 Who is the plan's designated agent for legal process? ▶

23 Give the name and address of each fiduciary (including trustees) to the plan ▶ _____

_____

_____

24 Is this plan an adoption of any of the plans below? (If "Yes," check appropriate box and enter IRS serial number):

(a) ☐ Master/prototype, **(b)** ☐ Field prototype, **(c)** ☐ Pattern, **(d)** ☐ Model plan, or **(e)** ☐ Bond purchase plan?

Enter the four or eight-digit IRS serial number (see instructions) . . . . ▶

25 (a) Is this plan integrated with social security? . . . .

(b) Is it intended that this plan qualify under Code section 401(a) or 405? . . . .

(c) If (b) is "Yes," have you received a determination letter from the IRS for this plan? . . . .

(d) Does the employer/sponsor listed in item 1(a) of this form maintain other qualified pension benefit plans? . . . .

If "Yes," list the number of plans including this plan ▶

284

		Yes	No
26	Information about employees of employer at end of the plan year. **(a)** Does the plan satisfy the percentage tests of Code section 410(b)(1)(A)? If "No," complete only (b) below and see Specific Instructions		
(b)	Total number of employees		
(c)	Number of employees excluded under the plan because of: *(i)* Minimum age or years of service		
	(ii) Employees on whose behalf retirement benefits were the subject of collective bargaining		
	(iii) Nonresident aliens who receive no earned income from United States sources		
	(iv) Total excluded (add (i), (ii) and (iii))		
(d)	Total number of employees not excluded (subtract (c)(iv) from (b))		
(e)	Employees ineligible (specify reason) ▶ --		

(f)	Employees eligible to participate (subtract (e) from (d))		
(g)	Employees eligible but not participating		
(h)	Employees participating (subtract (g) from (f))		

27	Vesting (check only one box to indicate the vesting provisions of the plan):		▨
(a)	Full and immediate vesting, or full vesting within 3 years		
(b)	No vesting in years 1 through 9, and full vesting after the 10th year of service		
(c)	For each year of employment, beginning with the 4th year, vesting equal to 40% after 4 years of service, 5% additional for the next 2 years, and 10% additional for each of the next 5 years		
(d)	100% vesting within 5 years after contributions are made (class year plan only)		
(e)	Other vesting		

		Yes	No
28 (a)	Did the employer receive plan assets (including a return of contributions) since the last return/report Form 5500, 5500-C or 5500-K which was filed for this plan (or during this plan year if this is the initial return/report)?		
(b)	If this is a defined benefit plan which provides for annual, automatic increases in the maximum dollar limitations under Code section 415, does the plan provide that any such increase is effective no earlier than the calendar year for which IRS determines that increase under Code section 415(d)?		
(c)	Is this a plan with Employee Stock Ownership (ESOP) features?		
	(i) If "Yes," was a current appraisal of the value of the stock made immediately before any contribution of stock or purchase of the stock by the trust for the plan year covered by this return/report?		
	(ii) If (i) is "Yes," was the appraisal made by an unrelated third party?		
29	Have any individuals performed services as a leased employee for this employer or for any other employer who is aggregated with this employer under section 414(b), (c), or (m)? . . . . If "Yes," see instructions for completing item 26.	▨	▨
30 (a)	Is this plan a top heavy plan within the meaning of Code section 416 for this plan year?	▨	▨
(b)	If (a) is "Yes," complete (i), (ii) and (iii) below:		
	(i) Has the plan complied with the vesting requirements of Code section 416(b)?		
	(ii) Has the plan complied with the minimum benefit requirements of Code section 416(c)?		
	(iii) Has the plan complied with the limitation on compensation of Code section 416(d)?		

If additional space is required for any item, attach additional sheets the same size as this form.

*U.S. Government Printing Office: 1985—423-268 E.I. 36-2249473

Form **5558**

(Rev. October 1982)

Department of the Treasury
Internal Revenue Service

Application for Extension of Time

to File Certain Employee Plan Returns

▶ For Paperwork Reduction Act Notice, see Instructions on back

OMB No. 1545-0212
Expires 8-31-85

File With IRS Only

File in DUPLI-CATE by the due date for filing the return. (See general instructions 2 and 3.)	Name of taxpayer or plan sponsor (see instructions)	Check applicable box and enter number (see specific instructions)
	Address (Number and street)	☐ Employer identification number ▶ .... **OR**
	City or town, State, and ZIP code	☐ Social security number ▶

1 I request an extension of time until (see specific instruction 1) ▶ .... (check appropriate block(s)):

(a) ☐ To file Form 5500, Annual Return/Report of Employee Benefit Plan (with related schedules).

(b) ☐ To file Form 5500-C, Return/Report of Employee Benefit Plan (with related schedules).

(c) ☐ To file Form 5500-K, Return/Report of Employee Pension Benefit Plan (with related schedules).

(d) ☐ To file Form 5500-G, Annual Return/Report of Employee Benefit Plan.

(e) ☐ To file Form 5500-R, Registration Statement of Employee Benefit Plan (with related schedules).

(f) ☐ To file Form 5330, Return of Initial Excise Taxes Related to Pension and Profit-sharing Plans for tax year beginning
▶ .... and ending ▶ ....

(g) If you checked (f) above, are you electing to be taxed under ERISA section 2003(c)(1)(B)? . . . . ☐ Yes ☐ No

2 Complete the following for the plan covered by this application (see general instruction 2):

Plan name	Plan number	Plan year ending		
		Month	Day	Year

3 (a) Has an extension of time to file the designated return(s) been previously granted for this tax year? . . . . ☐ Yes ☐ No

(b) If "Yes," show the date(s) to which the extension was granted . . . . ▶ ....

4 Attach a detailed statement of why you need the extension (see specific instruction 4).

5 If the extension is for Form 5330, enter the amount of tax estimated to be due on Form 5330. Pay this amount with this application . . . . ▶

Caution: *Interest on late payment of tax accrues at the rate established under section 6621 of the Internal Revenue Code from the regular due date of the return until paid. (For the penalty for late payment of tax, see specific instruction 5.)*

Under penalties of perjury, I declare that to the best of my knowledge and belief the statements made on this form are true, correct, and complete and that I am authorized to prepare this application.

Signature ▶ _____ Date ▶ _____

Note: *The person who signs this form may be an employer or plan administrator filing Form 5500, 5500-C, 5500-K, 5500-G, 5500-R or 5330; a disqualified person filing Form 5330; an attorney or certified public accountant qualified to practice before the IRS; a person enrolled to practice before the IRS; or a person holding a power of attorney.*

Notice to Applicant.—THE INTERNAL REVENUE SERVICE WILL INDICATE BELOW WHETHER THE EXTENSION IS GRANTED OR DENIED AND WILL RETURN THE ORIGINAL OF THE APPLICATION

☐ The application **IS** approved to ▶ .... (You MUST attach a copy of this form to each return you file for which an extension is granted.)

☐ The application **IS NOT** approved. (You MUST attach a copy of this form to each return you file for which a grace period is granted.) However, in view of your reasons stated in the application, a 10-day grace period is granted from the date shown below or due date of the return, whichever is later. This 10-day grace period constitutes a valid extension of time for purposes of elections otherwise required to be made on timely filed returns.

☐ The application **IS NOT** approved.

After consideration of the reasons stated in your application, we have determined the extension is not warranted. (The 10-day grace period is not granted.)

☐ The application cannot be considered, since you filed it after the due date of the return.

☐ Other ▶ ....

_____ _____ By: _____
(Date)   (Director)

287

If you want the original of this application returned to an address other than that shown on page 1, please fill in the address below.

Please Print or Type	Name
	Address (Number and street)
	City or town, State, and ZIP code

General Instructions

Paperwork Reduction Act Notice.— The Paperwork Reduction Act of 1980 says we must tell you why we are collecting this information, how we will use it and whether you have to give it to us. We ask for it to carry out the Internal Revenue laws of the United States. We need it to determine if you are entitled to an extension of time to file your employee plan returns. If you want such an extension you are required to give us this information.

1. Purpose.—Form 5558 may be used to apply for an extension of time to file Form 5500, 5500–C, 5500–K, 5500–G, 5500–R, or 5330. No extension will be granted if you are electing to be taxed under section 2003(c)(1)(B) of the Employee Retirement Income Security Act of 1974 (ERISA).

2. How and Where to File.—In general, you must file a separate Form 5558 for each return for which you are requesting an extension. However, if you are a single employer and all of your plan years end on the same date, you may file one Form 5558 to request an extension of time to file more than one Form 5500, 5500–C, 5500–K, 5500–R or 5500–G. Attach a list showing the plan names and numbers of all of the plans for which you are requesting an extension and show the month, day, and year the plan year ends.

Complete this form in duplicate and file it with the Internal Revenue Service Center shown in the list below.

If the principal place of business, office or agency (or legal residence, if you have no principal place of business or office or agency in the United States), is located in	Use the following Internal Revenue Service Center address
New Jersey, New York City and counties of Nassau, Rockland, Suffolk, and Westchester	Holtsville, NY 00501
New York (all other counties), Connecticut, Maine, Massachusetts, New Hampshire, Rhode Island, Vermont	Andover, MA 05501
Alabama, Florida, Georgia, Mississippi, South Carolina	Atlanta, GA 31101
Michigan, Ohio	Cincinnati, OH 45999
Arkansas, Kansas, Louisiana, New Mexico, Oklahoma, Texas	Austin, TX 73301

Alaska, Arizona, Colorado, Idaho, Minnesota, Montana, Nebraska, Nevada, North Dakota, Oregon, South Dakota, Utah, Washington, Wyoming	Ogden, UT 84201
Illinois, Iowa, Missouri, Wisconsin	Kansas City, MO 64999
California, Hawaii	Fresno, CA 93888
Indiana, Kentucky, North Carolina, Tennessee, Virginia, West Virginia	Memphis, TN 37501
Delaware, District of Columbia, Maryland, Pennsylvania	Philadelphia, PA 19255

If you have no legal residence, principal place of business or principal office or agency in any Internal Revenue district, file your return with the Internal Revenue Service Center, Philadelphia, PA 19255.

3. When to File.—You should file this application in sufficient time for the Internal Revenue Service to consider and act on it before the return's regular due date.

Specific Instructions

Name and address.—If you are a single employer and are requesting an extension to file the annual return/report Forms 5500, 5500–C, 5500–K, 5500–R, and 5500–G, you must enter your name and address in the heading. If you are filing for other than a single employer, enter the plan sponsor's name and address on the application. The plan sponsor listed on this application should be the same as the plan sponsor listed on the annual return/report filed for the plan.

Employer identification number or social security number.—If you are filing this application for an extension of time to file Form 5330 and you made excess contributions to either a Code section 403(b)(7)(A) custodial account or a Keogh (H.R. 10) plan or you are a disqualified person other than an employer, enter your social security number. In all other cases, enter the employer identification number of the person listed in the name and address block.

Line 1.—Check the box or boxes to indicate the return for which you are requesting an extension.

If your application for an extension to file Form 5500, 5500–C, 5500–K, 5500–R, or 5500–G is approved, you will be granted an extension of not more than 2½ months.

If you are filing for a single employer plan or for a plan of a controlled group of corporations that file a consolidated income tax return when the plan year and the tax year coincide, and you have been granted an extension of time to file your income tax return beyond the due date of the Forms 5500, 5500–C, 5500–R, and 5500–K, the extension also applies to the Forms 5500, 5500–C, 5500–R, and 5500–K.

Attach a copy of the approved IRS extension to file the income tax return to each Form 5500, 5500–C, 5500–R, or 5500–K that is filed after the normal due date.

If your application for extension of time to file Form 5330 is approved, you may be granted an extension of up to six months.

Line 4.—Attach a detailed statement explaining why you need an extension. The Internal Revenue Service will grant a reasonable extension of time for filing a return if you file a timely application showing that you are unable to file the return because of circumstances beyond your control. Generally, an application will be considered on the basis of your own efforts to fulfill this filing responsibility, rather than the convenience of anyone providing help in preparing the return. However, consideration will be given to any circumstances that prevent your practitioner, for reasons beyond his or her control, from filing the return by the due date, and to circumstances in which you are unable to get needed professional help in spite of timely efforts to do so.

Applications that give incomplete reasons, such as "illness" or "practitioner too busy," without adequate explanations, will not be approved. If it is clear that a request for extension is frivolous, solely to gain time, the Internal Revenue Service will deny both the extension request and the 10-day grace period.

Line 5.—If you are applying for an extension of time to file Form 5330, estimate the amount of tax due with Form 5330 and enter the total on line 5.

The extension of time to file does not extend the time to pay the tax due. Therefore, you must pay the amount of tax due with this application.

The law imposes a penalty for late payment of tax. The penalty is ½ of 1% of the unpaid amount for each month or part of a month it remains unpaid. The maximum penalty is 25% of the unpaid amount.

Interest is also charged at the rate provided by law from the due date of the return until the date the tax is paid.

☆ U.S. Government Printing Office: 1983—421-108/229

Plan Termination

Forms to be used for terminating an ESOP.

☒ 9898   ☒ VOID   For Official Use Only

			OMB No. 1545-0119
Type or machine print PAYER'S name	1 Amount includible as income (Add boxes 2 and 3)	2 Capital gain (For lump-sum distributions only)	**1984** Statement for Recipients of
Street address	3 Ordinary income	4 Federal income tax withheld	**Total Distributions from Profit-sharing, Retirement Plans, Individual Retirement Arrangements, etc.**
City, State, and ZIP code			
Federal identifying number	5 Employee contributions to profit-sharing or retirement plans	6 Net unrealized appreciation in employer's securities	
Type or machine print RECIPIENT'S name (first, middle, last)	Recipient's identifying number	7 Category of distribution	For Paperwork Reduction Act Notice and instructions for completing this form, see Form W-3G.
Street address	8 IRA, SEP or DEC distributions	9 Other: $ %	
City, State, and ZIP code	This does ☐ does not ☐ qualify as a lump-sum distribution.		**Copy A**
	Your percentage of total distribution.▶ %		**For Internal Revenue Service Center**
	Death benefit exclusion does ☐ or does not ☐ apply.		

Form **1099-R**   **Do NOT Cut or Separate Forms on This Page**   Department of the Treasury - Internal Revenue Service

☒ 9898   ☒ VOID   For Official Use Only

			OMB No. 1545-0119
Type or machine print PAYER'S name	1 Amount includible as income (Add boxes 2 and 3)	2 Capital gain (For lump-sum distributions only)	**1984** Statement for Recipients of
Street address	3 Ordinary income	4 Federal income tax withheld	**Total Distributions from Profit-sharing, Retirement Plans, Individual Retirement Arrangements, etc.**
City, State, and ZIP code			
Federal identifying number	5 Employee contributions to profit-sharing or retirement plans	6 Net unrealized appreciation in employer's securities	
Type or machine print RECIPIENT'S name (first, middle, last)	Recipient's identifying number	7 Category of distribution	For Paperwork Reduction Act Notice and instructions for completing this form, see Form W-3G.
Street address	8 IRA, SEP or DEC distributions	9 Other: $ %	
City, State, and ZIP code	This does ☐ does not ☐ qualify as a lump-sum distribution.		**Copy A**
	Your percentage of total distribution.▶ %		**For Internal Revenue Service Center**
	Death benefit exclusion does ☐ or does not ☐ apply.		

Form **1099-R**   **Do NOT Cut or Separate Forms on This Page**   Department of the Treasury - Internal Revenue Service

☒ 9898   ☒ VOID   For Official Use Only

			OMB No. 1545-0119
Type or machine print PAYER'S name	1 Amount includible as income (Add boxes 2 and 3)	2 Capital gain (For lump-sum distributions only)	**1984** Statement for Recipients of
Street address	3 Ordinary income	4 Federal income tax withheld	**Total Distributions from Profit-sharing, Retirement Plans, Individual Retirement Arrangements, etc.**
City, State, and ZIP code			
Federal identifying number	5 Employee contributions to profit-sharing or retirement plans	6 Net unrealized appreciation in employer's securities	
Type or machine print RECIPIENT'S name (first, middle, last)	Recipient's identifying number	7 Category of distribution	For Paperwork Reduction Act Notice and instructions for completing this form, see Form W-3G.
Street address	8 IRA, SEP or DEC distributions	9 Other: $ %	
City, State, and ZIP code	This does ☐ does not ☐ qualify as a lump-sum distribution.		**Copy A**
	Your percentage of total distribution.▶ %		**For Internal Revenue Service Center**
	Death benefit exclusion does ☐ or does not ☐ apply.		

Form **1099-R**

Department of the Treasury - Internal Revenue Service

PAYER'S name, address, ZIP code, and Federal identifying number.

1 Amount includible as income (Add boxes 2 and 3)	2 Capital gain (For lump-sum distributions only)	OMB No. 1545-0119
3 Ordinary income	4 Federal income tax withheld	**19 84** Statement for Recipients of
5 Employee contributions to profit-sharing or retirement plans	6 Net unrealized appreciation in employer's securities	**Total Distributions from Profit-sharing, Retirement Plans, Individual Retirement Arrangements, etc.**

RECIPIENT'S name, address, and ZIP code.

Recipient's identifying number	7 Category of distribution	**This information is being furnished to the Internal Revenue Service.**
8 IRA, SEP or DEC distributions	9 Other: $ %	
This does ⌷ does not ⌷ qualify as a lump-sum distribution.		**Copy B**
Your percentage of total distribution.▶ %		
Death benefit exclusion does ⌷ or does not ⌷ apply.		**For Recipient**

Form **1099-R**   Department of the Treasury · Internal Revenue Service

---

PAYER'S name, address, ZIP code, and Federal identifying number.

1 Amount includible as income (Add boxes 2 and 3)	2 Capital gain (For lump-sum distributions only)	OMB No. 1545-0119
3 Ordinary income	4 Federal income tax withheld	**19 84** Statement for Recipients of
5 Employee contributions to profit-sharing or retirement plans	6 Net unrealized appreciation in employer's securities	**Total Distributions from Profit-sharing, Retirement Plans, Individual Retirement Arrangements, etc.**

RECIPIENT'S name, address, and ZIP code.

Recipient's identifying number	7 Category of distribution	**This information is being furnished to the Internal Revenue Service.**
8 IRA, SEP or DEC distributions	9 Other: $ %	
This does ⌷ does not ⌷ qualify as a lump-sum distribution.		**Copy B**
Your percentage of total distribution.▶ %		
Death benefit exclusion does ⌷ or does not ⌷ apply.		**For Recipient**

Form **1099-R**   Department of the Treasury · Internal Revenue Service

---

PAYER'S name, address, ZIP code, and Federal identifying number.

1 Amount includible as income (Add boxes 2 and 3)	2 Capital gain (For lump-sum distributions only)	OMB No. 1545-0119
3 Ordinary income	4 Federal income tax withheld	**19 84** Statement for Recipients of
5 Employee contributions to profit-sharing or retirement plans	6 Net unrealized appreciation in employer's securities	**Total Distributions from Profit-sharing, Retirement Plans, Individual Retirement Arrangements, etc.**

RECIPIENT'S name, address, and ZIP code.

Recipient's identifying number	7 Category of distribution	**This information is being furnished to the Internal Revenue Service.**
8 IRA, SEP or DEC distributions	9 Other: $ %	
This does ⌷ does not ⌷ qualify as a lump-sum distribution.		**Copy B**
Your percentage of total distribution.▶ %		
Death benefit exclusion does ⌷ or does not ⌷ apply.		**For Recipient**

Form **1099-R**   292   Department of the Treasury · Internal Revenue Service

Lump-sum Distribution.—Generally, this is a payment, within one tax year, of the balance of an employee's credit in a retirement plan payable to the recipient (a) on account of the employee's death, (b) after the employee reaches age 59½, (c) on the employee's separation from service, or (d) when the employee becomes disabled (see section 72(m)(7)). For additional information, see **Publication 575**, Pension and Annuity Income.

If this form reports distributions from an individual retirement arrangement (IRA), simplified employee pension (SEP) or from a qualified employer plan classified as deductible employee contributions (DEC), the amount will be included in Box 8 and there will be no entries in Boxes 1, 2, or 3.

Death Benefit Exclusion.—If you receive a plan distribution as the beneficiary of a deceased employee (or deceased disability retiree who died prior to attaining retirement age), you may be entitled to a "death benefit exclusion" of up to $5,000. Taxable amounts shown in Boxes 2 and 3 are without regard to this exclusion. Allocate the exclusion between capital gain and ordinary income and include the reduced amounts on your tax return.

Note: If the total distribution is made to more than one person, the percentage you received is shown in the space below Box 9. Enter the percentage on **Form 5544**, Multiple Recipient Special 10-Year Averaging Method, if you elect the 10-year averaging method.

Box 2.—This part of the lump-sum distribution qualifies for capital gain treatment. Report it on Schedule D (Form 1040 or Form 1041) and identify it as "Lump-sum Distribution." See **Death Benefit Exclusion** above. Also, see the instructions for **Form 4972**, Special 10-Year Averaging Method, or Form 5544 for election to treat this amount as ordinary income for the 10-year averaging method.

Box 3.—This part of the total distribution is taxable as ordinary income and may be eligible for a special 10-year averaging method. See Form 4972 or 5544. Also, see the instructions for **Death Benefit Exclusion** above.

Note: If there is an entry in Box I, but no entries in Boxes 2 or 3, ask the employer to furnish the information for Boxes 2 and 3.

Box 4.—This is the amount of Federal income tax withheld on designated distributions made during 1984. You may take a credit on your income tax return for the tax withheld.

Box 5.—Amounts contributed or considered contributed by the individual that were not deductible by the individual when the contribution was made (minus nontaxable amounts previously distributed) are not taxable to the individual when distributed. This box will **not** show any contributions to an IRA, SEP or DEC, but will show premiums paid on commercial annuities.

Box 6.—If the distribution consists in part of securities of your employer's corporation, the net unrealized appreciation in these securities is not taxed until you sell the securities.

Box 7.—No code may be present if the amount in Box 1 is a normal distribution. The code listed identifies the type of distribution you received, as follows:
1—Premature Distribution (other than codes 2, 3, 4, or 5); 2—Rollovers; 3—Disability; 4—Death (includes payments to a beneficiary); 5—Prohibited Transactions; 6—Other; 7—Normal IRA, SEP or DEC Distributions; 8—Excess contributions refunded plus earnings on such excess contributions; 9—Transfers to an IRA for a spouse due to a divorce.

Box 8.—Amounts received from an IRS, SEP or DEC may be includible in income depending on the type of distribution. See **Publication 590**, Individual Retirement Arrangements (IRA's), for more information.

Box 9.—If you receive an annuity contract as part of a distribution, the value of the contract is not taxable when you receive it. When you receive periodic payments from the annuity contract, they are taxable, but only to the extent the payments are more than your basis in the annuity. If the distribution is made to more than one person, the dollar amount and the percentage of the annuity contract distributed to you are shown in this box. You will need this information if you elect the special 10-year averaging method on Form 5544.

If an annuity contract has been transferred to another trustee, an amount will be shown in this box and Code 2 will be shown in Box 7.

If you receive a death benefit payment as a beneficiary from the employer of a deceased employee, the amount will be shown in this box and Code 4 will be shown in Box 7. See **Publication 525**, Taxable and Nontaxable Income.

☆ U.S. GOVERNMENT PRINTING OFFICE: 1983-390-164 E.I. 11-1897126

Lump-sum Distribution.—Generally, this is a payment, within one tax year, of the balance of an employee's credit in a retirement plan payable to the recipient (a) on account of the employee's death, (b) after the employee reaches age 59½, (c) on the employee's separation from service, or (d) when the employee becomes disabled (see section 72(m)(7)). For additional information, see **Publication 575**, Pension and Annuity Income.

If this form reports distributions from an individual retirement arrangement (IRA), simplified employee pension (SEP) or from a qualified employer plan classified as deductible employee contributions (DEC), the amount will be included in Box 8 and there will be no entries in Boxes 1, 2, or 3.

Death Benefit Exclusion.—If you receive a plan distribution as the beneficiary of a deceased employee (or deceased disability retiree who died prior to attaining retirement age), you may be entitled to a "death benefit exclusion" of up to $5,000. Taxable amounts shown in Boxes 2 and 3 are without regard to this exclusion. Allocate the exclusion between capital gain and ordinary income and include the reduced amounts on your tax return.

Note: If the total distribution is made to more than one person, the percentage you received is shown in the space below Box 9. Enter the percentage on **Form 5544**, Multiple Recipient Special 10-Year Averaging Method, if you elect the 10-year averaging method.

Box 2.—This part of the lump-sum distribution qualifies for capital gain treatment. Report it on Schedule D (Form 1040 or Form 1041) and identify it as "Lump-sum Distribution." See **Death Benefit Exclusion** above. Also, see the instructions for **Form 4972**, Special 10-Year Averaging Method, or Form 5544 for election to treat this amount as ordinary income for the 10-year averaging method.

Box 3.—This part of the total distribution is taxable as ordinary income and may be eligible for a special 10-year averaging method. See Form 4972 or 5544. Also, see the instructions for **Death Benefit Exclusion** above.

Note: If there is an entry in Box I, but no entries in Boxes 2 or 3, ask the employer to furnish the information for Boxes 2 and 3.

Box 4.—This is the amount of Federal income tax withheld on designated distributions made during 1984. You may take a credit on your income tax return for the tax withheld.

Box 5.—Amounts contributed or considered contributed by the individual that were not deductible by the individual when the contribution was made (minus nontaxable amounts previously distributed) are not taxable to the individual when distributed. This box will **not** show any contributions to an IRA, SEP or DEC, but will show premiums paid on commercial annuities.

Box 6.—If the distribution consists in part of securities of your employer's corporation, the net unrealized appreciation in these securities is not taxed until you sell the securities.

Box 7.—No code may be present if the amount in Box 1 is a normal distribution. The code listed identifies the type of distribution you received, as follows:
1—Premature Distribution (other than codes 2, 3, 4, or 5); 2—Rollovers; 3—Disability; 4—Death (includes payments to a beneficiary); 5—Prohibited Transactions; 6—Other; 7—Normal IRA, SEP or DEC Distributions; 8—Excess contributions refunded plus earnings on such excess contributions; 9—Transfers to an IRA for a spouse due to a divorce.

Box 8.—Amounts received from an IRS, SEP or DEC may be includible in income depending on the type of distribution. See **Publication 590**, Individual Retirement Arrangements (IRA's), for more information.

Box 9.—If you receive an annuity contract as part of a distribution, the value of the contract is not taxable when you receive it. When you receive periodic payments from the annuity contract, they are taxable, but only to the extent the payments are more than your basis in the annuity. If the distribution is made to more than one person, the dollar amount and the percentage of the annuity contract distributed to you are shown in this box. You will need this information if you elect the special 10-year averaging method on Form 5544.

If an annuity contract has been transferred to another trustee, an amount will be shown in this box and Code 2 will be shown in Box 7.

If you receive a death benefit payment as a beneficiary from the employer of a deceased employee, the amount will be shown in this box and Code 4 will be shown in Box 7. See **Publication 525**, Taxable and Nontaxable Income.

☆ U.S. GOVERNMENT PRINTING OFFICE: 1983-390-164 E.I. 11-1897126

Lump-sum Distribution.—Generally, this is a payment, within one tax year, of the balance of an employee's credit in a retirement plan payable to the recipient (a) on account of the employee's death, (b) after the employee reaches age 59½, (c) on the employee's separation from service, or (d) when the employee becomes disabled (see section 72(m)(7)). For additional information, see **Publication 575**, Pension and Annuity Income.

If this form reports distributions from an individual retirement arrangement (IRA), simplified employee pension (SEP) or from a qualified employer plan classified as deductible employee contributions (DEC), the amount will be included in Box 8 and there will be no entries in Boxes 1, 2, or 3.

Death Benefit Exclusion.—If you receive a plan distribution as the beneficiary of a deceased employee (or deceased disability retiree who died prior to attaining retirement age), you may be entitled to a "death benefit exclusion" of up to $5,000. Taxable amounts shown in Boxes 2 and 3 are without regard to this exclusion. Allocate the exclusion between capital gain and ordinary income and include the reduced amounts on your tax return.

Note: If the total distribution is made to more than one person, the percentage you received is shown in the space below Box 9. Enter the percentage on **Form 5544**, Multiple Recipient Special 10-Year Averaging Method, if you elect the 10-year averaging method.

Box 2.—This part of the lump-sum distribution qualifies for capital gain treatment. Report it on Schedule D (Form 1040 or Form 1041) and identify it as "Lump-sum Distribution." See **Death Benefit Exclusion** above. Also, see the instructions for **Form 4972**, Special 10-Year Averaging Method, or Form 5544 for election to treat this amount as ordinary income for the 10-year averaging method.

Box 3.—This part of the total distribution is taxable as ordinary income and may be eligible for a special 10-year averaging method. See Form 4972 or 5544. Also, see the instructions for **Death Benefit Exclusion** above.

Note: If there is an entry in Box I, but no entries in Boxes 2 or 3, ask the employer to furnish the information for Boxes 2 and 3.

Box 4.—This is the amount of Federal income tax withheld on designated distributions made during 1984. You may take a credit on your income tax return for the tax withheld.

Box 5.—Amounts contributed or considered contributed by the individual that were not deductible by the individual when the contribution was made (minus nontaxable amounts previously distributed) are not taxable to the individual when distributed. This box will **not** show any contributions to an IRA, SEP or DEC, but will show premiums paid on commercial annuities.

Box 6.—If the distribution consists in part of securities of your employer's corporation, the net unrealized appreciation in these securities is not taxed until you sell the securities.

Box 7.—No code may be present if the amount in Box 1 is a normal distribution. The code listed identifies the type of distribution you received, as follows:
1—Premature Distribution (other than codes 2, 3, 4, or 5); 2—Rollovers; 3—Disability; 4—Death (includes payments to a beneficiary); 5—Prohibited Transactions; 6—Other; 7—Normal IRA, SEP or DEC Distributions; 8—Excess contributions refunded plus earnings on such excess contributions; 9—Transfers to an IRA for a spouse due to a divorce.

Box 8.—Amounts received from an IRS, SEP or DEC may be includible in income depending on the type of distribution. See **Publication 590**, Individual Retirement Arrangements (IRA's), for more information.

Box 9.—If you receive an annuity contract as part of a distribution, the value of the contract is not taxable when you receive it. When you receive periodic payments from the annuity contract, they are taxable, but only to the extent the payments are more than your basis in the annuity. If the distribution is made to more than one person, the dollar amount and the percentage of the annuity contract distributed to you are shown in this box. You will need this information if you elect the special 10-year averaging method on Form 5544.

If an annuity contract has been transferred to another trustee, an amount will be shown in this box and Code 2 will be shown in Box 7.

If you receive a death benefit payment as a beneficiary from the employer of a deceased employee, the amount will be shown in this box and Code 4 will be shown in Box 7. See **Publication 525**, Taxable and Nontaxable Income.

☆ U.S. GOVERNMENT PRINTING OFFICE: 1983-390-164 E.I. 11-1897126

Form **2848-D**
(Rev. October 1983)
Department of the Treasury
Internal Revenue Service

Tax Information Authorization and Declaration of Representative

▶ **See separate Instructions.**

OMB No. 1545-0150

PART I.—Tax Information Authorization

Taxpayer(s) name, identifying number, and address including ZIP code (Please type or print)

For IRS Use Only		
File So.		
Level		
Receipt		
Powers		
Blind T.		
Action		
Ret. Ind.		

hereby authorizes (name(s), CAF number(s), address(es) including ZIP code(s), and telephone number(s))

to receive from or inspect confidential tax information in any office of the Internal Revenue Service for the following tax matter(s).

Type of tax (Indivdual, corporate, etc.)	Federal tax form number (1040, 1120, etc.)	Year(s) or period(s) (Date of death if estate tax)

Initial here ▶ _ _ _ _ _ _ _ _ if you do NOT want the above named designee(s)* to act as the representative(s) of the taxpayer(s) before the Internal Revenue Service and to make written or oral presentations of fact or argument on behalf of the taxpayer for the above tax matters.

Send copies of notices and other written communications (excluding refund checks and routine mailings of tax forms) addressed to the taxpayer(s) in proceedings involving the above tax matters to:

1 ☐ the representative first named above, or

2 ☐ (names of not more than two of the above named representatives) _

Unless specified to the contrary below, this tax information authorization automatically revokes all earlier tax information authorizations, but does NOT revoke earlier powers of attorney, on file with the Internal Revenue Service for the tax matters and years or periods covered by this authorization.

_ (Specify any exceptions to the above, indicating to whom granted, date, and address.) _ _ _ _ _ _ _ _ _ _ _ _ _ _ _

Signature of or for taxpayer(s)

(If signed by a corporate officer, partner, or fiduciary on behalf of the taxpayer, I certify that I have the authority to execute this tax information authorization on behalf of the taxpayer.)

_ _
(Signature)   (Title, if applicable)   (Date)
(Also type or print your name below if signing for a taxpayer who is not an individual.)

_ _
(Signature)   (Title, if applicable)   (Date)

*If you initial this space, thus authorizing your designee(s) only to receive and inspect confidential information about your tax matters, your designee(s) may be an organization, firm, or partnership. If you do not initial this space, intending that your designee(s) act as your representative(s), your representative must be an individual who must complete Part II.

For Privacy Act and Paperwork Reduction Act Notice, see page 1 of separate Instructions.

Form **2848-D** (Rev. 10-83)

295

PART II.—Declaration of Representative

I declare that I am not currently under suspension or disbarment from practice before the Internal Revenue Service, that I am aware of Treasury Department Circular No. 230 as amended (31 C.F.R. Part 10), Regulations governing the practice of attorneys, certified public accountants, enrolled agents, enrolled actuaries, unenrolled return preparers, and others, and that I am one of the following:

1 a member in good standing of the bar of the highest court of the jurisdiction indicated below;

2 duly qualified to practice as a certified public accountant in the jurisdiction indicated below;

3 enrolled as an agent pursuant to the requirements of Treasury Department Circular No. 230;

4 a bona fide officer of the taxpayer organization;

5 a full-time employee of the taxpayer;

6 a member of the taxpayer's immediate family (spouse, parent, child, brother or sister);

7 a fiduciary for the taxpayer;

8 an enrolled actuary (The authority of an enrolled actuary to practice before the Service is limited by section 10.3(d)(1) of Treasury Department Circular No. 230);

9 an unenrolled return preparer pursuant to section 10.7(a) (7) of Treasury Department Circular No. 230;

10 Commissioner's special authorization (see instructions for Part II, item 10) _____ ;

and that I am authorized to represent the taxpayer identified in Part I for the tax matters there specified.

Designation (Insert appropriate number from above list)	Jurisdiction (State, etc.) or Enrollment Card Number	Signature	Date

Form **4972**

Department of the Treasury
Internal Revenue Service

Special 10-Year Averaging Method

(For Total Distribution from Qualified Retirement Plan)

▶ **Attach to Form 1040 or Form 1041.**   ▶ **See separate instructions.**

OMB No. 1545-0193

1984

74

Name(s) as shown on return	Identifying number

By checking this box ▶ ☐ , I agree, for this and all other lump-sum distributions I receive for the same employee, not to treat any part **as** capital gain. I know this decision cannot be changed. (See Instruction F.)

Note: Read instructions B. and C. to see if your distribution qualifies for the special 10-year averaging method.

Part I	**Use Part I if You Have Not Filed Form 4972 for Any Year after 1978**		

1 Capital gain part from payer's statement (Form 1099R, box 2) **1**

If you are using the 10-year averaging method for the capital gain from the distribution as well as for the ordinary income, leave line 1 blank and include the capital gain on line 2 (see instruction F). Otherwise, enter the capital gain from your payer's statement (Form 1099R, box 2). If you are filing Schedule D and cannot take the exclusion on line 4 below or do not have to decrease the capital gain for Federal estate tax, enter the capital gain on your Schedule D also. See the separate instructions for line 1.

2 Ordinary income part from payer's statement (Form 1099R, box 3). Enter here instead of on Form 1040 or Form 1041 . . . . **2**

3 Add lines 1 and 2 . . . . **3**

4 Death benefit exclusion (see instructions for line 4) **4**

5 Total taxable amount (subtract line 4 from line 3) **5**

6 Current actuarial value of annuity, if applicable (from Form 1099R, box 9) **6**

7 Adjusted total taxable amount (add lines 5 and 6). If this amount is $70,000 or more, skip lines 8 through 11, and enter this amount on line 12 also **7**

8 50% of line 7, but not more than $10,000 . . . . **8**

9 Subtract $20,000 from line 7. Enter difference. If line 7 is $20,000 or less, enter zero . . . **9**

10 20% of line 9 . . . . **10**

11 Minimum distribution allowance (subtract line 10 from line 8) **11**

12 Subtract line 11 from line 7 . . . . **12**

13 Federal estate tax attributable to lump-sum distribution. Do not deduct on Form 1040 or Form 1041 the amount entered on this line that is attributable to the ordinary income entered on line 2. (See instructions for line 13) **13**

14 Subtract line 13 from line 12 . . . . **14**

15 Enter $2,300 plus 10% of line 14 . . . . **15**

16 Tax on amount on line 15. Use Tax Rate Schedule X (Single Taxpayer Rate) in Form 1040 Instructions **16**

17 Multiply line 16 by 10. If no entry on line 6, skip lines 18 through 23, and enter this amount on line 24 also **17**

18 Divide line 6 by line 7 (carry to four decimal places) **18**

19 Multiply line 11 by line 18 . . . . **19**

20 Subtract line 19 from line 6 . . . . **20**

21 Enter $2,300 plus 10% of line 20 . . . . **21**

22 Tax on amount on line 21. Use Tax Rate Schedule X (Single Taxpayer Rate) in Form 1040 Instructions . **22**

23 Multiply line 22 by 10 . . . . **23**

24 Subtract line 23 from line 17. . . . . **24**

25 Divide line 2 by line 3 (carry to four decimal places) **25**

26 Tax on ordinary income part of lump-sum distribution (multiply line 24 by line 25). Show this amount on Form 1040, line 39, or Form 1041, line 26b. . . . . ▶ **26**

For Paperwork Reduction Act Notice, see separate instructions.

Form **4972** (1984)

Part II | Use Part II if You Filed Form 4972 for Any Other Year After 1978 or if You Received an Annuity Contract after 1978

		(a) Total received 1984	(b) Total received after 1978 and before 1984	(c) Total of columns (a) and (b)
1	Capital gain part from payer's statement (Form 1099R, box 2) **1**			
	If you are using the 10-year averaging method for the capital gain from the distribution as well as for the ordinary income, leave line 1 blank and include the capital gain on line 2 (see instruction F). Otherwise, enter the capital gain from your payer's statement (Form 1099R, box 2). If you are filing Schedule D and cannot take the exclusion on line 4 below or do not have to decrease the capital gain for Federal estate tax, enter the capital gain on your Schedule D also. See separate instructions for line 1.			
2	Ordinary income part from payer's statement (Form 1099R, box 3). Enter here instead of on Form 1040 or Form 1041 . . . . **2**			
3	Add lines 1 and 2 . . . . **3**			
4	Death benefit exclusion (see instructions for Part I, line 4) **4**			
5	Total taxable amount (subtract line 4 from line 3) . . **5**			
6	Current actuarial value of annuity if applicable (from Form 1099R, box 9) **6**			
7	Adjusted total taxable amount (add lines 5 and 6, column (c)). If this amount is $70,000 or more, skip lines 8 through 11, and enter this amount on line 12 also **7**			
8	50% of line 7, but not more than $10,000 . . . . **8**			
9	Subtract $20,000 from line 7. Enter difference. If line 7 is $20,000 or less, enter zero **9**			
10	20% of line 9 . . . . **10**			
11	Minimum distribution allowance (subtract line 10 from line 8) **11**			
12	Subtract line 11 from line 7. . . . . **12**			
13	Federal estate tax attributable to lump-sum distribution. Do not deduct on Form 1040 or Form 1041 the amount entered on this line that is attributable to the ordinary income entered on line 2. (See instructions for Part I, line 13) **13**			
14	Subtract line 13 from line 12. . . . . **14**			
15	Enter $2,300 plus 10% of line 14 . . . . **15**			
16	Tax on amount on line 15. Use Tax Rate Schedule X (Single Taxpayer Rate) in Form 1040 Instructions . **16**			
17	Multiply line 16 by 10. If no entry on line 6, skip lines 18 through 23, and enter this amount on line 24 also **17**			
18	Divide line 6, column (c), by line 7 (carry to four decimal places) **18**			
19	Multiply line 11 by line 18 . . . . **19**			
20	Subtract line 19 from line 6, column (c) **20**			
21	Enter $2,300 plus 10% of line 20 . . . . **21**			
22	Tax on amount on line 21. Use Tax Rate Schedule X (Single Taxpayer Rate) in Form 1040 Instructions . **22**			
23	Multiply line 22 by 10 . . . . **23**			
24	Subtract line 23 from line 17 . . . . **24**			
25	Divide line 2, column (c), by line 3, column (c) (carry to four decimal places) **25**			
26	Tax on ordinary income parts of lump-sum distributions (multiply line 24 by line 25) **26**			
27	Tax on ordinary income part of lump-sum distribution shown on Form 4972, Part I or Part II, for 1979 through 1983 . . . . **27**			
28	Tax on ordinary income part of lump-sum distribution (subtract line 27 from line 26). Show this amount, but not less than zero, on Form 1040, line 39, or Form 1041, line 26b . . . . ▶ **28**			

Form **5310**
(Rev. Nov. 1982)
Department of the Treasury
Internal Revenue Service

Pension Benefit
Guaranty Corporation

Application for Determination Upon Termination; Notice of Merger, Consolidation or Transfer of Plan Assets or Liabilities; Notice of Intent to Terminate

(Under sections 401(a) and 6058(b) of the Internal Revenue Code and section 4041(a) of the Employee Retirement Income Security Act of 1974)

OMB No. 1545-0202
Expires 5–31–85

For Agency Use Only

Complete every applicable part of this form. If an item in an applicable part does not apply, enter N/A.
Multiemployer plans covered by PBGC insurance program, see Purpose on page 1 of the instructions.

Reason for filing (check applicable box(es); see General Instructions):

A ☐ Notice of plan—*(i)* Merger, *(ii)* Consolidation, or *(iii)* Transfer of plan assets or liabilities to another plan.

B ☐ Application for ONLY an Internal Revenue Service (IRS) determination letter regarding a plan termination. (This is NOT a notice of intent to terminate for the Pension Benefit Guaranty Corporation.)

C ☐ Defined benefit plan filing "ONE STOP" (One-Stop filing is a voluntary choice in lieu of separate filings under B and D for):
   (i) Notice of intent to terminate under the Pension Benefit Guaranty Corporation (PBGC) termination insurance program AND
   (ii) Application for an IRS determination letter upon plan termination.

D ☐ Defined benefit plan filing ONLY a notice of intent to terminate under the PBGC termination insurance program. (This is NOT a request for an IRS determination letter.)

| **Part I** | **All Filers Complete This Part** |

1 (a) Name of plan sponsor (see instructions):

Address (number and street)

City or town, State, and ZIP code

2 (a) Name of plan administrator (if same as 1(a), enter "same")

Address (number and street)

City or town, State, and ZIP code

2 (b) Administrator's employer identification number

1 (b) Employer identification number

1 (c) Sponsor's telephone number
( )

1 (d) Employer's tax year ends
Month   Day   Year **19**

1 (e) Business code number

1 (f) Date business incorporated or began

2 (c) Administrator's telephone number
( )

2 (d) Name, address, and telephone number of person to be contacted if more information is needed (see instructions):
Name _____ Telephone number ( )
Address

2 (e) Office of the District Director of the key district where sponsor is located (see instructions):

3 If you checked reason for filing B, C, or D, has each party who is required to be notified been properly informed of this filing (see instructions)? . . . . ☐ Yes ☐ No

4 Type of plan entity (check only one box; see instructions):
(a) ☐ Single-employer plan
(b) ☐ Plan of controlled group of corporations or trades or businesses under common control
(c) ☐ Multiple-employer-collectively-bargained plan (other than a multiemployer plan)
(d) ☐ Multiple-employer plan (other)
(e) ☐ Other (specify) _____

5 (a) Plan name

(b) Plan number

(c) Plan year ends

6 (a) Is this a defined benefit plan covered under the Pension Benefit Guaranty Corporation termination insurance program (see Part IV instructions)? . *(i)* ☐ Yes *(ii)* ☐ No *(iii)* ☐ Not determined

(b) If you checked "Yes" or "Not determined," have you ever used an employer identification number or plan number in any prior filing with PBGC other than the ones entered on lines 1(b) or 5(b) above? . . . . . . ☐ Yes ☐ No
If "Yes," enter the number(s) previously reported. ▶

7 Indicate type of plan (see General Instruction E):
(a) ☐ Defined benefit
   (i) ☐ Fixed benefit
   (ii) ☐ Unit benefit
   (iii) ☐ Flat benefit
(b) ☐ Money purchase
(c) ☐ Profit-sharing
(d) ☐ Other (specify) ▶

Under penalties of perjury, I declare that I have examined this application, including accompanying statements, and to the best of my knowledge and belief it is true, correct and complete.

Signature ▶_____ Title ▶_____ Date ▶_____

Signature ▶_____ Title ▶_____ Date ▶_____

For Paperwork Reduction Act Notice, see page 1 of the instructions.

299

Form 5310 (Rev. 11–82)   Page **2**

Part II | Complete This Part if You Checked Reason for Filing A

8 Other plan(s) involved in transaction (see instructions):

(a) Plan name ....

(b) Name of employer

(c) Employer identification number

(d) Plan number | (e) Date of merger, consolidation or transfer

(f) If the plan listed in 5(a) is a defined benefit plan attach an actuarial statement of valuation evidencing compliance with the requirements of Code section 401(a)(12) and the Income Tax Regulations under Code section 414(l).

Part III | Complete This Part if You Checked Reason for Filing B, C, or D

9 Effective date of plan

	Yes	No
10 (a) Has the plan ever received an IRS determination letter?		
(b) If (a) is "Yes," enter the file folder number and date of the most recent determination letter and complete (d) through (g). File folder No. .... Date ▶--------------------------		
(c) If (a) is "No" and your reason for filing is B or C, attach a copy of the executed original plan document or joinder/adoption agreement, all plan amendments, trust agreement, group annuity contracts and custodial agreements (do not complete (d) through (g)).		
(d) If (a) is "Yes," has the plan been amended since the last determination letter?		
(e) If (d) is "Yes," and your reason for filing is B or C, attach a copy of the amendment(s) and complete (f) and (g).		
(f) Do any of the amendments alter the plan's vesting provisions?		
(g) Do any of the amendments decrease plan benefits?		

11 (a) Proposed date of plan termination ▶--------------------------

(b) Attach copies of records of all actions taken to terminate the plan (see instructions).

(c) Last contribution to the plan:

    (i) Date   (ii) Amount (see instructions) $ (iii) For plan year ended

12 Reason for termination (check only one box to indicate primary reason for termination):

(a) ☐ Change in ownership by merger

(b) ☐ Liquidation or dissolution of employer

(c) ☐ Change in ownership by sale or transfer

(d) ☐ Adverse business conditions (see instructions and attach explanation)

(e) ☐ Adoption of new plan (see instructions and attach explanation)

(f) ☐ Other (specify) ▶

13 Indicate funding arrangement:

(a) ☐ Trust (benefits provided in whole from trust funds)

(b) ☐ Trust or other arrangement providing benefits partially through insurance and/or annuity contracts

(c) ☐ Trust or other arrangement providing benefits exclusively through insurance and/or annuity contracts

(d) ☐ Custodial account described in Code section 401(f) and not included in (c) above

(e) ☐ Other (specify) ▶

14 (a) Name(s) of trustee(s) or custodian(s)   **(b)** Date trust's accounting period ends

Address (number and street)

City or town, State, and ZIP code

	Yes	No	Not Certain
15 Participation (see instructions): Collectively bargained plans and plans filing only a notice of intent to terminate (reason for filing D) do not complete (a) and (c).			
(a) (i) Is the employer a member of an affiliated service group? . . . . If there is uncertainty whether the employer is a member of an affiliated service group, check the "Not Certain" column.			
(ii) If (i) is "Yes" or "Not certain," did a prior ruling letter rule on what organizations were members of the employer's affiliated service group or did the employer receive a determination letter on this plan that considered the effect of Code section 414(m)?			
(iii) If (ii) is "Yes," have the facts on which that letter was based materially changed?			
(b) Is the employer a member of a controlled group of corporations or a group of trades or businesses under common control?			

15 (Continued):

(c) Complete the following as of the proposed date of plan termination (current year) and as of the end of the 2 prior plan years:

	19........		19........		Current year 19........	
	Yes	No	Yes	No	Yes	No
(i) Did the plan satisfy the percentage tests of Code section 410(b)(1)(A)?						
(ii) Total number of employees (if more than 100 enter "100 plus"). .						

(d) Enter the number of participants employed for the current plan year and each of the 5 prior plan years on the schedule below:

	19........	19........	19........	19........	19........	Current year 19........
(i) Number at beginning of plan year . .						
(ii) Number added during the plan year .						
(iii) Total (add lines (i) and (ii))						
(iv) Number dropped during the plan year .						
(v) Number at end of plan year (subtract (iv) from (iii))						
(vi) Total number of participants in this plan separated from service during the plan year without full vesting . . .						

16 Summary of Participant or Claimant by category:

	Total number	Amount of monthly benefits as of the most recent payment date
(a) Retirees and beneficiaries (including disability retirees) receiving benefits . .		
(b) Active participants eligible for normal retirement		
(c) Active participants eligible for early (but not normal) retirement		
(d) Active participants vested before termination (other than normal or early retirement)		
(e) All other active participants		
(f) Participants separated from service with deferred vested benefits		
(g) Total (add lines (a) through (f))		

17 Miscellaneous:

	Yes	No	Not Applicable
(a) As a result of the termination, are accrued benefits or account balances nonforfeitable as required under Code section 411(d)(3)?			
(b) Will the trust continue to operate after termination of the plan (see instructions)?			
(c) Were any funds contributed in the form of, or invested in, obligations or property of the employer or any group of corporations or group of trades or businesses under common control?			
(d) Will distribution include property other than cash?			
(e) For a defined benefit or money purchase plan, do you estimate there will be an accumulated funding deficiency as of the end of the plan year during which the proposed termination date occurs, if no additional plan contributions are made?			
If "Yes," enter the estimated accumulated funding deficiency $_____			
(f) (i) If there are unallocated funds which can be reallocated to participants without exceeding the limitations of Code section 415, have these funds been reallocated?			
(ii) If (i) is "Yes," did the plan originally contain a provision allowing this allocation?			
(iii) If (ii) is "No," was the plan amended to provide for this allocation?			
(g) Will any funds be, or have any funds been, returned to the employer? If uncertain check "Not Applicable." If "Yes," enter the estimated amount ▶ $_____			
(h) Is this plan or trust currently under examination or is any issue relating to this plan or trust currently pending before the Internal Revenue Service, the Department of Labor, the Pension Benefit Guaranty Corporation or any court? . . . . If "Yes," attach a statement naming the agency(s) and/or court and briefly describing the issues.			
(i) Did any plan participant during the current plan year or in the 5 prior plan years receive a lump-sum distribution (see instructions) or have an annuity contract purchased by the plan from an insurance company on his or her behalf? . . . . If "Yes," state the largest amount so distributed or applied to purchase an annuity contract $_____			
(j) Is this a Keogh (H.R. 10) plan? . . . . If "Yes," is an owner-employee covered under the plan? . . . . If an owner-employee is covered under the plan, will distribution be made to him or her before he or she reaches age 59½? . . . . • . . .			
(k) Does the plan have ESOP/TRASOP features?			

18 Defined contribution plans (other than money purchase plans) such as profit-sharing, stock bonus, or other such plans where forfeitures are credited to individual account balances, enter the information for the current plan year and the 5 prior plan years on the following schedule:

	19.......	19.......	19.......	19.......	19.......	Current year 19.......
(a) Employer contributions						
(b) Forfeitures						

(c) Explain basis on which forfeitures were allocated_____

_____

_____

19 Indicate how distributions will be made on termination (check applicable box(es)):

(a) ☐ Lump-sum distribution

(b) ☐ Annuity contract

(c) ☐ Periodic payments from trust

(d) ☐ Transfer of assets and liabilities to another plan

(e) ☐ Other (specify) ▶

20 Statement of net assets available to pay benefits as of the proposed date of plan termination. Read specific instruction **20**, and if you checked Reason for Filing C or D, read specific instruction 25(c) before completing this item.

Assets

(a) Cash and cash equivalents . . . .

(b) Receivables—

    (i) Employer contributions . . . .

    (ii) Other . . . .

(c) Party-in-interest investments—

    (i) Loans to employer . . . .

    (ii) Employer securities . . . .

    (iii) Other . . . .

(d) Other investments—

    (i) Government securities · . . . .

    (ii) Pooled funds/mutual funds . . . .

    (iii) Corporate (debt and equity instruments) . . . .

    (iv) Real estate and mortgages . . . . . .

    (v) Other . . . .

(e) Buildings and other depreciable property . . . .

(f) Unallocated insurance contracts . . . .

(g) Other assets . . . . · . . . .

(h) Total assets (add lines (a) through (g)) . . . .

Liabilities and Net Assets

(i) Accounts and notes payable—

    (i) Past due benefits . . . .

    (ii) Employer . . . .

    (iii) Other . . . .

(j) Accrued expenses . . . .

(k) Mortgages payable . . . .

(l) Acquisition indebtedness . . . .

(m) Other liabilities . . . .

(n) Total liabilities (add lines (i) through (m)) . . . .

(o) Net assets available to pay benefits (subtract line (n) from line (h)) . . . . . .

Part IV **Complete This Part If You Checked Reason For Filing C or D and checked "Yes" on line 6(a).**

If you checked Reason for filing C or D and "Not determined" on line 6(a), completion of this part is optional. However, if you do not complete this part, you must file the plan document, any amendments to the plan document, and the IRS determination letter(s) for the plan as described for lines 22(b), (c) and (g). If PBGC later determines that the termination insurance program covers the plan, you must file the remainder of the information required by this Part (see Part IV instructions).

21 **(a)** Name(s) of labor organization(s) representing plan participants

| **(b)** Telephone number ( )

Address (number and street)

| **(c)** Name of principal officer

City or town, State, and ZIP code

| **(d)** Title of principal officer

22 Indicate the applicability of items (a) through (i) by checking the appropriate column. Attach each item that is applicable (see instructions):

	Applicable	Not applicable
(a) Power of attorney. File 2 copies if you are filing "one-stop" (see General Instruction H)		
(b) Copy of executed plan document		
(c) Copy of executed amendment(s) to the plan document		
(d) Copy of executed group annuity or group insurance contract(s)		
(e) Copy of executed trust agreement(s)		
(f) Copy of executed collective bargaining agreement(s)		
(g) Copy of IRS determination letter(s)		
(h) Copy of the most recent actuarial report		
(i) Copy of the most recent financial statement of plan assets		

23 Indicate the sufficiency of plan assets (see instructions):

	Yes	No
(a) Are any participants entitled to receive benefits assigned to categories 1 through 4 under ERISA section 4044? If "Yes," complete (b); if "No," enter N/A in (b), (c), (d), and (e).		
(b) Do you estimate that plan assets (excluding any amount described in (d) below) are adequate to provide all the benefits assigned to categories 1 through 4 on the proposed date of plan termination? If "Yes," enter N/A in (c) and complete item (d); if "No," complete (c) and (d).		
(c) Indicate the estimated amount by which the value of benefits in categories 1 through 4 exceeds the value of plan assets on the proposed date of plan termination ▶ $...............		
(d) Is the employer making a commitment (in the form prescribed in the PBGC regulation on determination of plan sufficiency) before the proposed date of plan termination to pay, on or before the date assets are distributed, the amount needed to provide all benefits in categories 1 through 4? If "Yes," attach a signed copy of the commitment; if "No," complete (e).		
(e) Has the plan sponsor paid or does the sponsor intend to pay employer liability as prescribed in the PBGC regulation on employer liability before PBGC's request for payment?		

Note: Interest on employer liability will accrue from the date of plan termination.

24 Submit participant data schedules in the format shown in the instructions for the following groups of participants:

(a) Retired participants and beneficiaries receiving benefits from the plan;

(b) Participants separated from service not yet receiving vested benefits from the plan; and

(c) All other participants with vested or non-vested accrued benefits.

25 Indicate the information you are filing with this notice by checking one of the following boxes (see instructions):

(a) ☐ I am filing a complete Form 5310 including required attachments.

(b) ☐ I am filing a complete Form 5310 except the information showing plan assets allocated to participants (see note below).

(c) ☐ I am filing a complete Form 5310 except plan asset information (line 20) and participant data schedules (line 24). I will file the information required by lines 20 and 24 within 90 days after the date of this filing. (See note below.) By not filing lines 20 and 24 with the form, I am agreeing to extend the 90-day period prescribed by ERISA section 4041(a) during which I will not make any distributions pursuant to the proposed termination of the plan.

(d) ☐ With this form I am filing a request for an extension of time to file the information required by line(s) _____ (other than the information required by lines 20 and 24). (See note below.) For more information about extensions see the instructions.

Note: If you checked reason for filing C and you are not sending all the information required in Parts I, III, IV, and either completed Form(s) 6088 or a second copy of the complete participant data schedules described in the line 24 instructions of Form 5310, the 270-day period prescribed by Code section 7476(b)(3) will not commence until you file the remaining required information.

☆U.S. GOVERNMENT PRINTING OFFICE 1982 381–108–39

Form **6088**
(November 1982)
Department of the Treasury
Internal Revenue Service

Pension Benefit Guaranty Corporation

Distributable Benefits from Employee Pension Benefit Plans

▶ Attach to application for determination—regarding a plan termination

OMB No. 1545-0202

Expires 5-31-85

This Form is NOT Open to Public Inspection

Name of employer

Employer identification number

(Money amounts should be in whole dollars. Round off to nearest dollar.)

Line no.	Participant's last name and initials (see instructions) (a)	Check applicable columns				Fill in columns			Compensation		Distributable Benefits			
		Officer/shareholder (b)	Owner-employee (c)	Other self-employed (d)	Benefits fully vested before termination (e)	Years of participation (see instructions) (f)	Age at plan termination (g)	Percent of business owned (1% or more) (h)	Current 12 month period (see instructions) (i)	Average compensation (see instructions) (j)	Defined contribution plans list account balance as of plan termination date (see instructions). Defined benefit plan (see instructions). (k)(1)	Defined contribution plans list account termination date benefit (see instructions). Defined benefit plan (see instructions). (k)(2)	Defined contribution plans other than money purchase plan enter the forfeitures for all full years of service or for the last 10 years whichever is lesser. Defined benefit plans (see instructions). (l)	Defined contribution plans enter amount determined by dividing (k) by the product of (f) and (j): $\frac{(k)}{(f)\times(j)}$. Defined benefit plans (see instructions). (m)
1														
2														
3														
4														
5														
6														
7														
8														
9														
10														
11														
12														
13														
14														
15														
16														
17														
18														
19														
20														
21														
22														
23														
24														
25														
26	Totals for above													
27	Totals for all others													
28	Totals for lines 26 and 27 .													

For Paperwork Reduction Act Notice, see page 1 of the Instructions for 5310.

General Instructions

(References are to the Internal Revenue Code unless otherwise indicated)

Every sponsor or plan administrator of a defined contribution or defined benefit plan who files only an application for an Internal Revenue Service (IRS) determination letter regarding a plan termination (Reason for Filing B on Form 5310) is required to attach thereto Form(s) 6088, which must be completed in all details.

For collectively bargained plans a Form 6088 is required only if the plan covers employees of the representative labor union(s) or of any plan(s) for union members, and if so, a separate Form 6088 is required for each such union or plan. For a plan, other than a collectively bargained plan, maintained by more than one employer (where all employers in each affiliated service group, controlled group of corporations, or group of trades or businesses under common control are considered one employer), a separate Form 6088 is required for each such employer.

Every sponsor or plan administrator of a defined benefit plan who files both a notice of intent to terminate under the Pension Benefit Guaranty Corporation (PBGC) termination insurance program and an application for an IRS determination letter regarding a plan termination (Reason for Filing C —"One Stop") on Form 5310 should attach either Form(s) 6088 or a duplicate copy of the schedules required in line 24 of Form 5310.

Prepare the participant census as of the date of termination or proposed termination.

Section 6104(a)(1)(B) provides generally that applications, filed with respect to the qualification of a pension, profit-sharing or stock bonus plan, shall be open to public inspection. However, section 6104(a)(1)(C) provides that information concerning the compensation of any participant shall not be open to public inspection. Consequently, the information contained in this form shall not be made available to the public, including plan participants and other employees of the employer who established the plan.

This form is to be used by the Internal Revenue Service in its analysis of an application for determination as to whether a plan of deferred compensation qualifies under section 401(a) or 405(a).

Specific Instructions

Column (a).—First list any participant who at any time during the 5 year period prior to the date of plan termination or proposed plan termination date owned directly or indirectly 10% or more of the voting stock or 10% or more (whether or not nonforfeitable) of the business. Next list the remaining participants in order of current compensation (see Note 2 and instructions for column "i") starting with the highest-paid participant followed by the next highest-paid, and so on. If there are fewer than 25 participants, list all the participants. Otherwise, only the first 25 who fall under the priorities listed above need be listed on lines 1 thru 25.

NOTE 1: *For purposes of this form, "participant" means any individual who satisfied the participation requirements prescribed by the plan and who is entitled to receive benefits under the plan. Included are employees as of the proposed date of plan termination with accrued non-vested benefits and individuals no longer employed as of the proposed date of plan termination but entitled to future benefits under the plan.*

NOTE 2: *"Compensation" for purposes of columns (a), (i) and (j) is defined as all amounts (including bonuses and overtime) paid to the participant for services rendered the employer.*

Column (f).—List years of participation prior to the earliest of proposed date of plan termination, retirement or separation from employment.

Column (i).—Current 12-month period can be the last calendar or plan year ending before the proposed date of plan termination or the 12-month period ending on the proposed date of plan termination; for participants that are no longer employed as of the proposed date of plan termination, compensation as defined in the note above is that received for the applicable period immediately before the earlier of retirement or separation from employment.

Column (j).—Determine average compensation by dividing compensation for all years of participation or for the last ten years of participation, whichever is lesser, by the lesser of 10 or the number of years of participation entered in column (f). For participants no longer employed as of the proposed termination date, use compensation and years of participation prior to the earliest of proposed date of plan termination, retirement or separation from employment.

Column (k).—Defined contribution plans list under (1) the total account balance of each participant attributable to employer contributions. Do not include amounts attributable to employee contributions.

Defined benefit plans list amounts allocated in accordance with section 4044(a)(1), (2), (3) and (4)(A) of the Employee Retirement Income Security Act of 1974 under column (k)(1), and list under column (k)(2) all other allocated amounts.

If the sum of the amounts in columns (k)(1) and (2) does not equal line 20(o) of Form 5310, attach an explanation of the difference.

Column (l).—Defined benefit plans list present value of total accrued benefit (whether or not nonforfeitable) as of date plan assets are proposed to be distributed or as of proposed date of plan termination for plans that are to be trusteed by PBGC. Also, attach a statement explaining how the present values were determined.

Column (m).—Defined benefit plans enter the ratio of distributable benefits to present value of accrued benefit: $\dfrac{(k)(1) + (k)(2)}{(l)}$.

☆U.S. Government Printing Office: 1982—381-108/34

Index